Labour Law and the Gig

CW01494606

This international book analyses the impact of digitisation in labour markets on labour relationships and also on labour processes.

The rapid progress of modern disruptive technologies and AIs, and their multiple applications to each phase of the labour production system, are changing the production rules on a global scale with significant impacts in every aspect of work. As new technologies transform work patterns and change the type of jobs available – destroying some while creating others – and even the nature of the tasks performed, numerous legal problems arise which are challenging to legislators and legal scholars who need to find appropriate solutions to them. Considering the labour law issues which have been created by technological developments and currently affect the work of millions worldwide, this book highlights the full scope of these issues, suggesting solutions to emerging problems and ways to mitigate the risks brought about through technological advancement.

Approaching the present debate with perspectives on legal problems with expertise from a wide range of different countries, this book presents informed and scholarly studies which answer the challenges that new technologies present in labour markets, private lives and labour processes.

Jo Carby-Hall is Professor of Law and Director of International Legal Research in the Centre for Legislative Studies at the University of Hull, UK.

Lourdes Mella Méndez is Professor of Labour Law and Social Security at the University of Santiago de Compostela, Spain.

Labour Law and the Gig Economy

Challenges Posed by the Digitalisation of Labour Processes

Edited by Jo Carby-Hall and Lourdes Mella Méndez

Routledge
Taylor & Francis Group

LONDON AND NEW YORK

First published 2020
by Routledge
2 Park Square, Milton Park, Abingdon, Oxon OX14 4RN

and by Routledge
605 Third Avenue, New York, NY 10017

First issued in paperback 2021

Routledge is an imprint of the Taylor & Francis Group, an informa business

British Library Cataloguing-in-Publication Data
A catalogue record for this book is available from the British Library

Library of Congress Cataloging-in-Publication Data
Names: Mella Méndez, Lourdes editor. | Carby-Hall, Jo, 1933- editor.
Title: Labour law and the gig economy : challenges posed by the
digitalisation of labour processes / Jo Carby-Hall and Lourdes
Mella Mendez
Description: Abingdon, Oxon ; New York, NY : Routledge, 2020. |
Includes bibliographical references and index.
Identifiers: LCCN 2019056473 (print) | LCCN 2019056474 (ebook) |
ISBN 9780367462482 (hardback) | ISBN 9781003033721 (ebook)
Subjects: LCSH: Labor laws and legislation. | Temporary
employees–Legal status, laws, etc. | Self-employed–Legal status, laws,
etc. | Independent contractors–Legal status, laws, etc. | Labor
supply–Effect of technological innovations on.
Classification: LCC K1705 .L327 2020 (print) | LCC K1705 (ebook) |
DDC 344.01–dc23
LC record available at https://lccn.loc.gov/2019056473
LC ebook record available at https://lccn.loc.gov/2019056474

Typeset in Galliard
by Integra Software Services Pvt. Ltd.

ISBN 13: 978-1-03-223716-9 (pbk)
ISBN 13: 978-0-367-46248-2 (hbk)

This book is a result of the following Research Project.

MINISTERIO DE ECONOMÍA, INDUSTRIA Y COMPETITIVIDAD. UNIÓN EUROPEA. Proyecto de Investigación nacional del MINECO, titulado "Nuevas (novísimas) tecnologías de la información y comunicación y su impacto en el mercado de trabajo: aspectos emergentes en el ámbito nacional e internacional" (DER2016-75376-R)

MINISTERIO DE ECONOMÍA, INDUSTRIA Y COMPETITIVIDAD. ESPAÑA. Red de Excelencia: Red de estudio y difusión del impacto de las nuevas TICS en la empresa (DER2017-90700-REDT). Financiaión de la Agencia Estatal de Investigación.

Contents

Contributors

Dr. Jo Carby-Hall. Professor of Law and Director of International Legal Research, Centre for Legislative Studies, Faculty of Business, Law and Politics, University of Hull (United Kingdom).

Dr. Daria Chernyaeva. Associate Professor, Faculty of Law, the National Research University "Higher School of Economics" (Russia).

Dr. Durgambini A. Patel. Professor and Head of the Department of Law, Savitribai Phule Pune University (India).

Dr. Alaa Eltamimi. Associate Professor of Law, Faculty of Law, Mansoura University (Egypt).

Duarte Abrunhosa e Sousa. Researcher in the Centre for Legal and Economic Research, Faculty of Law, University of Porto (Portugal).

Dr. Julia Tomassetti. USA/Assistant Professor at City University of Hong Kong, School of Law (China).

Dr. María Carmen López Aniorte. Professor of Labour Law and Social Security, University of Murcia (Spain).

Dr. Francisco Miguel Ortiz González-Conde. Assistant Professor of Labour Law and Social Security, Murcia University (Spain).

Antonio Megías-Bas. Pre-doctoral Consultant in the Department of Labour Law and Social Security. University of Murcia (Spain).

Dr. Artur Rycak. Advocate, former judge. Faculty of Law and Administration, *Łazarski* University (Poland).

Dr. Tatsiana Ushakova. Belarusian State University, Minsk (Belarus).

Dr. Sarai Rodríguez González. Assistant Professor, Faculty of Law and Social Security, University of La Laguna (Spain).

Dr. Loïc Lerouge. Director of Research at the COMPTRASEC UMR 5114. CNRS-University of Bordeaux (France).

Dr. Lourdes Mella Méndez. Professor of Labour Law and Social Security, University of Santiago de Compostela (Spain).

Dr. Francisca Ferrando García. Professor of Labour Law and Social Security, University of Murcia (Spain).

Dr. Monserrate Rodríguez Egio. Lecturer of Labour Law and Social Security, University of Murcia (Spain).

Foreword

Law affects everyone. It determines what taxes people pay, how their children are educated, and what they are prohibited from doing. Bad law can have disastrous consequences. It is important that legislators enact clear laws, drafted to deliver what is expected of them. Laws are subject to interpretation. Cruel and unusual punishment may be prohibited by law, but where is the dividing line between punishment that is cruel and unusual and that which is not? Drafting matters. To be prohibited, the punishment has to be cruel and unusual, not cruel or unusual.

It is thus important not only to know what the law says, but also what it means. Explaining and interpreting law is core to making sense of how a nation is regulated. Works on law that complement the formal wording of legislation play an essential role in understanding and are of value not only to lawyers and parliamentarians, but also to all those wishing to understand the significance of what has been enacted. Understanding the law empowers citizens.

I therefore warmly welcome the publication of this volume. Society cannot function without workers. The scope and nature of how labour is deployed has become more complex as nations have industrialised and become more specialised. Laws to protect workers have developed over time, though the nature of the development has varied from nation to nation. Labour law is now substantial and often complex. That complexity is compounded by new technology. Given the speed of development, there is a challenge for ensuring that the legislative framework is sufficiently robust to cope with the changes. To what extent is it possible not only to keep abreast of new means of communication, but also those still in gestation? Law may become dated very quickly. Technological change impacts massively on labour processes, creating opportunities as well as threats to traditional practices. How does one regulate labour in the light of those changes, including communication through social media, e-mail and electronic means of surveillance?

The contributions to this volume help make sense of this complex body of law. The volume is notable for its breadth and depth. Drawing on the impact of new technology on labour law in a range of countries – drawn in this case from Europe, Asia and Africa – provides analyses and insights that can inform law in other nations. The volume is substantial both in scale and coverage. It is a welcome, and timely, addition to the literature.

Philip Norton
(Lord Norton of Louth)

A reflection on the challenges posed by digitalisation of labour markets

Lourdes Mella Méndez

The introduction of a new collective book is always both a responsibility and a true pleasure for the editors. This book, entitled *Labour Law and the Gig Economy: Challenges Posed by the Digitalisation of Labour Processes*, is made up of chapters from the United Kingdom, Russia, India, China, Portugal, Egypt and other Arab states, Spain, Belarus, Poland and France. This international scope is relevant to analyse the topic related to the impact of the digitalisation in labour markets and labour processes.

From an introductory and explanatory perspective, the three main research issues analysed into this international book are the following:

1) *The main changes that the introduction of new technologies produces in the labour market, from a general viewpoint.* The rapid progress of modern technology, ICTs and AI and their multiple applications to each phase of the labour production system is changing the production rules on a global level and has a significant impact in every aspect of work. New technology transforms work patterns and changes the type of jobs and even the nature of the tasks performed. A new term appears for the new labour market and economy, which is 'gig economy', and it reflects the temporary and flexible jobs that now are commonplace, as companies prefer to hire independent contractors (freelancers) or part-time or temporary employees instead of the traditional full-time employees (who rarely change positions and focus on a lifetime career).

   Flexibility for both parties is an advantage of the new employment, as is indicated in chapters two and three. In the modern digital world, it is becoming increasingly common for people to work remotely or from home. This enables flexible work as many of those jobs do not require the freelancer or employee to come into the office to provide services. Employers also have a wider range of applicants to choose from around the world. Another advantage of digitalisation is the huge possibilities of new businesses and services to provide to the world market with efficiency (fast and immediate service and cost savings). So, special interest is paid in blockchain technology and all its applications in execution of labour contracts in chapter two or in social networks related to employment relationship and noncompete clauses in chapter five.

On a negative perspective, this new economy and digitalised employment, which is possible thanks to new technologies and online platforms (as these connect workers with customers), brings new challenges for the workforce, such as the clarification of their employment status, as it will not always be self-employed or autonomous worker status. In a digitalised labour environment it is possible to have employees coexisting, self-employees or even the so-call third option 'economically dependent autonomous worker'. The national legislators should provide some criteria to protect workers from employer fraud, which deprives employees of their traditional labour status and, consequently, labour rights. Chapter one deals with this issue in a splendid manner and so does chapter six. In the last chapter, the author highlights how pre-industrial companies' allegation of property rights emerges again to justify the control over employees and limit the scope of labour protection. Another negative effect of this new digital revolution is the possible increase of unemployment. Computers with intelligent programmes and robots could take many routine tasks and jobs away from workers in next few years. Chapters three and four examine – from different countries (India and Arab States) and legal systems – this global challenge and point out the urgency of providing specific training for upskilling and reskilling the workforce that will be affected by automation.

2) *The principal effects of the interaction of new technologies with an employee's private life.* Three key and interconnected aspects are examined here: the first, the limits of employer control – increased by new technologies – in relation to the protection of employee's fundamental rights to privacy. Two chapters, on a complementary basis (the seventh from a theoretical approach and the eighth from a more judicial and practical method), analyse this burning issue. The second aspect is the right of the employee to a work-life balance and the third is the right to disconnection from the workplace and the limitation of corporate control of working time. On this point, two complementary studies from France and Spain – chapters 10 and 11 – defend the importance of clearly separate times both for health protection and to guarantee the immunity of rest time from the employer whose power is amplified by digital tools. All these risks are relevant in the new employment generated by digitalisation, as flexibility in a gig economy often means that workers have to make themselves available any time gigs become available, regardless of their other needs. So, flexibility of working gigs is prone to disrupt work-life balance, sleep patterns, and activities of daily life. The solutions offered in these chapters could be helpful for social agents and legislators.

3) *The impact of digitalisation on the labour process.* Digitalisation of the employment relationship has consequences on labour process too, although very few authors pay attention to these important effects. Due to the scarcity of doctrinal analysis, and with the intention of filling the gap, this book includes two specific and complementary chapters devoted to examining the nature of digital evidence on labour procedure and its connexion with the fundamental rights of the employee. When an employer uses new technologies

to control an employee and then makes decisions based on them, digital evidence appears as a new type of evidence, with a specific legal regime. Despite the fact that two authors are from Spain, the research done has a global interest as the problems caused by new technologies and digital evidence are similar in different countries.

The selection of countries included in this book is not random, but intentional, as the phenomenon of digitalisation is universal and facilitates a global economy and society too. So, it is important to analyse the current situation of the digital revolution not only in the main European countries (e.g., France, Spain, Portugal, Poland) and the USA (as many books and conferences do), but also in very far and different economic, social and legal systems around the world. This enables us to offer the reader a new, fresh and unique approach to this important topic from Arab States, Russia and Asia (India) and show how the common challenges and risks emerge in a similar way everywhere.

The previous political and economic countries' situation determines the nature of the answer given by national political institutions to this digital change so far. So, in Arab States the delay in enacting appropriate legislation in connection with the development of technology in the Arab labour market is due to political unrest and revolution that has occurred in many of these countries, and led to a greater focus on constitutional amendments as to the exercise of political rights and criminal legislation. This requires a stronger effort by social agents (trade unions and employers' organisation) to raise awareness about the importance of tackling the current problems of the labour market, which is related to national economic growth and social welfare. The conditions in these Arab countries are ideal to develop this digital revolution, i.e. a great interest by young people in learning engineering and applied technological sciences in universities and institutes, which will contribute significantly to the absorption of this technology by a wide sector of Arab citizens. Arab countries also have huge financial resources (especially the Gulf countries) to acquire advanced technology and employ it in different workplaces.

In the case of Russia, the inexistence of a specific regulation about digitalisation can be explained by the inflexibility of the governmental decision-making system or a lack of political will to promote the necessary changes. This delay may also partly be attributed to the simplified approach that the Labour Code presents with regard to the classification of platform workers (and other cases where new technologies are involved) thanks to which the Russian judicial system does not experience a rise in claims related to this issue despite the wide network of Uber-like services. The Russian Labour Code has an old provision that presumes employment relations to exist in case of doubts that cannot be ruled out when a court considers a dispute on the recognition of such relations to be employment relations. Finally, for India, the 4th Industrial Revolution brings great opportunities to jump many stages of progress, speeding the process to become a developed economy. Companies are adopting different technological advances in diverse ways, some cautiously, some in a confident manner and many companies are still waiting and watching. From the negative perspective, India is afraid of unemployment. Automation and robotics in industrial manufacturing suits countries with low productive populations, but it does not suit countries like India, where more than 12 million people enter the job market every year. So, there is a natural fear of job loss resulting from automation and robotics in India. Which is why, in this book the author's chapter on India stresses the need to train a workforce that is able to face the current digitalisation in a positive manner.

The principal aim of this book is to expose the huge and global importance of new technologies in labour markets, and their challenges, and then to alert governments and international organisations about them so that they can take the necessary action to combat some of the most important risks to protect people from them.

Divided into three parts, this book will enrich the present debate with new approaches to legal problems from different countries.

In the first part, entitled "The impact of new technologies in the labour market", the reader will find, in chapter one, a critical appreciation on a selection of legal aspects of the 2017 Taylor Review, written by Professor Jo Carby-Hall, of University of Hull (United Kingdom). In general, this Review treats a rich variety of industrial relations and other topics and generally makes realistic and wide-ranging recommendations for changes in specific laws for the British government and Parliament to consider prior to enacting legislation. The "Good work: Taylor Review of Modern Working Practices", published in July 2017, deals with each of the "four conversations" or aspects selected by the ILO's Future of Work Centenary Initiative (namely "work and society," "decent work for all," "the organisation of work and production" and the "governance of work") in the British context. Thus, the British Government set out its "Good Work Plan" in response to the Taylor Review recommendations.

This chapter makes an interesting critique on a selection of some legal topics of content of that Review. This critique includes the following crucial issues related to the British labour market: (a) the importance of employment status; (b) the worker status conundrum in comparison to employee status; (c) greater transparency of rights in the particulars of employment; (d) one/two sided flexibility; (e) continuity of employment; (f) agency workers and HRMC rules; (g) corporate governance and social dialogue; (h) corporate transparency; (i) enforcement and (j) a summation. Although the Taylor Review is criticised for failing to provide clear recommendations to distinguish the three main status categories (namely employee, worker and self-employed or independent contractor), the chapter does not hold the same opinion. On the one hand, the Taylor Report makes constructive suggestions in respect of this complicated issue and, on the other hand, the author does not believe that the laws are falling behind when faced with cases involving modern technological and innovative advances. Recently, British tribunals and courts have been very effective in dealing with the most up-to-date digital and technological innovations which have encouraged the establishment and rapid development of the gig economy which is why the author is against any fundamental changes being made to the laws relating to status, which could generate new problems. However, the author suggests some discreet changes to take into account employers who abuse the system to the detriment of the worker.

What is clearly missing in this Review is the solving of an imminent problem facing the British flexible labour market, namely providing a definition of the *genuine* independent contractor status or *genuine* self-employment status. The independent contractor status currently is one that applies to those who are not employees or workers and is therefore a default category of individual or body. It would be useful to have a concise definition in the near future.

According to the author, this Review has much merit and is rich in ideas that could prove seminal for both working practices as well as developing trends in the British labour market. Indeed, the Review has raised the profile of the debate surrounding the importance of good employment practices in non-standard working arrangements, which cannot be ignored by legislators, employers or other stakeholders.

In the second chapter, Professor Daria Chernyaeva, of the Law Faculty of the National Research University "Higher School of Economics" (Russia), draws up some relevant considerations related to the impact of the 4th Industrial Revolution on individual employment relationship under the regulatory regime in Russia. The main advantages and disadvantages of the major new technologies associated with the current Industrial Revolution are exposed in the context of the labour framework, elaborating on the ways to eliminate or reduce disadvantages and boost the benefits derived from them. Special attention is paid to blockchain technology, which offers a distributed and shared ledger (or a database, or digital platform) based on cryptographic algorithms which store information on all verified transactions performed on a certain asset (digital or digitised). The penetration of blockchain-based technologies is increasing in several spheres. Apart from cryptocurrencies or internet of things (IoT), the blockchain can be used to provide digital identity, support digital voting, financial services or even be used in contractual relationships to execute the terms of regular contracts through the computerised transaction protocol that the blockchain provides.

According to the author, technically the new technologies have no imminent features that would automatically protect workers involved with them. Therefore, a very smart regulation is needed to step in and establish a system of minimal standards applicable to workers involved in such relationships.

The chapter also contains a short review of the Russian position on the regulatory efforts on the use of new technologies in labour relationships (i.e. regulating remote work, health and safety or the use of electronic technologies in human resource management, employee record keeping and document processing), as well as an analysis of responses to this by the Russian courts.

The following chapter, by Professor Dr. Durgambini A. Patel, Professor of Law at Savitribai Phule Pune University (India), and entitled "Digitalisation *vis-à-vis* the Indian Labour Market: Pros and Cons", gives the reader a clear and interesting view on the impact of digitalisation in another important Asian country, India. At the beginning of the chapter, the author compares the two interrelated phenomena "digitalisation" and "digitisation" and links the 3rd Industrial Revolution to the first (digitalisation) and the concept of outsourcing. The researcher then deals with the meaning of this latter concept and the advantages and disadvantages on labour markets. On the positive side, it increases growth in business along with cost savings and allows for an efficient utilisation of resources. From a negative perspective, the author emphasises the constant feeling of job insecurity and the loss of jobs in the domestic workforce.

As noted by Professor Durgambini, the 4th Industrial Revolution is characterised by automation. So, several traditional methods of working would be replaced by automated technologies which reduce labour time and cost. The inventions of robots and automatable technologies are posing a threat to the existing industrial setup as the tasks which were previously not automatable are now under the radar of automation.

The analysis leads to the conclusion that routine jobs performed by the population are amongst the ones most likely to be automated by machines. It is relevant to note that such jobs are mostly performed by people with lower educational qualifications who aspire to rise above the minimum wage. Replacing such workers will lead to social security problems, including both societal and economical imbalance, so the Indian policy maker must formulate the right policies in the coming times to help mitigate the impact of such replacements. Educating the soon to be replaced workers and inculcating new skills will help them survive. The Skill India campaign launched by the government in 2015 aims to train over 40 million people by 2022 in various skills.

According to the author, the government must also consider the impact of digitalisation on the economic system of India. The disruptive nature of technologies will ultimately result in the concentration of wealth in the hands of the owners of such technological assets, who are not in the majority. This justifies the immense importance of education of the masses and especially those in the workforce in the age of rapid digitalisation.

In the fourth chapter, Professor Alaa Eltamimi, from the Faculty of Law of Mansoura University (Egypt), analyses the impact of new technologies in the current labour market of selected Arab States which include Egypt, Oman, the United Arab Emirates, Qatar, Jordan, Lebanon, Kuwait, Yemen and Saudi Arabia. The author shows how the Arab states have taken important measures to adopt modern technology systems in numerous fields of work. These measures are described by the author who illustrates the effects of changes being made to labour laws in the various Arab countries and the importance of training programmes. In the first part of the chapter, the author analyses the challenges arising from modern technology. In the second part, the author deals with future job development in relation to the developing technology, followed in the third part by recommendations and concluding remarks.

In the fifth chapter, Professor Duarte Abrunhosa e Sousa, of the Centre for Legal and Economic Research of the Faculty of Law, University of Porto (Portugal), delves into a specific and good example of the current digitalisation of labour markets: the impact of social networks in the employment relationship. Social networks – such as Facebook, Twitter or LinkedIn – allows the construction of a new online public space with interactions and consequences in the labour market, because they have moved discussion forums into a virtual reality that can have an unlimited reach. The author starts from this idea to analyse the potential impact of social networks in the breach of employment non-compete clauses. In other words, the objective is to know how employment non-compete clauses can be breached by workers with posts, tweets or profile updates on social networks, with an emphasis on Portuguese law.

These types of clauses should be well regulated in each country's legal framework since they can promote important restrictions on workers' rights to work. These restrictions are more relevant if their effects continue in a post-contractual period because employers can claim damages if a non-compete clause is breached by a former worker. So, it is easy to appreciate the importance of this new topic. For example, in 2015, a Danish court decided that updating a LinkedIn profile could be a violation of a covenant not to compete. This way, only by studying the importance of social networks in society and the economy, is it possible to determine if the information shared by a worker on social networks can cause damage to a former employer. Some conclusions are that industry analysis is essential to determine if the use of social networks for professional purposes is a breach of a covenant not to compete; and social networks are a new paradigm that must be interpreted sufficiently well by courts in order to avoid their use to evade liability by workers.

In the sixth chapter, Professor Julia Tomassetti, of City University of Hong Kong, School of Law (China), reflects on the necessary balance between worker rights and property rights in digitalised work. The author explains how companies appeal to property rights to limit the scope of labour legislation, focusing on disputes over employment status involving service work (with customer interaction) and work coordinated through digital technology. The analysis exposes a potential legal consequence of the digitalisation of work: the restoration of the pre-industrial master's property rights to the servant's labour.

As the legal basis of the right to control the labour of others is ambiguous, companies draw on this ambiguity by arguing that they direct labour not in their capacity as employers, but rather in their capacity as disposers and protectors of their property (entrepreneurs). So, companies dismiss the relevance of labour controls to their labour law obligations. As illustrated by lawsuits involving the digital platforms Uber and Lyft, companies exploit the worker-customer encounter and the embedding of managerial controls in software to increase the relational space over which they can redefine employer authority as the prerogatives of the enterprise owner.

However, according to the author, the appeals to entrepreneurial prerogatives in disputes over employment status are debatable. The origin of the employer's authority to control the enterprise was the employment contract, not property. Besides, there is no reason that the legal standards for employment status should cede to property rights.

The second part of the book, entitled "The impact of new technologies in the employees' private life", consists of five chapters related to concrete aspects of the influence of the technological innovation on the employee's private life. Two chapters deal with the relation between the employer powers and the employee's fundamental rights. So, in the seventh chapter, Professors López Aniorte, Ortiz González-Conde and Megías-Bas, from University of Murcia (Spain), examine, from a legal point of view, the conflict between the fundamental right to privacy of the employee and the exercise of managerial power by means of capturing images of employees by using CCTV and hiring detectives. In the first instance, the authors analyse the traditional doctrine of the Spanish Constitutional Court, which admits that such means of control is legal provided that the control measure is justified, appropriate, necessary and balanced. However, the casuistic nature of the so-called "proportionality doctrine" allows the adoption of contradictory judicial solutions in analogous or identical cases, generating situations of legal uncertainty.

In the opinion of the authors, this flexibility will have to be nuanced after the judgments of the European Court of Human Rights (ECHR) in the well-known cases of Bărbulescu II and López Ribalda, that require a rethinking of the theory of fundamental rights of working people in many countries, within the framework of the new digital and technological era. The ECHR Judgment of January 9, 2018, case of López Ribalda and others *versus* Spain, emphasises the need for prior, express, specific and unequivocal information to the employee about the employer control. The authors agree with the idea that this ruling will allow deepening transparency and the protection of privacy and personal data of workers in an environment of intensification of employer control through new technologies.

In a similar way, the eighth chapter also explores the limits of new technologies and the need of protection of employee's fundamental rights through different important judgements. The author, lawyer and researcher Professor Artur Rycak, from Łazarski University (Poland), considers that the use of modern technologies (by the employee as part of an employment relationship) is linked with the threat of a violation by the employer of the right to privacy and the confidentiality of the employee's correspondence. The author reviews the most relevant rulings of the ECHR, in which the Court has ruled that the right to privacy includes the sphere of employment within the framework of industrial relations, both in the public and private sectors. At the same time, the Court specified the boundaries of the employer's interference with the employee's private sphere based on several international laws, in the light of Art. 8 of the European Convention for the Protection of Human Rights and Fundamental Freedoms, adopted by the Council of Europe.

Special attention is also paid here to the Bărbulescu case (2017), as the Court established minimum standards for the protection of the right to employee privacy and the secrecy of correspondence, which governments must consider in their legislative process. These standards are addressed to employers too. So, according to the author, it is clear that since that judgement it is necessary to take seriously the duty to inform employees about the monitoring of their activity (the notification should be clear, complete and given in advance) to avoid the violation of the right to privacy and to respect the principle of proportionality. In any case, the extent of monitoring by the employer and the degree of intrusion into the employee's privacy should be measured in each specific situation taking into account all circumstances of the case.

The ninth chapter is related to another important topic linked to the employee's private life: namely, the influence of new technologies in the employee's work-life balance. The author, Professor Tatsiana Ushakova, of Belarusian State University, Minsk (Belarus), reflects on the theme under the legal framework of the European Union. In the field of labour law, work-life balance is always relevant and should be taken into account for two reasons: on the one hand, it is connected to other significant issues (such as labour rights, equality and non-discrimination, safety and health at work, organisation of working time and new forms of work); on the other hand, work-life balance is a dynamic concept that has experienced the same transformations that has affected the world of work so far. From this starting point, the author revisits this concept within the European Union legal framework as it is necessary to define the impact of the European Pillar of Social Rights and the phenomena of Industry 4.0 on it.

The European Pillar includes a comprehensive approach to the work-life balance, however the author is critical of the document's vague proposal in terms of its legal nature and effectiveness. In this sense, according to the author, the recognition of the fundamental right to work-life balance should be considered including a set of effective measures, mainly the organisation of working time and positive protection measures. Even more, a framework directive with a comprehensive approach and a genuine balance between organisational and technological aspects and negative and positive protection should be devised.

The two following chapters are related to a specific aspect that enables the effectiveness of the work-life balance, i.e. the right to disconnection from the workplace. Certainly, the need of establishing rigid limits to the possibility of permanent communication, permitted by new ICT, is essential to protect health and other workers' rights. The technological availability of workers for indefinite periods of time, beyond traditional working hours, blurs the lines between working and rest time, and even creates a new kind of (working) time, known as "technological connectivity time", in which the worker is not free to completely rest. This is analysed in the tenth chapter authored by Rodríguez González, from the University of La Laguna (Spain), related to the digital disconnection as a limit to corporate control of working time. The author studies in greater depth whether digital disconnection should be incorporated into the Spanish legal system as a "new" right or, by contrast, if it should be considered a specific part of the "right to rest" and a mandatory minimum content of collective bargaining. According to this author, within the Spanish judicial framework, technological disconnection need not be incorporated as a novel right but may instead be simply upheld as a specific subset of the established "right to rest". To that end, a modification of Articles 34 and 85.3 of the Workers' Statute in Spain is recommended, in order that the notion of technological disconnection is duly upheld and considered as part of collective bargaining, and so that the right and duty to disconnect is accompanied by global company policies implemented to raise awareness of this issue.

In a complementary way, the eleventh chapter is focused on the French legal model. Professor Loïc Lerouge, of the COMPTRASEC, University of Bordeaux (France), examines the right to disconnect in his country, which was the first to regulate this important issue. Indeed, the French Labour Code was modified, by Law n° 2016-1088, in 2016 (the so-called "El Khomri" law), to include this new right to disconnection. According to the researcher, that means that the public sector is not directly concerned and that creates an unbalance in terms of this right between the private and the public sectors. So, in order to implement the right to disconnect, the public service has to bargain and conclude an agreement without any legal incentives.

In relation to the private sector, at first, the arrangements to exercise this right by the employees are defined by collective bargaining which must be implemented by companies with at least 50 employees and a trade union representative at the time of the annual negotiation on the professional equality between women and men and the quality of life at work (Article L. 2242-8 of the Labour Code). However, the employer is not compelled to reach an agreement. If companies do not have any union representative or the bargaining fails, the law provides that the employer must still implement the right to disconnect in the form of a charter. However, the absence of a charter is not sanctioned whereas the obligation to negotiate is punishable with one year in prison and a fine of €3,750 under the article L. 2242-8 of the Labour Code.

In the author's opinion, the analysis of the agreements concluded on the quality of life at work in France shows that the right to disconnect is more focused on a technical and organisational approach rather than on an approach based on health at work. It is important to take into account that recognising legally a right to disconnect from the workplace is related not only to the employer's management power, but also to matters of health and psychological harassment generated by some methods of managing employees. This link has even been recognised in France by the Court of Cassation, which the reader will be able to peruse during the reading of the chapter.

The third part of the book is related to "the impact of new technologies on the labour process," and consists of two chapters. Both chapters are written by Spanish researchers but it is important to bear in mind that the type of problems which new technologies are causing in the Spanish labour process are similar to the problems experienced in other countries, especially when the violation of the worker's fundamental rights is alleged, so the solutions suggested here have a general interest and are thus of great importance. Chapter 12 deepens the digital evidence in the labour process and the fundamental rights of the employee. The author, Professor Mella Méndez, of the University of Santiago de Compostela (Spain), reflects on the use of e-mails as a software tool commonly employed in the workplace, which by facilitating easy storage and the recording of all information transmitted through them, serve as a means of digital evidence in the labour process. So, this work analyses its real probative value, for which it is necessary to verify its authenticity and accuracy of content. In addition, the researcher focuses on the process of obtaining this digital evidence, as when the employer violates the fundamental rights of the employee in obtaining the evidence, such evidence is illegal and ineffective. Additionally, this illegality is transferred to any possible sanction that the employer imposes on the employee (as a result of the information obtained), although legal doctrine and jurisprudence are in doubt between the two classical positions: qualification of the nullity or the unfairness of the dismissal (when this is the sanction).

The author considers that the best solution is to take into account all circumstances of the concrete case (as it is also defended by the so-called intermediate position) and then reach a decision. Thus, in that situation in which first an employer violates the fundamental rights of the employee and, later, a contractual breach of the employee is discovered, it is logical that the illegality of that employer surveillance and, consequently, the nullity of the technological evidence, also implies the nullity of the subsequent dismissal. This brings the cause of that unlawful conduct, that is, the employer acquires knowledge of the contractual breach of the employee as a result of his own irregular conduct.

However, the situation is very different when the employer has certain knowledge or a well-founded suspicion of an employee's non-compliance and, in order to prove it, decides to perform surveillance behaviour to gather objective evidence to submit to the proceedings. In this case, if that surveillance violates fundamental rights, it will be null and void and will not have any effect on its own, but the extension of the nullity to the employer's decision to dismiss may be excessive.

In the final chapter, Professors Ferrando García, Rodríguez Egio and Megías-Bas, of the University of Murcia (Spain), insist on the probative value and effectiveness of the evidence obtained through e-mail and messaging in the control of the workplace activity. Special attention is paid to the compatibility of those means of surveillance of labour activity with the constitutional right of the worker's privacy, in order to verify the legality or illegality of the evidence obtained.

Related to the key issue of the effects of the unlawful evidence, obtained with the violation of fundamental rights, in the classification of the disciplinary action, it is concluded that it is necessary to defend "the irradiation thesis" which entails the nullity of the disciplinary decision. Therefore, in this way, it considers that the transgression of a fundamental right not only involves the nullity of the act constituting the infringement, but also the restitution of the situation prior to the moment at which the infringement occurred and the reparation of all the consequences derived from the referred act.

Bearing in mind the analyses and evaluation which have taken place in the 13 chapters of this volume, the relevance and interest of the book is clear for two reasons: first, the challenging topic and second, the volume's international scope. Very few books – if any – offer such a broad variety of legal issues and countries' studies in relation to the impact of new technologies in labour markets, private lives and labour processes.

In general terms, the main conclusions of the research included in this book are the following:

1) The 4th Industrial Revolution is already influencing the global economy and society, as shown in the different chapters. All countries around the world are making changes to adapt their labour markets and companies to the huge challenges that these new technological advances (ICTs, robots, 3D printing, AI, digitalisation of manufacturing process) will pose in the coming years. One is the emergence of the gig economy based on flexibility and occasional work, which are elements that lead to the discussion about the nature of the new services provision. Most national legislations have not kept up with those technological and innovative changes and employers and individuals working for those employers find themselves in a legal limbo in relation to the legal status (i.e. employee, worker, economically dependent autonomous worker, independent contractor or self-employed worker) (see chapter one). The specific status must be determined in each situation according to the concrete circumstances, avoiding employer fraud in misclassification, with the intention of removing labour rights for employees.

2) Digitalisation presents some important risks, such as the increase of the unemployment, as exposed in chapters two, three, four and six. The experts conclude that routine and basic jobs performed by the population are amongst the ones most likely to be automated by machines; humans are not needed at all for many tasks, as computers gradually replace them. For example, driving jobs will disappear as vehicles become self-driven. To the extent that those type of jobs are mostly performed by workers having lower educational qualifications, their replacement will lead to social security problems, including both societal and economical imbalance, so the governments must articulate the right policies to mitigate the impact of such replacement (i.e., unemployment benefits, social basic income). Furthermore, a key and urgent measure is workforce training to acquire new skills and competences, especially related to the use of digital tools.

3) New technologies clearly impact the private life of employees, particularly with regard to fundamental rights (i.e. dignity, privacy and secrecy of communications), as analysed in chapters seven and eight. Employers can search for people online and maybe see them expressing controversial opinions in social media. Digital cameras watch and record our movements in public and private places. Currently, it is much harder to have personal privacy in the digital world, specifically when the person becomes an employee and the employer has power augmented by ICTs. The European Court of Human Rights has ruled about some important cases and emphasises the need for an employer to give employees prior, express and unequivocal information about the use of these cameras and tools to record the labour activity. This judicial doctrine will allow more transparency and the protection of privacy and personal data of workers in an environment of intensification of business control. The infringement of the employee's fundamental rights has serious consequences in the labor procedure when the employee files a claim against the employer, as elaborated in chapters 12 and 13.

4) Governments and social agents have to take care of employee's health and safety in the digital labour context, as claimed in chapter 10 and 11. On the one hand, the physical isolation imposed by remote and digital work (i.e. telework) increases the tendency for people to socialise and communicate via digital devices rather than through real life contact. This can easily lead to several health problems as studies suggest that the lack of real-life contact is causing depression and other forms of mental illness in many people. On the other hand, the limitation of working time and digital disconnection are important actions to protect workers from overtime and psychological risks (technostress, techno-addition, anxiety). Collective agreements and social dialogue are good ways to adopt effective measures to avoid these risks.

5) It is crucial to ensure a good work-life balance in the context of the 4th Industrial Revolution and for that the organisation of working time is the key issue, as concluded in chapter nine. Flexible working hours, part-time work and even working from home have been shown to considerably raise job satisfaction, productivity and lead to higher motivation in employees. A good work-life balance is related to nondiscrimination and equality policies in labour markets with important results in increasing productivity too.

The editors believe that the reader will find within the pages of this volume numerous theories and solutions presented in an informed and scholarly manner in answer to the challenges resulting from the digitalisation of labour markets and processes. We wish to thank the publishers for their constant professional support throughout the preparation of this international book. The editors also wish to thank the authors for their painstaking work in contributing their chapters and collaborating with the editors' numerous suggestions, demands and constructive criticisms.

Santiago de Compostela,
August 2019

Part I

The impact of new technologies in the labour market

1 The Taylor Review 2017 – A critical appreciation on a selection of its legal content

Jo Carby-Hall

Preliminary matter

The ILO's "centenary conversations" versus the Taylor Review 2017

Driven primarily by the digital revolution and rapid technological advances, the world of work is changing to such an extent that the International Labour Organisation (ILO) established a high-level body to examine the relationship between work and society. The Commission on the Future of Work will address how the future of work can deliver decent and sustainable jobs thereby contributing to decent work and economic growth. Launched on 21st August, 2017 under the ILO's Future of Work Centenary Initiative, the Commission will organise its work round four centenary conversations, namely "work and society," "decent work for all," "the organisation of work and production" and the "governance of work."[1] The global body's examination will seek to provide the analytical basis for the delivery of social justice in the 21st century.

Coincidentally, and although no mention but one[2] of the ILO initiative is made therein in a different context, the Taylor Review of Modern Working Practices entitled "Good Work" and published in July 2017,[3] treats each of the aforementioned "four conversations" in the British context referred to on several occasions in that Review as "the British way."[4]

The approach of the Review is based on a single overriding ambition, namely "All work in the United Kingdom economy should be fair and decent

---

1 Source: "ILO launches Global Commission on Future of Work (21st August 2017)" http://sdg.iisd,org/news/ilo-launches-global-commission-on-t... (retrieved 14th October, 2017).
2 See "Good Work: The Taylor Review of Good Working Practices" July 2017, at p. 104 quoting the CIPD submission to the Review in the context of the ILO Decent Work construct for emerging economies or similar ideas of Good Work and Meaningful Work
3 The team consisted of Matthew Taylor (Chair), Greg Marsh, Diane Nicol and Paul Broadbent.
4 See e.g. "Good Work: The Taylor Review of Good Working Practices" July 2017 at pp. 7, 9, 33, 51, *etc.* hereinafter called "Taylor Review." See a brief commentary on this Review by Jo Carby-Hall entitled *"Le Rapport Taylor de 2017"* in Revue du Droit Comparé du Travail et de la Sécurité Sociale, Presses Universitaires de Bordeaux Vol 3, 2018, pp. 182–185.

with realistic scope for development and fulfilment."[5] Good work matters because (a) "fairness demands...that people, particularly those on lower incomes, have routes to progress in work, have the opportunity to boost their earning power and are treated with respect and decency at work," (b) "the quality of people's work is ... a major factor in helping people to stay healthy and happy which benefits them and serves the wider public interest" (c) "better designed work that gets the best out of people can make an important contribution to tackling our complex challenge of low productivity," (d) "we should as a matter of principle, want the experience of work to match the aspirations we have of modern citizenship; that people feel they are respected, trusted and enabled... to take responsibility, and (e) "the pace of change in the modern economy and particularly technology and the development of new business models, means we need a concerted approach to work which is both up to date... responsive and based on enduring principles of fairness."[6]

These are indeed high principles achieved only in an ideal world of work but to which the British industrial relations system should aspire and strive towards. The Taylor Review is comprehensive, treats a rich variety of industrial relations and other topics[7] and generally makes realistic and wide-ranging recommendations for changes in specific laws for the British government and Parliament to consider prior to enacting legislation.[8] The government set out its "Good Work Plan"[9] in response to the Taylor Review recommendations and described it as "the largest upgrade in workers' rights in over a generation" which "is a key part in building a labour market that continues to reward people for hard work, that celebrates good employers, and is boosting productivity and earning potential across the UK."[10]

Outline plan of this chapter

Parameters of space do not allow for a discussion to take place on all aspects of this Review. What is proposed is to attempt a critique on a selection of some legal topics therein. These will include (a) the importance of the employment

5 "Taylor Review", *op, cit.* at p. 6.
6 *Ibid.*
7 For example, quality of work, clarity in the law, one-sided flexibility, responsible business, fairer enforcement, incentives, self- employment, scope for development, progress opportunities, lasting change, *et al.*
8 See however the polemic article written by Katie Bales, Alan Bogg and Tonia Novitz "'Voice' and 'Choice' in modern work practices: Problems with the Taylor Review", *Industrial Law Journal*, 46, 2018 at pp. 1–18 where the Taylor Review is subjected to much criticism (retrieved from Westlaw UK in 2018).
9 Published on 17th December, 2018 Com. 9755 https://www.gov.yk/government/publica tions/good-work-plan (retrieved 10th February 2019).
10 See commentary by Jo Carby-Hall "Justice au Travail – Lutes à armes égales" in *Revue du Droit Comparé du Travail et de la Sécurité Sociale*. Presses Universitaires de Bordeaux. Vol. 1 2019 pp. 234–237.

status; (b) the worker status conundrum in comparison to the employee status; (c) greater transparency of rights in the particulars of employment; (d) one/two sided flexibility; (e) continuity of employment; (f) agency workers and HRMC rules; (g) corporate governance and social dialogue (h) corporate transparency; (i) enforcement and (j) a summation.

The importance of employment status

The Law Society of England and Wales[11] submission to the Taylor Review commented as follows:

> Determining whether you are an employee, a worker or genuinely self-employed requires the ability to understand complex legislation, which is spread over many Acts, and be aware of a mountain of case law. For individuals, not knowing your employment status means not knowing what employment rights you deserve. For businesses, this situation can lead to uncertainty about their responsibilities and what can be demanded from workers. The situation does not need to be so complicated.[12]

For individuals to know what employment rights they enjoy, they first need to know their employment status. As the Taylor Review rightly states "Employment status is the gateway through which an individual must go to access statutory rights."[13] Individuals working in traditional full-time employment – which, in spite of the rapid developments taking place in new employment forms[14] – still

---

11 The Law Society of England and Wales is the professional association that represents and governs the lawyers' (solicitors') profession for the jurisdiction of England and Wales. It provides services and support to practising and training solicitors as well as serving as a sounding base for law reform.

12 "Taylor Review", *op. cit.,* p. 34.

13 *Ibid,* p. 35.

14 For a detailed evaluation of those new forms of employment which developed by reason of technological and digital developments from *circa* the latter part of the 1970s onwards, see Jo Carby-Hall "Novel Forms of Employment: Quid Juris?" in "Nuevas Technologías y Nuevas Formas de Trabajar en el Derecho Español y Comparado" (Lourdes Mella Méndez y Pilar Núñez Contreras (Eds)) in e-journal Colección Monografías Derecho Social y Empresa. No. 1 (2016) Dykinson publishers at pp. 32–78 and for even newer forms of employment in the gig economy which took place from *circa* 2016 see, by the same author, "Innovatory Forms of Employment in the 21ˢᵗ Century versus Employment Status" in *Sociedade de Permutas e Combinações: Problemas Jurídicos da Economia Colaborativa* scheduled for publication by Cambridge Scholars Publishing in 2020. See too Jo Carby-Hall "New Frontiers of Labour Law: Dependant and Autonomous Workers" in *Du Travail Salarié au Travail Indépendant: Permanences et Mutations* (Professors Bruno Veneziani and Umberto Carabelli (Eds)) European SOCRATES Programme (2003) Cacucci Editore. Italy, for more established and traditional employment statuses in the UK as for example, crown employees, office holders, probationary employees, merchant seamen, fixed-term contracts, call centres, piece workers, home workers, temporary workers, apprentices, etc. at pp. 225–246. For the status of seafarers which includes

constitute a majority of persons employed and thus enjoy the employee status[15] and the employment rights which automatically go with that status. Individuals who are *genuinely* independent contractors or self-employed do not generally enjoy any employment rights.

The problems of employment status arise where individuals are neither "employees" nor "independent contractors" but enjoy the status of "worker." That latter status is defined in a most complex manner by legislation.[16]

The reality is that, resulting from digital and technological innovation the world of work is changing rapidly and will continue to do so in the future at a relentless and unprecedented pace. Three important matters need to be stressed at the outset. First, British laws – both statutory and common law based on judicial precedent[17] – need to keep pace with technological and digital advances to meet the needs of the modern labour market. Second, and just as important, is that (a) employment of whatever kind needs to be fair and decent so as to give, not only protection to the individual at work, but also (b) to alert businesses which wish to know what their legal responsibilities are toward those whom they employ. Third, the laws – whether statutory provisions or common law – are not overly clear and are open to a variety of interpretations which encourage unscrupulous employers (a) to exploit individuals working for those kinds of employers and at the same time (b) undercut other employers who respect the legal provisions and therefore have an unfair economic advantage over those latter types of employers.

merchant seamen and fishermen see Jo Carby-Hall "The Legal Impact of Brexit on Seafarers' Employment" in *Retos Presentes y Futuros de la Política Marítima Integrada de la Unión Europea* (Professor Laura Carballo Piñeiro (Coordinatora)) (2017) J.B. Bosch Editor, pp. 273–299.

15 The Employment Rights Act 1996 s. 230 (1) defines the employee as "an individual who has entered into or works under... a contract of employment" which includes a "contract of service or apprenticeship whether express or implied and (if express) whether oral or in writing." (s.230 (2)).

16 *Ibid.*, s. 230 (3) (b). Also known as the "limb (b) workers." This subsection of section 230 will receive special attention at pp. 27–30 *infra*.

17 Judicial precedent (sometimes referred to as case law) is a process whereby judges follow previously decided cases where the facts are identical or sufficiently similar. The doctrine of judicial precedent involves the application of the principle of *stare decisis et non quieta movere* (meaning, standing by what has been decided and not unsettling the established.) Once a point of law has been decided in a particular case, the law must be applied in all future cases containing the same material facts. The binding element is the *ratio decidendi* (the judge's legal reasoning for coming to the conclusion in respect of a case.) *Obiter dicta* (issues stated in the course of the judgment) are not binding but may provide persuasive evidence. The basic rule in the hierarchy is that a court must follow the precedents from a higher court, but they are not bound to follow decisions from courts lower in the hierarchy. The hierarchy consists of the Court of Justice of the European Union (in the UK following Brexit on 31 January 2020 until the end of the Transition Period ending 31 December 2020 and in this writer's opinion, possibly thereafter), the Supreme Court, the Court of Appeal and the Divisional Courts. All other courts which include the County, Crown, Magistrates' and tribunals cannot create precedents. "Distinguishing" is a way of avoiding following judicial precedent because the material facts are different or because the statement of fact in the previous case cannot be adequately applied to the new case because it is too narrow.

Although the Taylor Review had received approbation from many who were consulted and who held the opinion that "the current framework – the British way – works well and is flexible enough to deal with new ways of working"[18] it nevertheless concluded that "through our discussions it became clear that how the law is interpreted varies widely."[19] The Review mentions the fact that over the years the courts tried to provide some clarity through the creation of tests for determining whether an individual enjoys the employment status of "employee" or that of an "independent contractor"[20] and more recently, cases relating to gig employment,[21] on whether the individual is a "worker" or an "independent contractor." The Taylor Review thus came to the conclusion that "the relevance of weight given to these varies depending on the circumstances; without an encyclopaedic knowledge of case law, understanding how this might apply to your situation is almost impossible."

That Review believes that there is a compelling case for greater clarity in determining employment status which will be necessary to provide the foundations of fair and decent work and recommends the development of "legislation and guidance that adequately set out the tests that need to be met to establish employee or independent contractor status. This should retain the best elements of case law and better reflect the reality of modern day casual work in terms of the control exercised by employers over their staff."[22] Thus, in the Review's opinion "legislation must do more and the courts less" if *clarity* is to be improved and unscrupulous employers are *dissuaded from exploiting* vulnerable individuals by misuse of their employment status.

The Review's opinion is that legislation should be updated to reflect the main characteristics of an employment status through primary legislation which should "respond dynamically to changing conditions and relevant case law, the detail that underpins these criteria should be specified in a way that can be updated quickly with greater use of secondary legislation and guidance."[23]

Scepticism

The recommendation on status is viewed with a great deal of scepticism by the author in spite of the fact that the Taylor Review members need to be congratulated for making such a bold and robust recommendation for the government to

---

18 "Taylor Review," *op. cit.* p. 33.
19 *Ibid.*
20 These tests, developed by the common law, include *inter alia*, the control test, the integration into the organisation test, the economic reality test, the intuitive test, the mutuality of obligations test and the intention of the parties' test. For a detailed analysis and evaluation of those tests see Jo Carby-Hall "New Frontiers of Labour Law: Dependent and Autonomous Workers," *op. cit.* at pp. 247–282.
21 For an analysis and evaluation of gig employment case law see Jo Carby-Hall "Innovatory Forms of Employment in the 21st Century versus Employment Status," *op. cit.*
22 "Taylor Review," *op. cit.* p. 40.
23 *Ibid.* at pp. 34 and 35.

consider. The Review's suggestion for enacting legislation is done with the very best of intentions, *inter alia*, to simplify the current complex laws on employment status; to help avoid the exploitation of vulnerable individuals by unscrupulous employers; to update laws to 21st-century employment market developments by taking into account the digital and technological advances; to allow for more flexibility; to understand better individuals' employment rights and employers' obligations; to streamline the laws and so on. This scepticism and its reasoning have already been expressed in greater detail elsewhere[24] but will be briefly treated below.

The Government's Department of Business, Innovation and Skills (BIS) Review, of 2015

The BIS Review of 2015[25] gives some support for this author's scepticism. That Review was commissioned "to consider what the UK labour market looks like and suggest ways in which the government could deliver a framework that strikes the correct balance between the rights of the individual and the needs of business, supporting growth and prosperity in the 21st century." The BIS Review considered that determining employment status is essential because it ensured, *inter alia*, knowledge of the rights of individuals as well as the employers' responsibilities.

The BIS admitted the complexities inherent in determining the employment status of the employee, the worker and the genuine self-employed (or independent contractor). These complexities are various and originate from different sources. An important source is that of the common law in which judges established a number of tests over a period of more than a century[26] to determine the "employee" or "worker" status. A second source in determining employment status derives from legislation that defines the "employee" and the "worker".[27] It will be particularly noted that there is no legislation that defines

---

24 In Jo Carby-Hall "Innovatory Forms of Employment in the 21st Century versus Employment Status," *op. cit.* pp. 26–30 of the manuscripts.

25 The BIS Employment status review 2015 was commissioned by the coalition government and its report was published on 9th February 2015 and submitted to the Minister of Employment Relations in March 2015 and updated in December 2015. On 9th February 2017 this Review was placed in the public domain in the interests of transparency and to assist in informing the Taylor Review as part of a wider range of evidence. Source: https://www.gov.uk/government/uploads/system/uploads/attachment_data/file/585383/employment-status-review-2015.pdf (retrieved 30th October 2017).

26 For example, the "hospital cases" and the employer's vicarious liability for torts committed by the employees at the end of the 19th century and the beginning of the 20th century to be followed more recently by decades of cases on employment rights heard in the courts. The various tests pronounced by judges that evolved through the years, are taken into account by the courts when deciding cases on modern practices and developments that are taking place in the current employment market.

27 See the Employment Rights Act, 1996 s. 230 (1) and (3) (a) (employee) and s. 230 (3) (b) (worker).

the "independent contractor" or the "self-employed"! To make matters even more complicated, legislation sometimes treats individuals who are not necessarily independent contractors as independent contractors for their own convenience, needs and/or purposes.[28]

The current approach taken by the tribunals and the courts is to determine which one of the three statuses – namely employee, worker or independent contractor – an individual fall into. They do so *in the absence of the key elements of the relationship between the parties being defined by legislation* by applying the general British contractual principles, the EU Directives and British case law that includes a plethora of common law cases and based on *the particular facts of the case*. This allows the tribunals and the courts the necessary *flexibility* to enable them to assess the *reality* of the *relationship* between the parties and thus *respond to digital and technological changes* that occur in the labour market.[29]

The BIS Review acknowledged the lack of clarity in cases of atypical working conditions and made some suggestions to clarify the current framework but came to the conclusion that "Even the most radical of options presented, flipping the presumption of one to employment of all unless another relationship would be established would not address all these cases".[30] There is thus just cause for scepticism on what the Taylor Review suggests, in that the BIS Review provides a déjà vu on the status theme. A root and branch change to the current long established and well-understood laws (at least by labour lawyers and judges) would not be advisable for a number of good reasons. It is not thought that the Taylor Review is recommending such drastic changes. What the Taylor Review is recommending is the improvement of *clarity* and *transparency* for both individuals and employers, clarifying the line between the *worker status* and that of the *independent contractor*, the *removal of incentives* for some businesses *to gain competitive advantage* by adopting models which are disadvantageous to workers and that *legislation does more of the work while the courts and tribunals do less*.

Submissions for reform on the employment status debate

Bearing in mind the above scepticism the following submissions are made for reform of the employment status conundrum.

(a) On the one hand it cannot be denied that the British legal framework which determines the employment status of an individual is complex. Nor can it be denied on the other hand that the current legal framework is

---

28 For example, Her Majesty's Revenue and Customs (HMRC) treats individuals who are not necessarily independent contractors as such for tax purposes.

29 The gig economy cases in 2016–2018 of *Uber, Pimlico Plumbers, City Sprint, Deliveroo* and many others constituting perfect examples on how the tribunals and courts take into their stride the 21st-century employment relations system created by digital and technological developments.

30 Source: BIS Employment Status Review, 2015 (published in 2017) at p. 50 (Conclusions).

highly flexible and has responded and adapted well to changes in employment market practices over numerous years and continues to do so in respect to challenges brought about by the novel forms of employment[31] and more recently, by the gig employment.[32] This high level of flexibility allows tribunals[33] and courts[34] to adapt to future situations, trends and developments in future labour markets. There is therefore no need to change the existing legal system on status by new legislation as recommended by the Taylor Review. Furthermore, and granted that, in spite of the growth of atypical employment in which there is significant scope for uncertainty on the status concept, it should be pointed out that there still is a majority of employees working in traditional employment and whose status of employee – apart from relatively few cases – is unquestionable and therefore not subject to litigation on the status issue.

(b) Most individuals and employers are provided through the current legislative and common law systems with all they need to determine status and thus abide by employers' legal responsibilities and employees' and workers' employment rights. Furthermore, judging from past experience the current tribunal/court flexible system would be able to adapt to all future developments and challenges that would occur. There is therefore no need to make any fundamental changes to the current, well-established and well-understood (at least by lawyers) laws. Making such changes, would result in the creation of a "spider's web." By attempting to correct perceived issues within the current legal framework, new and unexpected challenges would inevitably be created in a different framework thus compounding the problem further and opening the floodgates to additional and unnecessary expensive litigation.

(c) There is however one big problem with the current flexible tribunal/court system in that one has to await the decision of a tribunal/court *before* the status of the individual is known. Such a situation is more prevalent in cases of atypical employment that constitutes a minority, albeit an important one, on the labour market.[35] There is no current mechanism in law that ascertains *ab initio* of employment the status of an individual. For those working in atypical forms of employment[36] this could cause anxiety, vulnerability, insecurity, uncertainty and indeed deprivation of employment rights entitlements. Unscrupulous employers could take advantage of this *lacuna* by exploiting the vulnerable, low-skilled and low-paid workforce.

---

31 Discussed and analysed in Jo Carby-Hall "Novel Forms of Employment: Quid Juris?" *Op. cit.*
32 Analysed in Jo Carby-Hall "Innovatory Forms of Employment in the 21ˢᵗ Century Versus Employment Status," *op. cit.* pp. 9–16 of the mms.
33 Such as Employment Tribunals (ET) and the Employment Appeal Tribunal (EAT).
34 Namely, the Court of Appeal (CA) and Supreme Court (SC).
35 There are 1.3 million individuals working in the gig economy or 4% of all employment (source: CIPD).
36 For example, amongst other forms of atypical employment, novel forms of employment or gig economy employment mentioned in this chapter.

In order to remedy this *ab initio* uncertainty as to employment status, it is suggested that there be established through primary legislation the setting up of a system whereby more *guidance* is given to prospective atypical individuals as well as to their prospective employers. This could be done through either Codes of Practice[37] or delegated legislation[38] on the identification of employment status.

A well-publicised and well-organised national education system on status for individuals working in atypical work would need to be set up by the government. It is submitted that a number of organisations would need to be involved in this venture thus the TUC, trade unions, Employers' Associations, CABs,[39] employment agencies, ACAS[40] and others would be represented. A new statutory executive body answerable to the government would need to be set up to co-ordinate the work of publicising issues on status for potential individuals working in atypical employment. In this manner, the parties[41] concerned would be aware *ab initio* of the employment status of the individual working in atypical employment which, according to recent jurisprudence would normally be that of "worker."[42] Knowing *ab initio* the individual's employment status would also enable that individual to know from the very beginning his/her employment rights entitlement. Furthermore, the above submission would send to an unscrupulous employer a strong signal by making him aware of his statutory and common law obligations towards the employed individual.

The aforementioned primary legislation could even make it compulsory for prospective employers recruiting atypical work individuals, or groups thereof, to *agree* the employment status of the individual *ab initio* and not to impose compulsorily an employment status, such as making that status a precondition of employment as has been the case in the gig

---

37 Codes of Practice under British law are not legally binding or enforceable but are invariably referred to by tribunals and courts as giving guidance and advice to the parties concerned, in this case, both prospective employers as well as prospective workers or employees. The provisions of Codes of Practice (of which there are many in the British industrial relations system) are taken into account by tribunals and courts and failure by one of the parties to observe the Code's provisions may well tip the balance of the case one way or another. Tribunals and courts thus take cognisance of the Code's provisions, even though they are not legally binding (as a law would be) in deciding the case before them.

38 As for example, Statutory Instruments, Regulations or Orders delegated to ministers by Act of Parliament.

39 Citizens' Advice Bureau.

40 Advisory, Conciliation and Arbitration Service.

41 Namely the prospective employer and the prospective individual seeking work in atypical employment.

42 Or "dependent contractor," if the Taylor Review suggestion for this change to be made is taken on board by the government (see pp. 28–30 *infra*).

employment jurisprudence heard by the tribunals and the courts.[43] This submission would give the silent and significant minority of individuals working in atypical work the *security* and *employment rights* enjoyed by the greater majority of employees and workers employed in traditional employment. Furthermore, individuals employed in atypical work should not be finding out that they do not have employment rights consequent to their bringing a case before the tribunals; they should know at the start of their employment what their status is and what rights they can expect as a result of that status.

Thus, the notions of *guidance, education* and *support* would have the effect of informing the individual working in atypical work of his/her legal employment rights and give such person confidence to complain to an Employment Tribunal should specific legal rights be infringed by an unscrupulous employer.[44]

It would be naïve to think that this proposed "arsenal" would constitute the *deus ex machina* that would solve all employment status problems. Employment Tribunals and the courts would still have an important role to play in this respect, but at least it is hoped that their task would be alleviated.

(d) It is submitted that a root and branch reform (created by new legislation) of the current and well-established system which enjoys flexibility and has an enormous pedigree, is retrograde, questionable, expensive on the national purse and therefore unnecessary. The *lacunae* identified in the current system can be remedied easily through less radical reforms and by hitting straight at the target where it is needed as suggested in (c) above. Nor may it be said that the current laws are *dépassé* or antiquated vis-à-vis the innovatory employment forms of the 21st century brought about by digital and technological developments. It would be folly to make any changes to the current laws where these are not required! In this manner the salvo will hit the targeted areas only – namely that of the important minority of vulnerable individuals and exploiting employers – where it is most needed and thus neutralising it to achieve fair and decent work, while leaving intact the

---

43 In the *Uber, City Sprint, Pimlico Plumbers* and other cases the employer made it a precondition of employment that the individuals would have the status of independent contractors. This status was imposed on those individuals compulsorily to enable the employer to rid himself of the individuals' employment rights.

44 See the three year research programme carried out on behalf of the Polish Government by J.R. Carby-Hall entitled "The Treatment of Polish and Other A8 Economic Migrants in the European Union Member States" (2008) Bureau of the Commissioner for Civil Rights Protection of the Republic of Poland, Warsaw. The results of this three years research programme commissioned by the Polish Government to this author and published in the English and Polish editions (each in two volumes) exposes the antediluvian, unfair, criminal and other exploitative practices used in the EU Member States by unscrupulous employers towards their economic migrant workers. Chapter 10 makes a number of significant recommendations for changes in the laws of some of those countries. The majority of those recommendations have been taken on board by the EU Member States.

long pedigree of the current established laws on status which work well. The targeting of this group in the manner suggested above should address the issue of *fair and decent work*; clarify the *employment status* of the individual *ab initio* and *prevent* the unscrupulous employer from controlling[45] the drafting of contracts to their advantage, namely one way flexibility[46] to the disadvantage of individuals; clarifying what *statutory rights* the individual enjoys and what the employer's *obligations* are. Thus, individuals and employers will have *clearer information*, a greater *understanding* of what rights and obligations apply and a greater level of *certainty*.

Changes in the law for changes' sake are not recommended! The wise statement made by N.F. Simpson[47] needs to be borne in mind. "And suppose we solve all the problems it presents? What happens? We end up with more problems than we started with. Because that's the way problems propagate their species. A problem left to itself dries up or goes rotten. But fertilise a problem with a solution – you'll hatch out dozens."

The worker status conundrum in comparison to the employee status[48]

The distinction

An important legal distinction is drawn between the status of "employee" and that of "worker." It is often said that "all employees are workers but not all workers are employees." This may have been true at one time when the term "worker" was not defined but it is no longer so today because workers, as defined by legislation, enjoy a *specific status* that allows them to enjoy basic statutory rights. The employee status enjoys all statutory and common law[49] rights while the worker status enjoys only limited or basic statutory rights.[50]

The status of worker introduced into British law by the European Union[51] is a status that is not clearly understood in the United Kingdom. It is defined[52] as:

---

45 As has happened in the gig economy cases heard in 2016 to 2018.

46 Bearing in mind what the Taylor Review's evidence found namely, that many individuals liked the flexibility offered by atypical work (*Ibid.* at p. 34).

47 An English playwright in "A Resounding Tinkle" (1958).

48 See Jeremias Prassl "Who is the worker?" *Law Quarterly Review* (2017), 133 (July) pp. 366–372.

49 Some examples of the employee's common law rights include, the common law *duty of care*, the employer's *vicarious liability* for torts committed by the employee towards fellow employees and third parties and the employee's ability to bring an action for *wrongful dismissal* (which is not to be confused with the unfair dismissal concept which is a statutory right).

50 They include the statutory right to the national minimum wage, protection under the Working Time Regulations, paid holidays, paid rest breaks, sick pay and protection from discrimination.

51 For a full and clear explanation of the EU influence see EurWORK – European Observatory of Working Life (1st March 2017).

52 The Employment Rights Act 1996 s. 230 (3) (a) (b).

an individual who has entered into or works under (or where the employment has ceased, worked under) (a) a contract of employment or (b) any other contact express or implied (and if it is express) whether oral or in writing whereby the individual undertakes to do or perform personally any work or services for another party to the contract whose status is not by virtue of the contract that of a client or customer of any profession or business undertaking carried on by the individual.

For the lack of a better English expression, the French would call the statutory definition of the worker status "un casse-tête chinois"!

Put into simple language the statutory definition would appear to include an individual who provides services to a firm PERSONALLY (which, to be noted, is a key requirement) and that firm has a MODICUM OF CONTROL over that individual in the provision of those services, and is not a customer of that firm – the likelihood is that that individual's status is that of "worker."

The Taylor Review rightly points out that the "employment status should be distinct and… not so ambiguous that only a court can fully understand the basic principles" The law should also ensure that where individuals are under "significant control in the way they work, they are not left unprotected as a result of the way their contract is drafted. It should not be as difficult as it is now for ordinary people or responsible employers to seek clarity on employment status."[53]

There is clearly an ambiguity in the above definition! In section 230 (3) (a) the definition or "worker" includes an individual working under "a contract of employment" (namely an "employee") whereas section 230 (1) has defined the employee as an individual who works, or has worked, under a contract of employment. How does one explain this duplication? Is that not another "casse-tête chinois"?[54]

The "dependent contractor" proposal

The Taylor Review holds the opinion that the "current three-tier approach is confusing and that the two categories of people that are eligible for "worker" employment rights should be easier to distinguish from one another. With that in mind, government should introduce a new name to refer to the category of people who are eligible for "worker" employment rights but who are not employees. The legislation should refer to this group as "dependent contractors."[55]

The government should retain however the current three tier approach because it remains relevant to the modern labour market. Furthermore, "in developing

---

53 "Taylor Review," *op. cit.* at p. 34.
54 Which led the RMT trade union in its submission to the Taylor Review to say "The meaning of the term "worker" is ambiguous. The legal definition is excessively vague" ("Taylor Review," *op. cit.* at p. 35).
55 "Taylor Review," *op. cit.* at p. 35.

the test of the new 'dependent contractor' status, control should be of greater importance, with less emphasis placed on the requirement to perform the work personally."[56] More emphasis on *control* and less emphasis on *personal service* will result in more individuals being protected by employment law. It will also be harder for employers to hide behind "substitution clauses"[57] which can only be challenged through the courts. Substitution clauses are common in contracts of employment. Sometimes they are included by unscrupulous employers with the specific intention of avoiding the employer's legal obligations towards the employee or worker. If the contract contains an unlimited/unfettered right to provide a substitute, the relationship will not be one of employer and employee/worker. In spite of any appearances to the contrary, the supposed employee/worker will have the status of an independent contractor.[58]

---

56 *Ibid*. at p. 36.

57 A "substitution clause" in the contract enables an individual to detail a third party, for example a colleague, a friend or an outsider, to perform that individual's work on his/her (the individual's) behalf.

58 In *Pimlico Plumbers Ltd and Another v Smith* [2018] UKSC 29 (*on appeal from [2017] EWCA Civ. 51*) a unanimous Supreme Court consisting of Lady Hale (President), Lord Wilson (who delivered the judgment), Lord Hughes, Lady Black and Lord Lloyd-Jones held that in order to qualify as a limb (b) worker, the Respondent, Mr Smith, had an obligation to perform *personally* his work or services to Pimlico. "Personal performance is a necessary constituent of a contract of service; so, decisions in that field can legitimately be minded for guidance as to what, more precisely, personal service means in the case of a limb (b) worker." (per Lord Wilson). However Lord Wilson quoted Mackenna J's dictum *in Ready Mixed Concrete (South East) Ltd. v Minister of Pensions and National Insurance* [1968] 2 QB 497 which added and important *qualification* when he said at p. 515 that "Freedom to do a job either by one's own hands or by another's is inconsistent with a contract of service, though a limited or occasional power of delegation may not be…" Mackenna J. cited Atiyah in his book entitled "*Vicarious Liability in the Law of Torts*" (1967) who said (at p. 59) that "it seems reasonably clear that an essential feature of a contract of service is the performance of at least part of the work by the servant himself." Taking into account the above and examining the contractual terms agreed between Pimlico and Mr Smith, Lord Wilson posited "The sole test is, of course, the obligation of personal performance; any other so-called sole test would be an inappropriate usurpation of the sole test. But there are cases, of which the present case is one, in which it is helpful to assess the significance of Mr Smith's right to substitute another Pimlico operative by reference to whether the dominant feature of the contract remained personal performance on his part." Mr Smith had established that he was a limb (b) worker. Nor was the Supreme Court in any doubt that the status of Pimlico by virtue of the contract was that of a client or customer of his. Thus, Pimlico's appeal was dismissed and the substantive claim for Mr Smith as a limb (b) worker would proceed to be heard in the Employment Tribunal. See too *Independent Workers' Union of Great Britain (IWGB) v RooFoods Ltd T/A Deliveroo* Central Arbitration Committee (CAC) Case Number TUR1/985 (2016) 14th November 2017 (where the CAC decided that the Deliveroo riders were independent contractors and not workers. Nor were they entitled to union recognition by the IWGB). The CAC is a non-departmental government organisation that resolves collective worker disputes. It decided that because the Deliveroo riders had a right (in a recently amended contract) to have a substitute to perform the work for them, they were independent contractors. The CAC posited "In light of our central finding on *substitution*, it cannot be said that the riders undertake to do *personally* any work or services to another party" (italics are the author's) and added that "the insuperable difficulty for the union

In redefining the "dependent contractor" status, the government should "adopt the *piece rates* legislation to ensure those working in the gig economy are still able to enjoy maximum flexibility whilst also being able to earn the National Minimum Wage."[59]

Greater transparency of rights to be given in the particulars of employment

Changes to the legislation

The Taylor Review suggests[60] that "changes to the legislation will be a significant step to improving the employment law framework and making the law do the work rather than the courts" but the government should consider ways to "enbed" (*sic*) the rights and responsibilities set out in legislation" to enable less misunderstanding or opportunity for avoidance. Under British law there is no requirement for the employer to provide the employee with a written contract of employment. There is however a requirement for the employer to provide the employee with a *written statement of the particulars of employment* within two months of starting the employment.[61] Such statutory particulars given to employees could be helpful to "dependent

is that we find that the substitution right to be genuine, in the sense that Deliveroo has decided in the new contract that riders have a right to substitute themselves both before and after they have accepted a particular job and we have also heard evidence, that we accepted of it being operated in practice." Factors which affect whether there is "control" by the employer were (a) the series of changes made to the contract allowing riders to *substitute* their work to third parties and (b) the requirement that riders were no longer to wear a *uniform*. Being independent contractors, the riders of *Deliveroo* were not entitled to union recognition. This case went contrary to the recent trend of cases such as *Pimlico Plumbers, City Sprint* and *Uber* where the tribunals and courts held that the individuals working for those companies had the worker status thus enjoying basic employment rights. The CAC Deliveroo decision is a boost to gig economy employers and a blow to the trade union movement. Although there is no appeal from the CAC decision, the trade union can challenge the CAC decision in the High Court by way of a judicial review. At the time of writing (25th June 2018) the IWGB challenged this CAC decision in the High Court and Simler J. who gave the IWGB permission for a full judicial review on the CAC ruling of November, 2017, rejected a number of the trade union's arguments but said that it was "arguable" that the CAC should have considered the right (through IWGB recognition by the employer) of Deliveroo riders to bargain collectively, as provided for by Article 11 of the European Convention of Human Rights. Simler J. has thus allowed a limited challenge on human rights grounds. This decision was reached "having considered the judgment of the Supreme Court in the 2018 *Plumbers case* and emphatically rejects the union's challenge based on that judgment." It is also worth noting *obiter* that a CAC decision is not binding on Employment Tribunals though it could constitute persuasive evidence.

59 "Taylor Review," *op. cit.* at p. 37.

60 *Ibid.* at p. 38.

61 Although the time limit and the giving of statutory particulars are frequently ignored by employers according to the evidence received by the Taylor Review.

contractors".[62] The Taylor Review suggests that the government makes it a statutory requirement for both employees and dependent contractors to be given the particulars of employment on the *first day* of obtaining employment.[63]

The information *currently* required for insertion in the written particulars of employment to employees includes the name of the employer, the place of work, wages, paid holidays, sick pay and pension rights. The Taylor Review seeks an extension to ensure that it is relevant to *dependent contractors* and includes the *statutory rights* which workers are entitled to from the *first day* of employment, how wages are *calculated* and how they will be *paid*. The Taylor Review suggests further that the laws specify the *format* of the written particulars of employment to enable information to be *transparent* in plain English and accessible. Furthermore, the Review suggests that the government takes steps "to prevent employers from attempting to bury information or using overly legalistic and unintelligible language." Thus, the development of the standard format could be easily adopted with specific information given by the employer. The recommendation addressed to the government is that "it should build on and improve *clarity*, *certainty* and *understanding* of all working people by extending the right to a written statement to dependent contractors as well as employees."[64]

The Review goes even further by asking the government to encourage employer compliance by introducing a *right* for individuals to claim *compensation* where the employer fails to provide a written statement. Such compensation could either be provided by legislation or by the government working with the Advisory, Conciliation and Arbitration Service (ACAS) and others to ensure that such information is accessible to all those who are entitled to receive it. In this manner clarity and transparency would exist around employment status and employment rights.[65]

On-line Tool

In order to improve further clarity and understanding, the Taylor Review suggests that the government should create and develop a free to use on-line tool which provides individuals with information on employment status and other relevant matters, thus taking advantage of the digitalisation and machine learning to

---

62 Assuming the government accepts the Taylor Review recommendation on the creation of the "dependent contractor" status.

63 See too the GMB trade union submission to the Taylor Review which said that "the employer should also be required to issue the written statement of terms from day one to all workers – not just those that might be employees" ("Taylor Review," *op. cit.* at p. 38).

64 "Taylor Review," *op. cit.* at p. 39.

65 See too the submission made to the Taylor Review by Law Works that "There can be and should be greater transparency for all workers as to the terms of their engagement and accrued rights such as pay. Extending to workers similar rights of employees as regards particulars of engagement as well as itemised information regarding pay and other accrued entitlements could be the first step to informing workers of the most basic level about their rights and obligations."

spread information. In addition to providing information to providing information on the employment status, it could give advice to employers on the employment status of staff hired; advice and information on entitlement to rights of such individuals, how to qualify for them; providing a determination between "dependant contractors" and the self-employed and build on these and other themes over time as the on-line tool develops. It recommends that the government "should build on legislative changes to further improve clarity and understanding by providing individuals and employers with access to an on-line tool that determines employment status in the majority of cases."[66] Future developments could include the determination of status, thus making the process of establishing what rights individuals are entitled to even simpler.

The Review thus recommends the provision of "maximum clarity on status and rights for all individuals by extending the right to written particulars to all in employment and developing an on-line tool providing a clear steer on what rights an individual has."[67] So much for matters relating to clarity on *status* and *employment rights* in the law!

One or two-sided flexibility?

Flexibility in the United Kingdom labour market

The United Kingdom labour market is renowned for its flexible nature! Flexibility plays a key role in enabling employers to respond to rapid changing market conditions and also to enable the maintenance of high employment rates. Thus, the flexibility concept that characterises the British labour market has many advantages. Flexibility in ideal circumstances suggests freedom between the employer and an individual (whether of employee status or more usually of worker status) to agree terms and conditions of employment (subject to the *minimum minimorum* stipulated by law) that best suits each of the parties.[68]

The Taylor Review research was concerned by the manner in which employers used the concept of flexibility to their own advantage thus exploiting and controlling workers. Nowhere is this situation more visible than in the 2016–2018 cases of *Uber, City Sprint, Pimlico Plumbers* and possibly[69] *Deliveroo*[70] and pending cases

---

66 "Taylor Review," *op. cit.* at p. 39.

67 *Ibid.* at p. 40.

68 The Labour Force Survey of March 2017 states that one in five of those employed on zero hours contracts are in full-time education and 68% of these individuals do not wish to have more hours.

69 "Possibly" because the CAC decided that the Deliveroo riders were independent contractors (contrary to the tribunal and court findings in the other cases) and the IWGB trade union petitioned for a judicial review in the High Court whose decision at the time of writing (18th June 2018) is awaited.

70 See the discussion on those cases in Jo Carby-Hall "Innovatory Forms of Employment in the 21st Century Versus Employment status," *op. cit.* at pp. 13–16 of the mms.

still to be heard, where, it is suggested, that the tribunals and courts will – by virtue of the June 2018 Supreme Court's decision in *Pimlico Plumbers* – uphold the decisions taken in these cases. In each of those cases (bar the CAC Deliveroo case) the respective employers used that flexibility to their own advantage by *unilaterally imposing* upon their workers the status of independent contractor. They *controlled* this policy by making it a "take it or leave it" situation. No negotiations were therefore allowed or suggested. This amounted to one-sided flexibility! The vulnerable individual on atypical work – as for example, individuals working on zero hours contracts and the gig economy – needs to be protected! Flexibility is important to the labour market, for the reason given above, and thus needs to be retained, but flexibility should not be used by unscrupulous employers solely to their own advantage without taking into consideration their workforces. Employers must therefore be discouraged from exercising one-sided flexibility!

Lack of reciprocity

Evidence given to the Taylor Review showed repeatedly that flexibility was not being reciprocated by employers when there was a requirement for individuals to be available for work at short notice without any guarantee that work would be made available. Individuals were thus unable to make private arrangements and if they refused the work offered, the employer would "punish" individuals by not offering them work in the future. Nor could the individuals complain for the same reason.

The Taylor Review suggests that:

> too many employers… are relying on zero hours, short hours or agency contracts when they should be more forward-looking in their scheduling. We want to incentivise employers to provide certainty of hours and income as far as possible and to think carefully about how much flexibility they can reasonably expect from their workers. Workers need to be able to make informed decisions about the work … to plan around it and to be compensated if arrangements change at short notice.[71]

The Review recognised the difficulty of remedying such a situation and left the matter to the government to find a solution while suggesting that it should ask the Low Pay Commission[72] "to consider the design or impacts of the introduction of a higher National Minimum Wage (NMW) rate for hours that are not guaranteed as part of the contract."[73]

---

71 "Taylor Review," *op. cit.* at p. 43.
72 *Ibid.* at p. 44.
73 This recommendation would be extremely difficult to bring about, for this higher NMW will need to be set to encourage employers to schedule guaranteed hours as far as is reasonable within the company. The issue of what is reasonable could prove problematic. Where there is a request

Continuity of employment

Continuous employment is when an employee has worked for one employer without a break. The length of continuous employment gives certain rights to employees which include, *inter alia*, maternity pay, flexible working requests, redundancy pay, unfair dismissal claims and so on.

The GMB trade union made a suggestion to the Taylor Review to the effect that:[74]

> the archaic rules about continuity of employment compound the problems associated with employment status so someone with many years of a relationship with the employer can often lose out through gaps in the provision of work. Government should seek to change the statutory definition of continuity so that accrued service is not lost through breaks

And suggesting further "the abolition of continuous service requirements altogether and provide for full employment rights from day one."

Although agreeing in part to the GMB's opinion, the Taylor Review did not recommend the abolition of the continuity of employment concept. The use of casual forms of labour does not necessarily mean that employment protection obligations owed by the employer towards the individuals concerned are reduced. Thus zero hours workers who work regular hours could enjoy employee status and thus be entitled to all employment protection laws. The problem with such individuals on zero hours contracts and who work regular hours is that they could find it difficult to prove eligibility to qualify for certain employment benefits by reason of *gaps*[75] in their continuity of employment. For example, in order for an employee to qualify to make a claim for redundancy payments or unfair dismissal,[76] the employee has to be *continuously* employed for two years as from the date the employment starts.[77] Those who are *casual* or *intermittent* individuals could thus find it difficult to establish the continuity of employment to entitle them to qualify for the particular employment right.

---

by the employer for an individual to work longer hours than was agreed in the contract, the employer would have to compensate the most vulnerable workers for the additional flexibility requested of them. The question is how vulnerable should the vulnerable individual be?

74 "Taylor Review," *op. cit.* at p. 45.

75 Some gaps or breaks in normal employment count towards a continuous employment period. These include sickness, maternity, paternity, parental or adoption leave, annual leave, employment overseas with the same company, the time between unfair dismissal and an employee being reinstated, when an employee moves between associated employers, military service with the reserve forces, temporary lay-offs, employer lock-outs, transfers of undertakings, where a corporate body gets taken over by another because of a legal change. See too the Employment Rights Act 1996 ss. 210–219.

76 Other employment rights that require continuity of employment include, *inter alia*, statutory paternity and maternity pay, statutory adoption pay, *etc.*

77 As shown in the contract of employment or/and the statutory particulars.

There do exist current statutory laws that permit less than a week's gap to be bridged in between assignments in circumstances where a break in between assignments has occurred due to a "temporary cessation of work."[78] These statutory rules are not sufficient to protect the casual or intermittent worker. The Review suggests "that more should be done to make the process of establishing continuity of employment easier"[79] by increasing that period to one month. This would mean that a casual individual who works for a week and then has been laid off for up to a month when a job is offered, the continuity of employment would accrue during that month. In that manner, casual and intermittent workers would be enabled to acquire employment rights in circumstances where qualifying periods apply.

The Taylor Review also suggests that the government "should consider classifying the casual situations where legitimate cessations of work for the same employer apply." Thus, should the cause be that work is not available or "should it apply to a wider set of situations."[80] The Review recommends that the government "should extend, from one week to one month, the consideration of the relevant break in service for the calculation [of the][81] qualifying period for continuous service and clarify the situations where cessations of work could be justified."[82]

Agency workers and Her Majesty's Revenue and Customs (HMRC) Rules

The back cloth

For purposes of transparency relating to the pay of agency workers, the British tax rules were changed in 2015. This means that agency works employed, in particular in the construction industry, who are classed as independent contractors,[83] are for tax purposes treated as employees and therefore have their tax liability as well as their contribution to the national insurance deducted automatically from their wages on the PAYE[84] scheme.

---

78 Continuity of employment is preserved under s. 212 (3) (b) of the Employment Rights Act, 1996 if the employee is absent from work for a period "on account of a temporary cessation of work." See too the EAT case of *Holt v E. B. Security (in liquidation)* where an establishment closed permanently, and an employee previously employed by that establishment was re-employed a short while later by an associated employer in an entirely different role.

79 "Taylor Review," *op. cit.* at p. 45.

80 Such other situations may include individuals who have worked for that employer over a long period but who take regular breaks such as students in term time or school holidays or who take breaks in between assignments for longer than a week which are not due to lack of work availability but because of other causes, for example work assignment to other workers.

81 Square brackets inserted by the author.

82 "Taylor Review," *op. cit.* at p. 45.

83 i.e. self-employed.

84 Pay as you earn.

At this stage it would be appropriate to interpolate by directing the reader to the Court of Appeal case of *Ferguson v John Dawson and Partners (Constructors) Ltd.*[85] where two Lord Justices (namely Megaw LJ and Lawton LJ) viewed public policy in different ways. In that case the intention of the parties was that the plaintiff who was working on "the lump"[86] was to have the status of independent contractor. As such, the defendant employer made no PAYE deductions from the plaintiff's wages for income tax and national insurance contributions. Megaw L.J. found it difficult to accept:

> that the parties, by a mere expression of intention as to what the legal relationship should be, can in any way influence the conclusion of law as to what the relationship is. I think that it would be contrary to the public interest if that were so, for it would mean that the parties, by their own whim, by the use of a verbal formula, unrelated to the reality of the relationship, could influence the decision on whom the responsibility for the safety of workmen, as imposed by statutory regulations, should rest.

Lawton L.J. – dissenting from the majority judgement – considered that the parties' intention was clear, that because they wanted to avoid the incidence of taxation they did not wish to have an employer-employee relationship, it would therefore "be contrary to public policy to allow a man to say that he is self-employed for the purpose of avoiding the incidence of taxation but a servant for the purpose of claiming compensation" (for unfair dismissal for example). Both Lord Justices considered public policy in different ways. Megaw L.J. considered that it would be against public policy to allow the employer to rid himself of his statutory liability for the safety of is employees, whereas Lawton L.J. considered that it is against public policy to allow a person the status of self-employment so as to avoid taxation and equally allow him the status of employee to enable him to take advantage of benefits such as the unfair dismissal remedies or redundancy pay.

This case serves as an illustration for *one* of the reasons as to why HMRC tax rules were changed.

Agency workers' woes

This change in the law made to combat the avoidance of tax has resulted in an important salary drop,[87] because of legitimate deductions made,[88] in the take-

---

85 [1976] 3 All ER 817 (CA).

86 This is an expression used in the construction industry meaning casual employment in that trade.

87 In some cases, the receipt of only half of the wages earned (source: "Taylor Review" findings at p. 46).

88 Namely, income tax and national insurance contribution deductions to wages made at source under the PAYE system. To be noted is the fact that, were the agency worker classified as an

home pay of agency workers. To add insult to injury, agency workers have experienced further wage deductions in respect of (a) handling fees charged amounting to between £15 to £35 per week and (b) secondary national insurance contributions[89] deductions. In addition, recruitment agencies often sub-contract the payment of wages and deductions thereof to intermediary companies known as "umbrella companies." Such recruitment agencies have a legal obligation to inform the workers of these arrangements, but many do not do so. As the Taylor Review points out "unscrupulous providers can bury important information in the small print of long contracts." The Review recommends that "Government should amend the legislation to improve the *transparency* of information which must be provided to agency workers both in terms of rates of pay and those responsible for paying them".[90]

There is another agency worker's woe! Some such workers are sometimes denied, or receive partial, holiday pay. All British workers are entitled to 5.6 weeks' paid annual leave but for those who are employed on casual work or have variable hours from one week to another, it can be difficult to calculate with any degree of accuracy their annual leave pay entitlement. Although there is a statutory formula for individuals who do not work normal hours[91] such a formula is not applicable to seasonal workers and to those subjected to peaks and troughs in work. In such situations the individual may well receive a smaller amount of annual leave pay.

The Review also found that some agency workers and those on zero-hour contracts were either not aware of their paid annual leave entitlement or being aware, were afraid to take it lest they should lose their job. An unscrupulous employer could well take advantage of this situation and exploit the agency workers' ignorance or fear.

The Taylor Review recommended that the government should do more to promote *awareness* of annual leave entitlements, "increasing the pay reference period to 52 weeks and take account of seasonal variations and give dependent contractors the opportunity to receive rolled-up holiday pay."[92]

The third woe relates to long-term agency workers. Companies operating in the flexible labour market, rely on temporary workers to fill longer-term positions with the same agency worker performing the same work over many years. Some[93] such

independent contractor, such worker – if he/she declared to HMRC the wages received – would still have to pay income tax and national insurance contribution, but at a lower rate.

89 Employers pay "Secondary" Class 1 National Insurance Contributions (NIC) on their employees' earnings. "Primary" Class 1 NICs are paid by the employee through the "pay as you earn" (PAYE) scheme. Employers are responsible for deducting income tax and National Insurance Contributions from their employees' wages at source. Employers pay the amounts deducted from employees' salaries to HMRC every month.

90 "Taylor Review," *op. cit.* at p. 46.

91 Holiday pay entitlement for a person who does not work normal working hours is calculated on the number of hours worked over a reference period of twelve weeks.

92 "Taylor Review," *op. cit.* at p. 47.

93 "Some" because many agency workers relish the freedom (as opposed to career prospects) they enjoy as agency workers.

workers see no future career development, experience insecurity and are afraid to take time off to find alternative employment lest they be disciplined or dismissed. The Taylor Review recommends that[94] "Government should introduce a right to request a…contract of employment for agency workers who have been placed with the same hirer for 12 months and an obligation on the hirer to consider the request in a reasonable manner."

The same is recommended for zero hours workers who after a long period of time, such workers should have the opportunity to request a fixed hours contract. The Review suggests "The average weekly hours worked over the previous twelve months should be the starting assumption of any new contract" and recommends[95] that the government "should act to create a right to request a contract that guarantees hours which better reflect the actual hours worked, for those on zero hours contracts who have been in post for 12 months."[96]

Good corporate governance and the social dialogue

Some general issues

The Taylor Review states the obvious – namely that "well run companies recognise the importance of the people who work for them" and "invest time and effort in good management relationships…between individuals and at a collective level."[97] For work to be fair and decent an effective social dialogue is imperative; workers need to be treated with respect and dignity; day-to-day business needs to be conducted in a civil manner and workers' views on how the work is performed should be considered by management to be relevant and potentially useful; workers need to have a broad and general understanding on what policies the company is pursuing, what its aspirations and future plans are and the role of workers in contributing to such company developments; and finally workers need to be informed of important strategic decisions which may affect them. Employee involvement and social dialogue constitute the essence of well-organised and successful companies. The Taylor Review heard of excellent examples of well-managed companies which put into practice some or all of the above criteria.

In addition to the above criteria, corporate governance and social dialogue include also statutory and common law requirements to be met in certain fields of employment law. Many of these statutory requirements emanate from EU Directives transposed into national laws while others emanate from

---

94 "Taylor Review," *op. cit.* at p. 48.

95 *Ibid.* at p. 48.

96 More will be said on agency workers in the "State Enforcement" part of this chapter at pp. 49 *et seq. infra.*

97 For example, trade union recognition, collective bargaining and disclosure of information by management, consultation of employee groups, such as health and safety committees if the employer does not recognise a trade union, works councils, and so on.

national laws *per se*. There is also the notion of a broader concept, namely that of corporate social responsibility of a company where social dialogue may feature prominently. Parameters of space do not allow for a full discussion on each of these but a few examples by way of illustration (and stimulation of the mind!) will be given as a way of expanding the notions of corporate governance and social dialogue.

An example of a European law being enacted into British law is the Acquired Rights Directive,[98] another is the Transfer of Undertakings (Protection of Employment) Regulations, 1981[99] (known as TUPE) which transposed the Directive into British law. Therein there is an obligation on the employer to inform and consult[100] the employee representative(s) that a relevant transfer is to take place, when it will take place and why, the legal, economic and social implications on employees, the measures envisaged by the employer in connection with the transfer and measures which the transferee employer envisages and how these will affect the employee.

A further example of a Directive being translated into British law is the *collective* redundancy Directive.[101] Therein there are important provisions on the employer's duty to consult prior to making collective redundancies with a view to avoiding dismissals, reducing the number of employees to be made redundant, mitigating the redundancy consequences and so on. Such consultations must be with the view of reaching an agreement with the employee representatives.[102]

---

98 Council Directive No.22/187 (O.J. 1977 L.61/26).

99 S.I. 1981 No. 1794.

100 *Ibid*. Reg. 10 (2). For a detailed analysis on TUPE see Jo Carby-Hall "Transfer of Undertakings in the United Kingdom" in *La Transmisión de Empresas en Europa* (Professors Bruno Veneziani and Umberto Carabelli (Eds)) European SOCRATES Programme, (1999) Cacucci Editore, Italy at pp. 187–263 especially at pp. 231–234.

101 Council Directive on Collective Redundancies 75/129/EEC (O.J. L 48/29) as amended by Directive 92/56 and Directive 98/59 (O.J.1998 L. 225/16.) See Dolding (1992) 21 ILJ 310 and Jo Carby-Hall "Redundancy in the United Kingdom" in *I Licenziamenti per Riduzione di Personale in Europa* (Professors Bruno Veneziani and Umberto Carabelli" (2001) Cacucci Editore, Italy at pp. 387–537. This chapter analyses both *individual* redundancies which is an example of a British law *per se* (pp. 387–490) and *collective* redundancies originating from the European Union (pp. 491–537).

102 For other examples of Directives translated into British laws where corporate governance and social dialogue feature see Jo Carby-Hall "Working Time: The British Experience" in *Regnare, Gubernare, Administrare in honour of Professor Jerzy Malec* (Professors Stanislaw Grodziski and Andrzej Dziadzio (Eds)) 2012 AFM publishers Krakow Poland at pp. 367-395 and by the same author "Opt Outs and Variations in Working Time- British style" in *Le Travail Humain au Correfour du Droit et de la Sociologie* Hommage au Professuer Nikitas Aliprantis (Vol. 1) (Professors Christian Mestre, Corinne Sachs-Durand and Michel Storck (Eds)) (2014) Presses Universitaires de Strasbourg at pp. 53–71. Health and safety laws see J. R. Carby-Hall "Health, Safety and Welfare at Work" *Managerial Law* Vol. 31 Nos 1/2 (1989) pp. 1– 45 especially at pp. 41 & 42.

As for national laws, *individual* redundancies are provided for by the Employment Rights Act 1996. Therein there are provisions for negotiations with a view to concluding a collective agreement and its contents cover, *inter alia*, the amount of severance payments, the method of selection, a point system assessment, alternative proposals to avoid redundancies and other principles.

There are also elements of corporate governance and social dialogue in British common law. Examples include the common law duty of respect towards the employee by the employer[103] and the common law duty of care[104] owed to the employee.

Elements of corporate governance and social dialogue will also be found in policies relating to corporate social responsibility schemes operated by some national and international establishments.[105]

Bad practices in leadership and management skills found by the Taylor Review

The Taylor Review also found that "the UK has traditionally not performed strongly on leadership and management skills"[106] which constitutes "the key component of the productivity gap and particularly pronounced in SMEs." This related sometimes to bad management practices. Only half of employees said that their manager is good in seeking their views and one third of managers say that they allow employees to influence decision making.[107] Research carried out by the Taylor Review also indicated that workers felt that they had "no say in or even visibility of, significant decisions that would affect their working lives" with some employers being "unwilling to permit employees to exercise any meaningful control over their work."[108] These bad corporate

---

103 Lord Denning "introduced" the common law duty of respect towards the employee in one his judgements. For a more detailed portrait of this distinguished judge and others see Jo Carby-Hall "The Digestive System of the British Judge" in *Variaciones Sobre Derecho del Trabajo en Perspectiva Comparada* (Vol 2) *Liber amicorum* Antonio Martín Valverde (Professor Joaquín Garcia Murcia (Ed)) (2016) Tecnos Madrid at pp.133–161.

104 See Jo Carby-Hall *Principles of Industrial Law* (1969) Charles Knight, (First Edn.) London at pp. 34–47.

105 See Jo Carby-Hall "Responsabilité Sociale de l'Entreprise en Common Law et Développement d'une Corporative Social Responsibility" in *Quelle Responsabilité Sociale pour l'Entreprise?* (Professor Philippe Auvergnon (Ed)) (2005) Presses Universitaires de Bordeaux at pp. 161–177.

106 BIS Research Paper No. 211 – Leadership and Management Skills in SMEs Managing Associations with Management Practices and Performance. 2015. https://www.gov.uk/government/uploads/system/uploads/attachment_data/file/407624/BIS-15- 95_Leadership_and_Management_skills_in_SMEs.pdf (retrieved 17th October 2017).

107 RSA at https://medium.com/@theresa/why-we-need-to-talk-about-good-work-728d7d82877c (retrieved 5th October, 2017).

108 The Taylor Review said that "It must be a matter of concern that the proportion of 'routine and semi-routine' workers who say that they have no freedom to decide the organisation of their work" This phenomenon increased from 42% in 2005 to 57% in 2015 (source: *Ibid.* above).

practices give atypical work a negative perception. The Taylor Review states that the "challenge is to extend the good practices we have seen more widely, especially to smaller companies and those engaging significant numbers of atypical workers."[109]

A "voice" in the workplace

The CIPD submission to the Taylor Review stated "Having a voice is essential not just at the moment of entering an employment relationship, but as it progresses, too".[110]

The Review expressed neutrality on whether workers in the United Kingdom should be represented on company boards as in Germany or have a system of representative establishment councils or employee representation as they have in France, Belgium and Luxemburg[111] but "very much share the view that company owners have a wider responsibility towards the people who work for them – both directly and their supply chains – and should take this responsibility seriously." The Review goes on to say:

> Effective worker voice has several purposes: for managers or company owners to receive timely feedback about business practices for those who are charged with delivering them every day, for individuals to get together (physically and virtually and with or without management) to discuss common issues affecting them; to have a safe route for the workforce to raise concerns and finally offer the ability for the workforce to hear and influence big strategic issues which may have an impact on them. These are clearly related to questions around formal trade union representation including for the purposes of collective bargaining...but voice can and should be exercised even where there is little of no trade union organisation and representation.[112]

The Information and Consultation of Employees Regulations[113] which apply only to companies employing 50 or more employees,[114] offer a framework to encourage long-term information and consultation arrangements between the social

---

109 "Taylor Review," *op. cit.* at p. 51.
110 "Taylor Review," *op. cit.* at p. 52.
111 See J.R. Carby-Hall *Worker Participation in Europe* Routledge Library Editions: *Employee Ownership and Economic Democracy*, Volume 2 (2018) Routledge, London and New York.
112 "Taylor Review," *op. cit.* at p. 52.
113 S.I. 2004 No. 3426 (known as ICE), which put into effect the Information and Consultation Directive 2002/14/EC. See too Mark Hall "Assessing the Information and Consultation Regulations" *ILJ* Vol. 34 Issue 2 (2005) at pp. 103–126.
114 To be successful in getting ICE applied, at least 10% of (and a minimum of 15) employees need to support this initiative. Because of those restrictions, the Taylor Review said that only 14% of workplaces had works councils or consultative committees in 2011.

partners. The employer must provide the employee representatives[115] with information on a variety of issues that includes substantial changes likely to lead to restructuring or redundancies taking place in the establishment. So as to change the culture in many organisations, the Taylor Review suggests that the threshold of employee sign up be reduced and all workers should count in that number. It recommends that the government should examine the effectiveness of the ICE Regulations "in improving employee engagement in the workplace. In particular it should extend the Regulations to include employees and workers and reduce the threshold for implementation from 10% to 2% of the workforce making the request."[116]

The Review points out that "the adoption of Information and Consultation practices might be a step…to greater involvement of collective representation more generally." It is hoped that this may well be the case but the reader should bear I mind that the ICE Regulations are based on the EU Directive provisions and as was suggested elsewhere,[117] could well become a victim of post Brexit legislation either because of its current ineffectiveness or, if the Taylor Review proposals are accepted, by the political colour of the government.

The Taylor Review's scepticism of legislation alone to make the necessary changes suggested by the Review was such that it recommended additional measures namely, that the government should "work with investors in People, ACAS, Trade Unions and others to promote further the development of employee engagement and workforce relations especially in sectors with significant levels of casual employment."[118]

Corporate transparency

Corporate transparency results in workers or potential workers being able to make informed decisions and choices on where and how they wish to work. Companies should take decisions about how to *structure* their workforces consciously rather than by default and there would be merit in organisations above

---

115 The Regulations provide, in some detail, procedures for the election of worker representatives where a trade union is not represented in the company. There also exist provisions that protect worker representatives against suffering any detriment.

116 "Taylor Review," *op. cit.* at p. 53.

117 See article by Jo Carby-Hall "The Effect of Brexit on British Industrial Relations Laws and its Commercial and Constitutional Consequences" in Revista Derecho Social y Empresa "*Eficiencia Económica y Protección Social*" No. 7 Julio 2017 (Professor Pilar Contreras (Ed.)) Dykinson Publishers. Spain at pp. 14 –199 re-printed as a chapter in *Trade and Labour Standards – New Trends and Challenges* (Professor José Luis Gil y Gil (Ed)) (2018) ADAPT University Press and Cambridge Scholars Publishing at pp. 189 –261. In the maritime sphere see the chapter by Jo Carby-Hall entitled "The Legal Impact of Brexit on Seafarers' Employment" in a book entitled *Retos Presentes y Futuros de la Política Marítima Integrada de la Unión Europea* (Professor Laura Carballo Piñeiro (Coordinadora)) (2017) J.B. Bosch (Ed.) at pp. 273–299 particularly at pp. 286–288 (information and consultation).

118 "Taylor Review," *op. cit.* at p. 53.

a certain size being publicly accountable for their workforce structure. With this in mind the government should introduce new duties on employers to report, and also bring to the attention of the workforce, information on workforce structure.

The Taylor Report thus recommends in the first instance, that companies of a certain size (such size not being specified by the Review) should "make public their model of employment and use of agency services beyond a certain threshold." Such a threshold not being specified, it is not proposed to invent a threshold here, for it is best to leave this to the government if it accepts this recommendation. The Review also recommends in the second instance, that companies should:

> report on how many requests they have received (and number agreed to) from zero hours contracts workers for fixed hours after a certain period in employment. Thirdly, companies should "report on how many requests they have received (and number agreed) from agency workers for permanent positions with a hirer after a certain period.

All these reports are planned to encourage companies to be more transparent regarding their respective workforce structures.

Enforcement

Because of an imbalance of economic power between employers and employees and recognising the vulnerability of employees to exploitation, discrimination and other undesirable practices, an efficient system of enforcement is essential. If employers –intentionally or accidentally – fail to observe the labour law provisions, employees and workers need to seek redress through the Employment Tribunals and the courts after ACAS conciliation has proved to be unsuccessful or otherwise failed them. In addition to the tribunals and courts, the State however does enforce some aspects of labour law where there is considered to be a higher risk of vulnerability or exploitation. The Taylor Review believes that there is room for "improvements in both those areas that could make the process more balanced."[119] It is proposed to treat Employment Tribunals first before discussing State enforcement through government organisations.

(a) Employment tribunals

The majority of statutory (and very limited common law) rights require an individual to bring an action in an Employment Tribunal which has jurisdiction over a very wide variety of statutory employment law issues.[120] Before an action

---

119 *Ibid.* at p. 57.
120 Which include unfair dismissal claims; redundancy payments claims; discrimination claims (race, sex, disability, religion or belief, sexual orientation, age); wrongful dismissal (at

is brought in an Employment Tribunal there is a statutory requirement to notify ACAS[121] of the dispute to enable it to conciliate or mediate with the aim of resolving the dispute out of court through the early conciliation process. Either of the parties to the dispute can refuse the early conciliation process opportunity that is not compulsory. In such situations the case will be heard by an Employment Tribunal. Although originally designed to be "do it yourself tribunals" – chaired by a legally qualified employment judge sitting either alone or with two lay members one with an employee background and the other with an employer background[122] – where individuals may present their case themselves without the aid of a lawyer in an entourage which is not as procedurally legalistic as is a court of law – although over the years such tribunals have become more legalistic and formal.

If the Employment Tribunal finds that there has been a breach of statutory rights it will order an employer to pay a financial award and in unfair dismissal cases re-instatement, re-engagement or compensation which includes a tranche for loss of future earnings, loss of employer perks, pension rights, and much more.[123]

Reversal of burden of proof

One important aspect brought up by the Taylor Review for reform is the *burden of proof* to prove individual status which currently rests fairly and squarely on the employees'/workers' shoulders. The Taylor Review suggests that the system be changed:[124]

> to create a presumption of employment or worker status...shifting the burden on the employer to prove that this is not the case. This means that if an individual brings a claim that requires them *(sic)* to be an employee, or a worker, it is for the employer to prove that they *(sic)* are *(sic)* not. The same would be true of dependent contractors which we have suggested replaces the current category of worker.

common law); particulars of employment; failure to inform and consult in cases of transfer of undertakings; equal pay claims; claims relating to deductions from wages and so on. Employment Tribunals do not have jurisdiction on contractual disputes that are dealt in the civil courts, namely the High or County Court in England, Wales and Northern Ireland and the Sheriff Court in Scotland. Thus, disputes relating to accidents at work, restrictive covenants, contractual claims for damages arising out of termination of employment, contractual breaches relating to non-payment of wages or benefits owing or pay in lieu of notice are heard in the civil courts.

121 i.e. Advisory, Conciliation and Arbitration Service.

122 Depending on the type of case brought before the Employment Tribunal.

123 For a more detailed study on compensation see J. R. Carby-Hall "Aspects of Unfair Dismissal Law" *Managerial Law* Vol 33 Nos. 1, 2, 3 (1991) MCB University Press particularly at pp. 36–47.

124 "Taylor Review," *op. cit.* at p. 62.

The Review recommended that "The burden of proof in employment tribunal hearings where status is in dispute, should be reversed so that the employer has to prove that the individual is not entitled to the relevant employment rights, not the other way round, subject to certain safeguards to discourage vexatious claims."

Tribunal fees

The issue of tribunal fees feature prominently in the Taylor Review[125] and recommendations for changes have been made therein but since 11th July 2017 when the Review was published, the British Supreme Court case of *R (on the application of UNISON) v Lord Chancellor*[126] of 26th July 2017 has abolished such fees. For this reason, the Taylor Review recommendations on fees are both irrelevant for the purposes of this exercise and are now of historical interest only. It is proposed however to discuss briefly the background to the Supreme Court's unanimous decision to scrap Employment Tribunal (ET) and Employment Appeal Tribunal (EAT) fees.

Unlawful and unconstitutional

The Supreme Court seven judges[127] were *unanimous* in holding that the government acted *unlawfully* and *unconstitutionally* in introducing ET and EAT fees in 2013.[128] ETs have jurisdiction to determine numerous employment related cases most of which are based on employment rights granted by Acts of Parliament, a number of which give effect to EU laws. They are the only forum in which such cases[129] may be brought. The function of the EAT is to hear appeals from ETs on points of law. Until the coming into

---

125 *Ibid*. See pp. 51 & 52 of the Review.

126 [2017] UKSC 1 on appeal from [2015] EWCA Civ. 935.

127 Lord Reed who delivered the judgement with whom Lord Neuberger (President), Lord Mance, Lord Kerr, Lord Wilson, Lord Hughes and Lady Hale (Vice President) agreed. Lady Hale in her judgement addressed the discrimination issues relating to the case.

128 The Fees Order was debated and approved by both the House of Commons and the House of Lords under the affirmative resolution procedure on 28th July and came into force on 29th July 2013. Charging fees was considered to be desirable for three reasons, namely (a) and most importantly, fees would help to transfer some of the cost burden from taxpayers to those who used the system; (b) a price mechanism could incentivise earlier settlements and (c) it could dis-incentivise vexatious or weak claims. See the January 2011 government consultation paper entitled "Resolving Workplace Disputes claims" announcing the intention to charge fees in ET and EAT cases.

129 It should be noted that claims before the ETs do not necessarily involve monetary awards. An example is a claim relating to written particulars of employment. Where the employer fails to provide such statement, or where such statement is incomplete, the employee is entitled to refer the matter to an ET (see too Directive 91/533/EEC articles 2 and 8).

force of the Employment Tribunals and Employment Appeal Tribunal Fees Order 2013[130] a claimant could bring and pursue proceedings in the ET and on appeal to the EAT without paying any fees. The 2013 Order changed this by charging fees to claimants. The Fees Order of 2013 prescribed a variety of fees payable. In accordance with the Supreme Court judgement as of 26th July 2017, the charging of fees was held to be *unlawful*; hence no fees will be charged in the future. The government will have to refund the thousands of individuals who were charged fees since 29th July 2013.[131] What is known is that because of the high fees charged, claims to Employment Tribunals had fallen sharply in the last four years;[132] what is unknown however is how many individuals did not bring claims because they could not afford the extortionate and disproportionate fees[133] charged due to the "tax" imposed on justice. The Supreme Court talked of the fees being "so sharp, so substantial and so sustained" that they were unaffordable to United Kingdom[134] low- and middle-income workers. The UNISON trade union[135] brought the case to the courts by way of judicial review. Its General Secretary said:

> The government is not above the law. But when ministers introduced fees they were … showing little concern for employees seeking justice following illegal treatment at work. Unscrupulous employers no longer have the upper hand. These unfair fees have let law-breaking bosses off the hook these past four years and left badly treated staff with no choice but to put up or shut up.

---

130 SI 2013/1893.

131 It is anticipated that that will cost the government (taxpayer) approximately £27 million.

132 Ministry of Justice revue of January 2017 entitled "Review of the introduction of fees in the Employment Tribunals: Consultation on proposals for reform" (Cm 9373) where there has been a reduction of claims in the region of 66%–70%. The Review concludes that "The actual fall since fees were introduced was much greater and we have therefore concluded that it is clear that there has been a sharp fall, substantial and sustained fall in the volume of case receipts as a result of the introduction of fees." (para. 105). It concluded that "the overall scale of the fall…is troubling" (para. 336).

133 Employment Tribunal fees were introduced on 29th July 2013 and started at about £160 for a Type A claim (e.g. breach of contract and wage claims). The Type B claim (e.g. sex and race discrimination, unfair dismissal) fee was £250. Were there to be a further hearing for a type A claim, the additional fee charged was £230 and for a type B claim it rose to £950. An appeal to an Employment Appeal Tribunal attracted an additional £400 *lodging fee* and a £1,200 *hearing fee*.

134 i.e. tribunals in Scotland, Northern Ireland, Wales and England.

135 With the support of the Equality and Human Rights Commission and the Independent Workers' Union of Great Britain as interveners. UNISON argued that the Fees Order of 2013 was not a lawful exercise of those powers, because the prescribed fees interfere unjustifiably with the right of access to justice under both the common law and the EU law, frustrate the operation of Parliamentary legislation granting employment rights and discriminating unlawfully against women and other protected groups.

On the *constitutional* aspects of this case Lord Reed's learned judgement explained the pedigree in British law of the right of access to the courts. He said:

> When Parliament passes laws creating employment rights... it does so not merely to confer benefits on individual employees, but because it has decided that it is in the public interest that those rights should be given effect... the possibility of claims being brought by employees whose rights are infringed must exist... Equally, although it is often desirable that claims arising out of alleged breaches of employment rights should be resolved by negotiation or mediation, those procedures can only work fairly and properly if they are backed up by the knowledge on both sides that a fair and just system of adjudication will be available if they fail. Otherwise, the party in the stronger bargaining position will always prevail.[136]

Lord Reed went to great pains to illustrate the *pedigree* behind a right of access to the courts in the enforcement of rights concept by quoting from Magna Carta (1215)[137] and which remain in the statute book in the closing words of the version issued by Edward I in 1297. "These words are not a prohibition on the charging of court fees, but they are a guarantee of access to courts which administer justice promptly and fairly" said the learned judge.[138] The significance of this guarantee was emphasised by Sir Edward Coke[139] in 1642 when he said "And therefore, every Subject of the Realme, for injury done to him *in bonis, terries, vel pesona*[140] by any other Subject... may take his remedy by the course of the law, and have justice and right for the injury done to him, freely without sale, fully without any denial, and speedily without delay."[141]

The learned Lord then mentioned Blackstone who cited Coke in his "Commentaries on the Laws of England" (1765–1769) on the individual

---

136 [2017] UKSC at para 72 p. 21.
137 Chapter 40 of Magna Carta "Nulli vendemus, nulli negabimus aut differemus rectum aut justiciam" (We will sell to no man, we will not deny or defer to any man either Justice or Right).
138 [2017] UKSC at para. 74 p. 22.
139 In "Institutes of the Laws of England" Part 2 written in the 1620s and published posthumously in 1642 citing chapter 29 of the 1297 Edward I charter.
140 i.e. in goods, in land, or in person.
141 "Hereby it appeareth that Justice must have three qualities, it must be *Libera, quid nihilini-quius venali Justitia; Plena, quia Justitia non debet claudicare; and Celeris, quiadilatio est quaedam negatio* and then it is both Justice and Right" (1809 ed. at pp. 55 and 56). The English translation of the above Latin words are "Free, because nothing is more iniquitous than saleable justice; Full, because justice ought not to be limp; and Speedy because delay is in effect a denial."

right of a person to apply to a court for redress,[142] as well as a sample of modern case law which give judicial recognition of the constitutional right of "unimpaired access to the courts."[143]

Does the fees order cut down statutory rights? Plus the enforceability of EU Laws issues

There were two further issues considered by the Supreme Court, First, the lawfulness of the Fees Order. Lord Reed stated that:

> in so far as the Fees Order has the practical effect of making it unafford-able for persons to exercise rights conferred on them by Parliament, or of rendering the bringing of claims to enforce such rights a futile or irrational exercise, it must be regarded as rendering those rights nugatory.[144]

In the second instance, the Court of Appeal in the UNISON case identified 24 of the rights enforceable in ETs as having their source in EU law.[145] The Supreme Court said that "the ET is the only forum in which those rights can be enforced. It follows that, so far as applicable to those rights, restrictions on the right of access to ETs and the EAT fall within the scope of EU law."[146]

---

142 A right of every person "is that of applying to the courts of justice for redress of injuries. Since the law is in England the supreme arbiter of a man's life, liberty and property, courts of justice must at all times be open to the subject, and the law be duly administered therein." (Book 1 Chapter 1 "Absolute Rights of Individuals").

143 Citing Lord Diplock in *Attorney General v Times Newspapers Ltd* [1974] AC 273 at 310; *Bremer Vulkan Schiffbau und Maschinenfabrik v South India Shipping Cornp Ltd* [1981] AC 909 and earlier 20th century cases. Quoting Lord Gardiner who "put the point in a nutshell" in a letter to the Treasury in 1965 (from Genn's "*Judging Civil Justice*" (2010) p. 46) Lord Reed said "(i) Justice in this country is something in which all the Queen's subjects have an interest, whether it be criminal or civil. (ii) The courts are for the benefit of all, whether the individual resorts to them or not. (iii) In the case of the civil courts the citizen benefits from the interpretation of the law by the Judges and from the resolution of disputes, whether between the state and the individual or between individuals" (Lord Reed's judgement in the UNISON case *op. cit.* 2017 paragraph 71. p. 22).

144 Based on the Court of Appeal case of R *v Secretary of State for Social Security, Ex parte Joint Council for the Welfare on immigrants* [1997]1 WLR 275, where Simon Brown LJ (at p. 292) stated that "these Regulations for some genuine asylum seekers… must now be regarded as rendering those rights nugatory."

145 Examples include, *inter alia*, Working Time Directive rights, maternity leave, discrimination, equal pay, collective redundancies, transfer of undertakings and so on.

146 See too the Charter of Fundamental Rights of the EU Art 47 which states" everyone whose right and freedoms guaranteed by the law of the Union are violated, has as the right to an effective remedy before a tribunal".

(b) State enforcement through government organisations

In addition to Employment Tribunals the State enforces some aspects of employment law where there is considered to be a higher risk of employee/worker vulnerability or exploitation. These organisations are tasked with enforcing compliance against a range of basic employment rights. They include Her Majesty's Revenue and Customs, the Gangmasters and Labour Abuse Authority, the Employment Agency Standards Inspectorate and the Health and Safety Executive. Each of these will be discussed briefly

Her Majesty's Revenue and Customs (HMRC)

HMRC is tasked with enforcing, prosecuting and naming and shaming employers who break the National Minimum Wage (NMW)[147] and National Living Wage (NLW) on behalf of BEIS.[148] The aim is to ensure that the lowest paid and most vulnerable receive the minimum wage required by law. It has the additional function of providing the enforcement for Statutory Sick Pay (SSP), which is a statutory payment redeemable by employers through the PAYE system. HMRC however does not have jurisdiction over holiday pay disputes. Where such disputes come about claimants have to use Employment Tribunals[149] for any redress. The Taylor Review is of the opinion that HMRC should assume responsibility for enforcing this right and recommends that "HMRC should take responsibility for enforcing the basic set of core rights that apply to all workers – NMW, sick pay and holiday pay for the lowest paid workers."[150]

Gang-masters and Labour Abuse Authority (GLAA)

The GLAA licences businesses that supply temporary labour in high risk sectors in the fresh food supply chain.[151] The Immigration Act 2016 gave the GLAA

---

147 The NMW relates to the legal wage entitlements per hour of workers of school leaving age (namely 16) by groups (16–18; 18–20; 20–24 and over 25) and regulated by the Low Pay Commission since 1999. The NLW is a new minimum wage rate for workers of 25 years of age and over. It is the NMW rebranded and is exactly the same with a different name!

148 In 2017 the Department of Energy and Climate Chance (DECC) was dismantled and merged with the Department of Business, Innovation and Skills (BIS). In their place, the Department of Business, Energy and Industrial Strategy (BEIS) has been created.

149 Tribunal decisions may go on appeal to the EAT, the Court of Appeal, the Supreme Court and even to the CJEU (until Brexit comes about) bearing in mind the Working Time Directive provisions.

150 "Taylor Review," *op. cit.* at p. 59.

151 The Gang-masters Licensing Authority (GLA) was founded in 2004 in the aftermath of the Morecambe Bay tragedy where 23 Chinese migrants lost their lives by the incoming tide. The Immigration Act 2016 gave the GLA additional powers to investigate cases of modern slavery, forced labour and other labour abuses across England and Wales regardless of employment status and sector. The GLA was renamed GLAA when the change came into

additional powers, which came into effect in April 2017, namely to investigate cases of modern slavery where forced/compulsory labour and other forms of abuse and exploitation have been identified across England and Wales regardless of employment status or sector.

Employment Agency Standards Inspectorate (EAS)

The EAS is responsible for ensuring compliance with the provisions of the Employment Agencies Act, 1973 and the Conduct of Employment Agencies and Employment Businesses Regulations, 2003. The legislation ensures that agency workers are treated fairly by their agency.

Health and Safety Executiv. (HSE)

The Health and Safety at Work Act 1974 places a duty on the employer to ensure, as far as is reasonably practicable, the health, safety and welfare at work of all employees and workers of whatever kind, whether temporary, casual, permanent, seasonal, those on atypical contracts, etc. There exist duties on the employer to have health and safety committees and representatives for information and consultation purposes.[152] The Working Time Regulations 1998 provide for the maximum weekly working time limits, night work, shifts and a rich variety of other issues which are enforced by the HSE.

Each of the above organisations is given "sharp enforcement teeth" where breaches occur resulting in civil and criminal penalties ranging from fines to imprisonment and thus having the important effect of dealing with unscrupulous employers.

Director of Labour Market Enforcement

This Office was created in 2016 and became operational in 2017. Its task is to produce an annual labour market enforcement strategy to set the strategic direction of the aforementioned GLAA, EAS and HMRC's NMW and NLW team. The aim of that office is to ensure that enforcement efforts are *coordinated* and *targeted*. Although all three organisations remain operationally independent of

---

effect in April 2017. For a detailed study of modern slavery in the European Union States and the GLA in the UK see J. R. Carby-Hall *The Treatment of Polish and Other A8 Economic Migrants in the European Union Member States* (a research and legal advice programme commissioned by the Polish Government) (English and Polish Editions each in two volumes) (2008) Bureau of the Commissioner for Civil Rights Protection Warsaw and Jo Carby-Hall "The Continuing Exploitation of Economic Migrants and Other Vulnerable Workers" in *Essays on Human Rights – A Celebration of the Life of Dr. Janusz Kochanowski* (Jo Carby-Hall (Ed)) (2014) Ius et Lex Foundation, Warsaw at pp. 94–134.

152 For further reading see J. R, Carby-Hall "Health, Safety and Welfare at Work," *op. cit.* especially pp. 38–41.

each other each one of these needs to plan its resourcing and operations to deliver against a single set of objectives and priorities. The Director will no doubt seek improvements that should enhance the safety net of the most vulnerable in the labour market.

Agency workers and the GLAA and EAS remits

The GLAA's remit includes all types of labour provider as well as ensuring that end users of the labour are dealing with licenced labour providers. On the other hand, the EAS inspectorate can only take enforcement action and apply penalties to recruiting agencies and not to the end user of the agency workers. In practice more employment businesses outsource payroll and other services to intermediaries such as umbrella companies[153] with workers being *compelled* in these arrangements or *signing up* to them with the detail *hidden* in the small print of the contract. This can result in the worker not knowing who the employer is or not understanding the manner in which the wages are calculated. Although umbrella companies generally perform their tasks well the Taylor Review found that "at the lower paid, lower skilled end their role is more questionable"[154] such as the umbrella company charging the worker an administration fee which would have been illegal had the agency paid the worker. The Taylor Review thus recommends that "The New Director of Labour Market Enforcement should consider whether the remit of EAS should be extended to cover policing umbrella companies and other intermediaries in the supply chain."

Furthermore, the GLAA is entitled to withdraw a licence if the gang-master or intermediaries operating in its sector are not complying with the Agency Workers Regulations,[155] which ensures that agency workers are not a source of cheap labour. The key protection is the right to equal pay.[156] An opt-out clause is however allowed under the legislation if workers sign with the employment agency a "pay between agreements" contract.[157] Such clause guarantees the agency worker some pay between assignments if the agency is unable to find him/her work.

Concerns had been raised by the Swedish Derogation during the Taylor Review on three grounds. Firstly, agency workers are forced to accept such contracts either at the start of their employment or after 11 weeks of

---

153 See pp. 36–38 *supra*.

154 "Taylor Review," *op. cit.* at p. 58.

155 Which has put into effect the EU Directive on Temporary Agency Work (2008/104/EC).

156 This means that agency workers are entitled to be paid the same wages as the permanent workers doing the same job after a 12-week qualifying period.

157 Also known as the "Swedish Derogation," so named after the original derogation in the Directive on Temporary Agency Work 2008. That derogation came about because while the Agency Directive was being negotiated, the Swedish government asked for a special exemption to reflect normal practice in the use of agency workers in Sweden.

employment. Such conduct is clearly unlawful.[158] In the second instance, it is easy for employment agencies and also umbrella companies to avoid paying workers in between assignments.[159] The third concern treats, the structuring by employment agencies of a short-term assignment to avoid their equal pay responsibility *simpliciter*. On those three grounds and in order to protect agency workers from being abused, the Taylor Review felt inclined to deal "effectively with abuses of 'pay between assignments' contracts and recommended that "The Government should repeal the legislation that allows agency worker to opt out of equal pay entitlements."[160]

Regarding the Employment Agency Standards Inspectorate (EAS) which does not have the legal means to enforce the Agency Workers' Regulations (AWR) thus "leaving hundreds of thousands of agency workers" to bring their cases to Employment Tribunals, the Review "did not believe this is right and think the system should adapt." It recommended that the "Government should consider extending the remit of the EAS Inspectorate to include compliance with the AWR."[161]

(c) Enforcement of employment tribunal awards

Where an individual is successful in winning a case, the Employment Tribunal will make a financial award by way of redress. Thus, in unfair dismissal cases redress may[162] include a compensation award made to the employee, in redundancy cases the redress would consist of an employee's entitlement to a redundancy payment,[163] in cases of unlawful deduction from wages, the award would be the unpaid wages, and so on. Statistics[164] show that following enforcement action taken by individuals, a significant number of employers do not respect the awards made by the tribunals, which means that individuals do

---

158 Because the Agency Workers' Regulations *specifically* prohibits the structuring of assignments to avoid equal pay.

159 Although this may not necessarily be the fault of the agency or umbrella organisation, for the agency worker may not bother to draw monies owed to him where such worker has subsequently found alternative employment.

160 "Taylor Review," *op. cit.* p. 59.

161 *Ibid.*

162 Although redress in the majority of successful unfair dismissal cases consists of compensation, reinstatement or re-engagement are also alternative remedies. See J. R. Carby-Hall "Aspects of Unfair Dismissal" *Managerial Law* Vol. 33 Nos 1, 2, 3 (1991) MBC University Press especially at pp. 31–48.

163 See Jo Carby-Hall "Redundancy in the United Kingdom" in *I Licenziamenti per Riduzione di Personale in Europa* (Professors Bruno Veneziani and Umberto Carabelli (Eds)) European SOCRATES Programme (2001) Cacucci Editore, Italy at pp. 387–537.

164 See the 2013 government commissioned research entitled "Payments of Tribunal Awards", 2013 Survey. IFF Research made by the Department of Business, Innovation and Skills, which shows (in Ch. 5 at p. 27) that in England and Wales 34% of Employment Tribunal awards remain unpaid, whereas in Scotland the figure is much higher at 46%.

not receive them. The Taylor Review found those percentages to be unacceptable. Civil tribunals do not have enforcement powers, so the Employment Tribunal award is treated as if it were a County Court order. The enforcement procedure is somewhat complicated and lengthy[165] and involves the claimant employees and workers filling forms and incurring additional fees with no guarantee whatsoever that they will recover the initial award made by the tribunal. This "catch 22" situation is unbelievable but true! The Taylor Review in finding this to be unfair recommends[166] that the "Government should make the enforcement process simpler for employees and workers by taking enforcement action against employers/engagers who do not pay employment tribunal awards without the employee/worker having to fill in extra forms or pay an extra fee and having to initiate additional court proceedings." Furthermore, the Review suggests the creation of "a deterrent for employers who think they can simply ignore the law" and recommends that the[167] "Government should establish a naming and shaming scheme for those employers who do not pay employment tribunal awards within a reasonable time."

(d) Applicability of tribunal and court judgements to the wider workforce

Talking of the *Uber* case the Taylor Review argues that:

> the reality is that the ruling only applies to the two drivers who brought cases. It is neither just nor efficient for the system to operate so that every single person in the organisation has to bring a case to be recognised as a worker for the judgment to apply to the whole workforce."

What the Taylor Review is talking about is the applicability of an Employment Tribunal ruling to the *wider workforce in the company*. With great respect to the Taylor Review's aforementioned statement, two matters need to be commented upon.

First, in practice, when a judgement had been passed by a tribunal or court as a result of an individual or a joint case hearing applying to the wider workforce,

---

165 There exist three optional enforcement routes. Firstly, the *Fast Track* route through a High Court Enforcement Officer in England and Wales, or in the second instance through the *County Court* (or in Scotland the Sheriff Court). Each of these has its limitations and in addition the employee or worker has to pay fees. The third route, which is free of charge, is through the *Department of Business, Energy and Industrial Strategy* (BEIS), which imposes a penalty on the employer who refuses to pay the employee/worker. The individual has to notify BEIS that the employer has not paid the award or settlement. BEIS after considering the matter will issue a letter to warn the employer that if he fails to pay the award, he will incur a penalty (fine) notice which if not paid the BEIS will instigate debt recovery action on the unpaid fine. The BEIS has no statutory powers to pursue the award itself. Thus, the BEIS collects the state enforced penalty fine and the employee/worker does not succeed in recovering the financial award to which he is entitled, made by the tribunal!

166 "Taylor Review," *op. cit.* p. 63.

167 *Ibid.*

employers normally extend the tribunal or court decision to all employees or workers in the company. Were the employer not to do so, it would mean that there would be in the company two different sets of employment contracts with two different sets of employment statuses. Such a situation would make the company unmanageable administratively and expensive financially. In addition, there could be confusion and inequalities in a variety of ways causing industrial unrest. A concrete example to affirm the above is the *Uber* decision in the Employment Tribunal, which was upheld on appeal by the Employment Appeal Tribunal.[168] It will be recalled that Uber drivers had the employment status of "workers" and not independent contractors as argued by Uber. Mr Nigel Mackay said on behalf of Uber that in theory any Uber driver in the UK would benefit from the EAT decision should it stand uncontested.[169] He expanded his previous sentence by saying:

> The judgment directly applies to the original 25 claimants in the claim and since, another 43 drivers joined…However, given that all Uber drivers work in essentially the same way, then there is no reason why the same principles would'nt (*sic*) apply across all drivers in the UK and they could all be free to join the claim and be entitled to compensation.[170]

The GMB trade union legal director said "Uber must now face up to its responsibilities and give its workers the rights to which they are entitled" while the General Secretary of the IWGB trade union said "Today's victory is further proof…that the law is clear and these companies are simply choosing to deprive workers of their rights."

This author would go even further and beyond the company level and suggest that if a legal trend establishes itself such as it has in the gig economy cases of *Addison Lee*,[171] *City Sprint*[172] *Uber*[173] and the Court of Appeal case of *Pimlico*

---

168   *Uber BV, Uber London Ltd and Uber Britannia v Aslam et al.* UKEAT/0056/17/DA. This case held that any Uber driver who had the Uber application (app) switched on was working for the company under a worker status contract. They were therefore workers and, as such were owed employment rights. It should be noted that there are some 50,000 drivers using the app in the UK.

169   It should be pointed out that *Uber* requested permission to appeal against the EAT decision directly to the Supreme Court thus bypassing the Court of Appeal in order to resolve this case sooner rather than later (on 5th December, 2017). This request was rejected, for the Court of Appeal would have to hear the case first. At the time of writing the date of the appeal hearing (if indeed this case is appealed) is unknown.

170   Source: BBC News 10th November 2017.

171   *Lange et al v Addison Lee Ltd* Case No. 2208029 July 2017 (London Central ET) (unreported) and *Gascoigne v Addison Lee Ltd.* Case No, 2200436/2016 (ET) (unreported).

172   *Dewhurst v City Sprint UK Ltd.* Case No. 2202512 (2017) (ETT (unreported) See too *Boxer v Excel Group Services Ltd. (in liquidation)* Case No. 3200365/2016 (ET) (unreported).

173   *Aslam v Uber BV* [2017] IRLR 4 (ET) and on appeal to the EAT it dismissed the appeal. At the time of writing, (1st March, 2018) this case is awaiting to be heard in the Court of Appeal.

Plumbers[174] other such firms operating in the gig economy would be influenced to reform their policies by observing the tribunal and court decisions.

In the second instance, there exists in British law the doctrine of judicial precedent.[175] Under that doctrine lower tribunals and courts are bound to follow the judgements of higher tribunals and courts where the facts of the case are either identical or very similar. The decision of the 2018 Supreme Court case of *Pimlico Plumbers* is binding on the lower tribunals and courts. In the gig economy cases such as cycle couriers, car delivery drivers and plumbers were all successful in arguing that they enjoyed the employment status of worker for the purposes of the Employment Rights Act 1996, the Working Time Regulations and the National Minimum Wage Act endowing them with a host of employment rights. The judicial precedent doctrine thus goes a long way towards influencing the application of court case decisions not only to a wider workforce in the companies concerned but also to a wider workforce in the whole of the industry or trade. By reason of these two facts it is submitted that the Taylor Review recommendations that[176] "Government should create an obligation on employment tribunals to consider the use of aggravated breach penalties and costs orders if an employer has already lost an employment status case on broadly comparable facts – punishing those employers who believe they can ignore the law" and that[177] "Government should allow tribunals to award uplifts in compensation if there are subsequent breaches against workers with the same or materially the same working arrangements" Such suggested legislative action would be both unnecessary and inappropriate.

The longstanding *Pimlico Plumbers* case heard in Supreme Court[178] could have implications by virtue of the doctrine of judicial precedent in the *wider gig economy* thus entitling individuals – who are considered to have the employment status of worker – to enjoy the statutory employment benefits.

Will the CJEU decision in *Asociación Profesional Élite Taxi v Uber Systems Spain SL*[179] which is binding on the UK tribunals and courts[180] affect in any way the trend in the current UK courts' and tribunals' decisions on the gig economy? It is not thought that it will! The Grand Chamber of the European court held that Uber[181] "must be classified as 'a service in the field of transport' within the

---

174 *Pimlico Plumbers Ltd. v Smith* [2017] EWCA Civ. 51 (CA) awaiting, at the time of writing (1st March 2018), the case to go on appeal to the Supreme Court.

175 The common law has developed by broadening itself from precedent to precedent. See footnote 14 *ante* for an explanation of the doctrine of judicial precedent.

176 "Taylor Review," *op. cit.* p. 63.

177 *Ibid.* at p. 64.

178 The *Pimlico Plumbers* case has been heard in the Supreme Court on 20 and 21st February 2018 and the judgment delivered on 13th June 2018. Resulting from the Supreme Court's decision in the *Pimlico Plumbers* case, it is not thought that *Uber* will appeal the EAT decision to the Court of Appeal.

179 Case C-434/15 heard on 20th December 2017.

180 The UK exited the EU on 31 January 2020 (see European Union (Withdrawal Agreement (Act) 2020 (c.1)). During the agreed transition period to 31 December 2020, the UK will remain subject to EU law.

181 Case C-434/15 para. 48.

meaning of Article 58(1) TFEU." In other words, a transport company for the purpose of employing taxi drivers and not the information society service claimed by Uber Systems Spain SL. It is for the EU[182] "Member States to regulate the conditions under which intermediation services... are to be provided in conformity with the general rules of the FEU Treaty." In the same vein, the Advocate General concluded that:[183]

> Uber's activity comprises a single supply of transport in a vehicle located and booked by means of a smartphone application and that this service is provided, from an economic standpoint ... by Uber or on its behalf. The service is also presented to users, and perceived by them, in that way. When users decide to use Uber's services, they are looking for a transport service offering certain functions and a particular standard of quality. Such functions and transport quality are ensured by Uber.

He then concludes that[184] "Uber is ... not a mere intermediary between drivers willing to offer transport services occasionally and passengers in search of such services. On the contrary Uber is a genuine organiser and operator of urban transport services ... While it is true ... that this concept is innovative, that innovation nonetheless pertains to the field of urban transport."

The Supreme Court case of *Pimlico Plumbers* confirmed that gig workers enjoy the employment status of "worker" rather than that of independent contractor or self-employed as stipulated in their respective contracts. Even prior to the *Pimlico Plumbers'* case the trend in the United Kingdom showed clearly that tribunals and courts favoured the status of worker for individuals working in the gig economy and were prepared to lift the veil of the contract to examine the *reality* of the relationship. The aforementioned CJEU decision, which is binding on the United Kingdom, will have the effect of making it harder for Uber and other employers employing gig workers to plead that it is a platform and that its drivers are therefore self-employed individuals.

Summation

The Review's seven principles

In his Foreword Matthew Taylor, the Chair of the Review, "calls for us as a country to sign up to the ambition of all work being good work" and that "this Review will come to be seen to have won the argument that good work

---

182 *Ibid.* para. 47.
183 Opinion of Advocate General Szpunar delivered on 11th May 2017 in *Asociación Elite Taxi v Uber Systems Spain SL* Case C-434/15 para. 53.
184 *Ibid.* para. 61.

for all should be a national priority."[185] The Review outlines in a practical manner its *seven principles*[186] towards achieving fair and decent work with realistic scope for development and fulfilment. Whereas this chapter limits itself to a critical appreciation of some of the Review's legal content, each of those seven principles are applicable to that limited list.

The first principle talks of the British strategy for work to "be explicitly directed toward the goal of good work for all, recognising that good work and plentiful work can and should go together." Although the government should be held accountable for good work, all stakeholders need to take responsibility. There should "be a fair balance or rights and responsibilities, everyone should have a baseline of protection and there should be routes to enable progression at work." The rights and entitlements of the self-employed need improvement while technological "change will impact work and types of employment and we need to adapt" though "technology can also offer new opportunities for smarter regulation, more flexible entitlements and new ways for people to organise."

The second principle states that "Platform based working offers welcome opportunities for genuine two-way flexibility" and allows opportunities for individuals who are unable to enjoy conventional employment. The "worker" status should be maintained but the Review's suggested "dependant contractor" status should make it clearer" about how to distinguish workers from those who are legitimately self-employed."

Thirdly, the law "and the way it is promulgated and enforced should help firms make the right choices and individuals to know and exercise their rights… 'Dependent contractors' are the group most likely to suffer from unfair one-sided flexibility and therefore we need to provide additional protections for this group and stronger incentives for firms to treat them fairly."

A further principle for achieving good work "is not national regulation but responsible corporate governance, good management and strong employment relations within the organisation, which is why it is important that companies are seen to take good work seriously and are open about their practices and that all workers are able to be engaged and heard."

The fifth principle treats individuals' realistically attainable future work prospects "and that they can from the beginning to the end of their working life, record and enhance the capabilities developed in formal and informal learning and in on the job and off the job activities."

The sixth principle talks of a more proactive approach to workplace health, which needs to be developed in the interests and to the benefit of workers, companies and the public at large.

Finally, the National Minimum Wage "is a powerful tool to raise the financial baseline of low paid workers." This seventh principle aims at people – and

---

185 "Taylor Review," *op cit*. at p. 5.
186 *Ibid*. pp. 9 and 110–111.

particularly the low paid – not being "stuck at the living age minimum or facing insecurity but can progress in their current and future work."

As already explained and analysed in this chapter, the Review outlines ways in which the aforementioned principles may be furthered.

How have individuals and organisations perceived the Taylor Review?

It is a well-understood fact that *Good Work: the Taylor Review on Modern Working Practices*, like any other review or report, is likely to divide opinion among stakeholders[187] each of whose interests differ.

On the one hand, the TUC General Secretary Frances O'Grady was critical of this Revue when she said that:[188]

> It's no secret that we wanted this revue to be bolder. This is not the game-changer needed to end insecurity at work. A "right to request" guaranteed hours is no right at all for many workers trapped on zero-hours contracts. And workers deserve the minimum wage for every minute they work, not just the time employers choose to pay them for.

The General Secretary of the GMB trade union called the Taylor Review[189] "a disappointing missed opportunity" which had the effect of allowing the system of insecure work to continue, while the General Secretary of the UNITE trade union who said that the Review lacked[190] "the serious programme the country urgently needs to ensure that once again work pays." Criticism also came from the Chief Executive of the Association of Independent Professionals and Self-Employed (IPSE) who posited[191] "any changes to employment status should bring clarity and not add to the confusion surrounding how government treats the way people choose to work."

On the other hand, the CBI's Managing Director for People and Infrastructure was of the opinion that the Review[192] "rightly recognises that labour market flexibility is a key strength of the UK economy, driving better outcomes for everyone. Businesses agree that flexibility must be matched with fairness, but building on our own approach, as the report concludes, is the right way forwards. The CBI is ready to work in partnership with the Government to address the challenges the report raises. Spreading good practice, not just focusing on new laws is something the CBI has always supported given the

---

187 Particularly employers and their associations and trade unions, employees and the TUC, as well as employment law practitioners, academics, politicians, HMRC, Low Pay Commission, ACAS and others affected or interested directly or indirectly by that Review.
188 Source: Rob Moss "*Personnel Today*" 11th July, 2017 p. 2. https://wwwpersonneltoday. com/hr/good-work-bad-reaction. (Retrieved 10th October, 2017).
189 *Ibid.* p. 2.
190 *Ibid.*
191 *Ibid.*
192 *Ibid.*

link between good employee relations and higher productivity, which is the only sustainable route to rising (*sic*) wages and better living standards. There is much for firms to like" but warned that there would also exist challenges, namely "A number of proposals in the report will be of significant concern to businesses, however. Changes to the application of the minimum wage, rewriting employment status tests and altering agency worker rules could have unintended consequences that are negative for individuals, as well as affecting firms' ability to create new jobs."

The Director General of the British Chambers of Commerce posited that the Review[193] "has rightly recognised that the UK's flexible labour market is a great source of strength and competitive advantage but has also recommended some common-sense changes where grey areas have emerged in recent years." He continued by saying that "Civic- minded business leaders across the UK have expressed concern over the consequences of insecure employment in their local communities in recent years and recognise there is a two -way bargain that needs to be struck that gives flexibility and security to both employers and employees...While the notion of a wage premium in exchange for uncertain working hours is superficially attractive, it could have unforeseen circumstances, and push up wage costs elsewhere. Further expert consideration of the potential impact of such a measure on jobs will be needed... If a new category of 'dependent contractors' proposed by the review is implemented, it must give a clear legal definition to prevent any ambiguity or unintended knock-on effects. The Government should consult widely with business and employees … to ensure any response to the … Review is proportionate, fair and above all un-bureaucratic."

An overall assessment of the Taylor Review

In spite of the criticism of "*feebleness*" which the Taylor Review received from trade unions and others,[194] this important, sensible, well balanced, wisely thought out and generally positive Review had, of necessity, to be published for it is a welcome contribution to a much needed debate about how we ensure the British labour market reflects the ways in which working people live their lives! Most of the recommendations made by the Review seen as a whole are both balanced and necessary.[195] Were

---

193 *Ibid.*
194 See pp. 58–59 *supra*. See too the criticism made by the CEO of Thompsons focused on both the Taylor Review and the government where he said "It is a limp response to a limp report, which offers nothing but vague platitudes" (*The Guardian*, 8th February 2018) and the UNITE leader Mr. Len McCluskey's negative comment on the seven principles of the Taylor Revue referred to as "The seven pillars of Taylor are very wobbly and tumble to rubble under first scrutiny."
195 See in particular the RSA's response in answer to the criticism directed at the Taylor Review. It was written by Brhmie Balaram and entitled "Taylor Review: pragmatism must prevail" RSA, 12th July 2017. Three key points need to be kept in mind for ensuring a level playing

these recommendations to be adopted by the government and eventually enacted by the Westminster parliament, a significant number of grey areas[196] currently existing in labour law would be clarified and employees and workers[197] would enjoy increased protection of their *existing* and *suggested* new employment rights. The employment rights recommendations that have been discussed above feature eminently[198] throughout this Review.

The two tier[199] *state enforcement* framework currently works well. It is important that those most vulnerable to exploitation are protected by the four government bodies (i.e., HMRC, GLAA, EAS and the HSE), which enforce compliance in a range of basic employment rights. Furthermore, the employment tribunals have jurisdiction over numerous employment issues. The two-tier system is thus effective. There are, however, a number of ways in which the system could be improved to address certain imbalances. One of these is to ensure more robust penalties to deal with employers who choose to ignore the

field for both workers and employers while also serving the public interest. This author sympathises entirely with the contents of that RSA document. The reader is strongly recommended to consult this very balanced document at https://www.thersa.org/discover/publications-and-articles/rsa (retrieved 25th December 2017).

196 Examples of grey areas do exist in labour law, the most flamboyant of which is the complexity of ascertaining the employment status of the individual analysed above at pp. 2–9. It will be noticed that this author is not in total agreement with the recommendations made by the Review on this topic. Reasons for such a disagreement have already been discussed within the aforementioned pages.

197 It should be noted that the Review recommended that a new status of "dependent contractor" should replace that of "worker."

198 Examples include, *inter alia*, clarity, certainty and understanding of all people at work by extending the information given in the *statutory particulars of employment* not only to the employee status as is currently the case, but also to the worker status (and dependent contractor status if that recommendation is taken on board by the government). Furthermore, it is recommended that such statement should be provided on the first day of employment. A recommendation was made for access to an *on-line tool* to assist employers, employees and workers to determine their employment status. Another recommendation was made for legislation that allows *agency workers* and those on *zero hours contracts* to request the formalisation of the reality of the working relationship. With regard to agency workers, the Revue recommends that if they worked with the same hirer for twelve months, they should be given the right to request a permanent contract with the hirer. Also, the hirer would be required, under this recommendation, to consider the request seriously. In the case of zero hours contracts it has been recommended to establish a higher national minimum rate for hours that are not guaranteed in the contract. Currently a week's gap in between employments would usually break *continuity of employment*. The Review recommends an increased gap of one month before continuity of employment be broken. Where an individual is on *a long period of sick leave* a new right is recommended by the Review, namely the right to return to the same job or to a similar one.

199 The two-tier state enforcement mechanism consists (a) of government bodies tasked with enforcing compliance against a range of basic employment rights which include Her Majesty's Revenue and Customs, (HMRC), the Gangmasters and Labour Abuse Authority (GLAA), the Employment Agency Standards Authority (EAS) the Health and Safety Executive (HSE) and (b) Employment Tribunals.

court/tribunal judgements either by failing to *pay financial awards* or failing to *apply judgements* to other relevant relationships in their workforce. The Review thus recommends that *aggravated breach penalties and costs orders* be made on employers who had previously lost employment status cases on broadly comparable facts or who fail to pay financial awards. A *naming and shaming scheme* for employers who fail to pay tribunal awards is also recommended by the Review.[200] All these suggestions would have the effect of punishing employers who believe that they can ignore the law.

Much has been said on "voice in the workplace" and information and consultation. The Revue recommended that the trigger threshold for employers to establish an information and consultation committee which is currently 10% of the workforce should be reduced to 2% of the workforce which would include persons enjoying the employment status of *worker* as well.

Growing *labour market flexibility*[201] and the effect this has on both *wages and conditions of employment* is stressed throughout the Taylor Review. The important and rapid development of the gig economy indicates that individuals' work patterns are evolving so as to adapt to technological advances. However, it is argued by many that legislation has not kept up with those technological and innovative developments and that both employers and individuals working for those employers find themselves in a legal limbo in such aspects as the legal distinction between the status of employee, of worker and of independent contractor. Furthermore, the Taylor Review is criticised for failing to provide clear recommendations[202] to distinguish each of those three status categories. With respect to that argument this author does not hold the same opinion. The Taylor Report does indeed make constructive suggestions in respect of this complicated issue.[203] Nor does this author believe that the laws are falling behind when faced with cases involving modern technological and innovative advances. For well over a century the courts have effectively dealt with employment status cases by developing a number of tests. Each case heard has been fact specific. More recently, the tribunals and courts have been effective in dealing with the most up-to-date digital and technological innovations,[204] which have encouraged the establishment and rapid development of the gig economy. Indeed, it would assist civic-minded employers if more clarity were available on the issue of employment status developed by the common law in that they would ensure

---

200 "Taylor Review," *op. cit.* at p. 63.
201 Through its flexibility the UK is recognised as having the fifth most efficient labour market in the world behind Switzerland, Hong Kong, Singapore and the United States (Global Competitiveness Report, 2016–17 of the World Economic Forum).
202 See "Taylor Review," *op. cit.* at pp. 34–40 where four recommendations are made in respect of status.
203 *Ibid.* at pp. 33–34 (current approach); pp. 34–35 (new approach); pp. 35–36 (retention of current three tier system); pp. 37–38 (dependent contractor) and p. 40 (the provision of maximum clarity on status and employment rights).
204 *Inter alia* the cases of *Uber* in the EAT, *City Sprint* in an Employment Tribunal and *Pimlico Plumbers* in the Supreme Court.

that their policies comply with the laws and thus treat their workforce fairly. Workers would also be assisted by more clarity on employment status developed through the common law in that they would know their employment rights and thus not be exploited by unscrupulous employers who would exploit any uncertainty and treat individuals as self-employed to circumvent their statutory rights. However in both cases of employer and worker either *ignorantia juris neminem excusat* (ignorance of the law excuses no one) or more likely *eorum quae quis scire tenetur non excusat* (ignorance of those things which one ought to know is no excuse) hence the reason why the Taylor Review recommends more clarity on the status issue[205] and this author disagreeing in part by suggesting an alternative.[206] The arguments of this author may be briefly epitomised in a few sentences. Firstly, the current legal framework which establishes the person's employment status and which has evolved through the common law since the early 20th century allows both employers and individuals a high degree of flexibility; secondly, this flexibility shows that the framework has adapted well to changes created by the latest technological and digitalisation advances in the labour market, a flamboyant example of which are the 2016 to 2018 tribunal and court decisions in the gig economy, namely the *Uber, City Sprint, Pimlico Plumbers* cases, and there is very little doubt that future employment tribunals and courts will be capable of adapting this further to any new – and currently unknown forms – of employment which may evolve in the labour market. In the third instance, for those who do not wish to have flexibility in their working arrangements their employment status is *usually* clear as are their statutory and common law employment rights. The employer's legal responsibilities towards the employee are also clear. However, in employment where individuals wish to take advantage of such flexibility, there can well be some uncertainty, insecurity and vulnerability with the unscrupulous employer taking advantage of such situations to the individual's detriment by exploiting low skilled and low paid workforces. Hence in the fourth instance, the reason why this author is against any fundamental changes being made to the laws relating to status, which changes would *per se* generate new problems and challenges of their own. However, some discreet changes have been suggested to take into account employers who abuse the system to the detriment of the worker.[207]

---

205   See "Taylor Review" *op. cit.* Chapter 5 entitled "Clarity in the law" at pp. 32–40 suggesting (a) secondary legislation containing additional detail which could be updated quickly to respond dynamically to changing market conditions as well as case law; (b) recommendations to improve clarity for individuals and employers to reflect emerging business models; (c) adaption of the current framework to developing circumstances to improve clarity and transparency in the field of worker and independent contractor; (d) efforts made to remove incentives for some employers to gain competitive advantage by adopting business models which may disadvantage workers and (e) legislative framework on the status aspect to do more of the work and the courts less.

206   See pp. 23–27 *supra.*

207   By better education, guidance and support and possibly by the strengthening of some laws. In such a manner the high levels of flexibility in the current system will be preserved.

What is clearly missing in this Review is the solving of a most imminent problem facing the British flexible labour market, namely providing a *definition of the genuine independent contractor* status or *genuine self-employment* status. Much is said in the Review of the statuses of worker, employee and dependent contractor but although the independent contractor is mentioned throughout the Revue, a *lacuna* exists insofar as the status of the genuine independent contractor in the flexible labour market lacks a statutory definition. The independent contractor status currently is one that applies to those who are not employees or workers and is therefore a default category of individual or body.

Numerous *other issues* feature in the Taylor Review most of which have been discussed in this chapter. They include, *inter alia*, the suggestion that HMRC should be given *enforcement powers* in connection with holiday pay and national minimum wage breaches; the alignment of tax status and employment status; in the case of the suggested dependent contractor status more *emphasis on control* should be made and *less emphasis on personal service* thus depriving individuals of statutory employment rights by virtue of there being a genuine right to *substitution* on the part of the individual; regarding the *written particulars of employment* the Review recommended that these should be extended to individuals enjoying the worker status (and that of dependent contractor); that these particulars be given on *day one* of employment and that *compensation* should be paid to the employee, worker, or dependent contractor by a non-compliant employer; the recommended introduction of *minimum piece work rates* where employers pay by the task rather than by the hour; and the recommended *abolition of the Swedish derogation* which provides agency workers with full employment rights.

According to the first study of its kind carried out for the government's Department of Business, Energy and Industrial Strategy,[208] it is alarming to note that a quarter of individuals working in the *gig economy*[209] are *paid less that the national minimum wage* of £7.50 an hour.[210] The Chairman of the House of Commons Work and Pensions Select Committee described the alarming figures shown by the research carried out on gig work as "the single biggest force in the

---

208 NatCen Social Research (Unweighted base) (YouGov omnibus): all GB adults (aged 18+) involved in gig economy. See too Robert Booth's article in *The Guardian* of 8th February 2018 which makes for interesting reading on the gig economy in the United Kingdom.

209 Namely, some 700,000 gig economy individuals between the ages of 18 and 34. There is an estimated total of 2.8 million individuals consisting of freelance workers and one person companies working in the gig economy in the 12 months to August 2017 most of whom use gig work to supplement other work. Those 2.8 million gig economy workers consist of minicab apps such as Uber; couriers in courier firms of various kinds such as *City Sprint, Deliveroo, DPD, Hermes, etc.*, marketplace apps or websites and takeaway deliveries [Furthermore 18% of the working age population are considering some form of gig work in the future which would make a total of 7.9 million such individuals (RSA written by Brhmie Balaram, "Taylor Review: Pragmatism must prevail" 12th July 2017)].

210 It should be noted that independent contractors – which is the status in which a great majority of gig workers are employed – are not entitled to the national minimum wage.

British economy undermining the national living wage" and indicated that the national minimum wage should be extended "to the small army of workers who are exposed to poverty pay because they are forced into forms of self-employment that are unrecognisable to most people."

Were the Taylor Review recommendations which recommend the enhancement of workers' employment rights[211] to a wider range of individuals to be implemented, the *pay roll to employers* would be considerably increased. The administration in implementing those changes could be complicated, and may lead to litigation that would also be costly on employers. In particular, the recommended dependent worker status will have the effect of adding heavy costs on gig platforms. Bearing in mind that the term "worker" is currently used in numerous pieces of legislation its reclassification could prove both problematic and expensive. It may even be that additional costs on employers will manifest themselves in unexpected and currently unknown areas.

The Taylor Review has been submitted to the government, which after considering it will respond in due course.[212] Some of the recommendations made by the Review will be easy to implement if they are adopted by the government while others – such as the employment status conundrum – will be more complicated. At the time of writing it is not known *what* changes will be made to the current legislation, nor is it known *when* changes (if any), will be made. What is known however is threefold namely (a) that this Revue which has much merit and is rich in ideas could prove seminal for both working practices as well as developing trends on the British labour market, (b) that it has the potential to change how the world of labour is perceived in the future, bearing in mind the effect(s) of Brexit on future labour laws,[213] and (c) in the words of Sir Brendon Barber the chairman of ACAS, that "it has raised the profile of the debate around the importance of good employment practices in these non-standard working arrangements." May this author add that this Revue is about

---

211 For example, the proposals relating to hours of pay, statutory sick pay, the national minimum wage, holiday pay, national insurance contributions of 13.8%. *etc*...

212 The Work and Pensions and Business, Energy and Industrial Strategy Committees published a joint report and draft Bill to close the loopholes which allow companies to use bogus self-employment status as a route to cheap labour and tax avoidance saying that the law must not allow willingness to exploit workers to be a competitive advantage (20th November, 2017). See too the Work and Pensions Committee Formal Minutes (15th November 2017) and the Government's response to this joint report on the framework of modern employment (close the self-employment loopholes) (16th April. 2018).

213 See the published interviews on the effects of Brexit in British labour laws in "*Entrevista al Prof. Jo Carby-Hall*" in *Orbitados* by Prof. Carmen Jover Ramírez, Cadiz University, 4th May 2017. pp. 1–11 interview by Ius Labor, Barcelona (7pp), (2017) and in maritime law "interviewed" by Dr. Annina Burgen, *Inaugural Newsletter* of the Maritime Institute of Campus do Mar, Vigo, to be published in 2020 (17pp). See too commentary by Jo Carby-Hall "'Brexit means Brexit:' Quels effets sur le Droit du Travail" *Revue du Droit Comparé du Travail et de la Sécurité Sociale, Presses Universitaires de Bordeaux* (2017) pp. 194–197.

quality of work and not merely quantity. Legislation (if any) may take some time to materialise but the Taylor Review sets a concrete and clear direction which employers and other stakeholders cannot ignore! There is little doubt that the Taylor Review's heart is pointing in the right direction with excellent recommendations having been made. It now remains to be seen if the *political will* and *time* exists to insert the Review's proposals, or some of them, into the statute book. At the time of writing much criticism has been expressed by employment lawyers who accuse the government of being "under-whelming" and calling upon it to respond to the Taylor Review's recommendations amongst fears[214] that significant reforms could be slow in coming. There was also growing concern over the Teresa May government's ability – by reason of the Prime Minister's lack of parliamentary majority which caused difficulty in implementing the Review's recommendations and indeed, appetite – to tackle the negative consequences of a sector which has developed under the advent of telephone apps[215] and the rapidly developing modern technology. This may well change with the Boris Johnson majority government elected on 12th December 2019, but it is too early at, the time of writing,[216] to know if that government will implement – immediately or eventually – the Taylor Review recommendations.

Mr Matthew Taylor said in his Foreword[217] "If policy makers and the public come to recognise the vital importance of good work to social justice, economic dynamism and civic engagement then the efforts of the Review team and all who have supported us would have been richly rewarded."

214 Possibly referring, *inter alia*, to the Brexit legislative and administrative programme which is currently occupying much of the government's time, thoughts and energies. There could also be an important element of political ideology therein.
215 See the research carried out by Mr Frank Field M.P (Labour) and Mr Andrew Forsey and their inquiry on the gig economy entitled "Inside the gig economy 'the vulnerable human underbelly' of the UK's labour market," *The Guardian*, 24th August 2017.
216 Namely, 7th January 2020.
217 "Taylor Review" *op. cit.* at p. 5.

2 The 4ᵗʰ Industrial Revolution and its impact on the individual employment relationship: general considerations and the regulatory context in Russia

Daria Chernyaeva[1]

Introduction

Despite the critics of the term and the concept, scholars got used to mentioning three "industrial revolutions."[2] Generally – and very superficially – speaking, the 1st Industrial Revolution is believed to have given us mechanisation. The 2nd is known for bringing mass and regionally distributed production. The 3rd one enriched us with automation and transnationally distributed production. Therefore, current technological – as well as related economic and societal – changes are usually called "the 4ᵗʰ Industrial Revolution", if not in scientific terms, then at least in a narrow sense.

Much research has been done on the features, essence and outcomes of industrial revolutions, and almost every author directly or indirectly has mentioned the effect a given industrial revolution produces in relations concerning

1 The author is deeply indebted to Polina Buyatova for igniting interest in the topic and for its extensive discussion.
2 This topic is not covered here, but the literature on it is abundant and includes both works that by now have become classical as well as those published recently. See f.i.: Horn, J., Rosenbland, L.N., & Smith, M.R. (Eds.). (2010). *Reconceptualizing the industrial revolution*. Dibner Institute studies in the history of science and technology. Massachusetts, MA: MIT Press; Freeman, Ch,, & Louçã, F. (2001). *As time goes by: From the industrial revolutions to the information revolution*. Oxford: Oxford University Press; De Vries, J. (1994). "The industrial revolution and the industrious revolution." *Journal of Economic History*, 54(2), 249–270; Church, R.A., & Wrigley, E.A. (1994). *The Industrial Revolutions*. 11 Volume Set. Hoboken, NJ: Wiley; Steams, P.N. (1993). *The industrial revolution in world history*. Boulder, CO: Westview Press; Steams, P.N. (1991). *Interpreting the industrial revolution*. Washington, DC: American Historical Association; Habakkuk, H.J., & Postan, M. (Eds.). (1966). *The Cambridge economic history of Europe 6, The industrial revolutions and after: incomes, population and technical change*. Cambridge: Cambridge University Press; Clark G.N. (1953). "The idea of industrial revolution." David Murray lecture. Glasgow University publications (Том 95). Lecture on the David Murray Foundation (Том 20). Glasgow: Jackson, 1953; Ashton, T.S. (1948). *The Industrial Revolution, 1760–1830*. Oxford: Oxford University Press, etc.

work and in employment relations in particular. Work is known to take up to one-third of an average person's life,[3] so it is hard to overlook the relations built around it. Even nowadays in this time of ubiquitous computerisation these relations still lie at the heart of most productive activities.

In this short chapter, the author makes an attempt to link technologies which are considered to represent the coming of the new technological era to people involved in – or influenced by – their application, and to discuss whether the new issues the technologies bring to employment relations and workers' legal status, are really detrimental to the workers' rights. Also the chapter aims at showing the advantages of the new technologies from the labour lawyer's viewpoint and the ways they can be consolidated. To that end, the author describes the state of the art in the regulation of work-related technological innovations in Russia.

Today's technical buzzwords

Recently few events or publications can afford not to mention new technologies in one way or another. We all know these buzzwords or have heard some of them more than once: digitalisation, "uberisation", distributed ledger (blockchain), smart contacts, cryptocurrencies (digital currencies), decentralised autonomous organisations (DAOs), big data, platform work, internet of things, cobots, neural networks, etc.[4] All these technological solutions bear several common features of

---

3 For this data see f.i.: World Health Organization. (1994). *Global strategy on occupational health for all: The way to health at work.* Recommendation of the second meeting of the WHO Collaborating Centres in Occupational Health, 11–14 October 1994, Beijing, China. Geneva: World Health Organization. Retrieved November 26, 2018, from http://www.who.int/occu pational_health/publications/globstrategy/en/index2.html.

4 Due to size limitations no technical details of these concepts and phenomena are given. However, they are extensively described in many research papers, white papers, articles, interviews, blogs, etc. To name a few: Hassani, H., Huang, X., & Silva, E. (2018). "Big-Crypto: Big Data, Blockchain and Cryptocurrency." *Big Data Cognitive Computing,* 2(34), 1–15. DOI: 10.3390/ bdcc2040034; Wigler, B., & Cary, N. (2018). *The Future is Decentralised: Block Chains, Distributed Ledgers, & the Future of Sustainable Development.* Geneva: UNDP. Retrieved November 12, 2018, from https://www.undp.org/content/dam/undp/library/innovation/The-Future-is-Decentralised.pdf; Hinchcliffe, D. (2018). "Digital transformation in 2019: Lessons learned the hard way." *ZDNet.* October 11. Retrieved November 12, 2018, from https://www.zdnet.com/ article/the-biggest-lessons-learned-in-digital-transformation/; McAfee, A., & Brynjolfsson, E. (2017). *Machine, Platform, Crowd: Harnessing Our Digital Future.* New York, NY: W. W. Norton & Company; Choudary, S.P. (2015). *Platform Scale: How an emerging business model helps startups build large empires with minimum investment.* Boston, MA: Platform Thinking Labs; Schwab, K. (2016). *The Fourth Industrial Revolution.* New York, NY: World Economic Forum; Bächle, T.C. (2016). *Digitales Wissen, Daten und Überwachung zur Einführung.* Junius Verlag; Berger, J. (2016). *Contagious: Why Things Catch On.* New York, NY: Simon & Schuster; Schrage, M. (2014). *The Innovator's Hypothesis: How Cheap Experiments Are Worth More than Good Ideas.* Massachusetts, MA: MIT Press, etc. Among the most popular blogs on these topics are: Cisco Digital Transformation Blog (blogs.cisco.com/digital), Reddit Digital Transformation

which the most obvious is their aim to exclude the possibility of human interference from as many processes and as many stages as possible, ideally excluding this interference completely. The ultimate goal is the same as for the newest technologies that have arisen during the previous industrial revolutions: to attain the highest level of incorruptibility, flexibility, objectivity, accuracy, and immunity to adverse influences. These technologies streamline and speed up processes they become a part of and allow entrepreneurs to cut costs.

For example, blockchain is known to embrace the following remarkable features: (1) direct interaction between the participants (computers) in a blockchain with no intermediaries involved (i.e. peer-to-peer networking); (2) the distributed nature of data storage and operation preventing data corruption and loss; (3) totally decentralised management and control with no single management centre and no third parties authorised to verify transactions – an approach which offers unprecedented levels of objectivity, accuracy and independence; (4) consensus-based control[5] where a transaction (or a number of transactions) in a block is (are) verified and included in the chain only if all computers of the respective blockchain confirm that it is correct (otherwise the block is rejected) – a feature which adds protection from intrusion and improper influence; (5) asymmetric (or public key) cryptography used to make the system secure through the verification of the source of transactions – possibly the best crack-proof technology of today. All other new technologies mentioned above share most of these features. Thus, smart contracts being – in a simplified interpretation – just a piece of code, are absolutely "human-free", and DAOs operating through them in a blockchain environment share all the advantages of these two.

Each of these five features was not *per se* brand-new at the time the blockchain emerged. For example, A. Wright and P. De Filippi mention that P2P (peer-to-peer) networks[6] and public-private key encryption[7] were developed in the late

(reddit.com/r/digitaltransformation), XenonStack Blogs (xenonstack.com/blog/), Digitalist Magazine (digitalistmag.com), InnovationLab Blog (innovationlab.net/blog/), etc.

5 A short (and quite digestible for non-IT people) description of the idea is given here: Kalinov, V. (2018). *Consensus mechanisms.* July 04. Retrieved December 10, 2018, from https://block chainhub.net/blog/blog/consensus-mechanisms-2.

6 Wright, A., & De Filippi, P. (2015). "Decentralized Blockchain Technology and the Rise of Lex Cryptographia." *SSRN Electronic Journal.* DOI: 10.2139/ssrn.2580664. Note 15 at p. 5. In regard to P2P networks they cite A. Oram (2001). *Peer-to-peer: Harnessing the benefits of a disruptive technology.* Sebastopol, CA: O'Reilly Media, where a history of the networks was pictured, and the Usenet introduced in 1979 was mentioned as the "grandfather of today's peer-to-peer networks".

7 Wright, A., & De Filippi, P. Op. cit. In regard to the concept of public key cryptography they cite original works of the founding fathers of the RSA and public-key cryptography: Diffie, W., & Hellman, M.E. (1976). "New Directions in Cryptography." *IEEE Transactions on information theory*, IT-22(6), 644–654. Retrieved December 10, 2018, from https://ee.stanford.edu/~hell man/publications/24.pdf; Rivest, R.I., Shamir, A., & Adleman, L. (1978). "A method for obtaining digital signatures and public-key cryptosystems." *Communication of the ACM, 21*(2),

1970s (and P2P networks gained mainstream acceptance in the early 2000s), consensus mechanisms (such as Proof of Work) have been around since the late 1990s,[8] and decentralised and distributed data storage has been used since some 2005.[9] However, when combined, these technologies have opened a revolutionary new world of opportunities.

Blockchain as a new "operating environment"

Technically a blockchain technology offers a distributed (decentralised) and shared ledger (or a database, or a digital platform)[10] based on cryptographic algorithms that stores information about all verified (approved) transactions[11] performed over a certain asset[12] (digital or digitised).[13] A transaction or several transactions written as datasets form(s) a separate *block*. The blockchain participants (computers pooled in the blockchain, or the blockchain *nodes*) verify transaction(s) in the block that causes the block to be transferred to another participant. If all participants approve the transaction(s), the respective block is added to the other already verified blocks in a *chain*. Blockchain blocks are organised in

120–126. DOI: 10.1145/359340.359342. See also: Mollin, R.A. (2003). *RSA and public-key cryptography*. Boca Raton, FL: Chapman & Hall/CRC Press; Lynn, J.C. (2013). *Cryptography: Its history and mathematical transformation of RSA and Diffie-Hellman algorithm*. Elizabeth City, NC: Elizabeth City State University, etc.

8 Wright, A., & De Filippi, P. Op. cit. Speaking about these mechanisms they cite: Back, A. (1997). A Partial Hash Collision Based Postage Scheme. Retrieved December 10, 2018, from http://www.hashcash.org/papers/announce.txt.

9 In regard to this technology Wright and De Filippi cite Chacon, S., & Straub, B. (2014). *ProGIT*. Apress. P. 5. Retrieved December 10. 2018, from http://git-scm.com/book/en/v2/Getting-Started-A-ShortHistory-of-Git.

10 Umeh, J. (2016). "Blockchain double bubble or double trouble?" *ITNOW, 58*(1), 58–61.

11 The word "transaction" here (and in the majority of research works on blockchain) is used to represent a concept of a legally meaningful action, an action capable of bringing about legal consequences. This meaning is now common among the researchers of the blockchain technology.

12 Asset here is used in its common meaning of "an object of a transaction." This meaning of the term also shows signs of being established in blockchain scholarship.

13 This particular definition is generally based on the formula given in: Saveliev, A.I. (2016). "Dogovornoe pravo 2.0: "Umnye kontrakty" kak nachalo kontza classicheskogo dogovornogo prava" [Contract law 2.0: "Smart contracts" as a beginning of an end of the classical contract law]. *Vestnik grajdanskogo prava [Bulletin of Civil Law], 3*, 35-59 (at 41). However, more or less similar definitions have been given in: Deshpande, A., Stewart, K., Lepetit, L., & Gunashekar, S. (2017). *Distributed Ledger Technologies/Blockchain: Challenges, opportunities and the prospects for standards*. Prepared for the British Standards Institution (BSI). Retrieved December 22, 2018, from http://k1.caict.ac.cn/yjts/qqzkgz/bgtj/201708/P020170818579005375876.pdf; Wright, A., & De Filippi. Op. cit.; European Securities and Markets Authority. (2016). *The Distributed Ledger Technology applied to securities markets*. Discussion Paper. Retrieved December 10, 2018, from https://www.esma.europa.eu/sites/default/files/library/2016- 773_dp_dlt.pdf. p. 8; Kakavand, H., Kost De Sevres, N., & Chilton, B. (2017). "The blockchain revolution: An analysis of regulation and technology related to distributed ledger technologies." *SSRN Electronic Journal*. DOI: 10.2139/ssrn.2849251, etc.

chronological order. Together with information on the verified transactions, each block contains a timestamp, a reference (link) to the preceding block in the chain (a *hash* pointer) and a solution to a computational (mathematical) puzzle the blockchain nodes use to validate the data associated with a particular block.[14]

We are currently witnessing the penetration of blockchain-based technologies into a constantly increasing number of spheres. Apart from cryptocurrencies or internet of things (IoT), blockchain can be used to provide digital identity (f.i. to be used in a so-called "smart government"[15]), support digital voting, financial services or supply chain management.[16] It can certainly be used in contractual relationships – to execute the terms of regular (legal) contracts through the "computerised transaction protocol"[17] that blockchain provides (this application of a blockchain technology seems to have given birth

14 Deshpande, A. et al. Op. cit. Pp. 6-7. See also: Bonneau, J., Miller, A, Clark, J., Narayanan, A., Kroll, J.A., & Felten, E.W. (2015). "SoK: Research Perspectives and Challenges for Bitcoin and Cryptocurrencies." IEEE Xplore Digital Library: 2015 IEEE Symposium on Security and Privacy, San Jose, CA, 17–21 May 2015, 104–121 (at 107). DOI: 10.1109/SP.2015.14.

15 See f.i.: The Conference Board of Canada. (2018). *Enabling digital government with blockchain*. Recorded webinar. March 1. Retrieved December 02, 2018, from https://www.confer enceboard.ca/e-library/abstract.aspx?did=9503; Kennedy, J. (2018). "Is blockchain key to an accountable, digital government?" *SiliconRepublic*, January 22. Retrieved December 02, 2018, from https://www.siliconrepublic.com/enterprise/digital-government-blockchain; Sweden, E. (2017). "Blockchains: Moving digital government forward in the States." *NASCIO*. Retrieved December 02, 2018, from https://www.nascio.org/Portals/0/Publications/Docu ments/2017/NASCIO%20Blockchains%20in%20State%20Government.pdf; Stone, M. (2016). "The tiny European country that became a global leader in digital government." *Forbes*. June. Retrieved December 02, 2018, from https://www.forbes.com/sites/delltechnol ogies/2016/06/14/the-tiny-european-country-that-became-a-global-leader-in-digital-govern ment/; Bhatti, Z.K., Kusek, Z., & Verheijen, J. (2014). *Logged on: Smart government solutions from South Asia*. Washington, DC: World Bank. Retrieved December 03, 2018, from https:// openknowledge.worldbank.org/handle/10986/20487, etc.

16 See f.i.: Marr, B. (2018). "How blockchain will transform the supply chain and logistics industry." *Forbes*, March 23. Retrieved December 02, 2018, from https://www.forbes.com/sites/ber nardmarr/2018/03/23/how-blockchain-will-transform-the-supply-chain-and-logistics-industry; Brody, P. (2017). "How blockchain is revolutionizing supply chain management." *Digitalist Magazine,* September 06. Retrieved December 03, 2018, from https://www.ey.com/Publica tion/vwLUAssets/ey-blockchain-and-the-supply-chain-three/$FILE/ey-blockchain-and-the-supply-chain-three.pdf; Gilbert, D. (2016). "Blockchain technology could help solve $75 billion counterfeit drug problem." *International Business Time*, April 19. Retrieved December 02, 2018, from http://www.ibtimes.com/blockchain-technology-could-help-solve-75-billion-coun terfeit-drug-problem-2355984, etc.

17 This description uses the interpretation of "smart contracts" given in: Szabo, N. (1997). *The idea of smart contracts*. Amsterdam Center for Language and Communication (University of Amsterdam). Retrieved December 02. 2018, from http://www.fon.hum.uva.nl/rob/Courses/Informa tionInSpeech/CDROM/Literature/LOTwinterschool2006/szabo.best.vwh.net/smart_con tracts_idea.html, though actually Szabo is widely known to have introduced the term yet in 1994. See f.i.: Tapscott, D., & Tapscott, A, (2016). "The blockchain revolution: How the technology behind Bitcoin is changing money, business, and the world." *Portfolio*, 71–72.

to an alternative interpretation of the term "smart contract"[18]). A contractual relation concerning work is no exception.

In the management of relations concerning work (including human researource management) the blockchain-based solutions are used mostly in two roles: (1) as an advanced database for a secure storage, retrieval and exchange of documents; (2) an advanced calculation system for accurate and reliable calculations of either vulnerable numeric data or large amounts of numeric data. Therefore, it would be not an exaggeration to say that in this field the main interest in the use of the blockchain-based solutions lies not in the blockchain technological specificity, but in the levels of security and accuracy it is able to provide. In this sense, any technology would do if it could provide the same or higher levels of these features.

Employment relations may more or less benefit from most of the features of the technologies brought about by the 4th Industrial Revolution as almost any social relations may. So long as direct interaction saves time and money spent before on intermediaries' involvement, employers may also enjoy this, substituting banks for smart contracts in wage payments, processing collective bargaining votes in a blockchain, and so on. It can also tempt us to test a platform or a DAO for having the actual legal status of "employer"[19] and making a new type of legal fiction (shall we call it a "digital person"?[20]) and as the current research shows, it is not all that much impossible.

Are new technologies a threat to employment relations and workers' legal status?

New technologies are often blamed[21] for the decay in traditional employment relations and even for "tempting away" workers from the protective umbrella of an

---

18 On the controversy concerning the interpretation of the term "smart contract" and on the essential features of the phenomenon please see Bourque, S. (2018). "Smart contract – an elusive definition." *Medium.* June 23. Retrieved December 02, 2018, from https://medium.com/coinmonks/smart-contract-an-elusive-definition-a3f3dbc2c799; Bourque, S. (2018). "Smart contracts are neither smart nor contracts." *Medium,* July 02. Retrieved December 02, 2018, from https://medium.com/@SamREye26/smart-contracts-are-neither-smart-nor-contracts-1799d6d30bb5; Bourque, S., & Tsui S.F.L. (2014). "A lawyer's introduction to smart contracts." *Scientia Nobilitat. Reviewed Legal Studies,* 4-23. Retrieved December 02, 2018, from https://github.com/joequant/scms/blob/master/doc/pdfs/A%20Lawyer%27s%20Introduction%20to%20Smart%20Contracts.pdf.

19 For an interesting exercise in "refocusing" control test to make it more suitable for platform work cases please see: Cunningham-Parmeter, K. (2016). "From Amazon to Uber: Defining employment in the modern economy." *Boston University Law Review,* 96(5), 1673–1728. Retrieved December 02, 2018, from https://www.bu.edu/bulawreview/files/2016/10/CUNNINGHAM-PARMETER.pdf.

20 The founding fathers of DAO state that it is not a legal person and doesn't hire people. However, this may change with time, because theoretically being a specific type of an employer is not impossible for DAO. Follow the development of the idea at the current DAO website: https://blog.daohub.org.

21 See f.i.: IR Global. (2018). "The changing employment landscape: Disruptive technology and the gig economy." Virtual Round Table Series Employment Working Group. Retrieved

"employee" legal status with the promise of more autonomy, higher compensation, and brighter career prospects. However, their influence is quite complex, multidimensional, and controversial.

First of all, to a classical model of employment relations – such as f.i. described in the ILO Recommendation No. 198 and the ILO guides to it – new technologies bring in an unprecedentedly high level of trust attainable between parties. The very idea of a blockchain as a decentralised system with innumerable nodes of verification of the data circulated in it makes violations of contractual terms and the parties' statutory responsibilities close to impossible.

If we lived in an ideal world, the ultimate result of the application of these technologies would produce completely error-free and deceit-free employment relations. There would be no wage arrears or non-payment of compensation, taxes or social contributions,[22] as well as no deceit with the calculation of working time,[23] with days of paid leave, with the number of votes in employee participation and workplace coordination cases, and no issues in the assessment of the number and gravity of workplace disciplinary offences leading to dismissal,

December 03, 2018, from https://www.irglobal.com/file/d40c6c88e28a211d82db1ca69e2c286c.pdf; O'Reilly, J., Ranft, F., & Neufeind, M. (2018). *Work in the digital age: challenges of the fourth industrial revolution*. Preprint. March. Retrieved December 03, 2018, from https://www.researchgate.net/publication/324091786; Aloisi, A (2016). "Commoditized workers: case study research on labour law issues arising from a set of 'on-demand/gig economy' platforms." *Comparative Labour Law and Policy Journal, 37*, 653–688; Albin, E., & Prassl, J. (2016). "Fragmenting work, fragmented regulation: the contract of employment as a driver of social exclusion." In: Freedland et al (eds.). *The contract of employment*. Oxford: Oxford University Press; Freedland, M. (2016). "The contract of employment and the paradoxes of precarity." University of Oxford, Legal Research Paper Series. Paper No 37/2016; Smith, R., & Leberstein, S. (2015). *Rights on demand: ensuring workplace standards and worker security in the on-demand economy*. New York: National Employment Law Project. Retrieved December 03, 2018, from http://www.nelp.org/content/uploads/Rights-On-Demand-Report.pdf; Ahsan, M. (2018). "Entrepreneurship and ethics in the sharing economy: A critical perspective." *Journal of Business Ethics*, 1–15 DOI: 10.1007/s10551-018-3975-2; Jacobs, D.C.D., & Yudken, J., (2004). *The Internet, organizational change and labor: The challenge of virtualization*. New York, NY: Routledge, etc. However, there are also well-known opponents to this viewpoint, f.i.: Braverman, H. (1974). *Labor and monopoly capital: The degradation of work in the twentieth century*. New York, NY: Monthly Review Press, p. 319.

22 One of the blockchain-based solutions implemented through smart contracts in order to secure wage payment, make it transparent and reduce the time between working and getting paid is Etch: https://www.etch.work/. Etch is "the payroll protocol built on top of the Ethereum blockchain". It boasts to guarantee the money flows into a worker's Etch wallet every second of his/her working day. Another example is a Bitcoin-based payroll and international wage payment service Bitwage: https://www.bitwage.co.

23 One of the already implemented examples of blockchain-based solutions built around the working time control and recording is a platform Gigachain: http://gigacha.in/. Gigachain keeps records time workers spent working in a tamper-proof blockchain-based store and calculates pay based on hours worked and agreed terms of respective contracts for work.

and no fraud with documents on qualification.[24] For example, a smart contract would guarantee that neither party would be able to alter the contractual terms and workers' entitlements once the work has started, suddenly and without the other party's consent because all the changes in the blockchain environment would be recorded and then undergo verification over and over again.[25] Cryptocurrencies would allow cutting transactional and administrative costs of transnational wage payment down to zero, giving entrepreneurs an opportunity to offer higher wages without detriment to their financial stability and opening to workers a whole new world of job offers worldwide. Big data would provide unprecedented analytical power that would possibly allow stakeholders to summarise instances of particular workers' or entrepreneurs' behavior and decisions thereby concluding whether there would be evidence of them being prone to improper or unlawful behaviour.[26] For example, it is quite natural to use big data analysis for tracing and bringing together scattered instances of workplace violence among workers or an entrepreneur's discriminatory decisions in hiring or promotion

However, these new technologies are not immune to being used for evil, as hardly any technologies are. Respecting the size limitations for this chapter, let us consider one of the simplest, clearest and possibly the most popular examples of evidence that the situation is far from being ideal. It is the emergence of the term "uberisation" in regard to platform work[27] and other work organised with the use of new technologies. Labour lawyers and workers' rights activists tend to see platform work mainly as an employers' attempt to deprive workers of the legal

24 Recently a number of interesting examples of such blockchain-based solutions have been developed, including: HumanTelligence (https://www.human-telligence.com) that combines self-assessment for workers with TalentFit and Culture Analytics features for employers; Path Framework (https://www.pathfoundation.io) that stores and allows to manage and share validated information on professional experience, education and skills (also with a reward system based on PATH tokens); TiiQu (https://tiiqu.com) which creates verifiable digital passports that include information on qualifications, etc.

25 Such solution has already been developed: *Grain* protocol (https://grain.io) allows entrepreneurs to process work agreements on the blockchain, with an instant payment mechanism.

26 A step in this direction made with the blockchain-powered anti-harassment platform Vault can serve as one such example: http://www.vaultplatform.com. The platform allows its users to record their harassment experiences, store evidence and personal memos thus forming a sort of registry of "serial perpetrators." Information a user enters about his/her case can be accessed only with the explicit consent of this user. The platform also informs its users about the presence of their perpetrator's name in its "registry." However, it's still the user's decision what to do with this information further. The platform will not act in place of the user to actively protect his/her rights.

27 In addition to the examples of a platform work given throughout the text of this chapter, it may also be recommended to have a look at A. Aloisi's paper where a number of other employment-related platform solutions are analysed in the light of the workers classification problem: Aloisi, A. (2016). "Commoditized workers. Case study research on labour law issues arising from a set of 'on-demand/gig economy' platforms." *Comparative Labor Law & Policy Journal*, 37(3), 653–690. DOI: 10.2139/ssrn.2637485.

and financial protection that employment law has traditionally been providing. With the blockchain technology, the more or less central "Uber entity" is replaced with a countless number of smart contracts and blockchain nodes ensuring their transparent and independent deployment, but it hardly helps to provide better worker protection.

For example, the smart contract technology that was shown above as a promising tool for safeguarding the interests of the parties to an employment contract lacks the flexibility that new technologies usually declare to provide. Once a contract is executed all alterations to it become technically complicated at the very least[28] thus hindering any improvement in the conditions of employment and making the bargaining power of the parties an almost empty word. The need to alter or novate all smart contracts involved in a particular employment relationship may dramatically increase costs instead of cutting them. It may seem not all bad though – at least initially – because it may motivate entrepreneurs to abstain from signing "contracts for services" in arguable cases where grounds to sign an employment contract obviously exist (because otherwise once a court decides in favour of the employment nature of a particular contract, they would immediately face enormous expenses on technical implementation of the decision). Generally, this may give employees a better protection for a while. However, it may shortly make the labour market in this sector shrink because of the increased costs so that many workers would find themselves unemployed. Leaving entrepreneurs little flexibility with regard to the nature of the contracts they sign with workers is a very controversial way of solving the problem with platform workers' protection. Actually, any other reason for the alteration of the smart contracts – be it a solicited increase in benefits, a promotion or a sudden change in a worker's ability to work – would equally increase costs and cause problems for the parties because it would require the smart contracts either initially form a very complicated structure that takes into account most of such reasons or sustain alterations or novation each time a new reason arises.

---

28 While most academic papers state that smart contracts are absolutely immutable, our readers may find it interesting to look for the most recent non-academic articles that addresses the ways and consequences of smart contracts alteration. See f.i.: Carbon Blog. (2019). "How (Not) to Upgrade Smart Contracts." *Medium*. February 8. Retrieved from https://medium. com/carbon-money/stablecoins-and-upgradability-98bc64a46bcb (accessed on March 06, 2019). Cardozo Blockchain Project. (2018). "Smart Contracts" & Legal Enforceability. Research Report #2. October 16. Retrieved March 06, 2019, from https://cardozo.yu.edu/ sites/default/files/Smart%20Contracts%20Report%20%232_0.pdf; Grincalaitis, M. (2018). "Can a Smart Contract be Upgraded/Modified?" *Medium*. February 06. Retrieved March 06, 2019, from https://medium.com/@merunasgrincalaitis/can-a-smart-contract-be-upgradedmodified-1393e9b507a, and possibly a worthy final paper a student from the University of Alicante wrote: Tulsidas, T. U. (2018). "Smart Contracts from a Legal Perspective" (final thesis for the degree in law, University of Alicante, Alicante, Spain). Retrieved March 06, 2019, from https://rua.ua.es/dspace/bitstream/10045/78007/1/Smart_Con tracts_from_a_Legal_Perspective_Utamchandani_Tulsidas_Tanash.pdf.

Smart contracts are also of no use in cases where there is not physically or legally feasible way to manage without humans. For example, to lawfully dismiss an employee for truancy (absence without a valid reason) many national laws require an employer not only to calculate the number of days of such absence (which can easily be traced with modern workplace monitoring techniques) and to obtain the employee's written explanation (which can nevertheless be given in a specific digital form) but also to have talks with him/her, sometimes in the presence of workers' representatives. As for now, this process can hardly be fully digitalised without risking workers' interests. To implement it entirely with digital means might require quite serious changes in both regulatory and organisational approaches, i.e. we would need not just to amend laws, but modify many procedures involved at all the stages of the task implementation. Thus, in the example given above we would need a digital system that could not just register the fact that the talks actually took place but check the sufficiency and lawfulness of the contents of talks. Besides, as of yet, despite all discourse about reliability, nobody is really ready to guarantee that such systems are, or would be, fraud-and-error-proof.

Cryptocurrencies' rates are still very volatile and apart from this, in most jurisdictions, they have been legally recognised to be not money but property.[29] The latter poses a question of compliance with national,[30] supranational,[31] and international

29 In Russia courts had recognised cryptocurrencies to be a "property" before the State Duma or financial authorities issued any documents on it. See: Order of the 9th Court of Appeal of May 15, 2018 No. 09АП-16416/2018 on the case No. A40-124668/2017. Retrieved December 10, 2018, from https://kad.arbitr.ru/PdfDocument/3e155cd1-6bce-478a-bb76-1146d2e61a4a/58af451a-bfa3-4723-ab0d-d149aafecd88/A40-124668-2017_20180515_Post anovlenie_apelljacionnoj_instancii.pdf. In October 2017 Putin ordered the Government to specify the legal status of cryptocurrencies before July 01, 2018 (see the news about this on the Russian Newspaper website: https://rg.ru/2017/10/24/vladimir-putin-poruchil-podgotovit-popravki-o-kriptovaliute-do-1-iiulia.html; in Russian). However, in the middle of July 2018 the Chairman of the Committee for Financial Markets said that the law on cryptocurrencies will be enacted in September 2018 (see the news about this n the RIA Novosti website: https://ria.ru/economy/20180717/1524781617.html. The draft law No. 424632-7 approved in the first reading by the State Duma on May 22, 2018, is available here: http://asozd2.duma.gov.ru/main.nsf/(Spravka)?OpenAgent&RN=424632-7). Among the EAEU countries only Belarus has issued such regulation where cryptocurrency (tokens) is not called a property explicitly but still not included into the concept of "money" throughout the text (see Decree of the President of Belarus Republic No. 8 "On the Development of Digital Economy" of December 21, 2017. Retrieved December 22, 2018, from http://president.gov.by/ru/official_documents_ru/view/dekret-8-ot-21-dekabrja-2017-g-17716/).

30 For instance, it is directly and strictly limited in the articles 130 and 131 of the Russian Labor Code, in full compliance with the ILO Convention No. 95.

31 On the EAEU level the talks on "digital cooperation" and "transborder space of trust" have been conducted since the EAEU creation in 2014, and in 2016 a Working group on "digital agenda" was created (Decree of the Council of the Eurasian Economic Union No. 6 of March 13, 2016. Retrieved December 22, 2018, from https://docs.eaeunion.org/docs/ru-ru/01410351/cncd_02062016_39). However, in regard to the technologies discussed in this chapter no particular decisions have been made as for now. It is supposed that new

norms on wage payment in kind (generally stipulated in article 4 of the widely ratified ILO Convention No. 95) for those entrepreneurs that think about cryptocurrencies utilisation in wage payment. In this sense, cryptocurrency-based wage solutions – such as Bitwage based on Bitcoin (already mentioned above) – may look a bit awkward unless the parties succeed in rendering the worker as "self-employed" (which automatically excludes her from the scope of the ILO Convention No. 95[32] and all other applicable laws which respect the ILO approach). However, this issue is complex enough to deserve a separate chapter.

To sum all this up, technically the new technologies have got no imminent features that would either automatically protect workers involved in relations concerning work organised with the help of such technologies or prevent people from using it in such relations at all. As history teaches us, technologies can be used for good and for bad. Therefore, we need a really *smart* regulation to step in and establish a system of minimal standards applicable for workers involved in such relations, and this regulation should utilise the capabilities of the new technologies to build a reliable and efficient framework. Furthermore, we need labour lawyers who know somewhat more than basics in these technologies.

The Russian context

Russia is comparatively good at utilising technical innovation, but the regulatory response usually tends to lag considerably. Thus, recent innovations in the Labour Code – such as the new Chapter 49.1 on remote work (where, for no apparent reason it was blended with telework which is just a specific case of remote work[33]) or provisions that implement risk management approach in Section X devoted to occupational safety and health – address issues which the majority of developed countries have regulated several decades ago.

Moreover, one of the few topical subjects for discussion with regard to new technologies the Russian authorities eventually decided to initiate[34] is that on

technologies will be addressed in the draft Conception of Formation of the Common Financial Market that is planned to be launched in 2025. An interview with the Chairman of the EAEU Board. July 10, 2018 is at the website of the Eurasian Economic Commission: http://www.eurasiancommission.org/ru/nae/news/Pages/Forms/EEC_RSS_News.aspx.

32 Article 1 of the Convention defines wages as "...remuneration or earnings, ...which are payable in virtue of a written or unwritten contract of employment by an employer to an employed person for work done or to be done or for services rendered or to be rendered."

33 Article 312.1 of the Russian Labor Code where the definition of remote work is given mentions the "use of ICT public networks including Internet" as an integral condition of a work being considered "remote".

34 Parliamentary hearings "Specificity of procedures related to employment relations in digital economy". 25.01.2018. Official website of the State Duma of the Russian Federation. Retrieved from http://duma.gov.ru/news/26028. Materials prepared for the hearings are available at the official website of the Committee for economic policy, industry, innovational

the reasonableness and appropriateness of electronic technologies in human resource management (mostly employee records keeping and document procession). This is the main and almost only aspect of "digitalisation" and "new technologies in employment relations" which is currently widely discussed at governmental level. Publications and debates about other, more up-to-date aspects of "digitalisation" are still rare and sporadic.

To some extent, this can be explained by the inflexibility of the governmental decision-making system or a lack of political will (or influence) to promote or lobby the necessary changes. Partly this lag may also be attributed to the simplified approach the Labour Code entertained with regard to the question of classification of platform workers (and other cases where new technologies are involved) thanks to which the Russian judicial system does not experience a rise in claims related to this issue despite the wide network of Uber-like services.[35] While many jurisdictions are concerned with the correct application of classical tests to these specific cases or employ scholars to suggest new ones, the Russian Labour Code uses a comparatively old "magic provision" that presumes employment relations to exist in case of doubts which cannot be ruled out when a court considers a dispute on the recognition of such relations to be employment relations.[36] If such relations become recognised as employment ones, they are recognised as existing since the date on which the worker was actually admitted (allowed) to do the work that is specified in the contract. Moreover, if a court re-qualifies the contract to an employment one, the employer is fined about 1,350 euros (and twice as such if the violation repeated)[37] because

development and entrepreneurship of the State Duma: http://komitet2-7.km.duma.gov.ru/ Novosti-Komiteta/item/15390457/(in Russian); materials of the hearings are available at the same website: http://komitet2-7.km.duma.gov.ru/Kruglye-stoly-seminary-soveshha niya-i-dr/item/15496727 (in Russian).

35 For example, in Moscow (Russia) about 10 platform taxi service providers currently operate (YandexTaxi, Gett, RuTaxi, Maxim, CitiMobil, Taxovichkoff, etc.) most of which have been in the market for about 5 years at least. However, a bill aimed to regulate this sector that was submitted to the State Duma in June 2018 contained almost no provisions addressing conditions of the drivers' employment and no provisions addressing the specificity of their legal status. As for March 2019 the bill undergoes the second reading and is available at the State Duma website http://sozd.duma.gov.ru/bill/481004-7.

36 Article 19.1 of the Russian Labour Code devoted to the conditions of recognition of employment relations in cases where they have initially originated in the "civil law" contract for services. By the way, this approach is fully compliant with Paragraph 11(b) of the ILO Recommendation No. 198 which allows "a legal presumption that an employment relationship exists where one or more relevant indicators is present", and other countries (like Netherlands) apply this approach as well – see: International Labour Organsation. (2013). "Regulating the employment relationship in Europe: a guide to Recommendation No. 198." International Labour Office, Governance and Tripartism Department. Geneva: ILO, 2013. pp. 28–29. Retrieved November 11, 2018, from http://www.ilo.org/wcmsp5/groups/public/@ed_dialo gue/@dialogue/documents/publication/wcms_209280.pdf.

37 Par. 4 and 5 of the Article 5.27 of the Code of Administrative Offences of the Russian Federation.

according to Article 15(2) of the Code, the conclusion of "civil law" contracts (i.e. contracts for services) that actually regulate employment relations is not permitted.

At the same time, the Russian Labour Code still contains provisions that may be difficult to apply in the new technological reality. For example, Article 67(1) sets the general rule for the form of every employment contract stating that "... an employment contract shall be concluded in a written form in two copies each of which shall be signed by the parties." This formula poses questions about what these "written form", "copies" and being "signed" should mean, for example, in the blockchain environment or with regard to other technological solutions the 4th Industrial Revolution gave rise to. Not many countries have currently developed a regulatory response to such questions, and nor has Russia.

Conclusion

As was the case before the 4th Industrial Revolution, technology can still be used for good and for evil. The chosen path and the outcomes of the choices still eventually depend on our morals and values. Public authorities and courts can support and promote the righteous decisions for the society to include it in its value system and for it to take roots even in the countries where case law is not a part of the legal tradition.

The research showed that new technologies can be really beneficial in the field covered by employment law, but they do not come automatically as an immanent feature of the technologies. They require regulatory support with appropriate amendments in law and procedures.

The research also shows that in the management of relations concerning work (including HRM) these new technologies are used – primarily or exclusively – to perform tasks that are actually quite traditional (document storage, values calculation). What is attained with the use of these technologies is the quality of the performance of these tasks. Therefore, the main interest in the use of new technologies lies not in the specificity of some particular technical features of a certain technology, but rather in the level they allow to reach in the performance of traditional functions.

3   Digitalisation *vis-à-vis* the Indian labour market: pros and cons

Dr. Durgambini A. Patel

Introduction

The debate regarding growing digitalisation and its impacts on the labour markets all over the world has been ever present and constantly growing since the first Industrial Revolution, which happened in the 18th Century. The Digital revolution or the third Industrial Revolution happened in the mid-20th century and saw the invention of computers, the widespread use of electronics, the swift transition from mobile phones to "smart" phones and the creation and destruction of jobs as an inevitable result of the same.[1]

The Fourth Industrial Revolution as a concept was introduced at the trade fair in Hanover in 2013 and the core aim of this concept was to introduce the idea of "smart factories" which will involve the use of automated-physical systems.[2] But, the Fourth Industrial Revolution as opposed to the Third Revolution is often considered as a new era of Revolution and not merely as a continuance of the digital revolution due to its breakthrough and disruptive nature. It inculcates technologies and trends such as robotics, artificial intelligence, machine learning, the Internet of Things (IoT), virtual reality, cloud computing, etc. and is transforming the future of work and way of living profoundly.[3] Many jobs and ways of working will certainly change, and while some will become old, others will be created to make the life of the working class easier. There are also studies that suggest that with digitalisation there exists a process of job destruction and construction, which usually affects the traditional businesses and industries. Undoubtedly, the impacts of this revolution will be seen not only in the labour

---

1 "What is the Fourth Industrial Revolution?", World Economic Forums, Available at https://www.weforum.org/agenda/2016/01/what-is-the-fourth-industrial-revolution/ [Accessed on 1st Feb, 2019].
2 "Impacts of digitization on employment and social security of employees", Pavel Kohout, Robot Asset Management, SICAV, Marcela Palísková, Faculty of business administration, VŠE, Prague, Available at: https://www.Digitalization%20of%20LM/1_IMPACTS_OF_DIGITALIZATION_2017.pdf [Accessed on 1st Feb, 2019].
3 *Ibid.*

market, but also on society as a whole.[4] This is main reason why the future of work and labour still remains unsure, in addition to the speed and spread of technological change that is unparalleled.

Digitalisation and digitisation: the interrelationship

Digitalisation can broadly be conceived as mixing virtual technologies into everyday life to make life easier.[5] Whereas, digitisation is a process where digital versions of physical versions are created, such as documents, pictures, etc. which makes it easily rectifiable and displayable with minimum human intervention.[6] Digitalisation refers to transforming operations and tasks with the help of innovative digital technologies and adopting a "smart" approach to stay ahead of the curve. Digitalisation is often seen as a process to inject new ideas in the market by replacing existing business models and functions with new and improved business models, mainly to generate more revenue by investing less on labour. In today's world where industries and enterprises including start-ups are in the zone of cut-throat competition, they need to make sure that the services they offer, the quality, cost efficiency, quickness are better than their counterparts in the market. Hence such setups are expected to address and withstand the paradigm shift that is constantly occurring in their line of business. Digitalisation and the development of Information & Communication Technology (ICT) has immensely helped impact the wide area of an enterprise's activity like understanding the consumer point of view better by votes on a digital platform or solving their problems through 24/7 online customer assistance or social media platforms for better marketing of products. Therefore, digitalisation will not be possible without digitisation.

The digital revolution can transform the way people live their lives. Things that were thought to be impossible ten years ago can now be easily done by just pressing a button. However, with digitalisation and the Industrial Revolution hitting the markets, the impact on the labour markets is also obvious. The future of work, intensity and skill set also requires a modern approach with the rapidly changing times and technology. The Third Industrial Revolution, also known as the digitalisation, saw the advent of digitised technologies making life and the way of working a lot easier, but along with this the labour market encountered the concept of *outsourcing*. Though it is a relatively new concept, it is usually referred to as the process of hiring an individual or a company to handle certain aspects of the business of the hiring company. Outsourcing can

---

4 "Emerging technologies and the future of work in India", ILO, June 2018.
5 "Digital Futures: final report, a journey into 2050 visions and policy challenges", European Union. Available at: https://ec.europa.eu/futurium/sites/futurium/files/DF_final_report. pdf [Accessed on 31st Jan, 2019].
6 Available at: https://www.i-scoop.eu/digitization-digitalization-digital-transformation-disrup tion/[Accessed on 2nd Feb, 2019].

be done domestically or internationally. The concept of outsourcing gained a lot of popularity and started becoming widespread in the 1990s, as by then, companies started to focus on cost saving measure as a way to make profit, which now is a formally identified business strategy. The reason for their growing popularity of this concept is that companies that outsource get the work done for considerably less money and overhead expenses as they do not have to provide benefits to the employees who work for them.[7]

There are many forms of outsourcing; two major forms are Information Technology Outsourcing (ITO) and Business Process Outsourcing (BPO). ITO includes a company's outsourcing of internet related work such as application development and maintenance, help desk services, IT infrastructure management, data centre management, cloud computing, customer support, insurance claims processing. On the other hand, BPO services are Human Resources (HR), payroll or accounting.[8] The company to whom the work is outsourced is known as third-party providers or service providers.[9]

The emergence of outsourcing

Industries these days are susceptible to neck and neck competition mainly due to globalisation and the increased availability of choices for the customers. In such a scenario, the existing set ups will strive ever harder to improve the quality of their products along with the services provided to the consumer of their goods. Having said this, not all industries todayhave the required resources or talent to develop and complete their desired product. This is where the concept of outsourcing comes into play, as such industries and setups are forced to outsource their work to specialists. Outsourcing, also known as subcontracting, is not a new practice. This practice has been prevalent since the 1960s. With the emergence of complex production mechanisms and the growing rate of company expansions, there has been an increase in outsourcing processes.[10]

The outsourcing of services is a relatively new practice and this type outsourcing has created a lot of buzz, especially in developing countries by creating over a million jobs in the past decade. Outsourcing of services is mainly possible because of the emergence of Information and Communication Technology (ICT) and is an employment that came into existence purely

7 "What is Outsourcing and how it actually works." Available at: https://www.chrisducker. com/how-outsourcing-works/ [Accessed on 2nd Feb, 2019].

8 "The Concept of Outsourcing", Sova Pal Bera, *IOSR Journal of Computer Engineering* (IOSR-JCE) e-ISSN: 2278-0661,Volume 19, Issue 4, Ver. IV. (Jul.–Aug. 2017), pp. 37–39. Available at: www.iosrjournals.org.,http://www.iosrjournals.org/iosr-jce/papers/Vol19-issue4/Version-4/H1904043739.pdf [Accessed on 6th Jan, 2020].

9 *Ibid.*

10 "Outsourcing and the fragmentation of employment relations: the challenges ahead", Ursula Huws & Sarah Podro, August 2012, ACAS future of workplace Relations discussion paper series.

because of the rise of digitalised technologies that enable organisations to connect better at a lower cost. Outsourcing of work reduces stress on the primary company and ensures the quality of work done by the service provider, as they are specialised in the field of work outsourced to them.[11]

Impacts of outsourcing on labour markets

The decision of outsourcing certain tasks seems more strategic today as it reduces and controls operation costs, improves the focus of the company and allows the access to world class capabilities along with freeing internal resources. However, this concept of outsourcing also has its own pros and cons that impact the economy of countries. Some positive impacts are:

a)   Increased growth in business along with cost saving. Outsourcing of services to third-party companies helps the primary company to get their work done at a cost-effective rate. Therefore, once this relationship between the primary company and the service provider companies is established, more and more companies would want to outsource their work and similarly more and more companies would like to provide their services to such primary companies. This will lead to increased growth in businesses, domestically and internationally.

b)   Efficient utilisation of resources. Outsourcing of services provides exposure to a wide array of resources. The service providers who take up the task outsourced make sure that they employ the most skilled resources and advanced technology available, along with advanced quality infrastructure at minimal costs.

c)   Low risk. Countries like India that follow strict data security laws are most likely to be preferred for outsourcing tasks by the companies in the US or UK. This is because such outsourcing reduces the risks of substandard services and data breaches. Once the process is outsourced, the service provider ensures that it is completelyefficiently without mishandling any data.

d)   Offshore expansion. Outsourcing processes provide an opportunity to the primary company to expand its business in centres off their own shore. This way, the company can increase business and settle in a new environment.

The negative impacts of outsourcing can be the following:

a)   Constant feeling of job insecurity. Amidst the constantly changing labour market dynamics, it is essential for every employee to have job security and it is the duty of every employer to make the employee feel secure. But with the tremendous rise in outsourcing processes, an employee is always aware

---

11 *Ibid* 10.

of the risk of his job being outsourced to a third party. This may lead to him losing confidence in his employer, and ultimately not putting in as much effort in the work he performs.

b)   Cutthroat competition. With the increasing number of companies that out-source work, the number of service providers has also considerably increased over time; this paves the way for new competition in the market. This competition leads to a feeling of corporate satisfaction due to which many companies force their workforce to work overtime and provide fewer off periods. This hampers its relationship with local communities and local labourers.

c)   Domestic workforces lose their jobs. This is the main side effect of outsourcing on any economy. When the primary company decides to outsource their process to a different country, the workforce of the country where the primary company is located faces major losses. Furthermore, outsourcing today is not only limited to unskilled jobs: even jobs requiring an intense amount of skill are being outsourced.

In the case of India particularly, outsourcing has helped a lot in employing the ever-growing workforce and has helped in building and maintaining infrastructure. India holds 37% shares of global outsourcing and was likely to touch $167 billion in the year in 2018–19, which shows a whopping 8% increase as compared to the years 2017–18.[12] Moreover, due to outsourcing, people in India get to kn ow the working of big multi-national corporations by getting an opportunity to work with them.[13] Flexible work hours of some outsourcing companies and good pay have also led to an increase in the participation of women in the workforce. This helps them to contribute to their household finances.

But, on the other hand, the negative impacts of outsourcing are also visible in India as we are slowly adapting to the culture of the dominating company, the holiday schedules, work culture, losing out on significant cultural and traditional values. Therefore, the government has come up with various campaigns, such as "Make in India" and "Skill India", to keep the traditional culture and skills of India intact.

The Fourth Industrial Revolution and automation

Generally, with digitalisation hitting the market several pre-existing techniques of working apparently change and are replaced by automated technologies

---

12 See: https://telecom.economictimes.indiatimes.com/news/indian-it-industry-revenue-to-touch-167-billion-nasscom/66079734 [Accessed on 31st Jan, 2019].

13 "India – A destination for sourcing of services", PWC 2014, Available at: https://www.pwc.in/assets/pdfs/publications/2014/india-as-a-destination-for-sourcing-of-services.pdf [Accessed on 4th Feb, 2019].

which reduce the time and cost of work. This change demands new skills to carry out the tasks, which means that the existent workforce has to be trained or be replaced by workers who already possess the required skill set. Estimates suggest that low and middle skilled jobs are amongst the ones that are most likely to be automated.[14]

In the Indian context, the impact seems a little hazy as them a jority of our country's workforce is in the unorganised sector and the bulk of these workers are engaged in unskilled or low skilled work that generates a low level of income. The unorganised sector comprises small-scale enterprises, daily wage and self-employed workers, who evidently lack the financial capital and necessary skills to support the adoption of advanced technologies. Added to this is the fact that fewer than 2 million jobs are being created every year for a workforce that exceeds 8 million people with a declining proportion of women.[15] Micro-technologies, for example digital banking, along with upgrades in transport and connectivity services, can improve labour productivly to a noticeable extent.

Research and development relating to Artificial Intelligence (AI) in the public sector in India is headed by the Centre for Artificial Intelligence and Robotics (CAIR) at the Defence Research and Development Organization (DRDO) and the various Indian Institutes of Technology (IIT). On the other hand, research and development in the private sector is handled by multinational companies like Infosys and Intel. Several other leading companies like Amazon, Flipkart, Uber, Ola, etc. which have gained mass popularity, make use of applications which are network based and can be operated through smart phones or tablets. With the government announcing in early 2018 that the *Niti Ayog* will include a national programme on AI research, it is likely that both, the government and the industry, including start-ups, will increase investments in advanced technologies over the coming decade.[16]

Automation and job displacement

Advanced automation with the use of Artificial Intelligence (AI) and robots is already disrupting the job market. However, in the case of India, the difference between the potential of automation and its adoption is to be noted closely as not many industries have the basic infrastructure to adopt such automation; therefore, they will be susceptible to potential automation but not immediate adoption. Approximately 300 million Indians live without power while only 25% have access to the internet.[17] Jobs requiring low to medium skills that are

14 *Supra* note at 4 (ILO).
15 "India's labour market: a new emphasis on gainful employment", discussion paper by McKin-sey & Company, June 2017.
16 *Supra* note at 4 (ILO).
17 World Bank, 2017"Access to electricity," Available at: www.worldbank.org [Accessed on 31st Dec, 2018].

routine and rule-based could be the first to be technically automated; but again, their adoption will depend upon various socio-economic conditions such as relative cost and availability of skilled labour. Thus, the wave of advanced automation may only hit selected industries and work processes, rather than leading to complete job displacement.[18] According to studies, estimated automation in India, based only on the task content of various occupations, ranges from 52% to 62%;[19] whereas, the impact is greater if this is considered in terms of skill level where less than 20% of the working population is engaged in high-skilled occupations requiring analytical skills.[20] Having said this, the Indian labour market offering jobs that need such low to medium skills has a lot of potential for the automation of jobs as the task content of various occupations such as cashier, travel agents, etc. can be easily automated. But such jobs are very few in number in India. Such automation of jobs is more likely to affect the unorganised sector than the organised sector as these are the jobs that most unorganised sector workers aspire to.

The averagely educated and skilled unorganised workers rely upon such jobs to lead them out of poverty and hence such automation can pose a serious challenge in the context of the Indian labour market and reduce the mobility of low skilled-middle skilled labourers to jobs requiring higher skills and providing higher income.

Jobs most suceptible to automation

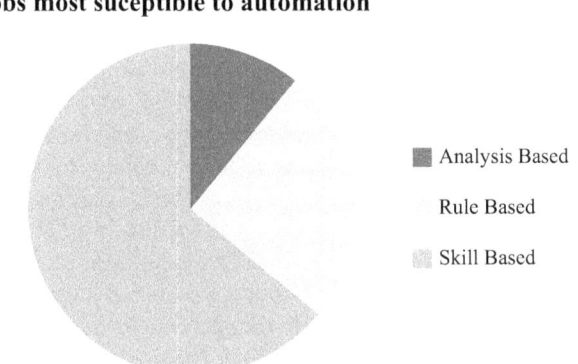

■ Analysis Based

   Rule Based

▦ Skill Based

Figure 3.1 Jobs most susceptible to automation

18 "Jobs lost, jobs gained: workforce transitions in a time of automation," McKinsey & Company, Dec 2017.
19 McKinsey Global Institute, "A future that works: Automation, employment and productivity" 2017.
20 *Ibid.*

The above chart shows the ratios of jobs which are most likely to be susceptible. As per the figure, analysis-based tasks including expertise driven tasks which involve developing, planning, decision making, creative works, etc. are most likely to be affected by Artificial Intelligence (AI) and augmented reality but are difficult to be automated. Rule based tasks including routine processing roles like cashiers, receptionists, travel agents, etc. are likely to be transformed by sensors and cloud computing. Whereas, skill-based roles include such tasks which require creativity and innovation and are least susceptible to automation.

Impacts of the Fourth Industrial Revolution and automation on the labour market

Another very important part of digitalisation of the labour market is the adoption of automation caused by digitalisation and the future of jobs in the sector which adopts such automation.

Impacts on the manufacturing sector

While reports suggest that manufacturing tasks in the organised sector have the maximum potential to be automated, with a recent study showing that 69% of the tasks in this particular line are susceptible to automation,[21] it does pose a question on the future of workmen in the manufacturing sector. However, adoption of automation will be affected by the relative cost of technological up grading to labour, among other social and economic varying conflicts of interests. Recent trends also indicate that manufacturing industries requiring a large amount of capital investment and are capital intensive in nature are more likely to be affected by the Fourth Industrial Revolution by adopting advanced automation and robotics. This is also reflected in the shift in the automobile sector, which is reportedly estimated to buy 60% of the industrial robots sold in India.[22] These robots have taken up routine jobs like welding, painting, etc. in various manufacturing units, shrinking the manual labour force from 32 to 4 people and this is expected to happen on a large scale in this industry given the high number of existing and inevitable routine jobs. Though the shift is already prevailing in the manufacturing sector, more precisely the automobile sector, this sector has contributed the most to growing employment rates over the last decade, which in the future will be affected by the adoption of automated technologies and advanced robotics.

21 World Bank Group Foresight Report. 2016: "World Development Report 2016, digital dividends." Available at: http://documents.worldbank.org/curated/en/896971468194972881/pdf/102725-PUBReplacement-PUBLIC.pdf [Accessed on 4th Jan, 2019].
22 Available at: https://auto.economictimes.indiatimes.com/news/industry/robots-are-no-hazard-but-beneficialsay-auto-industry-experts/48008181 [Accessed on 6th Jan, 2020].

Impact on labour intensive industries

Industries such as textile, leather, paper manufacturing, etc., which require high proficiency and are labour intensive, will experience automation at a comparatively slower pace. But certain processes in such industries, e.g. textiles, are experiencing automation in routine jobs and have replaced 20 workers with 2 workers. Due to such automation, the expected target of the government to create 1 million jobs in the textile sector is likely to remain unfulfilled.[23]

Impact on enterprises and start-ups

Digitalisation of labour and the impacts of the Fourth Industrial Revolution will be visible in entrepreneurial ventures, as it can provide better access to the suppliers and the market, or by enabling opportunities to start-ups working in remote areas. The development of new technologies is also helping to curb transaction costs that lead to imbalance in trading. These also help the enterprises to focus on production and distribution processes, as there is a fair chance to access the markets. Technological changes also bring about a change in the manner of trade by ensuring the entry of new products or bettering existing ones or by targeting unexplored limits of the market. This in a way ensures that incumbent companies pull their socks up and stand unshaken in the storm of increasing competition.

Impacts on business

The technologies which accompany the Fourth Industrial Revolution will have a huge impact on the existing and upcoming businesses. These impacts will be twofold: one on the supply side and the other on the demand side. On the supply side, the industry will have to create novel ways of balancing quality, speed and price of delivering goods and to catering to the need of the consumers, especially in a time where demands of the market are rapidly increasing day by day. New and improved technology can help increase production speed and reduce the cost of labour and hence help earn profits, provided the business has the required capital to invest in automated technologies to earn the returns they wish. Whereas the demand side will help businesses to maintain their balance between quality, quantity and price having daily changing patterns of consumer behaviour and growing transparency in the market. Technologically advanced platforms will provide access to new ways of consuming goods and services along with helping businesses to provide a good personal and professional environment to workers.

---

23 The Hindu "India labour market update", *India*, July 2016 and July 2017.

Conclusion

The global economy is on the doorstep of the inevitable Fourth Industrial Revolution, the impacts of which are going to be seen on the labour markets in India in the coming decades. According to the various research cited in this chapter, this Revolution, unlike the previous Revolutions, is not of a substitutive nature, but of a destructive nature. The inventions of robots and automatable technologies are posing a threat to the existing industrial setup as tasks that were not automatable are now under the radar of automation. In this regard, this chapter has analysed the impact of such a Revolution on the existing labour market setup and the changes that would take place in the future.

The analysis leads to the conclusion that routine jobs performed by the population are amongst the ones to be automated by machines. Such jobs are mostly performed by people with lower educational qualifications who aspire to move away from the minimum wage. Replacing such workers will lead to social security problems, including both societal and economical imbalance. Instead the government must formulate the right policies in the coming times to help mitigate the impact of such replacement.

Educating the soon to be replaced worker and inculcating new skills in him/her will help them survive. The Skill India campaign launched by the government in 2015 is a campaign, which included various initiatives by the government and aims to train over 40 million people by 2022 in various skills.

While framing laws and policies, the government must also consider the impact of such digitalisation on the economic system of India. The disruptive nature of technologies will ultimately result into the concentration of wealth only in the hands of the owners of such technological assets, who are not in the majority in today's scenario. This justifies the immense importance of the education of the masses, especially of those in the workforce in the age of rapid digitalisation.

Bibliography

Abraham, V. A. (2005). "New Technology and the Emerging Labour market: A study of Indian IT industry", *The Indian Journal of Labour Economics*, 48 (4), 789–801.

Banerjee, Brojendra Nath (1991). *Globlisation: Rough and Risky Road*, New Age International Limited, New Delhi.

Chenery, H. B., S. Robinson and M. Syrquin (1986). *Industrialization and Growth*, Oxford University Press, New York.

Illiyan, A. (2008). "Performance, Challenges and opportunities of Indian software export", *Journal of theoretical and applied Information Technology* (JATIT), 1088–1106, available at: http://jatit.org/volumes/research-papers/Vol4No11/11Vol4No11.pdf (last accessed 6th Jan, 2020).

Little, Ian M.D., Tibor Scitovsky and Mauricio Mesquita Maurice Scott (1970), *Industry and Trade in Some Developing Countries. A Comparative Study*, Oxford University Press, London.

NASSCOM (1999). "The Informational Technology Workforce", India's National Association of software and Service Companies, New Delhi.

Syed, S. H. (2016). "The role of Information Technology industry in India", *Kaav International Journal of Economics, Commerce and Business Management*, 3 (4), 87–108.

Useful websites

Digitalisation, migration and the future of work: https://www.lowyinstitute.org/the-interpreter/digitalisation-migration-and-future-work.

Digital India initiatives: http://digitalindia.gov.in/content/vision-and-vision-areas, https://www.ibef.org/industry/information-technology-india.aspx.

Digital Workplaces: Trends Shaping The Future Of Work-https://inc42.com/resources/digital-workplaces-trends-shaping-the-future-of-work/.

How workspace digitization enhances employee engagement: https://www.people matters.in/article/change-management/how-workspace-digitization-enhances-employee-engagement-15385.

4 The impact of new technologies in the current labour market of selected Arab states

Dr. Alaa Eltamimi

Introduction

Undoubtedly, modern technology in the Arab workplaces will result in serious legal consequences. It is important that employment should be fair and appropriate not only to protect the rights and interests of employees, but also to inform employers of their legal responsibilities towards them.[1] Also, there is a serious legal problem in that Arab labour laws are ambiguous and their provisions contradictory, which may pave the way to different interpretations that serve certain special interests away from justice and as a result leading to the loss of employees' rights. This requires new legislation that takes into account possible exploitations making Arab laws keep pace with the needs of the modern labour market.

The most important reason behind the delay by many Arab countries (such as Egypt, Tunisia, Libya, Jordan, Iraq and Syria) in enacting appropriate legislation in connection with the development of technology in the Arab labour market is the political unrest and revolution that has occurred in many of these countries, and led to a greater focus on constitutional amendments[2] regarding the exercise of political rights (such as the legislation on the election of the Head of State and the election of members of Parliament), and the criminal legislation (demonstrations, money laundering and tax evasion laws).[3] Although the trade unions have

---

1 The employment issue has been the focus of attention of the Arab world and the International Labour Organization, the employment relationship within the framework of the Declaration on Fundamental Principles and Rights at Work, which aims to provide decent work as a strategic objective for employment and to provide appropriate opportunities in accordance with labour market statistics and information and the wishes of those seeking employment and limit the exploitation of job applicants in their non-specialization according to international labour standards.

2 Mahmoud Hamad, "Comparative Survey of Constitutional Reforms in the Arab Region since 2011," Constitutional Book of the Arab Organisation of Constitutional Law, 2015–2016, p. 15.

3 The world is witnessing the worst economic and financial crisis since the 1930s. There is no doubt that the Arab world has been negatively affected by this crisis. The most important of these is the increase of unemployment, which could lead to a humanitarian disaster that could affect the security and stability of the region. This is in addition to the lack of

contributed significantly to these revolutions, after the stability of the political situation they did not put enough pressure on governments and the legislative authorities to enact legislation to meet their demands.[4]

All this shows the magnitude of the challenge, especially as the Arab countries seek economic development and wish to attract investment. Investors are keen to make sure that flexible and modern employment laws are available in the state where they wish to invest, to be strongly linked to their success in investing. There is also a need to maximise benefits from information and knowledge[5] that have become the norm because "development and increase in production and productivity are dependent on the value of knowledge, rather than on the physical factors of production, such as land, capital, abundant natural resources, and even the abundance of the labour force. The cost of knowledge in most cases exceeds the cost of all physical factors of production, and their added value represents

employment opportunities, inadequate policies of some countries towards employment, rehabilitation, training and education, and their inability to attract the necessary investments to create jobs and revive economic development. Statistics show that there are more than 20 million unemployed, mostly young people seeking work for the first time, and the lack of women's right to rehabilitation and work is one of the most important problems facing development in the Arab countries. The growth rates in the Arab countries are very low for the first time, both for the oil-exporting and importing countries. The reasons for the decline are conflicts and weak investment. Moreover, the oil countries suffer from the decline in oil prices, which affected national income and the growth rate of the investment resulting from it and that is one of the sources of growth. All these factors lead to increased risk and uncertainty, causing investors to refrain from expanding their investment. See: Badr Ismail Mohamed Makhlouf (2010) "The Role of Information Technology in the Development of Labour Statistics, Statistical Session on 'Development of Labour Statistics'," Sana'a, Republic of Yemen, 28–30 November 2010.

4 Adnan Almansir: "Political and Social Dialogues in the Labour Union", article available at: https://www.dohainstitute.org/ar/politicalstudies/pages/art142.aspx.

5 It should be noted that access to technology is not the only effective factor in achieving economic development. It is also hard to say that technology is the only factor influencing social and economic change, but it plays a big and influential role in this direction. This requires social adaptation with this technology. It is essential that the management structures be consistent with the development objectives and associated technological tasks. It should be noted that the method used to achieve this varies from State to State. But it is a firm fact that building a technology-based economy in Arab countries will require the creation of governance structures that reflect the dynamics of the common development of technology and institutions. Calestous Juma and Lee Yee-Cheong (2005), "Innovation: Applying Knowledge in Development, UN Millennium Project", Earthscan, UK and USA.

The information revolution is linked to the technical advances of the means of telecommunications, which helped to disseminate information and exchange information very quickly. Information technology is fundamentally different from previous technologies because of its interaction with all human and physical elements of society, which make information technology a common denominator. In all humanitarian activities, information technology in human society has fused into an overwhelming economic and media globalisation. Technology can be defined in general as "the state of knowledge concerning ways of converting resources into outputs" (OECD, 2011A: Estimate of support to agriculture) or as the "machinery and equipment developed from the application of scientific knowledge" (Oxford English Dictionary).

a multiplication of the returns of other production revenues".[6] These new knowledge-based standards have become a challenge for societies. Illiteracy is no longer the inability to read and write, but the inability to use the information technology and its applications in all aspects of life, especially in the workplace.[7]

Importance of this study

This study is particularly important because it seeks to research one of the most significant topics in the Arab countries in recent times, namely the impact of modern technology on their labour market. These countries have taken great steps to accommodate modern technology systems in numerous fields of work. This has led to many effects on the percentage of employment and wages, the high rate of unemployment, changes in the concept of labour law and the importance of training courses and measures to be taken by Arab labour markets. Unfortunately, these effects have no real or direct legal treatment in Arab laws. This study identifies those problems and makes proposals and recommendations directed to the Arab legislative institutions, especially in Egypt, Saudi Arabia, Kuwait, United Arab Emirates and Tunisia.

Problem of the study

There is a legislative vacuum in many Arab employment laws to absorb the implications of adopting technological systems. It is noteworthy that this legislative vacuum sometimes appears in the absence of a law, and sometimes in the existence of a law not taking into consideration the specificity of the economic and social implications of relying on modern technology in Arab workplaces. This is a big problem because the courts in Arab countries find it difficult to resolve many cases, as most Arab legal systems belong to the systems of written law. This occurs when there are already many cases before these courts, and the judge does not find an appropriate legal text to resolve the case, as will appear later.

Methodology

Because addressing the legislative vacuum in Arab employment laws requires an analysis of the existing legal texts and knowledge of the shortcomings and weaknesses in the absorption of the effects of modern technology as well as making appropriate proposals, it is necessary in this chapter to rely on *the conceptual*

---

6 Badr Ismail Mohamed Makhlouf, op. cit. See also: "New Sources OF Growth: Knowledge-Based Capital – Key Analyses and Policy Conclusions – Synthesis Report", OECD 2013, p.6.
7 "Literacy in the Information Age, Final Report of the International Adult Literacy Survey", Organization for Economic Co-operation and Development, Paris, and the Minister of Industry, Canada, 2000, p.x; S. Nickerson Bolt Beranek and Newman Inc. (1985), "Adult Literacy and Technology", Raymond, Technical Report No. 351, Centre for the Study of Reading Technical Reports, p.3

analytical approach. This research will also be based on an *evaluation approach* to test whether the proposed solutions will suit the practical reality, and whether they conform to the specificity of the ethical, political and economic rules in Arab countries, taking into account the other important differences in the legal systems concerned.

Part one: Challenges arising from the use of modern technology in the labour market of Arab countries

It is expected[8] that new technology will compete with workers in Arab countries for every future job and is likely that many jobs will be fully replaced with this technology. This means that future jobs will be either digital jobs or functions using digital tools[9] especially since the dominant culture in Arab society tends to trust modern technology more than human beings.[10]

Thus, Arab companies and institutions rely increasingly on technology by reason of their multiple advantages. This can adversely affect employment, especially in terms of inequality. This will allow some individuals to benefit greatly, while others may find themselves discriminated against.[11]

---

8 Jan Peter aus dem Moore, Vinay Chandran and Jorg Schubert (2018), "The Future of Jobs in The Middle East, World Government Summit", McKinsey Company, January, p.6.

9 Digital technology has dramatically changed the way individuals, businesses and even governments communicate. The digital economy has become a major engine of economic growth and job creation, so the adoption of technology is important to improve productivity and reach new markets. The World Bank is keen to support countries and their citizens in taking advantage of these opportunities. This support provides access to the Internet at reasonable prices for more than 4 billion people who are unable to communicate, in addition to building the skills necessary to benefit from the digital economy and infrastructure development. In October 2016, the World Bank launched a Digital Development Partnership (DDP) in cooperation with the public and private sectors to make real use of world development in 2016.

   DDP has helped to bridge the global digital gap in order to ensure that everyone can benefit from the economic and social benefits of communication. This has significantly increased access, improved quality and reduced the cost of international connectivity by up to 90% through market competition reforms and thousands of kilometers of investment infrastructure networks. The World Bank, Annual Report 2018, available at: http://www.worldbank.org/en/about/annual-report/our-work.

10 Shih-Yi Chien (2016), "The Influence of Cultural Factors on Trust in Automation", submitted to the Graduate Faculty of The School of Information Sciences in partial fulfillment of the requirements for the degree of Doctor of Philosophy, University of Pittsburgh, p. 4.

11 The degree to which different sectors of modern technology are receptive to future sustainability varies depending on the creation of new jobs. For example, businesses that rely on routine tasks such as manufacturing, transport and storage can absorb technology by 50%. The sectors that rely on human interaction and service, creative and non-routine activities absorb technology at a rate of less than 29% to 37%. In this regard, we can monitor the important result that the largest share of the possibility of employing technology can be done in Egypt compared to the economies of the Gulf countries, because of the large volume of employment within the sectors of industry and agriculture. A certificate of higher education or the equivalent of professional experience is a guarantee for a future job. The average probability of job completion is

It is worth mentioning that the Arab countries have almost equal technological capabilities in terms of equipment and expertise. This is because these countries have followed similar paths in technology adoption (from reverse engineering to cumulative innovation of products and processes). However, this did not prevent some administrative obstacles in some countries, as will be explained later.[12]

Furthermore, the following issues need to be addressed:first, the possibility of replacing jobs with technology and the legal protection against the dramatic decline in wages and an increased unemployment rate; second, the risk of inequality in the types of jobs and wages and increasing tensions in Arab societies; and third, the development of labour relations as well as the risks involved therein and the legal system regulating this.

Section one: Legal protection against the possibilities of replacing jobs with technology in Arab law

Forecasts since the 1950s and early 1960s suggest that technology will lead to the complete abolition of many jobs and a great increase in unemployment for many years. This expectation has increased recently due to the high dependence on the means of technology in many business sectors in Arab countries. It has been shown that they abolish more jobs than they create.[13]

In our view, the reason behind this is that many Arab countries (e.g., Egypt)[14] have for long suffered from bureaucracy in many workplaces, which has strained employers (in terms of salaries, pensions and health insurance), and strained customers who suffer from the multiplicity of procedures and their complexity. In addition, Arab governments have been encouraged to adopt technology (even if this means that technology replaces human beings), because corruption in many workplaces (bribery and personal interests) has spread on a large scale.

It should be noted that the elimination of some professions in Arab countries because of modern technology does not mean that these professional workers will be unemployed. Rather, it means that they will seek other work or will be retrained for new jobs. It may thus be said that technology in Arab workplaces has created new jobs which were previously unknown. According to the Elance

---

reduced to 33% for highly qualified employees. This means the possibility of a decline in the value of high-paying jobs that require high skills. Jean Peter, Vinay Chandran and Joerg Schubert (2018), "Future Jobs in Middle East 'World Summit of Governments'," McKinsey & Company, January, p. 16.

12 "Technology Report and Innovation 2012, United Nations Conference on Trade and Development, Innovation, technology and South-South Cooperation, United Nations", New York and Geneva, 2012, p. 5.

13 "The Effects of Technology on Employment and Implications for Public Employment Services", The World Bank Group Report Prepared for the G20 Employment Working Group Meeting, Istanbul, Turkey 6–8 May 2015, p. 5.

14 "Tackling the Leviathan: Reforming Egyptian Bureaucracy for Improved Economic Growth", Series of White Papers to Promote Transparency & Combat Corruption in Egypt, The Centre for International Private Enterprise (CIPE), p.13.

online platform[15] (Job Classifying Platform) of April 2015, some of these jobs required online marketing, blogging, and e-commerce functions. There were about 26,000 open positions, and hourly rates ranged from $16 to $22 on average.[16]

The use of technology in workplaces in some Arab countries, namely Egypt, Saudi Arabia, Bahrain, Kuwait, Oman and the United Arab Emirates, is relatively small compared to the major industrialised countries such as the United Kingdom, the United States and China.[17] The average use of technology in these countries exceeds 50%, while in Egypt, for example, the percentage use of technology in the different fields of work is estimated at 48%, while Saudi Arabia and Oman have a lower share (41%).[18]

Increasing reliance on technology in the Arab workplace has positive effects. The most important of which are increasing production, raising the level of product quality and reducing expenses, which encouraged many commercial companies to employ technology. Nevertheless, one of the most important negative effects, which is a serious challenge, is the increase in unemployment rate, because technology has replaced humans. This replacement was perhaps more serious than at the time of the Industrial Revolution, when machines replaced blue-collar workers. This is because machines could not be used in all business sectors, nor did they completely replace human beings. Technology has been able to penetrate all sectors of the business, whether in production or services, and has in many cases completely replaced the presence of human beings.[19]

15 Upwork, formerly Elance-oDesk, is a global freelancing platform where businesses and independent professionals connect and collaborate remotely. In 2015, Elance-oDesk was rebranded as Upwork. It is based in Mountain View and San Francisco, California. The full name is Upwork Global Inc. Upwork has twelve million registered freelancers and five million registered clients. Three million jobs are posted annually, worth a total of $1 billion USD, making it the largest freelancer marketplace in the world. Upwork allows clients to interview, hire and work with freelancers and agencies through the company's platform. The platform includes a real-time chat aimed at reducing the time it takes to find, vet and hire freelancers. The platform offers a time sheet application that allows freelancers to track their actual time spent working on projects with verified screenshots. In April 2017 Upwork started a US only job filter for freelancers in the United States and announced this in the Upwork freelancer community. In September 2018 a UK only, filter was established. In October 2018 Upwork's CEO Stephane Kasriel said in an interview with CNBC that Upwork had taken steps to help US-based freelancers protect against being undercut by their global counterparts, "Last year, we launched a U.S.-only website, where U.S. freelancers are only competing against other U.S.-based freelancers. And that means they can have rates that are compatible with what they would expect to get in the U.S." Upwork, Wikipedia, available at: https://en.wikipedia.org/wiki/Upwork.
16 "The Effects of Technology on Employment and Implications for Public Employment Services," The World Bank Group Report Prepared for the G20 Employment Working Group Meeting, Istanbul, Turkey 6–8 May 2015, p. 6.
17 Richard B. Freeman (2008), "The New Global Labour Market", University of Wisconsin–Madison Institute for Research on Poverty, Volume 26, Number 1, Summer/Fall, p. 4.
18 See: Ayad Al-Ani, Inji Borai, Sandra Farid, Bassant Helmi and Soha Rashed (2019), "Digitalization Strategies for The Arab World," Working Document, February, p. 11.
19 Most of the current research and reports focused on the impact of modern technology on developed industrialised countries such as the OECD member countries, but this chapter

The biggest negative impact of the use of technology is the high rate of unemployment. Thus, this negative impact will have a dramatic effect in the Arab countries, due to high unemployment rates in most Arab countries even before the use of technology,[20] beside low demand for skills, erratic growth of domestic

seeks to identify the future scenarios for the development of jobs in the Arab countries, in the light of the latest studies in this regard from the McKinsey World Institute.

The study focuses on six Arab countries: Egypt, Bahrain, Saudi Arabia, Kuwait, Oman, and the United Arab Emirates. The six countries collectively comprise more than 147 million people and their combined GDP in 2016 was more than $ 5.1 trillion. According to many studies conducted on these countries, several results can be monitored:

1. Modern technology can be used in 45% of the total activities in the Arab countries based on existing technologies, which is less than the global average of 50%. The difference between Arab countries is small. The highest percentage of technology utilisation is in Egypt, with 48% in Saudi Arabia and Oman with 41%.
2. The technological transformation of different businesses in Arab countries requires a significant economic cost estimated at about $366.6 billion US of wages and about 20.8 million employees with technological transformation activities.
3. Different business sectors in Arab countries vary in technology assimilation. The sectors that are based on routine activities such as manufacturing, transportation, storage and the information sector can absorb technology by 50%. The sectors that depend on the human element in a large way, such as the arts and entertainment, absorb technology at rates ranging between 29% and 37%.
4. The risk of job losses in the Arab countries increases for workers with low and medium education and experience levels. The average job loss is 50–55%, while the percentage of those with higher qualifications is 22%. It is worth noting that 75% of the total number of workers in the Arab countries mentioned above are of low and medium qualifications.
5. The penetration of technology into the Arab labour markets, especially in sectors where labour productivity is low or suffers from a scarcity of domestic resources, can lead to increased economic growth and the creation of future jobs with competitive advantages, which may require governance of these businesses relating to the identification of targeted investments and the visa regime, as well as training and education programs.
6. Modern technology in Arab countries is expected to create new jobs and economic growth is estimated from 0.3% to 2.2% of GDP by 2030 because productivity is expected to increase, especially in the oil, gas and consumer goods marketing sectors.
7. In the future, workers will be given more time to perform tasks that require thought more because activities that require movement and muscle activity will be reduced, as well as new intermediate functions involving a common human-machine interaction. "Digital Globalisation: The New Era of Global Flows", McKinsey World Institute, March 2016; Jean Peter, Vinay Chandran and Joerg Schubert (2018), "Future Jobs in Middle East World Summit of Governments", McKinsey & Company, January, p. 5.

20 "ILO: Unemployment and decent work deficits remain high in 2018", World Employment and Social Outlook – Trends 2018, available at: https://www.ilo.org/global/about-the-ilo/newsroom/news/WCMS_615590/lang–en/index.htm; see also: "List of Countries by Unemployment Rate", Wikipedia, The Free Encyclopedia, available at: https://en.wikipedia.org/wiki/List_of_countries_by_unemployment_rate.

Some international estimates indicate an increase in unemployment rates among youth in the Arab countries compared to other geographical regions, where it is estimated at 28% of

investment, low rates of foreign direct investment, and labour migration. Also, the latter countries do not have strategic plans to deal with this problem.[21]

However, the chances of confronting this negative impact of technology in the Arab countries appear to be greater in comparison with other countries (European and American countries) for the following reasons.

First, the percentage of young people of the total population of Arab countries compared to other countries gives real hope of the possibility of absorbing the elements of modern technology, dealing with it, and then finding suitable jobs, provided that the study and training courses are provided in a developed modern scientific method (away from traditional existing courses that do not provide any real addition), and accompanied by scientific planning done by governments and legislative authorities through issuing laws and regulations to provide appropriate training courses.

Second, there is great interest in the Arab countries in learning engineering and applied technological sciences in universities and institutes, which will contribute significantly to the absorption of this technology by a wide sector of Arab citizens.

Third, Arab countries have huge financial resources (especially the Gulf countries) enabling them to acquire advanced technology and employ it in different workplaces. They can also spend on education and training courses.

Fourth, Arab countries have a strong interest in acquiring and benefiting from modern technology because they are developing countries seeking to attract different investments.

Lastly, but not the least, statistical data[22] show that Arabs prefer to study information technology and engineering sciences to keep abreast of modern technology.

While the best solution to unemployment resulting from the use of technology is to employ trained and qualified workers, this solution may take some time. The temporary solution is undoubtedly unemployment insurance. In fact, Arab laws suffer from inadequate and ineffective regulation of unemployment insurance in general compared to the laws in Europe that provide unemployment insurance up to 90% of the salary of the worker for four years until the worker gets a new job.[23] It is noteworthy that the Arab legislation in recent years has begun to deal with the problem of unemployment more positively, but has not reached the required level yet.

the total population aged (15–24) years compared to the world average of 12.4 youth unemployment rates, about 9.5 in East Asian countries, 11.6 in sub-Saharan Africa and 18.1 in European countries. See: Mohamed Ismail and Heba Abdel Moneim (2015), "Youth Unemployment in Arab Countries", Arab Monetary Fund, August, p. 7.

21 Riadh Ben Jelili, "The Arab Region's Unemployment Problem Revisited", available at: http://www.arab-api.org/images/publication/pdfs/300/300_wps1015.pdf.

22 "UNESCO and World Bank statistics reveal that Arab women actively pursuing STEM fields e.g. in 2014, comprises 59% of total students enrolled in computer science in Saudi Arabia while UK and USA women enrolment were 16% and 14% respectively", Samira I. Islam (2017), "Arab Women in Science, Technology, Engineering and Mathematics Fields: The Way Forward", *World Journal of Education* Volume 7, Number 6, p. 12.

23 "Employment Covered Under the Social Security Program, 1935–84", *Social Security Bulletin*, April 1985, Volume 48, Number 4, p. 33.

It seems that protection against the prospect of replacing jobs with technology in Arab countries should be addressed not only in terms of fighting unemployment, but also in terms of sustainable development, which must begin with government actions supported by careful legislation. First, such legislation should consider appropriate action plans which should be adopted to deal with modern technology, in order to provide real opportunities for development, including permanent solutions to development challenges, respond to pressing priorities in the economic and social sectors, and include effective plans to take advantage of modern technology in all sectors to improve production.

Second, raising awareness of the various sectors of society as to the correct use of this technology through conducting training courses that suit local needs taking into account ethical standards and ensuring their access to all sectors of society, especially women is vital.

Third, modern technology should be used to create new job opportunities, and this requires flexible policies that accommodate positive opportunities and avoids the negative effects of technology, especially in the job market, to ensure the availability of trained cadres in order to achieve development.

Fourth, labour market policies should be rethought to suit technology needs, especially in the continuous training of graduates, the introduction of new departments in academic studies, and a reduction in the number of graduates in disciplines that are no longer required.

Fifth, it is important to provide special treatment to marginalised and vulnerable labour groups (large numbers in Arab countries), because they will be most affected by technology, in terms of job losses, salary cuts and low social insurance programmes.

Lastly, accurate standards must be established to achieve the digital access and binding government agencies to apply them fairly to all, including people with disabilities.

The success of the previous recommendations requires strong support by the government, and a clear strategy must be adopted with a clear vision and objectives as well as the means to ensure its success. It is thought that if these criteria are applied by Arab governments, they will contribute to establishing a strong infrastructure for keeping abreast of modern technology.

Section two: Risks of inequality in wages and increasing tensions in Arab societies

There is little doubt that differences and disparities in wealth and income greatly affect social justice, economic prosperity and hence political decision-making.[24] According to the World Economic Forum's 2017–2018[25] and 2019 survey[26]

---

24 Federal Law No. (8) of 1980 concerning the organisation of labour relations.
25 The Global Risks Report 2017, 12th Edition, Insight Report, World Economic Forum, 2017.
26 The Global Risks Report 2019, 14th Edition, is published by the World Economic Forum, available at: http://www3.weforum.org/docs/WEF_Global_Risks_Report_2019.pdf.

wage inequality is one of the most expected issues in the wake of the reliance on modern technology in the Arab workplace. However, wage inequality may have the least impact, and there are many forms of inequality.[27]

Several studies confirm that the spread of modern technology in Arab countries will lead to layoffs, except for a few who have experience in modern technology, and certainly can choose one of multiple jobs with the highest wages. Others (who do not have the technological expertise) will not have the same choice and they will have fewer job opportunities than before.[28]

Few Arab studies in this regard provide much information on wages in the Arab world. Many observers expect a wage recession in the future, except for some strong economies such as Saudi Arabia and the United Arab Emirates, which will continue to experience rising wages. Some Arab forecasts suggest that by 2028 the wage recession in many Arab countries could be exacerbated by the middle-income trap.[29]

This disparity in relation to wages and job accessibility will prevent Arab countries from achieving the desired social justice that promotes the economic growth. This is because this social justice is closely connected with a fair distribution of wages, and a real link between productivity and wages.[30] For many Arab countries (such as Saudi Arabia and the United Arab Emirates), although they have strong economies by virtue of having large production in the field of energy and oil, they have not been able to achieve social justice in the true sense due to the absence of a fair distribution of wealth in addition to the lack of transparency and disclosure.[31]

The Egyptian Parliament has established a National Wage Council, headed by the Minister of Planning, with the aim of setting a minimum wage at the national level. Parliament recommended considering the cost of living and how

27 Thereza Balliester and Adam Elsheikhi (2018), "The Future of Work: A Literature Review", Research Department Working Paper No. 29, International Labour Office, March, p. 26.

28 Mona Said (1996), "Public Sector Employment and Labour Markets in Arab Countries: Recent Developments and Policy Issues", Economic Research Forum.
   Forecasts also suggest that modern technology in Arab countries will reduce employment opportunities in middle jobs at the expense of other jobs. Also, it is expected to increase unstable jobs and high-skill jobs, and will increase the bias of technology-savvy people, which will exacerbate wage inequality in Arab countries. Tullio Jappelli and Luigi Pistaferri (2010), "The Consumption Response to Income Changes," *Annual Review of Economics*, Volume 2, pp. 479–506.

29 Mona Said, "Public Sector Employment and Labour Markets in Arab Countries: Recent Developments and Policy Issues", *op. cit.*

30 Michael R. Strain (2019), "The Link Between Wages and Productivity Is Strong, Part III: Promoting Private Sector, Wage Growth and Job Creation168", available at: https://assets.aspe ninstitute.org/content/uploads/2019/01/3.2-Pgs.-168-179-The-Link-Between-Wages-and-Productivity-is-Strong.pdf.

31 It should be noted that wages and employment in Arab countries after the global financial crisis in 2008 have stagnated, although some of the economies of these countries have seen some recovery in terms of GDP and job growth. It should be noted that this increase in the employment rate did not reduce the rates of low wages of the total national income, because most of the wealth created after 2008 went to the rich, and this explains the low consumption rates and the inability of fiscal policies to address inflation.

to balance wages and prices. It also has delegated the National Wage Council to lay down a minimum annual periodic bonus, which should not be less than 7% of the amount of social security contributions.[32]

Similarly, the Saudi Parliament said that, "The Council of Ministers may, at the request of the Minister, set a minimum wage.[33]

In the United Arab Emirates, Article (63) of Federal Law No. (8) of 1980 on the regulation of labour relations, stipulated that:

> The minimum wage and the cost of living shall be determined by a federal decree based on the proposal of the Minister of Man force and Social Affairs and the approval of the Council of Ministers. The Minister shall submit his proposal to determine or reconsider the minimum wage after consulting with the competent authorities and professional bodies of both employers and workers. Based on the studies and tables of fluctuations in the cost of living set by the competent authorities in the State, so that these minimum limits are enough to satisfy the basic needs of the worker and ensure a good living level.[34]

It is noteworthy that despite the existence of the previous texts, they did not achieve any benefit in the field of justice such as for the distribution of income in the countries where they were issued. The Arab countries suffer most from the imbalance in the distribution of income. The evidence for this is that the average salaries in these countries are in recession, although most of their economies improved after the financial crisis in 2008 in terms of Gross Domestic Product and job growth. The reasons for this are threefold.

First, most of the wealth generated in the Arab countries after the 2008 global financial crisis went to the wealthy. This explains the low consumption rates and the failure of monetary policies to reduce inflation. Second, job creation in the Arab countries following the application of modern technology has moved in a different direction. Third, companies were able to make huge profits from the use of modern technology but did not match this with an increase in wages because the wealth generated by these profits went to the suppliers of this technology and not the workers.[35]

The consequence is that those wages no longer play the central role in the redistribution of income as they did in previous years. Increasing capital productivity no longer leads to a real increase in average wages, in violation of the social contract

---

32 Article (34) of Egyptian Labour Law No 12 of 2003, available at: https://www.egypt.gov. eg/arabic/laws/labour/Law_12/F_worklow_law12.aspx.
33 The text of the Saudi Labour Law promulgated by Royal Decree No. 51 dated 23/8/1426 H. Article (89).
34 Federal Law No. (8) of 1980 on the organisation of labour relations, Article (63), available at: http://www.dubaichamber.com/documents/mediation/9.pdf.
35 "The Impact of Technology on The Labour Market and Its Relations", available at: http://www.samehnews.com/?p=191756.

on which the liberal economies were founded.[36] The revolutions that have taken place in many Arab countries (Egypt, Tunisia and Syria) have been the main driver of economic insecurity, which has led to hostility towards the rich and politicians.[37]

The automation of human functions is changing the requirements of the labour market. There are only jobs which electronic devices cannot perform, either because they require simple or high skills. This raises the question of the mechanism through which Arab governments can address the serious consequences of the use of modern technology and thus ensure sustainable development. There is no doubt that a set of structural reforms will be needed in labour legislation and management systems aimed at enabling workers to compete with technology, thereby greatly reducing the negative effects on the labour market. This disparity must be reduced by proposing real reforms in education and taxation systems and shifting the tax burden from labour to capital. Arab countries will also need to create new redistribution systems to encounter low wages and address the imbalance between productivity and wages. Accurate and organised data plays a crucial role in achieving those reform.[38]

This situation has put the law makers in the Arab countries in real difficulties regarding appropriate legislation to ensure the fair distribution of wages and striking a balance between productivity and wages. There are some recommendations in this regard as follows.

First, there must be legislation that ensures equality for all members of society in education and training, especially in the field of computer science and information technology.

Second, it is necessary to provide appropriate funding opportunities for education and training in modern technology, especially tax funds that can be relied upon to redistribute wealth and establish a social security system. Civil society should be involved in identifying needs and priorities in a way that benefits all.

Third, it is important to develop databases, update and analyse their data periodically and rely on these data to determine the required jobs and appropriate qualifications, and the necessary programmes for training in relation to modern technology to suit each job. The budget of different families should be recognised, and salaries and taxes should be determined in the light of income level and price fluctuations.

Fourth, there must be a focus on the requirements of the Fourth Industrial Revolution, establishing the digital economy, developing information networks and mastering the sciences of artificial intelligence in all fields, to ensure that there is no discrimination in treatment among different sectors within the country.

It is thought that it is time for Arab governments to start keeping abreast with the modern technology requirements, and detracting from its negatives effects,

---

36 *Ibid.*
37 *Ibid.*
38 Manuel Muniz, "The Impact of Technology on The Labour Market and Its Relations with The Deviation of Economic Tracks", translated article available at: https://www.ommah wahda.com (accessed 2 January 2019).

especially in terms of inequality of wages as it is a very important matter, not only with regard to workers' interests, but also to achieve the necessary development.

Section three: The risks involved in the development of labour relations and the legal system regulating them

Job loss in Arab countries is moving rapidly with robots and technology, creating many economic and social complexities.[39] Over the next 20 years, 75% of the current jobs are expected to disappear, although other jobs will be replaced (which will take some time). One of the most striking examples is the self-driving electric car, which will lead to the unemployment of millions of drivers around the world. Also, in the field of engineering, medicine and many professions and disciplines, computer programmes will design buildings in accordance with the highest professional standards. These computers will also diagnose diseases accurately, determine

39 "The Future of Jobs and Skills in the Middle East and North Africa, Preparing the Region for the Fourth Industrial Revolution", World Economic Forum, May 2017; "Jobs Lost, Jobs Gained: Workforce Transitions in A Time of Automation", December 2017,Mickinsey & Company, New York.
     Expectations are that employment may be at high risk due to modern technology, especially low-skilled labour with low wages. Some believe that tasks that require social intelligence in Arab countries are unlikely to be replaced with computerisation and that current polarisation trends in this market will probably not continue.
     There are other views that medium-skilled jobs involving technical and interpersonal skills will continue and may gain a wide range of tasks where technology helps.
     The World Bank reports that modern technology will contribute significantly to attracting more of labour to labour market. On the other hand, modern technology may create new job opportunities in Arab countries, especially in the creative industries and some service sectors, although the expected numbers are not precisely defined. But it is hard to say that technology will affect Arab labour markets. Apart from the fact that modern technology will cause workers to increase their skills and abilities, at the same time they will create new professions and require special training. This is confirmed by LinkedIn's 2018 US Employment Report, which says that machine-learning engineers, data scientists, and large data engineers are among the first to emerge from jobs that were only recently known. On the other hand, some functions such as digital platforms and large data will not only create new occupations in the highly skilled and high-paying sector, but also in the medium-term category, for example the emergence of trade content modification as a new profession in both industrialised and developing countries. The new technology will increase the demand for many new skills in Arab Countries and will also strongly contribute to the creation of new professions that require specially trained competencies, such as computer learning engineers, data scientists, and large data engineers. Coming ten years will greatly affect many companies and factories in this respect. The digital platforms will not only create new jobs in the sector that need high skills and high wages but also in the middle professions. Moreover, during the transition period (digital platform economy), it will be necessary to focus on traditional industries that will migrate from European countries due to technological progress and environmental legislation, to seek stability in Arab markets (e.g., the automotive industry). Another important influence of modern technology on labour markets is the division of tasks and actions into different places, which in the past were concentrated in one place. Carl Benedikt Frey and Michael A. Osborne (2017), "The Future of Employment: How Susceptible Are Jobs to Computerization?", University of Oxford Press, UK.

treatment methods, the quality of medicines and will include economic legal advice, which will result in the loss of millions of jobs in those vital sectors. In some Arab countries, hundreds of pilots are expected to be made redundant in the future after the introduction of self-propelled aircraft, especially as this will reduce the cost of air transport, thus increasing the preference for relying on technology and replacing human beings.[40]

The industry and agriculture sectors will be fully automated. This will include banking and financial services, including consultancy, investment guidance, sale and purchase of shares and securities through sophisticated programmes which control sales and purchases according to the conditions, performance and profitability of companies. Such developments will create economic and social problems that will necessarily change the nature of ownership and affect the relationship between employers and employees in terms of the nature of obligations and the basis of liability, proof and exemption. Although alternative jobs will exist (as we have already mentioned), these new jobs will not meet the bulk of the demand for jobs and will result in a greater focus on wealth and capital.[41]

In contrast, Ayman Al-Sheikh, Director of Digital Solutions at Red Hat Middle East and North Africa, believes that the overall shift in digitalisation will create new job opportunities over the next five years, especially in the banking and insurance sectors, after the education infrastructure has adapted to these changes. He also believes that the United Arab Emirates tops the spending on digitalisation infrastructure in the countries of the MENA region that is the Greater Middle East which includes Middle East, North Africa, Afghanistan and Pakistan, pointing to the various initiatives of government agencies with regard especially to the financial services and insurance. Demand for digital transformation and smart open infrastructure networks in the country is expected to increase over the next few years, with the most attractive sectors being banking, transport, financial services and telecommunications. Currently there are many transformations in the UAE[42] to complete the switch to smart services.[43]

---

40 Mohammed Al-Assoumi (2017), "Technology and Employment Opportunities", 5 October, available at: https://www.alittihad.ae/wejhatarticle/95900.

41 *Ibid.*

42 It is noted that in the United Arab Emirates alone there are more than 95% of the businesses that will be implemented using technology means and this is deemed to be an unprecedented rate in the said country. According to the results of the report by Accenture and SAB in 2016, the digital transformation of the UAE's GDP could increase to US$ 14 billion by 2020. Modern technology accelerates economic growth across Arab countries and helps create jobs. In 2011, these jobs provided revenues of $ 193 billion to boost the economy and 6 million new jobs. However, digitization differs depending on the stage of economic growth from one Arab country to another. The largest beneficiary of digitisation is the global export sectors, while other non-export sectors may lose local jobs due to digitization. During 2011, 377,772 new jobs were secured in Arab countries due to digitization. See: "The Future of Digitalization in the Middle East", available at: https://saneoualhadath.

43 "Digitalization Reduces Employment Opportunities in Insurance and Banks", available at: https://www.alroeya.com.

The question is whether bias[44] connected with high-skilled employees will continue to persist, accelerate, or potentially even reverse with the next set of emerging technologies over the coming decades?

As noted by economists Erik Brynjolfsson and Andrew McAfee[45] in the "Second Machine Age" the dependence on technologies will increase in favour of high-skilled employees. Since the 1980s, computers have been able to capture a large percentage of jobs that provide income for the middle classes, such as making books and works of a repetitive nature in factories. But works that need creativity, problem-solving skills and some technology support have developed and grown. Low-income workers, such as restaurant workers, guards and other jobs that are difficult for modern technology to do, are gaining popularity. All this led to the emptying of the middle class of its workers.

Daron Acemoglu holds another opinion. He assumes that the future direction of research towards automation and the creation of new tasks is endogenous and dynamic. Namely, he assumes that technology will be a powerful catalyst that will induce the weak worker to learn and the strong worker to increase his skill.[46]

In Daron's opinion, the spread of modern technology in Arab countries will encourage workers to develop their abilities to retain their jobs or have better job opportunities. Therefore, they will be keen on education and training to keep abreast of technological developments. It is thought that the real problem that could hinder education and technology training in Arab countries is finance. Consequently, there is a need to allocate resources to finance education and training in relation to modern technology through the following proposals

First, there must be a law that allocates part of the tax revenues in the Arab countries for education and training in connection with technology.[47]

Second, it is essential to allocate a government tax on all applications and documents submitted to any government service, and for these revenues to be directed to the financing of education and training in relation to modern technology.

Third, Arab parliaments should redraft laws on technology transfer, and oblige multinational corporations to make a real and effective commitment to training national manpower in accordance with the required needs. These corporations should be subject to the supervision of the host Arab state to ensure that training programmes are in line with national needs.

44 Erik Brynjolfsson and Andrew McAfee (2012), "Thriving in the Automated Economy", *The Futurist*, March–April, p. 27.
45 "Skill-biased technological change. Skill-biased technological change is a shift in the production technology that favours skilled (e.g., more educated, more capable, more experienced) labour over unskilled workers by increasing its relative productivity, hence its comparative demand" (Giovanni L.Violante, (2006), Skill-Biased Technological Change, New York University Press).
46 Daron Acemoglu and David Autor (2011), "Skills, Tasks and Technologies: Implications for Employment and Earnings", Chapter 12, *Handbook of Labour Economics*, Volume 4b, Elsevier B.V.; see also: "New Economy for the Middle East and North Africa, Middle East and North Africa MENA Economic Monitor", World Bank Group, October 2018, p. 56.
47 Mohammed Al-Assoumi, "Technology and Employment Opportunities", op. cit.

In the fourth place, it is necessary to amend laws to regulate the granting of incentives, bonuses and periodic allowances to workers according to the extent of commitment by the worker to the training courses imposed on him/her.

However, the disparity in the capabilities of each country will cause different living standards among these countries. The lion's share will not be for those countries that have natural resources (such as minerals and agriculture) but for the owners of software and modern technologies. The equation is therefore expected to change and there will be a reordering of the rich and poor countries, where many developing countries will have the opportunity to change their situation by focusing on education and research centers to develop software and digital techniques through curricula and innovations[48, 49].

According to the report issued by the World Intellectual Property Organization (WIPO), approximately half of the Arab countries on the list of innovative countries are seven countries from Asia: namely, Saudi Arabia, the United Arab Emirates, Qatar, Lebanon, Jordan, Kuwait and Yemen. It will be noted that four Arab countries are absent, namely Tunisia, Morocco, Egypt and Algeria.[50]

48 The word "innovation" is used to describe something new and unfamiliar. Adnan Farhan Al-Jawareen, "The Reality of Innovation and Technology in The Arab World", available at: https://www.academia.edu/9420316/THE_REALITY_OF_INNOVATION_AND_TECHN OLOGY_IN_THE_ARAB_WORLD.
    Access to scientific and technological knowledge and the ability to exploit it are becoming increasingly strategic and decisive for the economic performance of countries and regions in the competitive globalised economy. The 50 leading S&T countries have enjoyed much higher long-term economic growth than the other 130 countries of the rest of the world. Between 1986 and 1994 the average growth rate of this heterogeneous group of countries was around three times greater than that of the rest of the world. The average economic wealth per capita of these 50 countries has grown by 1.1% per year. On the other hand, the per capita income of the group of 130 countries that perform less well in education, science and technology has fallen over the same period by 1.5% per year. These trends prefigure a new division of the global economy, based on access to knowledge and the ability to exploit it" (OECD Statistics 1997: ix).
49 Carl Benedikt Frey and Michael A. Osborne (2017), op cit..
50 According to the report issued by International Organization of Intellectual Property in 2017 "Ranking of total (resident and abroad) IP filing activity by origin, 2017" Syria came in first place with 86 inventions and Egypt ranked second with 85, Morocco with 71, then the United Arab Emirates 50 and Saudi Arabia with 29. In 2015 Saudi Arabia was ranked first in the Arab world and 28th globally, with 364 patents in 2015, Kuwait ranked second in the Arab world and 44th globally, with a big difference with 64 patents in 2015 and 448 in all years. In Saudi Arabia, Aramco received 118 patents, the largest number obtained by an Arab company in one year. King Fahd University of Petroleum and Minerals received 91 patents, King Saud University 42 patents and King Abdelaziz City for Science and Technology 27 patents. In Kuwait, individuals received the largest share of patents with a score of 57 patents, while Kuwait University obtained four patents. In the UAE, individuals also received the largest share of patents with a score of ten patents, while Khalifa University for Science, Technology and Research received seven Patents. Saudi Arabia holds 66% of the patents in the Arab world. Saudi Arabia itself has acquired 7% of the patents in the Arab world in general and nearly 92% in patents registered in Arab universities in 2015, while the rest of the universities were only 8%. See: "World Intellectual Property Indicators 2018", Geneva: World Intellectual Property Organization.

In our view, taking advantage of the new technology data at present is no longer optional. Arab countries can compare its advantages and disadvantages, but it is an indispensable necessity for these countries to maintain their place on the global economic map. It is therefore a heavy burden on the Arab legislations, which should strive to review many of the legal texts governing the relationship between the employer and employee with the Fourth Industrial Revolution,[51] especially about the nature of mutual obligations between the parties, which must focus on the employer's commitment to training and development, a commitment required in good faith in the performance of the contract of employment. In other words, relying on technology does not mean layoffs, but developing workers' capabilities to deal with them and take advantage of their data. The worker is also committed to developing his abilities to suit the needs of the labour market. There is no doubt that such developments will be reflected in the concept of labour within the labour market in the Arab countries.

Technological innovation contributes significantly to major changes in economic activity, broadening competition, creating new industries and developing products. This requires flexible legislation that can absorb modern technology to achieve real development. Rigid and old regulations disrupt the process of innovation and long-term growth, leading to reduced quality and poor choice of goods and services, leading to higher costs and impeding the emergence of new industries.[52]

Inventions affect human development in different ways:[53] first, they increase the skills of workers and reduce poverty by increasing the capacity of science and

The careful reading of the reality of the Arab countries reveals that the figures in the international reports indicate the weakness of the culture that encourages innovation in Arab countries, but at the same time we should not underestimate the efforts of some Gulf countries in the last five years in relation to innovation and innovators through several encouraging strategies and operational steps.

However, technology and information experts believe that there is a lack of interest in Arab countries in inventions due to the following reasons:

1. Weak capacity and material resources as for innovators and scientific research, and this leads many of them to lose enthusiasm even if they have the qualifications to do so.
2. The absence of a structural legislation that facilitates the process of patent registration, which in some countries is a tragedy considering the obstacles.
3. Lack of innovators and ambitious youth in Arab countries due to the lack of support and encouragement by their governments and civil society.

51 The Fourth Industrial Revolution is the title launched by the World Economic Forum in Davos, Switzerland, in 2016, on the last episode of the series of industrial revolutions, which is currently under way. The previous three revolutions, which began in the late eighteenth century, made major changes to our lives, the evolution of primitive agricultural life, which lasted about ten thousand years, into a technology-based life at the individual and societal levels.
52 "The OECD Report on Regulatory Reform Synthesis", Organization for Economic Co-operation and Development Paris, 1997, p. 7.
53 Adnan Farhan Al-Jawareen, "The Reality OF Innovation and Technology in The Arab World", available at: https://www.academia.edu/9420316/THE_REALITY_OF_INNOVATION_AND_TECHNOLOGY_IN_THE_ARAB_WORLD.

technology programmes in public health, agriculture and energy use, ICTs and so on. Second, they increase productivity and raise the wages of workers. Third, technology indirectly affects the well-being of workers by increasing the production volume and increasing economic growth as productivity is boosted by increased labour output and improved service efficiency.

Part two: The legal future scenarios of job development and its relation to modern technology in Arab countries

There are numerous future scenarios in which Arab legal, economic and political studies seek to find effective solutions to the problems caused by technology in the Arab workplaces. The most important ones are:

1. insurance against the unemployment caused by technology, after it proved that the problem of unemployment is the most important and most serious and needs more attention by lawmakers in Arab countries;
2. establishing special conditions for unemployment insurance resulting from modern technology in the Arab States, because the unemployment resulting therefrom is not like any other. They need to be helped with education and training, and hence their access to insurance must be linked to their pursuit of training and qualification in order to be able to have an appropriate job;
3. knowing whether the concept of employment law is influenced by technological development (whether wide or narrow) that will determine the nature of appropriate legal treatment to deal with the problems of modern technology, whether by labour law mechanisms or other mechanisms.

Section one: The need for insurance protection against unemployment resulting from technology

It should be noted that there are two types of unemployment insurance: the first type is related to people who were employed and lost their jobs because of modern technology. The State in cooperation with social protection institutions needs to develop support programmes for these unemployed under certain conditions. This insurance is regulated by many Arab laws for all who lose their jobs in general. The second type is related to people who have never worked, and technology has delayed their employment. Governments will provide financial support to those who are waiting for a job during this transition period. What is paid here is not a salary but compensation, nor is it permanent but applied within a specified period and is conditional on the continuation of the person in search of work.

The social insurance versus unemployment resulting from technology plays a major role in reducing the negative effects of this unemployment, both on the unemployed and on his family and society. This imposes the need for special legislation regulating the Government's supervision of such insurance.

Despite the importance of this insurance in this sense, there are many financial and administrative obstacles to its success.

Financial considerations

Any insurance scheme seems ideal and logical. But one of the biggest obstacles is to provide financial resources to cover the needs of the participants. This difficulty sometimes deprives some groups of access to insurance due to a lack of resources (they are relatively stable and less vulnerable to unemployment) or to provide insurance services to all but with few benefits that make it useless.

It is expected that technology will increase the problem of unemployment and it is difficult to provide the necessary financial resources to encounter it.[54]

It is believed that this issue needs urgent and immediate consideration. Arab countries need to set upon unemployment insurance fund, financed through the payment by each five-year-old insured child of an annual or one-time payment as determined by actuaries and experts (the subscription in this insurance should be compulsory) and contributions by governments and trades unions.

The fund issues an insurance policy against the risks of modern technology. The money raised from periodic contributions must be invested in large projects that generate substantial profits. The profits resulting from these projects are allocated for anyone who loses his job due to technology or is unable to find a suitable job after the completion of his various educational stages and he will receive a salary suitable for living conditions. Participants' data should also be updated on a regular basis, and the beneficiaries of insurance services should be guided by the importance of education and training in modern technology so that they can find suitable jobs according to the needs of companies and institutions. There should be alternatives to jobs through which the worker can choose the job best suited to his or her circumstances.

It is thought that such measures would not only contribute to encountering the negative effects of unemployment but would also help many Arab countries achieve the desired development.[55]

Administrative and moral consideration

The problems of unemployment insurance arising from technology may not be solved solely by the collection of the necessary financial resources, but might be by addressing the administrative and ethical problems related to the collection of these funds, and the formulation of regulatory mechanisms to distribute them to the beneficiaries fairly and away from administrative corruption such as bribery and cronyism.[56]

---

54 Salah Ali Hassan (2013), "Unemployment Insurance in Law No. 135 of 2010 'Comparative Study'", New University House, p. 34.
55 Omar Helmy, "Unemployment Insurance Between Reality and Fiction", available at: https://almalnews.com.
56 "The US Unemployment Insurance, a Federal-State Partnership: Relevance for Reflections at the European Level", Policy Paper No. 129, May 2017.

In addition, there are many unethical practices in the field of unemployment insurance such as claiming benefits after returning to work or illegal work or submitting false or incorrect data to government agencies and not disclosing the real reason for leaving the job, or refusing a job without justification to receive the benefit. There are also many practices in some Arab countries, such as corruption, bribery and cronyism in relation to obtaining subsidies or accessing a suitable job.

It is necessary to establish accurate accounting systems governing the collection, investment and distribution of contributions. Such systems must be governed by transparency and disclosure, and the work of the insurance fund must be subject to the supervision of parliament and the judiciary, in a manner that ensures justice and equality and eliminates corruption. On the other hand, the right to complain must be activated for all those affected and quick and effective procedures should be put in place to investigate a complaint and respond to the demands of those affected.

Social protection must expand in the face of technology-related unemployment, not only to protect those who lose their jobs in the formal sector, but also to those in the informal sector who often cannot provide adequate resources for their retirement or job losses.[57] This problem is not new. A large percentage of workers who do not have insurance coverage in the "informal sector" in the Arab countries may find the non-contributory social assistance more important. Perhaps this is becoming increasingly important in some Arab countries such as Egypt, as energy and food subsidies have been reduced or eliminated. Consequently, the government has to take responsibility in this regard. Arab countries face real difficulties (e.g. Egypt, Tunisia and Sudan) due to the adherence by governments to traditional social protection programmes based on contributions, which are no longer fair or equitable. Moreover, the absence of the influential role of many trade unions has made the tragedy of vulnerable groups of workers more difficult. This shows the significance of adopting social protection policies in the Arab countries, which include a comprehensive package of programmes, benefits and services, which extend protection to all and ensure a minimum income benefit.[58]

Section two: Conditions of applying unemployment insurance to Arab countries

The application of unemployment insurance has witnessed many stages. The ILO has issued several international conventions that have attempted to develop the scope of this type of guarantee. International Convention No. 2 of 1919[59] on unemployment made the obligation on Member States under the provisions of the Convention on Unemployment Insurance, except in cases where it was impossible to apply in accordance with the circumstances of the Member State and cases of necessity.

---

57 "New Economy for the Middle East and North Africa, Middle East and North Africa MENA Economic Monitor", World Bank Group, October 2018, p.56.
58 *Ibid.*
59 C002 Unemployment Convention, 1919 (No. 2).

The social protection problem of unemployment at the international level has developed through International Convention No. 44 of 1934.[60] Article (2-1) of the convention stipulated that it should apply to every worker who receives a salary or wage. This general wording of the text implies a desire to extend the scope of the Convention to all employees, whether governmental or non-governmental, formal and informal. Nevertheless, Article (2-2), of the Convention ensured that Member States had the right to make exceptions to this expansion under their domestic law and listed some examples.[61]

It applies to all wage earners. This Convention does not specify any exceptions that deprive workers in public bodies and institutions of obtaining compensation or allowances in case of unemployment.

The Convention allows States to exclude certain categories from this provision in their national legislation, which are exceptions to the categories of extraordinary workers and may be impractical to apply the provisions of the Convention to them.

In a remarkable development, this agreement extended the scope of its application to include cases of partial unemployment where workers who are partially unemployed are entitled to unemployment compensation when their wages fall below the limit prescribed in their national legislation. It should be noted that the aforementioned provisions do not include a special provision for unemployment arising from the use of modern technology. It is worth mentioning that many Arab legislations (as in Egypt, Saudi Arabia and Kuwait) do not have special legislation that provides special guarantees to address the effects of unemployment resulting from technology, although many studies have confirmed that these countries are the most affected by the negative effects of technology.[62]

In Egypt, Article 17 of the constitution has regulated the right to pensions and health protection for the Egyptian citizen and it provides that "The State shall guarantee social and health insurance services. All citizens have the right to pensions in cases of incapacity, unemployment and old age in accordance with the law".

60 C044 Unemployment Convention, 1934 (No. 44).
61 Any member state may in its national laws or regulations make such exceptions as it deems necessary in respect of: (a) persons employed in domestic service; (b) homeworkers; (c) workers whose employment is of a permanent character in the service of the government, a local authority or a public utility undertaking; (d) non-manual workers whose earnings are considered by the competent authority to be sufficiently high for them to ensure their own protection against the risk of unemployment; (e) workers whose employment is of a seasonal character, if the season is normally of less than six months' duration and they are not ordinarily employed during the remainder of the year in other employment covered by this Convention; (f) young workers under a prescribed age; (g) workers who exceed a prescribed age and are in receipt of a retiring or old age pension; (h) persons engaged only occasionally or subsidiarity in employment covered by this Convention; (i) members of the employer's family; (j) exceptional classes of workers in whose cases there are special features which make it unnecessary or impracticable to apply to them the provisions of this Convention.
62 Salah Ali Hassan (2013), "Unemployment Insurance in Law No. 135 of 2010 'Comparative Study'", New University House, 2013, p. 42.

Egypt's social insurance system is one of the oldest in the world. It was founded in the mid-19th century by a decree of 1854 on civil pensions. The system was based on the collection of contributions, determining some benefits of the pension even for non-contributors to extend the scope of protection.[63]

It is noted that developments in various forms of social, economic and political life due to globalization, the provision of means of telecommunications and exchange of information, the opening of international markets and the abolition of exchange restrictions in the fields of trade, labour and the use of information technology in Egyptian workplaces have led to many results. All these factors influenced the determinants of economic planning and development, which in turn affected production and employment rates, wage levels and inflation rates. This has led to the need for an efficient social security system to strike a balance between the resources and obligations of the system to provide a decent life for the working class as the most important element of social stability.[64]

It should be stressed that Egyptian legislation, despite all the previous developments that have already affected many of the legal legislations in various countries of the world, did not keep up with it. In view of the draft law submitted by the Egyptian government in 2019, which has been approved by the Manpower Committee of the Egyptian Parliament, it is noted that this law is free from special rules to unemployment resulting from modern technology while Article 87 has itemised the general conditions for getting a pension as a result of unemployment, as follows.

In the first instance, the beneficiary must have been involved in social insurance for at least one year. Second, the participant will have the unemployment benefit for a maximum of 28 weeks, depending on the duration of his insurance contribution. Third, the insured shall not have resigned from service. Fourth, the insured's service shall not be terminated as a result of a final judgment in a felony or misdemeanor that violates honor, honesty or public morals, or if he

---

63 Egypt's legislation on social insurance has evolved since its application to the social insurance law promulgated by Law No. 79 of 1975, which defines the scope of application of the law by way of exclusion. Article 91 of this law stipulates that unemployment insurance shall be applied to workers subject to the Social Insurance Law in articles (2, 3) The following categories shall be excluded from unemployment insurance:

1. workers in the administrative body of the State and public bodies;
2. members of the family of the employer in the individual establishments up to the second degree and the partners who work in their companies;
3. employees who reach the age of 60 and may, by a decision of the President of the Republic, according to the terms and conditions of use of the categories referred to have the benefits of this insurance, provided that this decision shows the method of calculating wages for them;
4. workers in casual or temporary work, construction workers and seasonal workers and loading and discharge workers.

64 "New economy for the Middle East and North Africa, Middle East and North Africa MENA Economic Monitor", World Bank Group, October 2018, p. 57.

impersonates someone or provides false certificates or papers. Fifth, the insured must have participated in this insurance for at least one year, including the six months preceding each related failure. Sixth, the insured must have registered his name in the register of the unemployed in the competent manpower office and visited the manpower office in which his name is registered on the dates specified by a decision of the Minister of Manpower.

It appears from this provision that Egyptian law is still adhering to the benefit of the pension as a result of unemployment by having a contribution of at least one year[65] which would deny the benefit to many unemployed, especially workers in the informal sector. Also, a worker was not obliged to undergo proper training and to seek a suitable job opportunity as a condition for obtaining the pension. It seems to me that this law has not added anything new and will not contribute to solving the problem of unemployment caused by modern technology.

The position of the Egyptian law was slightly tempered by the fact that Article 92 provided for the suspension of unemployment compensation in two cases:

1) if the insured does not visit the Manpower Office in which his name is registered, and he is unemployed within the specified dates, unless with acceptable reasons.
2) if the insured refuses the training prescribed by the competent manpower office.

Article 91 also stipulates that the right to pay unemployment compensation shall be forfeited if the insured refuses a job the competent manpower office sees appropriate and shall be considered appropriate if the following conditions are met. (His wage is equivalent to at least 75% of the wage for which unemployment compensation is paid; the work must be in accordance with the insured's qualifications, experience and professional and physical abilities; the candidate's work should be in the same governorate where he was working at the time of his employment.)

In Saudi Arabia, a new law has been enacted known as "Sanad". It was aimed at providing more support to the Saudi worker and his family during the loss of his job for reasons beyond his control. The aim of this law is to provide a minimum wage that provides him and his family during the transition period between losing his job until being able to get another. In addition, it is vital to provide the necessary training and to assist him in the search for another job. Sanad applies to all Saudis provided they are no more than 59 years old.[66] This

---

65 According to the draft law, unemployment insurance is calculated as follows: 75% of the insurance subscription fee for the first four weeks; 65% of the insurance subscription fee for the second four weeks; 55% of the insurance subscription fee for the third four weeks; 45% for the remaining weeks. Also, the bill stipulates that the duration of the disbursement shall be 12 weeks (3 months) if the duration of the insurance subscription is less than 36 months, while it shall be 28 weeks (7 months) if the duration of the subscription exceeds 36 months.
66 The system was issued by Royal Decree No. (M/18) dated 12/3/1435 H. The system was implemented in the Kingdom as of 1/11/1435 AH for the establishments that follow the Hijri

system is for all Saudis who have lost their jobs, regardless of whether they work for the public or private sectors. This law did not require from the unemployed to receive the unemployment compensation proof that he has previously paid contributions to the insurance system. It is also mandatory and not optional. Although this law did not specifically address unemployment as a result of modern technology, it may include provisions that take into account the specific circumstances of such unemployment. Article (8) stipulates that the participant shall be entitled to the compensation contained in this Law on the following conditions: not having been dismissed from work due to a reason attributable to him; serious search for work; commitment to training specified by the Ministry and complying with the instructions and directives issued by the Ministry.

Any Saudi citizen can benefit from it if he has met the above conditions, especially if he left his job because of modern technology. Despite the advantages of the Sanad Act, many details have been missed in relation to the provision of social security for technology-related unemployment. The law did not adopt a clear vision on how to take into account unemployment due to technology or the appropriate mechanisms to provide social security services to those workers. Plus, the training courses offered to them were not adequately addressed in detail. This system only protects the Saudis and has not provided any form of protection for foreign workers, despite their abundance in Saudi Arabia, and there may be an urgent need for special protection to the unemployed due to technology.

In Kuwait, the unemployment Insurance Law is keen to regulate the terms and conditions of compensation for unemployment in general.[67] Namely, it comes free from special provisions dealing with the specificity of unemployment arising from modern technology.[68] Similar treatment should be provided to foreign workers, especially from the Gulf countries, where their number is large. Special legal provisions and access to training programmes are required after they lose their jobs due to modern technology.[69]

Some might think that talking about unemployment insurance in the Arab Gulf countries such as Saudi Arabia, the UAE and Kuwait, is strange. This is because they have strong economic indicators and provide tens of thousands of jobs every year to foreigners, so how is there unemployment!

In fact, these countries suffer from unemployment. This fact confirms the validity of my analysis of the impact of modern technology on labour markets in the Arab

---

calendar. As of 1/9/2014 M for establishments that follow the Gregorian calendar; available at: https://www.gosi.gov.sa/GOSIOnline/Unemployment_Insurance_%28SANED%29.

67 See: Kuwaiti Law on Unemployment Insurance, No. 101 of 2013; available at: http://gcc-legal.org/LawAsPDF.aspx?opt&country=1&LawID=4113.

68 Federal Law No. (7) of 1999 on the issuance of the Pension and Social Insurance Law and its amendments; available at: https://www.dxbpp.gov.ae/Law_Page.aspx?Law_ID=6368&Grand_ID=6368.

69 Dau-Schmidt, Kenneth G. (2015), "Labour Law: The Impact of New Information Technology on the Employment Relationship and the Relevance of the NLRA" Maurer Faculty, pp. 1589–1609; available at: http://www.repository.law.indiana.edu/facpub/1778.

countries. Many jobs now require technological qualifications that do not exist among nationals, so these countries seek to appoint qualified foreigners. This leads to increasing unemployment among nationals. In our view, the reasons for this situation are the weaknesses of employment policies and unemployment insurance, especially addressing the unemployment issue by more than one authority.

Furthermore, there is an urgent need to amend Arab legislation to address the risks of unemployment in general and unemployment resulting from technology in particular. Proposed suggestions include the following.

First, the need to establish a special fund to insure against unemployment resulting from technology, and that the savings are individual and mandatory contributions by employers, and that the workers also contribute between 3% and 9% of their salary.

Second, there should be an accurate plan for how to invest the funds collected from these contributions, to pay salaries to the unemployed, and to provide a decent life to them as well as to pay salaries to the unemployed non-participants while having priority in relation to the unemployed for a long period of time.

Third the adoption of decentralisation in the collection and disbursement of contributions to ensure the extension of social security to all regions in the country, and according to the circumstances of each case.

Fourth, adopting effective and realistic training plans to improve the capabilities of the unemployed in dealing with modern technology, according to each discipline.

Fifth, adopting strict rules to ensure transparency and disclosure in the work of the unemployment insurance fund, and for the government to have strict supervision in this regard.

Sixth, inventories must be strictly restricted, with the need for cooperation among all government agencies and organizations to determine their numbers and to give them social protection appropriate to the circumstances of each case.

Section three: The impact of modern technology on the concept of labour law

The jurists are keen to highlight the most important characteristics of work according to labour law as the work done by a person for the account of another person or a legal person under his authority and supervision for a wage.[70]

Egyptian labour Law[71] has defined the worker as "every natural person who works for a wage for the employer and is subject to his supervision and control". Also, the UAE Labour Law[72] has defined such workers as "Any male or female working for a wage of any kind in the service of the employer and under his

---

70 Dr. Ehab Eid, Lectures on The Work System and Social Insurance, available at: http://fac.ksu.edu.sa/sites/default/files/md_lml_w_ltmynt_ljtmy_yhb_.pdf.

71 Unified Egyptian Labour Law No. 12 of 2003, Official Gazette, Issue (bis), on April 7, 2003.

72 Federal Law No. (7) of 1999 on The Issuance of the Pension and Social Insurance Law and its amendments, available at: https://www.dxbpp.gov.ae/Law_Page.aspx?Law_ID=6368&Grand_ID=6368.

management or supervision, even if away from his eyes. Employees and users who serve the employer and who are subject to the provisions of this law, shall fall under this concept".

The Saudi labour law[73] issued by the Royal Decree No. 51 dated 23/8/1426) defines the worker as "a natural person working in the interests of an employer under his direction or supervision for a wage, even if he works away from his workplace". It is thought that these definitions will not undergo major changes in the respective countries' labour laws, except in connection with the master-servant relationship. The worker may be more proficient in technology than the employer, and this makes the worker somewhat independent in relation to carrying out the work required from him and is therefore not fully subject to the directions of the employer. In other words, the employer gives tasks to the worker experienced in technology and this worker carries out the tasks in his own manner.

Also, modern technology causes a lack of physical communication among workers, in a way that reduces their ability to negotiate and to represent their interests before the various trade unions. Moreover, the worker cannot communicate with the employer in the workplace to make a specific complaint regarding his job and the nature of his work, nor can he hold elections and form trade unions, and express his opinion with his colleagues about common matters in the workplace.

All these variables have revealed many shortcomings in Arab legislation, which require new and more appropriate provisions, especially to allow workers to communicate among themselves so that they may meet in the workplace and exercise their freedoms and claim their legitimate rights.

Section four: Training and rehabilitation for employment

Arab countries are aware of the significance of training in the use of modern technology so that they can benefit from it to improve the digital economy and to achieve economic and social development. At the same time, training helps to cope with the negative effects of the use of technology.[74]

Training in relation to modern technology – compared to other developments in the workplace– is characterised by continuity. This technology is evolving very quickly over short periods of time, which needs continuous and permanent training of workers.[75] On the other hand, training in modern technology is characterised by the fact that it is not aimed at educating the worker to do a new type of work but for the worker to do the same work that he was doing, but in a different way (using technological means). Thus, this training aims to

---

73 Saudi Labour Law Promulgated by Royal Decree No. (51/m), Issued by Royal Decree No. (24/m) dated 23/8/1426, as Amended by Royal Decree No. (24/m) dated 12/5/1434, and Amended by Royal Decree No. 46/m) and the date of 5/6/1436, available at: https://hrdf. org.sa/Content/files/labor_system.pdf.

74 International Labour Conference, 97th Session, 2008, Skills for Improving Productivity, Employment Growth and Development, Fifth Report, International Labour Office, Geneva.

75 *Ibid.*

address weaknesses that affected the performance of the worker, which is reflected in the gap between the traditional worker experience and knowledge on how to deal with technology and apply it in his work.[76]

Despite the importance of training in modern technology, there are many obstacles to the achieving its objectives in the Arab countries, as follows.[77]

First, the absence of a national strategy in many Arab countries (Egypt, Saudi Ariba, Tunisia) regarding training in modern technology.[78] And when it exists, it is often not evaluated, nor performance measured, and deviations are not corrected in a disciplined scientific manner.

Second, the weak contribution by the private sector in terms of partnership with education and training institutions or in terms of owning and managing modern technology education and training institutions: the overall burden is on most governments (for example: Egypt, Tunisia, and Libya) with limited funding capacity, and this leads to limited possibilities for technological training to achieve its objectives.

Third, the weakness of the scientific content provided in many training programs related to technology for workers. This is a serious issue, as these training programmes appear superficial and weak and do not provide real training to benefit the trainees.

Fourth, weakness of the abilities and training skills of the trainers, which means that the vocational and technical human capital in Arab countries is weak and unable to keep up with the technical developments. Training methods often rely on indoctrination without real understanding.

The above obstacles are accompanied with a set of challenges that make technology training more difficult to achieve its aims in the Arab countries. It is in the following detail:[79] first, the large number of people required to be trained in modern technology, especially in some countries with large housing and labor density (such as Egypt and Saudi Arabia). Second, the multiplicity and overlap of training programmes related to modern technology on the labour market. The challenge is not only the modernity of the training programme, but the real challenge is its suitability with the qualification requirements of the worker. Third, the need for adequate funding, since training in modern technology requires the provision of

76 The importance of Training Courses in Institutions, March 16, 2016; available at:https://euromatech-me.com.

77 Majid bin Mubarak bin Khalfan Al-Shuaili, "The Role of Vocational Training in Raising the Capabilities of Workers and Enabling Them to Compete on the Labour Market, (Modern Innovative Methodologies)", a Working Paper Submitted to the Executive Office of the Council of Ministers of Labour of the Gulf Cooperation Council States, Oman, 2016, p. 13.

78 "Arab Refractions: Citizens, Countries, Social Contracts, Carnegie Middle East Center", available at: https://carnegie-mec.org/2017/01/18/ar-pub-67650.

79 Mohammed Al-Jamni (2006), "The Use of Information and Communication Technology in Educational Institutions and Technical and Vocational Training, International Symposium on Teaching and Learning Development as for Technical and Vocational Education and Training Programs Using Information and Communication Technologies", UNESCO Offices in Beirut and Rabat, Tunisia, 20–22 November, p. 3.

modern equipment and programmes, and this will entail huge expense, especially in the field of development and maintenance.

It is important to note that the organisation of training in modern technology in Arab countries has not yet risen to the required level. Legislation, decisions and regulations have emerged in a general formulation that do not consider the specific difficulties and challenges of training in modern technology. In Egypt, the government has signed a cooperation protocol between the Ministry of Manpower and the Training and Rehabilitation Fund to finance vocational training centres in the different governorates and to train workers and qualify them for the internal and external labour market. The Minister stressed that the training centres affiliated to the Ministry need to develop and provide modern equipment and devices that contribute to progress in the process of vocational training and graduate trainees at a high level of skill and professionalism. He instructed the competent department in the ministry to develop its new proposals to create new ideas in training in order to remove obstacles of the training process and to develop mechanisms to implement development plans.[80]

Also released was the prime Minister's Decree No. (1543) of 2003 Concerning the Formation and Operation of the Board of Directors of the Training and Rehabilitation Fund, as amended by Decree No. (526) of 2011. Article 2 states that the Fund will finance the establishment, development and modernization of training centres and programs aimed at adapting to the needs of the labour market.

The Prime Minister's Decree No. 1543 of 2003 was issued on the formation and working system of the Board of Directors of the Training and Rehabilitation Fund, which was amended by Decree No. 526 of 2011. Article 2 states that the Fund shall finance the establishment, development and modernisation of training centres and programmes aimed at harmonising the needs of the domestic and external labour market and provides for the following:a) the drawing up of general policies to finance the establishment, development and modernisation of training centres and programmes in line with the needs of the local and foreign labour market; b) the setting of the conditions and rules governing the training process of the programmes, the duration of training, systems of tests, certification, graduation levels and teaching and training bodies; c) conducting research and studies, holding seminars and conferences and issuing relevant publications in order to promote

---

80 The minister said in a press release after the signing the protocol: "It aims at raising the efficiency of technical cadres of trainers, developing curricula, updating training programs and adding new curricula and characters required by the labour market, both internal and external, through different training system for whoever wishes to train to enable young people to acquire a craft or master the skill to obtain an opportunity on the labour market. The minister pointed out that the ministry will prepare a list of the priorities required to develop and modernise the training centres of the ministry and study the components and conditions of the selected training centres in terms of the infrastructure of these centres, especially the required equipment for the training process, the extent of effectiveness, as well as the cadres based on the training process, and the adequacy of their theoretical and practical experience on the implementation of programs offered by the Center." Available at: https://www.youm7.com.

human and material investment in all productive and service field; d) providing the necessary technical advice in support and development of vocational training and rehabilitation of the parties wishing to do so through the evaluation and preparation of feasibility studies required for them; e) participating in the support, development and financing of national projects in the field of vocational training and rehabilitation; f) coordinating with the authorities concerned in the development of plans to finance training and vocational training so as to optimise the use of available financial resources locally and internationally; g) encouraging all parties to develop their own resources to finance training through production training, organising exhibitions and relevant local and international markets.

However, the recommendation of the Law and Legislation Committee of the Egyptian State Council stated that: joint stock companies should pay 1% of their annual net profit for the benefit of the Training and Rehabilitation Fund of the Ministry of Manpower. This recommendation was issued pursuant to the provisions of the Egyptian Labour Law (Articles 133 and 134) No12 of 2003. This law stipulates that one of the resources of this fund should be 1% of the net profits of the enterprises if the number of their employees exceeds ten workers in addition to donations, and subsidies.[81]

In accordance with Article (76) of Egyptian Labour Law No 12 of 2003, "an employer may not derogate from the conditions agreed upon in the individual employment contract, the collective labour agreement, or assign a work to the employee other than what is agreed upon, unless necessary, to prevent an accident, to repair the consequences of such accident, or in the case of force majeure, provided that it is temporary and may assign a work to the employee which is not agreed upon, if not substantially different. In all cases, the rights of the worker shall not be prejudiced. However, the employer may train the worker and qualify him to perform different work with the technical development in the establishment."

Subject to the aforementioned text, it is noticeable that the Egyptian legislator adopts an advanced situation commensurate with modern technology in the labour market for two reasons: first, to prevent the employer from assigning the employee to do any acts not contained in the employee's employment contract, and therefore cannot assign the worker to perform works (technical or electronic) not agreed upon in the contract. Thus, for example, he cannot dismiss the worker simply because he is unable to do so if it is not agreed upon in the contract.

Second, that text has the effect of encouraging the employer to train the worker and qualify him to perform different work commensurate with the technical development. This means that the Egyptian legislator recognises the importance of rehabilitation to enhance the worker's abilities. The employer is responsible for training the worker even if the contract does not include explicit text to this effect.

It should be noted that Egyptian law has organised the training in general, and not provided for a special treatment to modern technology. It has not considered the importance of preparing a special programme for training, in connection with

81 Article (34) of Egyptian labour law No 12 of 2003.

technology requirements, whether from the view of curriculum or equipment. Also, this law has not presented a general strategy in technology training in the country as a whole and has ignored the huge number of Egyptian workers who need technology training to avoid layoff. Emphasizing the validity of this analysis, the technological qualification of Egyptian workers at present has not reached the required levels, although the law was issued in2003, and this confirms its ineffectiveness in achieving the optimum status of training in modern technology.

The position of the Saudi legislator is not much different from that of the Egyptian legislator. Chapters I and IV of the Saudi Labour Law contain several provisions regulating the training of workers in general, and not training related to modern technology. Article (42) stipulates that "every employer shall prepare his Saudi workers and improve their level of technical, administrative, professional and other works, in order to gradually replace them with non-Saudis and a register shall be prepared in which the names of the Saudi workers who have replaced the non-Saudis shall be written subject to the conditions and rules specified in the Regulations". Also, Article (43) stipulates that "...each employer with fifty or more workers shall qualify and train in his work his Saudi workers at least 12% of the total number of his workers annually. This percentage shall include Saudi workers who complete their studies if the employer bears the costs of studying." Furthermore, Article (44) stipulates that "the training programme shall include the rules and conditions followed in the training, its duration and hours, theoretical and practical training programs, the method of testing and the certificates granted in this regard. The Regulation shall specify the general standards and rules that should be followed in this regard in order to raise the level of performance of the worker in terms of skill and productivity".

There is no significant difference between the position of Saudi labour law and Kuwaiti labour law,[82] or UAE[83] or Tunisian labour law.[84]

It is very clear that the Saudi legislator did not take into account the special needs of training in modern technology, as the previous provisions were very general. It lacks any special provisions that consider the special treatment of what this technology requires.

According to some data released in this regard, Saudi Arabia intends to increase its interest in training in modern technology, and since 2017 it has allocated SAR 8 billion to develop the human resources sector and enable entrepreneurs and companies to improve the business sector in line with technological development. The Government seeks to discuss the relationship between human resource development and modern technology. Some experts expect redistribution of labour

---

82 Kuwait Labour Law No. (6) of 2010, available at:http://www.manpower.gov.kw/docs/LabourLow_Dir/2.pdf.

83 Law No. 27 of 1966 of 30 April Official Gazette No. 20 of 3, 6 May 1966, Tunisian Labour Magazine, 2018, Publications of the Official Press of the Republic of Tunisia, available at: http://www.legislation.tn/sites/default/files/codes/travailArabe.pdf.

84 Law No. 27 of 1966 of 30 April Official Gazette No. 20 of 3, 6 May 1966, Tunisian Labour Magazine, 2018, Publications of the Official Press of the Republic of Tunisia, available at: http://www.legislation.tn/sites/default/files/codes/travailArabe.pdf.

and increased demand for training, especially as all organisations must make pre-
parations to take advantage of human resources. Some experts said that the real
challenge is to adopt a clear strategy to cope with technological changes not only
in terms of employment, but everything related to the existence of comprehensive
and real shifts in all sectors in Saudi Arabia.[85]

It appears that Arab legislation has not paid enough attention to training in
modern technology, although this is one of the most needed solutions for Arab
countries at present. I also believe that this subject needs more urgent legal,

85 In the Kingdom of Bahrain: the Vocational Training Centre was established in 1975. The
Ministerial Decree No. 31 of 1979 on the regulation of conditions for the vocational training
of Bahraini workers in private sector establishments was issued. In 1991, the Bahrain Training
Institute was established. This is in addition to the establishment of training centres in major
industrial establishments such as: Alba, Arab Shipbuilding and Repair Company (ASRY), Gulf
Petrochemical Industries Company (GPIC) and others. Some of these centres have developed
and are providing training services to other companies and institutions. At the beginning of
2000, the foundation stone for the project for the development of emerging industries south
of Hadad (Industrial Incubators) was established. It is interested in embracing all entrepreneurs interested in establishing small industrial enterprises, in addition to incubators for
innovative entrepreneurs in technology.
   In the Kingdom of Saudi Arabia: Royal Decree No. M/30 of the year 1400 Hijri was issued
approving the establishment of the General Organization for Technical Education and Vocational Training to carry out the programmes of training and technical education in the Kingdom. The number of institutes and centres under its supervision in different regions of the
Kingdom (411) including 40 technical institutes, 101 technical training institutes, 270 technical training centres. Jubail Industrial College offers training programmes aimed at linking and
strengthening the link between training and basic and secondary industries in Jubail. Large
companies such as SABIC, the Human Resources Fund was established in 2001. It provides
financial support for employment programmes in private sector units. The Fund provides 50%
of the training and salary costs for the first two years. The Fund is one of the effective solutions
developed by the State to expand the private sector employment. The Fund relies on its revenues on bodies and donations, in addition to the annual fees added to the value of issuing
annual residence permits for foreign workers in the private sector. Data and institutions that
have benefited from the Fund's support in its first year include more than 60 organizations and
companies, except for the companies that have benefited from the national project for joint
training fund which contributes to the financing, and the evaluation and monitoring of the
training programme, which is estimated at about 36 companies, and succeeded in the Fund to
employ about 7,000 young men and women in its first year.
   In Oman, the Institute of Public Administration, which started its activities in 1977, was
established with the aim of raising the level of performance among Omani employees through
training programmes and conducting research, advising the administrative units in administrative areas,) and began its activity in 1984, with the aim of preparing a skilled and skilled
manpower to meet the needs of the comprehensive development of the Sultanate of Oman. It
also provides training opportunities for citizens who wish to gain a new profession or upgrade
their skills and rehabilitation of national manpower in the public and private sectors to raise
their efficiency in the field of labour. The technical college was established in Salalah, which
started its activities in 1993, in addition to the establishment of a technical college in Ibra, in
order to prepare and qualify Omani specialised cadres. See also: "Human Resources Technology Summit Opportunity for Development", Al Eqtisadi, UAE, 12 October 2017, available
at: https://aliqtisadi.com.

economic and social studies to identify obstacles to training in modern technology and propose appropriate mechanisms to solve them. I suggest some proposals for training in modern technology.[86]

First, planning and preparation for training connected with modern technology modern technology, with its ability to collect and store data, has contributed to planning for training, identifying training needs and proposing appropriate training programmes through:

1. *Measuring technology needs:* providing the required information on identifying and analysing the strengths, weaknesses, opportunities and challenges with respect to the needs of companies and institutions of labour trained in technology, and in the light of which the objectives, guidance and policies are identified.
2. *Planning for the needs of technically trained workers:* the planning process allows the identification of the required training technology programmes accurately and realistically. Besides, there are some electronic statistical programmes that help to achieve this (such as *SPSS* and *PARYS*),which allows the identification of training programmes appropriate to the reality of the Arab labour market.
3. *Selecting implementation method:* this step is of great importance because many training programmes in Arab countries are formulated in an ideal way, but their implementation is disappointing. It is therefore very significant to establish precise mechanisms for the implementation of the planned plans, and to have strict control over this implementation to ensure that it achieves its objectives. It should be noted that there are many ways in which modern technology training can be carried out. For example, training can be done remotely, through a television lesson, video or software programme. Distance training is easy and simple because it does not require the presence of the person to be trained in the place of training, and this method is characterised by low costs, especially if the training is distributed to many trainees through an internal network. It should be considered that training programmmes are designed with varying degrees, considering the relative disparity in the level of qualification of workers. Training can also be done at home outside working hours. This easy method also helps to continuously train them as to all new developments in the field of modern technology. It appears that there is a need to review the training programmes on modern technology in the Arab countries and I recommend the Arab governments to accelerate the adoption of a general strategy in training as to this technology at the level of the entire country and not in a particular sector. All ministries and agencies are obliged to cooperate to implement this strategy. I believe that Arab universities and research centres can contribute a great deal in this field,

---

86 "The Impact of The Use of Information Technology on The Performance of Human Resources – A Field Study on the Australian Feminist Academy" (no publisher mentioned, 2002, p. 75).

especially to design training programmes for technology according to the latest international standards. This step is important not only to train workers well, but also to gain community confidence in the feasibility of these training programmes. In the Gulf countries, technology-intensive production policy can be adopted, as opposed to labour intensive ones in other countries. It also aims to strengthen Arab cooperation to provide more employment opportunities and take appropriate measures to facilitate the orderly mobility of Arab labour and to give priority to aspects and considerations related to identity and culture, to avoid any negative consequences that may result from the expansion of the employment of foreign workers. Second, evaluating the training as to modern technology: special methods should be designed to assess workers' access to modern technology training programmes in accordance with approved international standards, and to identify strengths and weaknesses in worker qualification. This should be done continuously throughout the training period and not just at the end. It should also assess the benefit of the worker and his ability to apply the practical training he received, and not only the theoretical benefit, especially since modern technology may include some complex processes, which require the worker to be well trained. Ensuring that evaluation methods are free from corruption and cronyism to ensure that the worker has received the required qualification.

It seems that there is a need to prepare periodic reports on the activity of training centres and the extent of follow-up with the competent institutions and bodies to identify the number of trainees and the needs of employers for training in modern technology, which may need to establish a central database for the registration of trainees data and data of sub-training centres and certification of trainees as well as the issuance of statistical report.[87]

Conclusion

This chapter clearly demonstrates the great challenge facing Arab countries after the recent widespread dependence on technology in most institutions, companies and even small workplaces. This challenge is reflected in the fact that there is a great opportunity to take advantage of this technology in the development and improvement of production and the provision of different services, as well as avoiding the negative effects, especially the rise in unemployment rate that the majority of Arab countries suffered from, which is expected to be aggravated by this technology. This negative effect will definitely prevent Arab countries achieving desirable outcomes.

This chapter shows that there is an urgent need to review many policies on labour relations, as an important pillar to improve the best rates of production, and thus achieve the economic development, which all Arab countries have

87 *Ibid.* p. 75.

been striving for. Laws that regulate labour relations do not keep many of their rules in line with the requirements of modern technology, especially in the relationship of dependency between the worker and the employer after some studies pointed to a change in the concept of labour law on the impact of modern technology. The latter has also posed some challenges to unemployment, which are expected to have multiple negative effects in Arab countries due to the unemployment in these countries by the emergence of technology and the inability of the Arab legislations to face them effectively. Therefore, technology is expected to make it more difficult because many workers in different sectors are less able to deal with it, so many of them may be laid off. There is also a problem related to social security legislation, which failed in many Arab countries to provide the right treatment for the unemployed, both in terms of giving him an unemployment salary that provides for a decent life, and in terms of providing suitable and effective training opportunities that qualify him to join the labour market.

The chapter also shows that the legislation in the Arab Gulf Countries does not provide special treatment for foreign workers in the case of unemployment resulting from modern technology, especially that there are so many foreigners of different nationalities in large numbers, and therefore it is expected that they will be adversely affected by modern technology. Legislation in the Arab Gulf Countries should therefore have given exceptional treatment to foreign labour working in such countries by making available specialist training programmes in the area of information technology to adapt to the new working conditions as well as giving them unemployment security, especially as their dismissal would be severely detrimental.for them.

In addition to all the above, Arab legislation does not provide the appropriate mechanisms to train workers in modern technology. The legal provisions in this regard have been weak and insufficient to meet this serious challenge, which depends largely on the success of these countries in taking advantage of modern technology to achieve the desired development.

Recommendations

This chapter concludes with several recommendations, the most important of which are as follows:

First, conducting the desired reform of Arab labour markets within national strategies, involving all parties to the production process, aimed at accessing modern technology by all business sectors with regard to the training of workers to deal with this technology as a top priority, and equality among all workers to benefit from it, especially women and the disabled.

Second, modernizing labour relations to accommodate the growth and development of modern technology, and the need to update Arab legislation and labour standards in a manner commensurate with the aim of achieving sustainable development.

Third, activating the legislations that called for employing persons with disabilities in different workplaces and allowing them to benefit from the data of modern technology, especially as they may not need a great physical effort to deal with them.

Fourth, institutions must develop innovative ways to manage human resources and measure their capabilities with dealing with modern technology, and adapt to these rapid developments with modern technology.

Fifth, emphasizing that the shift to technology in the business sector does not mean relying on technology and marginalizing the role of the human element, rather focusing on individuals, innovation and investing in talent, caring for talented people and supporting them; especially since technology is expected to create new jobs.

Sixth, there is a need for the Arab governments to provide the appropriate financial support to deliver social security for the unemployed because of modern technology.

Seventh, Arab labour laws must ensure that there is a balance between the legal rights and responsibilities of the employer and the workers so as to ensure that the employer is committed to providing the worker with appropriate training in modern technology, while obliging the worker to undergo the required training on time, otherwise he will be denied social security. Such provisions shall be enshrined so that the parties may not agree to breach them in their employment contract.

Eighth, all educational institutions in the Arab countries should provide students with some form of qualification on modern technology in various ways to enhance their abilities and capabilities to work.

Lastly, a minimum unemployment allowance due to modern technology must be guaranteed to provide the unemployed with a decent life, with some incentives that can motivate them to develop their own abilities to suit technological development.

5   Impacts of social networks in the employment environment – from the traditional subjects to the particular case of employment non-compete clauses

Duarte Abrunhosa e Sousa[1]

Introduction[2]

At present we live in a society undergoing profound change. Indeed, contrary to past generations, today's society is able to pass through faster variations in daily life. It is thus important to know the causes of these rapid changes.

One of the major factors to point out is the agile way in which information is transmitted. Indeed, nowadays it is possible to share positive or negative news with a large number of people in only a few minutes. The example of terrorist attacks in *Bataclan*[3] is a relevant example because the news was shared worldwide while the incident was still happening. In this manner we receive information that sometimes could be occurring at the precise moment that we perceive it.

But, can we be certain that this evolution was expected?

During the course of history, there were always people who dreamed of the distant future. Some of these "dreamers" were able to share their expectations through different methods, such as literature, painting or cinema. Jules Verne, for example, was able to imagine with some competence submarines, airplanes or travels to the moon. However, in these imagined modern societies it was never suggested that in 2018 the world was going to be dominated by a concept known as "social networks".[4]

---

1 Lawyer. PhD candidate at the University of Santiago de Compostela. Member of the Executive Committee of CIELO Laboral network. Founding member of Young Labour Lawyers Association (AJJ). Member of the Portuguese Labour Law Association (APODIT) and European Employment Lawyers Association (EELA). Member of COMPASS's Committee of Experts.

2 This chapter is one of many results of the National Research Project carried out by MINECO (Spain), entitled 'New (newest) information and communication technologies and their impact on the labour market: emerging aspects at the national and international levels' (DER2016-75376-R), led by Prof. Lourdes Mella Méndez.

3 The author is referring to the terrorist attacks that happened on 12th November 2015 in Paris.

4 Just think about the 2019 world imagined in *Blade Runner* (Ridley Scott, 1982), or the inspiring book *Do Androids Dream of Electric Sheep?* (Philip K. Dick, 1968) or the *Back to the Future* original movie (Robert Zemekis, 1989), which considered likely the existence of flying cars in 2015. In all examples the idea of a social network was not suggested.

As much as we thought about today's society 20 years ago, we could never have imagined the revolution that social networks would generate in our lives. The space of dialogue between people and groups is still very important, but now it's not always accomplished personally. Social networks occupy the place that belonged to public spaces.

For the dissemination of social networks, the common access to these platforms through mobile instruments, such as smartphones, tablets or portable computers, was crucial. This means that to use a social network people only need to have access to the internet, regardless of where they are. So, social networks can be followed by everyone at any time.

In this society where the exchange of information is always faster, social networks have a key role in this mutation. The velocity that some information is shared could be directly connected with the number of shares on platforms such as LinkedIn, Twitter or Facebook. On the other hand, it is important to realise that media use social networks to share their news. Paper versions of newspapers are being replaced by others in online formats directly connected to posts or tweets. This fact shows that social networks are recognised as a powerful way to reach a larger number of recipients. Therefore, social media stimulate the sharing of news through social networks. Moreover, the challenge is even bigger if we take into account that sometimes news has its origin in shares made directly by people in their social network profiles.

With these societies in constant change, it is expected that social networks will grow their influence further afield rather than the opposite. For this reason, it's important to know how to deal with social networks because they are here to stay. In fact, it's no longer just an asset of the youngest generation, but also of the older generation. This way, the use of social networks is transversal to all society's generations and activity sectors.

Global perspectives on social networks and work

The traditional overview of the impact of social networks in employment is usually linked to their use by an employer to dismiss a worker. It's common to debate nationally if a worker's post on Facebook, for example, could be the motive for a dismissal for due cause. So, two key points are usually argued when debating these cases in court: i) the right to freedom of speech, and ii) the right to privacy in this environment. This is the main subject of social networks in an employment context in Portugal.

Additionally, social networks can shed light on workers' behaviour during sick leave and stimulate the end of any payment from social security or an insurance company. Once again, the right to privacy is one of the major aspects in discussion.

So, most case law is directly connected with this context of employment disputes. This way, the court's decisions on these subjects are very helpful to explore new themes related to the impact of social networks in a work environment like the breach of covenants not to compete.

Competition law

The economic activity in societies that allows the principle of free enterprise accepts the existence of competition between companies. Competition between economic agents is desirable when it is not the result of an unlawful act. As the Portuguese Supreme Court has decided, the act of competition is the one that, in the development of an economic activity, is able to cause damage to another economic agent, such as the diverting of customers to the benefit of a competitor.[5] This means the act of competition is lawful if it aims to change the behaviour of customers of an industry.

What is often forbidden is the practice of unfair competition. As pointed out by Nuno Sousa e Silva, unfair competition between economic agents needs to accomplish three requirements: i) the practice of an act of competition; ii) the act must be practiced with deceit; and iii) the act is contrary to honest rules and habits of the economic activity. So, only acts in respect of those principles are undesirable.[6]

However, sometimes it's difficult to understand the boundaries between a fair or an unfair act of competition. Consequently, Competition Law is growing faster not only as an autonomous discipline, but also in the European Court of Justice and national courts across Europe.[7]

Furthermore, it is important to take into account the fact that from a legislative policy point of view, the excess of restrictive regulation can damage the principle of free enterprise, while the absence of regulation can leave the weakest economic agents unprotected. This way, in the war between economic agents for their position in the market, all the means are important to fulfil the same goal. Therefore, it is vital to question if the rules of competition can have an impact in the employment relations.

Covenants not to compete in employment relations

Non-compete rules during an employment relationship

There is no doubt that during the employment contracts, workers are bound not to compete against their employer. This obligation is an expression of workers' duty of loyalty. For example, according to article 128 of the Portuguese Labour

---

5 Cfr. Decision of the Portuguese Supreme Court (26th September 2013), case number 6742/ 1999.L1. S2, consulted in www.dgsi.pt.

6 Cfr. *Trabalho e segredos de negócios: pode um (ex)-trabalhador ser proibido de trabalhar*, Questões Laborais, 47, 2015, Coimbra Editora, p. 237. Portuguese Competition Authority exemplify in their web page that the unfair act of competition could be the creation of confusion about the company, goods or services of a competitor or the false statements with the purpose to discredit competitors (cfr. http://www.concorrencia.pt/vPT/A_AdC/FAQs/Paginas/ FAQs-Praticas-Proibidas.aspx, consulted on 18 October 2016).

7 There are some very important cases with media coverage where competition law was in the spotlight, like the attempt of a takeover of PT by SONAE or the sponsorship contracts of football teams with telecommunication companies.

Code, duty of loyalty comprises not only the obligation not to make deals in competition against the employer, but also the prohibition of sharing information about the employer's organisation, production method or business.

In this context, when establishing a general prohibition of workers' competition against an employer during the employment contracts, the above-mentioned article of the Portuguese Labour Code imposes an obvious exclusivity clause regarding the company's industry. This way, duty of loyalty does not allow workers to work for their employer's competitors. For this purpose, the nature of the contract concluded between the worker and employer's competitor is irrelevant, since it could be exercised by different kinds of contracts.[8] All that matters is that workers do not perform any act of competition against their employer. Thus, having an exclusivity clause in an employment contract adds very little to article 128 of the Portuguese Labour Code.[9]

Thereby, it's possible to defend that workers are not forbidden to work for another employer if the activity is not in direct competition. Nevertheless, an employer could try to impose an exclusivity contractual clause that forbids workers from working in any industry. The enforceability of such a clause will depend on the application of principles of adequacy and proportionality.

At this point, we are able to conclude that the prohibition of a worker's competition against their employer is a key element regarding an employment relationship. In general, it results *ope legis* that workers can only exercise an activity in competition with their employer's express consent. On the other hand, the existence of an exclusivity clause is not essential for an employer to demand damages against their workers or to promote disciplinary action, because the Portuguese Labour Code already protects these interests.

So, if workers' competition against an employer during an ongoing employment relation is duly included in Portuguese and other legal frameworks, things could be different regarding the period after the employment termination.

Non-compete rules after the employment termination

The biggest problems related to workers' duty not to compete against their employer only arise after the termination of the employment contract. In fact, the use of these clauses with post-contractual effects could endanger the workers' right to work, because they are bound not to compete against a former employer after employment termination. So, they could not work for any competitor company or start a new business in direct competition with the former employer.

8 We strongly believe that this competition can be exercised by a worker through any kind of contract, such as employment contract, service agreement, or agency contract, among others agreed with a competitor company.

9 About this subject, the Portuguese Supreme Court decided that when the obligation of exclusivity results from a contractual clause that limit this restriction only to activities in competition against the employer, it doesn't have any autonomy because this issue is already regulated by the Portuguese Labour Code (cfr. Decision of the Portuguese Supreme Court (10th December 2009), case number 09S065, consulted in www.dgsi.pt).

In general, European legal frameworks accept the enforceability of agreements that limit the ability of workers to be hired by a former employer's competitor.[10] In turn, the USA deals with different frameworks. In some states, the use of non-compete clauses is tolerated, but in three states they are unlawful. The most relevant example of a prohibitive state is California where this restriction is considered the engine of the economy.[11]

In relation to Portugal, covenants not to compete are regulated in the Labour Code's article 136. So, in order to be lawful, a post-contractual clause not to compete must fulfil the following requirements: i) agreement should be in writing; ii) the worker's activity in competition should be able to cause damages to the employer; and iii) the worker must be financially compensated during the pending restriction but this can be reduced if the employer invested heavily in his professional training. The agreement can be concluded in the employment contract, during the contract, in the termination agreement or at a subsequent date.[12] The agreement duration is limited to two years. However, if a worker's position depends

---

10 There are different solutions in the EU member states, but almost all accept these clauses or agreements. There was some resistance in the Baltic countries on using non-competition clauses due to the influence of USSR law (in Russia, they are unlawful). However, courts used the civil law rules to turn these agreements lawful. This way, Baltic countries' labour reforms are starting to accept non-compete agreement. On the other hand, in 2015, Denmark also dwelt on this subject and decided to limit the access of clauses not to compete. Finally, even Norway (a non-EU member) reformed the rules of non-competition agreements by limiting them.

11 This position of California state is even more relevant if we take into account that some of the most important companies in the IT sector are located in the region of Silicon Valley (Adobe Systems, Apple, Cisco Systems, Ebay, Facebook, Google, Intel, Netflix, Yahoo!, among others). For a more developed approach of this subject: Hyde, Alan, and Menegatti, Emanuelle (2013), "Legal protection for employee mobility (draft)", available at: https://portal.upf.edu/documents/3298481/3410076/2013-LLRNConf_HydexMenegatti.pdf/5a45954c-3569-4c3a-a7c5-8a617f710f7c; Hyde, Alan (1998), "The Wealth of the shared information: Silicon Valley's High-Velocity Labor Market, endogenous economic growth, and the law of trade secrets", available at: http://andromeda.rutgers.edu/~hyde/; Hyde, Alan (2013), *Working in Silicon Valley: Economic and Legal Analysis of a High-Velocity Labor*, 1st Edition, Routledge, UK; Saxenian, Annalee (1996), *Regional Advantage: Culture and Competition in Silicon Valley and Route 128*, Harvard University Press; Gibson, Ronald J., (1999) "The legal infrastructures of high technology industrial districts: Silicon Valley, Route 128, and covenants not to compete", *New York University Law Review*, Volume 74, number 3, USA, pp. 575–629. The author's position on this subject is already shared in (2017), *Pactos de não concorrência laborais como instrumento de (des)incentivo da economia – o case study da Califórnia*, Los actuales cambios sociales y laborales: nuevos retos para el mundo del trabajo. IV, Cambios en la relación laboral individual y nuevos retos para el contrato de trabajo, Peter Lang, Switzerland, pp. 295–317.

12 Joana Vasconcelos defended that the Portuguese lawmaker solution in article 136 solved the interpretation problems of the previous Labour Code, because now there is no doubt that a non-competition agreement can be signed in the employment contract or in a termination agreement [, Código do Trabalho Anotado, 9.ª Edição, Almedina, Portugal pp. 351–352]. On the other hand, we can have some doubts if a non-competition agreement put into contract after the contract's termination has employment effects.

on a particular reliance on or access to important information, the agreement's limitation can reach three years.

As we can see, for the Portuguese legal framework, non-compete clauses do not depend on the complexity of a worker's position. The requirement is that the worker's activity in competition can cause damage to the former employer. Only for this reason the extension to three years stated by article 136 of the Portuguese Labour Code makes sense. Therefore, we can ask the relevancy of this framework when the Portuguese Constitution protects freedom of professional choice and the right to work in articles 47 and 48. Still, the Portuguese Constitutional Court has already decided on this matter stating that, in an abstract overview, covenants not to compete respect the Portuguese Constitution.[13] The Court underlined the importance of balance between workers' right to work restrictions and some employers' protected interests, such as avoiding that a competitor could use confidential information shared by a former worker.[14]

What we must do here is to highlight that when a worker builds a career in one determined field, he expects to be able to find new job opportunities relying on that experience. Acquired professional skills are a major asset for any worker in a job application. This way, it's not difficult to admit that competitor companies will seek the same candidates. Also, workers' experience developed with a competitor is always desirable for a new employer. However, this interest could not be totally connected with any particular knowledge about the competitor, but only because experience in any particular industry is very well appreciated.

So, we can conclude that the simple fact of starting a new professional relationship with a former employer's competitor is not enough to provide damages.[15] Therefore, it's important to have some caution in the interpretation of the concept of a competitor's business and damages for this purpose. If we take into account the values that we must conciliate, this subject is very sensitive. Yet, we cannot forget that it's perfectly legitimate for a worker to wish to use his experience to seek better working conditions. So, the restriction of the right to work is only acceptable in proportionality with the former employer's protected interests.

Finally, it's important to point out that even if a worker didn't sign any non-competition agreement he could cause damages to a former employer with the acquired knowledge. However, in these cases, the former employer can ask for damages through different fields of law, such as civil, corporate or criminal law.[16]

---

13 Cfr. Portuguese Constitutional Case number 256/2004 (14th April 2004), available at: www.tribunalconstitucional.pt.

14 For a bigger development of the Portuguese Constitutional Court case, please see Martins, João Zenha (2007), "Pactos de não concorrência com projeção laboral: Anotação ao Acórdão do Tribunal Constitucional nº 256/04", Jurisprudência Constitucional, n.º 9, Coimbra Editora.

15 For a development of the Spanish reality, please consult Lourdes Mella Méndez, *La responsabidad indemnizatória del trabajador durante la vigência del contrato de trabajo*, La Ley/Wolters Kluwer, Spain, with the particular theme on worker's liability from p. 256.

16 Portuguese Criminal and Intellectual Property Codes protects confidential information.

Danish case

At this stage, in order to study the impact of social networks in a non-competition agreement, we must start with the analysis of a pioneer Danish case decided by the Western High Court on 16th December 2014. So, let's revisit the case's facts for a better understanding:[17] 1) Two workers ended their employment contracts with the same employer with the goal of starting a new employment relationship with a competitor. 2) The workers were bound to a non-competition agreement, therefore they settled with their new employer that the contract would only start after the agreement's termination. 3) While they were bound to the non-compete clause, both workers updated their profiles on LinkedIn with information identifying a new employer and a link to the company's web page. 4) Because LinkedIn doesn't have any function dedicated to future employers, it seemed in both workers' profiles that they were already working for the new employer. 5) The workers' former employer demanded damages in court claiming the breach of the agreement.

The court of the first instance[18] decided that the update of a profile in LinkedIn was a breach of the covenant not to compete. This decision was supported by the fact that this social network aims to promote professional contacts. For this reason, according to this court, when both workers shared their new employer, they benefitted from that company's commercial interests. So, it was considered that the workers' behaviour was unlawful and breached the agreement not to compete.

Nevertheless, after an appeal, the Western High Court decided in a different way. According to the decision of the appeal, updating LinkedIn is not a direct or indirect act of work for the new employer. In the decision it was taken into account the following facts: i) even though these workers had a large number of contacts on LinkedIn, they worked in brokerage and financial markets, so, for this industry, personal relationships were irrelevant; and ii) the former employer did not assure his position by a written clause in both workers' non-competition agreements regulating the use of social networks.

For these reasons, the workers were absolved of charge and did not have to pay any damages to their former employer.

The role of social networks

The Danish Western High Court did not give special value to the impact regarding the update of profiles by both workers on LinkedIn. One of the major arguments was that in brokerage and financial markets personal contact is irrelevant.

---

17 Even though the author had access to the original version of the case's ruling, due to difficulties in translation from the Danish language, it was decided to describe this case with the help of the text prepared by Tina Reissmann (2015), *Updating LinkedIn profiles and non-competition clauses*, available at: http://www.internationallawoffice.com/Newsletters/Employment-Benefits/Denmark/Plesner/Updating-LinkedIn-profiles-and-non-compete-clauses.

18 The first court decision was made by the District Court of Aarhus.

Consequently, the court probably admits that in some industries the update of LinkedIn can be relevant and a source of workers' liability for damages.

LinkedIn is a social network that self-proclaims to be the biggest professional network with 400 million users in 200 different countries.[19] The mission of LinkedIn is to encourage online professional contacts and to make them more productive. In fact, through a simple search for a person on Google, most of the time the first line is occupied by their professional profile on LinkedIn. Contrary to Facebook, LinkedIn is a social network that aims to boost all their users' professional skills. So, there are a lot of complaints about some "unprofessional" interventions or shares made by users. The reason for these complaints is in the aim to avoid that LinkedIn becomes a kind of Facebook. Therefore, LinkedIn is an exclusively professional network.

Facebook has very different characteristics and is far more extensive than LinkedIn. Thus, Facebook started the first quarter 2018 with more than 2 billion active users.[20] On this social network we can find people with different usages of the platform's potential. While some use Facebook for leisure and contacting friends and family, others use it for professional purposes. If we take into account that this social network encompasses more users with different motivations, sometimes it's difficult to recognise the true purpose of some specific use. Still, Facebook can have a huge professional impact in some contexts, such as the following: 1) dissemination or advertising of a professional activity that already exists outside the network;[21] 2) personal marketing of a professional with the aim of gaining reputation among his contacts; 3) development of an economic activity directly through Facebook; 4) service agreement with other agents that wish to use Facebook for any of the above-mentioned professional purposes.

This way, even though it is not considered as a professional network, Facebook allows the development of commercial or professional activities. We may also add that the fact of having more users with a great variety of interests is an advantage when compared to LinkedIn.

Recently, Instagram has become a fast-growing social network. In 2015 it reached 400 million users[22] and is very well implemented by the younger generations. This social network is boosted by the share of photos with special effects and short messages. However, we can still use this platform for leisure or professional purposes. For example, Coca-Cola has 1.1 million Instagram followers,[23] while McDonalds has a total of 1.2 million.[24] Nevertheless, in some industries, Instagram can have a similar size as Facebook because it has got a big visual impact and it is

19 Information available on the LinkedIn webpage at https://www.linkedin.com/about-us? trk=uno-reg-guest-home-about (last consultation on 20th October 2016).
20 Data available at https://www.statista.com/statistics/346167/facebook-global-dau/.
21 Facebook stimulates this activity by selling the advertising of pages or information to whoever wants to reach a wider public than his contacts.
22 Numbers presented by Instagram on https://www.instagram.com/press/ (last consultation on 7th March 2016).
23 Cfr. https://www.instagram.com/cocacola/ (last consultation on 7th March 2016).
24 Cfr. https://www.instagram.com/mcdonalds/(last consultation on 7th March 2016).

growing with younger generations. In addition, both Instagram and Facebook have a great interaction that helps their operation.

Finally, it's important to mention Twitter. Although it is not used much in some countries like Portugal, this social network has 332 million active users all over the world. Twitter is based on the share of information through tweets. These tweets have a maximum size of 280 characters. So, the information shared is very short and limited. In fact, the first idea was to create a social network with a concept similar to text messaging in cell phones. Presently, Twitter has a strong implementation in the academic world and with the dissemination of news by social media. In the USA, Twitter is also used by people with or without notoriety for sharing ideas.

Social networks do not treat anyone differently. While receiving his *honoris causa* PhD at the University of Turin, Umberto Eco said in his speech that social networks were giving voice to a legion of fools, because any user could have the same impact on public opinion as a Nobel Prize winner.[25] So, the key role of social networks in our society is notorious. Even though we share the opinion of Umberto Eco regarding the size of the legion of fools that benefit from the use of social networks, it is important to point out that his words show a vital evidence for our study: social networks give a stage to common people that once was given to Nobel Prize winners. The reach of an update, post or tweet doesn't have any borders.

So, we strongly believe that currently social networks are not irrelevant in our society. Every time we need to understand the different phenomena that occur in society, we cannot only evaluate social networks as a simple tool for leisure.

Commentary on the Danish case solution

At this point, it is fundamental to make an approach to the Danish case decision when applied to the facts.

First of all, we consider that the Western High Court decided well when it tried to create a causal link between the influence of LinkedIn and the workers' industry. The court was very precise when it explained that brokerage and financial markets were industries without a relevant impact on social relationships. Therefore, it seems vital to understand what effect a social network could have in a determined industry. We cannot deny this impact without an analysis of each concrete situation.

This way, if we are studying a case of a worker in the sales industry with a high customer loyalty, the simple change of employer might be complemented with a change of customer. Imagine if this was the situation in the Danish case. The mere profile update in LinkedIn could easily provide damages to the former employer. As a matter of fact, the anticipated change of customers from one company to another could be a likely consequence of the public announcement of a new employer. This way, these acts would probably create damages for the employer

25 News about Umberto Eco's speech can be found in several links. However, we recommend the following link: http://www.lastampa.it/2015/06/10/cultura/eco-con-i-parola-a-legioni-di-imbecilli-XJrvezBN4XOoyo0h98EfiJ/pagina.html.

bound to a non-competition agreement with former workers. Now, the non-compete clauses with effects after the employment termination aim to avoid this very situation. For this reason, in the USA and UK these agreements have different categories inside the concept of restrictive covenants. One of these categories is the agreement of non-solicitation where a worker accepts not only not to work for a competitor, but also not to contact the former employer's customers with whom he had a professional relationship during the employment. Covenants not to compete do not merely have the purpose of avoiding trade secrets' migration from one company to a competitor that had lured its workers, but also to prevent workers from benefitting from access to customers to compete against a former employer while pending the agreement.

We believe that the analysis of the industry is the premise for any court decision that wishes to evaluate social networks' impact on the breach of a non-compete clause.

Regarding the second point of the Western High Court decision – the absence of any agreement in order to limit the dissemination of a new employer on LinkedIn – it's the author's opinion that the decision was not fair. In fact, it must be evaluated if a worker's action could or could not breach a covenant not to compete. So, employers do not need to put into a contract that workers cannot use social networks in competition. Because social networks are part of our daily life, they are a means as much as any other to breach the agreement. Defending the opposite is allowing the impunity of acts through social networks.

It is only on this last point that the author does not agree with the court's decision. It's also worthy of some merit that the court in the first instance decided to give dimension and visibility to the impact that an updating of LinkedIn can have on a commercial and professional relationship. In this Danish case, even if workers didn't work for the new employer, the anticipated dissemination of that information created that idea in the market, namely to workers, customers and competitor companies that have access to LinkedIn.[26]

The use of social networks as a relevant element for the breach of a covenant not to compete and the right to privacy

Social networks are now the new "public space" of our society.[27] Common talks in bars or pubs were partially replaced by the contact made through Facebook or other platforms available on the internet.[28]

---

26 We must remember that it's not necessary to be a LinkedIn user to analyse profiles. The research through Google allows the reach of that important information.

27 The author already also defended this idea in a different multidisciplinary path (cfr. Abrunhosa e Sousa, Duarte (2016), "Non-competition clauses – Impacts of social networks", Interdisciplinary Approach to Law in Modern Social Context – Conference Papers, Vilnius University, pp. 9–15).

28 This idea is also followed by Raúl Trejo Delarbe (2009), "Internet como expressão e extensão do espaço público", *MATRIZes*, Ano 2, n.º 2, available at: https://rtrejo.files.wordpress.com/2012/04/internet-e-espaco-pc3bablico-matrizes-2-2009.pdf.

On the other hand, social networks can also be a "public space of action".[29] Nowadays, there are many public protests performed through social networks. A simple disagreement regarding a political decision can lead to strong protests on Facebook, for example. Thus, there is no doubt that people feel free to use social networks to express beliefs, opinions and intentions. At present, these platforms are not a space of strict individual intimacy. Information shared in social networks is not much different from that shared at a restaurant's table with friends and colleagues. However, it has a major aggravating factor: the information shared stays in the platform and it is quite difficult to control all the recipients. So, it can go "viral".

Now, the Portuguese Constitution's article 26 establishes that everyone has the right to privacy. This is a recognition of the statute of personal right, freedom and guarantees. So, it is the general personality right's defence.[30] Regarding the right to privacy, it is important to remember the three spheres theory adopted by Jorge Miranda and Rui Medeiros:[31] i) intimacy sphere; ii) private sphere; and iii) social sphere. This way, which sphere is included in the use of social networks for professional or commercial purposes? Despite the traditional critics of this theory, it continues to be vital for the qualification of private life intimacy. Subsequently, the use of a social network where the user has, for example, 500 contacts allows an expectancy of putting aside the intimacy of his private life. What is the difference between sharing information on Facebook with 500 contacts or at a dinner with the same number of people? The law usually does not make any relevant approach to this concept, so the courts have to deal with the appropriate decision for each case.

As already mentioned, social networks became the new public space. This way, the right to privacy must be adjusted to the new reality. Social network users are increasingly better informed and know the possible reach of everything they share.

From an employment law perspective, article 16 of the Portuguese Labour Code protects the right to privacy[32]. This article is included in a subsection about personality rights. In this case, Portuguese lawmakers expressly recognised

---

29 This expression is used by Dayo de Araújo Silva Côrbo and Márcio Gonçalves (2015), "Redes Sociais Digitais na esfera pública política: Exercícios de Cidadania, Revista do programa de Pós-Graduação em Mídia e Cotidiano", *Artigo Seção Dossiê Mídia e Cidade*, Número 6, Volume 6, available at: http://www.ppgmidiaecotidiano.uff.br/ojs/index.php/Midecot/art icle/view/146/156.

30 Jorge Miranda and Rui Medeiros defend that article 26 of the Portuguese Constitution is a manifestation of the right of human dignity Miranda, Jorge, and Medeiros, Rui (2005), *Constituição Portuguesa Anotada, Tomo I*, Coimbra Editora, Portugal, p. 282.

31 Cfr. *op. cit.*, p. 290.

32 According to article 16 of the Portuguese Labour Code, the worker and employer should respect the other part's personality rights and privacy rights. About this subject, Maria Regina Redinha made an important development in 2004 (cfr. Regina Redinha, Maria (2004), *Os direitos de personalidade no Código do Trabalho, A Reforma do Código do Trabalho*, Coimbra Editora, Portugal, p. 169).

some cases that should be protected:[33] i) personal data; ii) use of biometric data; iii) medical exams and tests; iv) surveillance systems; and v) confidentiality of messages and access of information.

The use of a social network for professional purposes by an employer to demand damages against a worker is lawful in an employment law perspective.

Now, regarding disciplinary action, there are some relevant cases already decided by Portuguese courts. The most famous case was related to the dismissal of a union representative because he made some injurious comments against the employer on Facebook.[34] Although all the evidence was supported in a post on Facebook, Oporto Appeal Court decided the dismissal was considered as according to the law. Here, the surprise was the way this court handled the fact that a social network should not be used as a means to avoid unlawful acts. Therefore, it's important to cite the court's ruling here.

Social networks created new spaces that do not connect easily with the traditional spheres that grow in the irreducible intimacy of workers' privacy, so, it's difficult to identify the privacy boundaries that deserve the protection of confidentiality supervision, wherefore it's always needed to make a case-by-case examination.

The author agrees with the rightfulness of the decision because, as already mentioned, the use of social networks is not a synonym for an intimate sharing of information between two people. In some cases, one shared post on Facebook can reach millions of recipients all over the world in a few hours. This impact would be impossible if the same information was shared in a simple conversation between three or four people in a bar or on a park bench. Additionally, it seems important to underline that the Oporto Court of Appeal reinforces the need to analyse the level of privacy according with each particular situation. This way we can avoid the danger of generalisation in this subject.

Still, in the same case, the Oporto Court of Appeal held a fundamental statement by defending that any "expectancy of privacy" doesn't result from the worker's post on Facebook. This way, he could not claim the private and personal nature of that post in order to benefit the protection provided by article 22 of the Portuguese Labour Code.[35]

---

33 On this theme, Diogo Vaz Marecos identifies articles 17, 19, 20 and 20 of the Portuguese Labour Code (Marecos, Diogo Vaz (2012), *Código do Trabalho Anotado*, Coimbra Editora, Portugal, 2.ª Edição, p. 111).

34 Decision of the Oporto Court of Appeal (8th September 2014), case number 101/13.5TTMATS.P1, consulted in www.dgsi.pt. However, there are several cases in the USA that also debated the breach of non-competes through Facebook – *Enhanced Network Solutions Group v. Hypersonic Techs.*, 951 N.E.2d 265 (Ind. Ct. of App. 2011); *Invidia v. DiFonzo*, 2012 WL 5576406 (Mass. Super. 2012); *Pre-Paid Legal Services v. Cahill*, 924 F. Supp.2d 1281 (E.D. Okla. 2013).

35 Lisbon Court of Appeal decided in the same way (Decision of the Lisbon Court of Appeal (24th September 2014), case number 431/12. TTFUN.L1-4, available at www.dgsi.pt). According to the court's decision, when a worker prepares a post on Facebook, he allows his "friends" the free will to decide if they want to share it

For this reason, we can bring this idea to the analysis of the impact of social networks in the breach of non-competition agreements. It's the author's opinion that everything must converge to the existence or not of a "worker's legitimate expectation of privacy". So, the use of social networks for professional purposes most of the time will be incompatible with a legitimate expectancy of privacy.

Let's revisit the Danish case. Workers did not update LinkedIn with the intention of having the information recorded only for themselves or for a small group of recipients. By updating their profile in this social network, workers pretended to announce to the entire professional world that they had an employer change. Instead of having an expectancy of privacy, workers had an expectancy of notoriety. Thus, the right to privacy could not prevail just because the means used for sharing information were social networks.

The cited ruling of Oporto's Court of Appeal gives strong leads for interpreting this new reality and shows that it's prepared to deal with this new phenomenon.

Conclusions

After this analysis, it is important to identify our conclusions about the impact of social networks in covenants not to compete as follows:

a) Social networks created a new public space, since they moved discussion forums into a virtual reality that can have an unlimited reach;

b) Facebook, LinkedIn, Instagram and Twitter are examples of social networks that can be used for professional purposes;

c) In a society that entrenches the freedom of enterprise principle, competition is not only permitted, but it is also desirable if lawful;

d) After the termination of an employment contract, as long as all the legal requirements are fulfilled, a worker can be bound to a non-compete clause with his former employer;

e) Covenants not to compete must be interpreted with great caution, because they restrict the right to work;

f) In Denmark, the Western High Court decided profile updating on LinkedIn with the identification of the future employer by workers bound to a non-compete clause signed with a former employer was not a breach of contract;

g) On the contrary, the first instance court decided that the update of LinkedIn was a breach of the agreement;

h) The industry analysis is essential to determine if the use of social networks for professional purposes could be a breach in a covenant not to compete;

i) Social networks are a new paradigm that must be interpreted with adequacy by courts in order to avoid that they are used to evade liability;

j) The use of social networks for professional purposes implies a nature of expectancy of notoriety;

k) In order to determine if the use of shared information in a professional con-
    text by a worker through social networks is a violation of the right of priv-
    acy, it is necessary to analyse the dichotomy between "legitimate expectancy
    of privacy" and "legitimate expectancy of notoriety";

l) Employment covenants not to compete when pending can be breached by
    workers through social networks for professional purposes.

6 Rebalancing worker rights and property rights in digitalised work

Julia Tomassetti[1]

Introduction

This chapter is intended as an intellectual gesture drawing to reveal and critique how businesses appeal to property rights to limit the scope of labour legislation. It theorises that these appeals exploit an ambiguity underlying the legal authority to control the labour of others. It hypothesises that these arguments appear more plausible in disputes over two kinds of work—service work involving customer interaction and work managed through digitalised technology. These disputes are potential vehicles for augmenting the assumed prerogatives of business to direct the enterprise with little interference from workers or government. While focused on the US experience, an apt UK case concerning the employment status of Uber drivers shows that appeals to property rights seeking to exploit the ambiguous legal basis of labour control are not confined to the US.

While scholars have quite thoroughly interrogated the construction and deployment of employer property rights in collective bargaining law,[2] they have not adequately examined the role of property rights in labour law outside of this context.[3] Of pertinence to this chapter, appeals to property rights appear regularly in disputes over employment status—legal contests about who is and who

1 I thank Kenneth Dau-Schmidt, Andrew Elmore, Ilana Gershon, Michael Harper, and Sherally Munshi for their generous feedback on this chapter. For the opportunity they gave me to present this work, I am also grateful to the organisers of *Technological Innovation and the Future of Work: Emerging Aspects Worldwide*, at the Universidade de Santiago de Compostela Faculty of Law. All shortcomings are my own.
2 See, for example, James B. Atleson, *Values and Assumptions in American Labor Law*, (Amherst: University of Massachusetts Press, 1983), Ch. 7; Martin H. Malin, "Extending Mike Zimmer's Cross-Border Comparative Work: The Role of Property Rights in U.S. and Canadian Labo(u)r Law," *Employee Rights and Employment Policy Journal* 20, no. 2 (2016): 417–444.
3 Cf. Dianne Avery and Marion Crain, "Branded: Corporate Image, Sexual Stereotyping, and the New Face of Capitalism," *Duke Journal of Gender Law & Policy* 14, no. 1 (2007): 41–42. Avery and Crain recognized that, when controlling a worker's body for corporate branding purposes, "the employer's property-based business management and marketing interests intersect with its common-law right to control and discipline its workforce."

is not in an employment relationship for purposes of accessing rights and benefits conditioned on this status. These appeals are common in employment status disputes involving interactive service work, including service work coordinated through advanced information technology. When seeking regulatory dispensations or defending lawsuits by workers, the on-demand ride platforms Uber and Lyft predictably invoke rights to their digital technology.

An example: in a London lawsuit, Uber drivers for the on-demand ride platform Uber alleged that the company violated wage and hour law in refusing to recognise them as "workers." The drivers noted that Uber exercised considerable control over their work. Uber contended that its interest in "preserving the integrity of the platform" made any controls it exercised over drivers via this technology irrelevant to the issue of its obligations under labour law.[4] The tribunal observed that the refrain about platform integrity was "a formula repeatedly employed" by Uber.[5] The company made a similar "overarching" argument to the Court of Appeal, claiming that the features of the work the tribunal found to be evidence of drivers' worker status were "simply conditions of the licence to use the App."[6] Uber's purpose was to explain why the company should be exempt from regulatory requirements that would otherwise attach to this kind of work relationship. Lyft has made similar arguments.[7]

These claims descend from a long lineage of attempts to subordinate worker rights by appealing to notions of property rights. They exploit an ambiguity underlying the legal basis of the authority to direct the labour power of others: is this authority based on the contractual rights of the employer or the property rights of the entrepreneur?

Many disputes over worker rights, including those concerning employment status, turn at least in part on how decision makers resolve this ambiguity. Yet they rarely confront the ambiguity. More troubling is when decision makers exploit it to defeat the statutory and common law rights of workers.

The stakes are particularly high in disputes involving interactive service work and work coordinated through digital means. Certain features of these work relationships make them susceptible to a creeping expansion of employer property rights by route of the ambiguity. Companies exploit the worker-customer encounter and embedding of managerial controls in software to expand the relational space over which they can redefine their authority *qua* employers as their prerogatives *qua* entrepreneurs who "own" the enterprise.

The chapter proceeds as follows. It explains why the legal basis for the authority to control the work of others is ambiguous. To illustrate the shifting rationalisations courts have used to justify employer authority, and to show their implications for

---

4 *Aslam and Farrar v. Uber,* Case Nos 2202550/2015, at 13, para. 47 (London Emp't Trib., Oct. 28, 2015), *aff'd Uber BV v Aslam,* [2017] No. UKEAT/0056/17/DA (London Emp't App. Trib., Nov. 10, 2017), *aff'd* [2018] EWCA Civ 2748 (Ct. of Appeal, Dec. 19, 2018).
5 *Ibid.*
6 *Uber BV v Aslam,* [2018] EWCA Civ 2748, at para. 73 (Ct. of Appeal, Dec. 19, 2018).
7 See Part II (3).

worker rights, it looks at jurisprudence on the scope of collective bargaining under the US National Labor Relations Act (NLRA). The chapter then examines appeals to business property rights in disputes over employment status, focusing on cases involving interactive service work and work subject to digitalised control. A critique of these appeals follows.

Ambiguity regarding the legal basis of labour control

Origins

The legal basis of the authority to control the labour of others can be understood as the contractual rights of the employer afforded under the employment contract, or, as the property rights of the entrepreneur. The potential for alternate characterisations originated in (1) the peculiar doctrinal expression of the employment contract, and (2) the tendency of labour-capital relations to assume the form of employment.

First, employment, though denominated a "contract," gives the employer an authority over the employee that is more kindred to property rights in its one-sided open-endedness. This is no coincidence: the employment contract in common law systems is based on the preindustrial master-servant relationship, in which the master had a property right to the servant's labour.[8] The formal basis of this authority shifted from property to contract, but the property-like substance of that authority remained largely intact.[9] The master's property rights were reconfigured as implied contractual terms giving the employer plenary authority over the performance of the contract.[10] Unlike other contracts, employment tries to render the capacity for voluntarist action—including the capacity to follow instructions—a commodity exchangeable through contract.

---

8 Christopher L. Tomlins, "Law and Power in the Employment Relationship," in *Labor Law in America: Historical and Critical Essays*, ed. Christopher L. Tomlins and Andrew J. King (Baltimore: Johns Hopkins University Press, 1992) 74–75. See also Christopher L. Tomlins, *Law, Labor, and Ideology in the Early American Republic* (Cambridge, England; New York: Cambridge University Press, 1993); Philip Selznick, *Law, Society, and Industrial Justice* (New York: Russell Sage Foundation, 1969); Robert J. Steinfeld, *The Invention of Free Labor: The Employment Relation in English and American Law and Culture, 1350–1870* (Chapel Hill: University of North Carolina Press, 1991).

9 Tomlins, "Law and Power," 74–83.

10 *Ibid.* See Simon Deakin, "The Many Futures of the Contract of Employment," in *Labour Law in an Era of Globalization: Transformative Practices and Possibilities*, ed. Joanne Conaghan, Richard Michael Fischl, and Karl Klare (Oxford: Oxford University Press, 2002), 180–181; Julia Tomassetti, "From Hierarchies to Markets: FedEx Drivers and the Work Contract as Institutional Marker," *Lewis & Clark Law Review* 19, no. 4 (2015): 1101–1106.

The origins of employer authority in master-servant law, later designated as contractual, were similar under English common law. In civil law jurisdictions as well, the employer's unilateral authority was implanted into contracts of hire. The juridical paths of employment later diverged to some extent. Employment underwent a process of contractualisation in other systems, while the US employment contract retained decisively anti-contractual features, such as its at-will nature.

This brings us to the second feature that helps explain the ambiguous legal basis of labour control: employment almost always involves applying one's own efforts to someone else's property. Employment was a relationship of servitude, and those who had productive property apart from their labour power to sell were disinclined to submit to it. In an economy that conditioned access to the means of reproduction on market exchange, employment was for the most part reserved for those who had no other productive assets to exchange for payment except their ability to dispose of their faculties at the discretion, and under the direction, of another.

By construing the master's unilateral and open-ended authority over the property-less servant as a "contract," the employment contract transposes the owner's property rights over the terms on which it would permit others to use its property on to the contractual terms of labour control. An employer, like any other property owner, has a sweeping right over the disposition of its property. This right includes the authority to determine the terms upon which it allows others to use its property, whether it be land, equipment, investment capital, or other production inputs. Employment, entailing the application of work effort to another's property, appears as the mirror image of these terms.

Sometimes, the employer was conceived of as a "host inviting the worker to come and make use of his property, but only on conditions that the owner of the property should dictate."[11] However, as Alan Fox noted, "Conceptually, managerial or paternal authority could be based upon property notions, as incidents of ownership, rather than upon contractual concepts. But *it was contract* and not property which lawfully gave employers power to direct the work force."[12] As the scale of production expanded in the 19th century, US courts used the employment contract, rather than property rights to give the employer legal control over the enterprise.[13]

A consequence of the semblance between employer authority and property rights is that one might rationalise control over workers as either. A factory owner's instructions to workers regarding how to use its machinery, even how fast to work on it, resembles, on the one hand, employer control over employee performance. On the other hand, it resembles an exercise of property rights: a factory owner, like any other owner, has a right to determine how others may handle its property.

Illustration

NLRA jurisprudence on the scope of collective bargaining illustrates the ambiguous rationalisations courts and employers have used to account for enterprise control and to limit worker rights. In deciding disputes over what subjects employers and unions

---

11 Thomas Cochran and William Miller, *The Age of Enterprise: A Social History of Industrial America* (New York: Harper & Row, rev. ed. 1961), 238

12 Alan Fox, *Beyond Contract: Work, Power and Trust Relations* (London: Faber, 1974), 188–189.

13 Tomlins, *Law, Labor, and Ideology*, 284, 295–29.

were required to negotiate over, the Supreme Court referred to the idea of "managerial prerogative," a realm of decision-making in which companies had unilateral discretion. The Court ostensibly recognised this realm of decision-making as an empirical phenomenon and crafted a legal test to preserve this state of affairs, based on policy reasons, not doctrinal ones. Others, however, interpreted managerial prerogative as the legal rights inhering in the company's "ownership" of the enterprise.

The NLRA is the principal US statute governing the formation and legal status of unions; it requires employers to bargain in good faith with their employees' representatives "with respect to wages, hours, and other terms and conditions of employment."[14] By prohibiting employer interference with worker association and requiring employers to bargain collectively, the NLRA protected workers' rights to negotiate the terms under which the employer could dispose of their ability to work. For well-organised workers, this portended, potentially, a big incursion on the employer's power.[15]

Early on, the agency charged with administering the NLRA and the courts began debating which subjects fell within "wages, hours, and other terms and conditions of employment."[16] Some, like rates of pay, they found to be mandatory bargaining subjects under this provision. Others they found to be "permissive," meaning employers and employees were free to bargain over them, but neither could insist on it.[17] Employers could not impose unilateral changes to mandatory subjects until reaching a bargaining impasse but were free to make changes regarding permissive subjects.[18]

The courts' creation of "managerial prerogative" as a realm of inherent entrepreneurial decision-making responded to the statutory protection afforded to employees' contract rights. Judges deployed the concept of managerial prerogative to delimit the subjects of mandatory bargaining upon which workers could insist and back their insistence through statutorily protected collective action.[19]

In *Fibreboard v. NLRB*, the Supreme Court had to determine whether an employer's decision to subcontract out maintenance work performed by its unionised employees was a mandatory bargaining subject—a "term and condition" of employment.[20] The outsourcing decision effectively terminated all the employer's unionised workers. The majority held that the employer had violated the NLRA by failing to bargain over the decision. It argued that, in this case, where the company terminated its own employees but contracted out work that would still be performed for the company, and in much the same way, by

---

14 29 U.S.C. § 158(a)(5), (d); Atleson, *Values and Assumptions*, 115–127.

15 Karl E. Klare, "Judicial Deradicalization of the Wagner Act and the Origins of Modern Legal Consciousness, 1937-1941," *Minnesota Law Review* 62, no. 3 (March 1978): 265–266.

16 James B. Atleson, "Management Prerogatives, Plant Closings, and the NLRA," *New York University Review of Law and Social Change* 11, no. 1 (1982–1983): 83–124.

17 *Ibid.*

18 *Ibid.*

19 *Ibid.*

20 *Fibreboard Paper Products Corp. v. NLRB*, 379 U.S. 203 (1964).

a contractor's workers, the outsourcing was a "term and condition of employment." The court signalled, however, that not all outsourcing decisions would be mandatory subjects.[21]

Cases after *Fibreboard* looked more to Justice Stewart's concurring opinion than to the majority opinion to distinguish mandatory from permissive bargaining subjects. Justice Stewart argued that, while certain issues might have a direct and substantial impact on employment, those that "lie at the core of entrepreneurial control," particularly issues involving the "commitment of investment capital and the basic scope of the enterprise" were not "terms and conditions of employment." [22] They were "prerogatives of private business management."[23]

If the majority in *Fibreboard* took a somewhat "literal" approach to interpreting "terms and conditions of employment,"[24] in *First National Maintenance v. NLRB*, the Court announced a policy-based rationale for "labeling" certain bargaining subjects as mandatory and thus demarcating managerial prerogative.[25] Citing an employer's "need for unencumbered decision-making," to determine whether bargaining was required, the Court would balance the benefit to collective bargaining against the "burden placed on the conduct of the business."[26] Putting the employer's "burden" in the scale reflected the current capitalistic piety that the means of production in a market economy must, for efficiency reasons, be under private, authoritarian direction.[27]

While the Supreme Court's policy reasons for recognizing managerial prerogative were clear, its legal rationale was not: was the prerogative some legal *right* the employer had, or was it a reference to the *power* that employers were accustomed to exercising in the absence of a statute intended to help workers exercise their contractual rights to negotiate the employment contract?

The most tenable explanation is that this prerogative referred to a power: the statute gave employees increased access to their freedom of contract regarding the terms under which they would apply their efforts to the employer's property. This threatened the employer's customary power to dispose of its property free from any contractual restraints under the employment contract, something that would "mark a sharp departure from the traditional principles of a free enterprise economy."[28] Thus, the Court felt that Congress did not intend employees to use their protected bargaining ability to negotiate employment terms that entailed contractual restrictions on the traditional powers of employers.

---

21 *Ibid.*
22 *Fibreboard*, 379 U.S. at 223 (Justice Stewart, concurring).
23 *Ibid.* at 226.
24 *Ibid.* at 210.
25 *First National Maintenance Corp. v. NLRB*, 452 U.S. 666, 678, 679 (1981); Atleson, *Values and Assumptions*, 122–145.
26 *First National Maintenance*, 452 U.S. at 679.
27 Atleson, *Values and Assumptions*, 122–123.
28 *Fibreboard*, 379 U.S. at 226 (Justice Stewart, concurring).

Nonetheless, many others, especially employers, suggested that companies enjoyed a *legal* prerogative to run the business based on their rights as enterprise owners.[29] The Supreme Court did little if anything to dispel this notion. For example, *First National Maintenance*, quoting another Supreme Court case, referenced the "rightful prerogative of owners independently to rearrange their businesses."[30] Other cases suggested that managerial prerogative was grounded in business ownership and included the rights to control "investment" and determine what to produce.[31] Courts, arbitrators, and employers frequently referred to managerial prerogative as a business' "reserved" or "residual" authority not ceded through collective bargaining.[32]

The ownership notion is flawed. If a business' legal authority over the enterprise was "reserved," it must have been reserved from the employer's contractual authority as master, the historical basis of the employer's authority to manage production. Property does not provide a legal right to dictate the terms

29 See Stanley Young, "The Question of Managerial Prerogatives," *Industrial and Labor Relations Review* 16 (1963): 240–253.

30 *First National Maintenance*, 452 U.S. at 678 (quoting *John Wiley & Sons, Inc. v. Livingston*, 376 U.S. 543, 549 (1964)).

31 See, for example, General Motors Corp., 191 N.L.R.B. 951 (1971), *aff'd*, *UAW Local 864 v. NLRB*, 470 F.2d 422 (D.C. Cir. 1972); *ibid* at 427–428 (Judge Bazelon, dissenting). Cases dealing with employee rights to self-organize under the NLRA provide another example where courts have used property rights to limit workers' statutory rights. An employer may prohibit organizational solicitation by *non*-employees on its property based on its right as property owner to exclude persons from real property. Only in limited circumstances can non-employees overcome this right. *Lechmere, Inc. v. NLRB*, 502 U.S. 527, 537 (1992). In contrast, an employer's right to restrict solicitation by employees is less extensive: once its employees are "rightfully on the employer's property," the "employer's management interests rather than his property interests were there involved" and the employer may restrict it only "to maintain plant production or discipline." *Eastex, Inc. v. NLRB*, 437 U.S. 556, 571–572 (1978). Although this jurisprudence involves the relatively straightforward right to exclude others from real property, the lack of clarity in the Supreme Court's explanations and contention over the distinction shows the shadow cast by the property/employment ambiguity. Scholars have debated whether the employee/non-employee distinction can be justified by analogy to trespass law. Martin, "Extending Mike Zimmer's," 423; Atleson, *Values and Assumptions*, 60–61; Cynthia L. Estlund, "Labor, Property, and Sovereignty after Lechmere," *Stanford Law Review* 46, no. 2 (1994): 312, 323. If so, this would seem to manoeuvre adroitly around the ambiguity: the Court would not need to reinterpret the same authority to exclude as an incident of employer rights rather than property rights when dealing with employees as opposed to non-employees. Instead, host-invitee rights could account for the distinction, in that, once the employer invited employees on to its property, it would have no more property rights to assert against the employees' statutory rights. Some judges, however, like the *Eastex* dissenters, have rejected the viability of the trespass analogy and tried to limit the right to self-organize by exploiting the ambiguity. *Eastex*, 437 U.S. at 579–583. For a recent NLRB decision using the management/property interest distinction in a dispute over access to the employer's email system rather than real property, see Purple Communications, Inc., 361 N.L.R.B. 1050 (2014).

32 Atleson, *Values and Assumptions*, 122–123 (citing Fairway Foods, 40 L.A. 161 (Soloman 1965) and other decisions); Neil W. Chamberlain, "The Union Challenge to Management Control," *Industrial and Labor Relations Review* 16 (1963 1962): 184–192.

of a contractual exchange.[33] And, nothing in the NLRA suggests that it was meant to give employers more property rights. Either the employer retained legal rights under the employment contract, or it simply retained power by virtue of its superior access to the means of production.

Exploiting the ambiguity in disputes over employment status

Basic form of company appeals to their prerogatives as owners

How do appeals to property rights work in employment status disputes? Most legal standards for defining employment status look towards the extent of the alleged employer's right to control the labour process, and courts also look to the extent that the alleged employer denies to the worker the right to entrepreneurial decisions.[34] In a typical appeal to property rights to avoid employment status, the worker notes that the alleged employer asserts discretionary controls over how it performs the required labour that resemble those of industrial employment. The worker argues that these controls constitute evidence of employment status. Perhaps the alleged employer controls the pace of its work, requires a uniform, determines the hours of work, dictates how to talk to customers or how to keep records, or assigns tasks not agreed to at the time of contracting. Rather than denying that it indeed has a right to exercise these controls, the alleged employer suggests that it is not doing so in its capacity as an employer, but in its capacity as property owner and entrepreneur. Therefore, the authority does not count as evidence of employment status, because such decisions should be unencumbered by employment regulation.

Companies tend to invoke three kinds of prerogatives: a right to protect and control non-labour factors of production, a right to determine *what* to produce, and a right to control the disposition of the product in the market, including its relationship with customers. These comport with the kinds of employer decisions promoted to the realm of managerial prerogative in the collective bargaining context.

Disputes over whether drivers for the package delivery company FedEx are "employees" or "independent contractors" illustrate how companies invoke these prerogatives to avoid labour regulation. One court agreed with FedEx that controlling drivers' hours of work was not evidence of employment, because: "It is in the very nature of the [drivers'] work—delivering and picking up packages—that obliged them to work on certain days and at certain times. Customers would surely not accept deliveries at all hours of the night."[35] In another

---

33 See Young, "Managerial Prerogatives," 248.
34 Breen Creighton and Shae McCrystal, "Who Is a Worker in International Law?" *Comparative Labor Law & Policy Journal* 37, no. 3 (2016): 691–726; *Nationwide Mutual Ins. Co. v. Darden*, 503 U.S. 318, 323 (1992); *Alexander v. FedEx Ground Package Sys., Inc.*, 765 F.3d 981 (9th Cir. 2014); *Uber BV v Aslam*, [2017] No. UKEAT/0056/17/DA.
35 *Johnson v. FedEx Home Delivery*, 2011 WL 6153425 at 14 (E.D.N.Y. Dec. 12, 2011).

case, FedEx invoked the "practical operational requirements of the small package home delivery business" to dismiss the relevance of its controls over the timing and location of package deliveries. Such controls were necessary to serve customers: "The 'when' and 'where' packages are to be delivered are obviously dictated by customers' timetables and their addresses."[36] The court agreed with FedEx in this case and also opined, "true, these drivers must wear uniforms and the like, but a rule based on concern for customer service does not create an employee relationship."[37] The company's relationship with customers fell within its entrepreneurial prerogative. Likewise, FedEx's decision to produce package delivery services meant that controlling the times of those deliveries and appearance of drivers all fell within its prerogative to decide *what* to produce. Given that the product is a customer encounter, the subtext here is that FedEx controlled that encounter as a matter of its entrepreneurial prerogative, not as an employer.

We also see these appeals in disputes over whether franchisors should be responsible for employment law violations perpetrated on the direct employees of their franchisees. For instance, employees of McDonalds franchisees have alleged that McDonalds, and not only the franchisee restaurants they work at, should be liable for wage and hour violations caused in part by McDonald's programming of franchise software.[38] Some franchises, McDonalds included, reserve an extensive right to control virtually all aspects of the work of fast food employees, even dictating the number of seconds it should take per customer order.[39] Some courts have held that nearly all the controls franchisors exert over franchisee employees are irrelevant to the issue of the franchisor's liability under labour law.[40] Their rationale is that the controls protect the franchisor's trademark, valuable property placed in the hands of workers as they interact with its customers.[41]

Appeals in service work involving customer interaction

Why do appeals to managerial prerogative gain traction in disputes over interactive service work, and what do they portend for the balance of worker rights and property rights?

---

36 FedEx Reply Brief at *23, *FedEx Home Delivery v. NLRB*, 563 F.3d 492 (D.C. Cir. 2009).

37 *FedEx Home Delivery*, 563 F.3d at 503.

38 *Ochoa v. McDonald's Corp.*, 133 F.Supp.3d 1228 (N.D. Cal. 2015).

39 See Deepa das Acevedo, "Invisible Bosses for Invisible Workers, or Why the Sharing Economy Is Actually Minimally Disruptive," *University of Chicago Legal Forum* 2017 (2017): 35–62; David Weil, *The Fissured Workplace: Why Work Became so Bad for so Many and What Can Be Done to Improve It* (Cambridge, Massachusetts; London: Harvard University Press, 2014).

40 See, for example, *Juarez v. Jani-King of California, Inc.*, No. 09-3495 SC, 2012 WL 177564, at *5 (N.D. Cal. Jan. 23, 2012).

41 *Ibid*. See Andrew Elmore, "The Future of Fast Food Governance," *University of Pennsylvania Law Review Online* 165 (2016 2017): 73–90.

What distinguishes the production of services from the production of goods is the coincidence of production and exchange in the former. Production of the service is simultaneous with its transfer from the service provider to the customer. Thus, a taxi company produces the taxi ride as it is exchanged with the passenger. A massage is produced at the same time it is consumed. In contrast, a car company first produces an automobile and then trades it. The worker engaged in the production of goods is usually not involved in the transfer of that product to the customer. In interactive service work, however, the worker takes part in the transfer.[42]

This overlap between production and consumption/exchange renders it virtually impossible in interactive service work to distinguish the employer's contractual authority over the employee from its putative prerogatives as enterprise owner—decisions about what to produce, how to engage in market exchange, and how to protect its property in the hands of workers.

The decision regarding *what* service to make and trade often entails extensive control over the labour process: the "what" is a customer encounter with a worker, and is therefore, at least in part, inalienable from the labour process generating the encounter. This also means that the worker's production of the service during the exchange of the service provides a greater relational surface area over which the alleged employer can assert entrepreneurial rights—the expanse of the customer interaction. Every point of the customer interaction implicates the alleged employer's control over what it decides to make and how to exchange its product. Every moment is part of the traded, consumable product.[43] In contrast, a manufacturer could not plausibly assert that supervising the speed of workers on an assembly line was an exercise of its right to determine what to produce or to control its product in commerce. Nor would a court likely entertain a manufacturer's contention that dictating the worker's hours of work, appearance, or demeanour and projected emotional disposition were incidents of its right to control the market disposition of its product or its contractual autonomy in its relationships with customers. Interactive service work is different: Where production and consumption overlap, it can be more difficult to distinguish a company's relationship with its customers—over which it claims entrepreneurial prerogatives—from its relationship with workers, which implicates employment law.

Rather than see any productive process within the worker-customer encounter, some courts have read all aspects of this encounter as an exchange between the alleged employer and its buyer, and thus within the domain of its prerogatives as owner. Several courts have characterised traditional aspects of employer control as "quality controls" in service work contexts. Consider the court's remarks below in a dispute over the employment status of cable technicians:

---

42 See Julia Tomassetti, "Digital Platform Work as Interactive Service Work," *Employee Rights & Employment Policy Journal* 22, no. 1 (2018): 1–58.
43 See, for example, *C.C. Eastern, Inc. v. NLRB*, 60 F.3d 855, 859 (D.C. Cir. 1995) (internal citation omitted).

Comcast's quality control procedures ultimately stem from the nature of their business and the need to provide reliable service to their customers, not the nature of the relationship between the technicians and Comcast. While Comcast's supervision and control may appear substantial in degree, it is qualitatively different from the control exercised by employers over employees.[44]

The court invokes Comcast's rights over the "nature of their business" to disregard "substantial" "supervision and control" over its technicians' performance. It did not explain why the control here was "qualitatively different" from employer control.

Decisions over the employment status of FedEx drivers also illustrate the opportunities that the customer-service interaction provides for an expansive reading of employer property rights. In *FedEx Home Delivery*, a federal appellate court found that FedEx drivers were independent contractors rather than employees and therefore had no right to collectively bargain with FedEx.[45] The court needed to deal with some problematic facts: FedEx reserved a right to control driver training, package handling, insurance, uniforms, grooming standards, vehicle specifications, assignments, and routes.[46] The majority acknowledged that in previous cases the NLRB had found work rules like those dictated by FedEx probative of employment status. However, the majority argued that in FedEx's case, "those distinctions, though not irrelevant, reflect differences in the *type of service* the contractors are providing rather than differences in the employment relationship."[47] The court invokes FedEx's right to decide *what* to produce. Where production and exchange overlap, companies have argued that control over how workers produce its service is simply control over the results—the thing to be traded with its customers.

Courts have also exploited the property/employment ambiguity in service work to find that the alleged employer may control the worker's use of its intangible property in its capacity as property owner rather than employer. Just as an industrial worker might handle a manufacturer's expensive and delicate equipment during production, the service worker often handles (and even produces)[48] the service producer's valuable property during a customer encounter, namely the company's brand and reputation. In *FedEx Home Delivery*, the majority referenced the company's intangible property—signified by the FedEx logo—that FedEx entrusts

---

44 *Jacobson v. Comcast Corp.*, 740 F. Supp. 2d 683, 691–692 (D. Md. 2010).

45 563 F.3d 492 (D.C. Cir. 2009).

46 *Ibid. Estrada v. FedEx Ground Package Sys., Inc.*, 154 Cal. App. 4th 1, 11–12 (2007) FedEx maintained strict control over drivers' work. The *Estrada* court remarked, "FedEx's control over every exquisite detail of the drivers' performance, including the color of their socks and the style of their hair, supports the trial court's conclusion that the drivers are employees, not independent contractors".

47 *FedEx Home Delivery*, 563 F.3d at 501.

48 See Avery and Crain, *Branded*.

to the use of drivers to rationalise control over *all* "conduct" in which drivers are exposed to FedEx customers: "And once a driver wears FedEx's logo, FedEx has an interest in making sure her conduct reflects favourably on that logo, for instance by her being a safe and insured driver."[49]

It might seem a little much if a manufacturer were to claim that dictating to its workers the proper methods of using its machinery was in no way an exercise of its authority as an employer but only a measure to protect its property. Why then do courts entertain or even accept such arguments in service work? Two hypotheses come to mind.

First, perhaps the alleged employer's intangible property appears more vulnerable to disruption and damage from worker mishandling. To protect tangible property like machinery and tools, the manufacturer need only control the worker's physical manipulation of that property. Given the importance of emotional labour in service production,[50] the company producing a customer service must also control the psychic manipulation of its intangible property.

Another hypothesis is that, in contradistinction to goods production, in interactive service production, several prerogatives merge in the same decisions regarding labour control. Controlling the worker's interaction with the alleged employer's customers appears to implicate prerogatives over the disposition of non-labour property (for instance, brand), what to make, and how to engage in commerce. We see a conjunction of putative property rights in the same activities and decisions by the company. In the manufacture of goods, perhaps one could rationalise dictating a worker's speed on the production line as the exercise of a property right—a condition of the worker gaining access to the manufacturer's productive property. Yet the speed of the work would still be independent of the decision regarding what to produce and how to trade it.

Put another way, courts and companies draw on the simultaneity of production and exchange in interactive service work to reinterpret decisions about coordinating *production* into decisions about market *exchange* that implicate its autonomy as protector and disposer of property.

Appeals in work coordinated through digital technology: Uber and Lyft

The ride platforms Uber and Lyft have deftly exploited the ambiguity between employment and property rights as bases of labour control. Rather than sign an independent contracting agreement, Uber and Lyft drivers sign a "software

---

49 *FedEx Home Delivery*, 563 F.3d at 501. Under the NLRA, when an employer restricts employees from wearing union insignia to protect its "public image," courts have held that this rationale implicates the employer's "management interests" rather than its "property interests," and thus subjects the restrictions to a balancing test less indulgent of the employer. For a recent example, see *In-N-Out Burger, Inc. v. Nat'l Labor Relations Bd.*, No. 17-60241, 2018 WL 3339549, at *4 (5th Cir. July 6, 2018).

50 See Robin Leidner, *Fast Food, Fast Talk: Service Work and the Routinization of Everyday Life* (Berkeley: University of California Press, 1993).

license."[51] They literally construct their authority over drivers as a right to decide how others (drivers) handle its property. In the "software license" drivers agree to submit to a host of employer-like controls over terms and conditions of work as a condition of "access."[52] The platform here is the "host inviting the worker to come and make use of his property, but only on conditions that the owner of the property should dictate."[53] The labour process is embedded in the company's proprietary software, and the company programs the software to design, direct, and surveil the worker.

These on-demand platforms go further than FedEx and other service providers in reinterpreting conventional incidents of the industrial employer's contractual authority as incidents of property rights. The employer's right to discharge a worker[54] becomes part of "managing access to the platform to help maintain an acceptable level of trust and safety among members of the ridesharing community."[55]

The labour process is also embedded in what the platform claims to be a technology "experience"—the customer experience of using the platform. Any control over the worker via the software becomes an incident of property rights, an entrepreneurial decision about what "experience" to sell, not employer control. Authority over the worker is part of the programming sold to the platform's customer. According to Lyft, for example, rather than submit to Lyft's discretionary supervision and direction on pains of discipline or termination, drivers simply agree to allow Lyft to monitor their use of its software in accordance with the license agreement:

The metrics identified by Plaintiffs (passenger rating, acceptance rate and reliability rating) are tools for ensuring that drivers and riders have the best experience possible and limit instances where individuals improperly interfere with the efficient functioning of the Lyft platform in violation of the TOS.[56]

Supervisory and managerial tasks are absorbed by the programming and now appear as part of the company's proprietary technology rather than human resource functions. Replacing flesh and blood management with digital algorithms enables companies to rationalise far-reaching control over service workers as exercises of property rights that they claim are in turn invulnerable to labour law.

Under the governing legal standards, requiring workers to perform assigned tasks in a certain manner and with certain alacrity, supervising execution of these tasks, and doling out discipline if drivers do not are evidence of employment status. However, in Lyft's parlance, these particular controls are exercises

---

51 See *Razak v. Uber Techs., Inc.*, No. CV 16-573, 2017 WL 4052417, at *3 (E.D. Pa. Sept. 13, 2017); Lyft Motion for Summary Judgment at 1, *Cotter v. Lyft, Inc.*, 60 F. Supp. 3d 1067 (N.D. Cal. 2015).

52 See *ibid.*

53 Cochran and Miller, *Age of Enterprise*, 238.

54 See *Cotter v. Lyft*, 60 F. Supp. 3d at 1076.

55 Lyft Motion for Summary Judgment, *Cotter v. Lyft*, 60 F. Supp. 3d 1067

56 *Ibid.*

of property rights: "To the extent any control is given to Lyft in the agreement, it is minimal and related mainly to ensuring that the platform is used in a lawful manner, to protect Lyft's intellectual property rights, and to avoid fraud and abuse on the platform."[57] Uber also characterises its corrective authority over drivers as an entrepreneurial prerogative: Requiring drivers with low ratings to take a training course was "providing drivers with an opportunity to mitigate the consequences of their failure to meet a quality standard."[58] This looks suspiciously like an employer correcting an employee's deficient performance.

Requiring someone to submit to the alleged employer's discretion in assigning tasks also suggests employee status.[59] However, Lyft described its right to assign ride requests at its discretion—and penalise drivers for failing to accept requests—as an incident of its prerogatives to determine its product, protect its technology, and control its relationship with customers. It noted that the licenses drivers signed "prohibit individuals accessing the platform from interfering or disrupting the ride-sharing services." According to Lyft, not accepting requests was "interfering or disrupting" ride services.[60]

Why does embedding these conventional incidents of employment, like termination and discipline, into software transform them into incidents of property? Perhaps the digital platform further merges different prerogatives in the same kinds of decisions—decisions now said to be about programming. And rarefied prerogatives, like controlling customer relationships or determining what to produce, perhaps resemble more solid property rights when suffused with claims about protecting proprietary software.[61] Not even franchises suggest that they have a right to terminate workers in their capacity as enterprise owners rather than employers. Uber and Lyft take the arguments further. FedEx and franchises have intimated that disciplinary authority might be an indirect means of protecting their reputations and right to control their products; however, the platforms turn disciplinary authority and control into a direct component of that property. Workers are subjected to more intensive and refined control at the hands of the algorithm, while the law is perched to excuse companies from the legal consequences of that control.

Critique

The appeals to entrepreneurial prerogatives in disputes over employment status are subject to critique. The origin of the employer's authority to control the enterprise—to assert many of the prerogatives we see in these disputes—was the employment contract.[62] But this status is precisely what the alleged employer

---

57 *Ibid.*
58 Uber Reply Brief, *O'Connor v. Uber Technologies, Inc.,* 82 F.Supp.3d 1133 (N.D. Cal. 2015).
59 See *Cotter v. Lyft, Inc.,* 60 F. Supp. 3d 1067, 1076 (N.D. Cal. 2015).
60 Lyft Motion for Summary Judgment at 13, *Cotter v. Lyft.*
61 See "Critique" below.
62 Tomlins, *Law, Labor, and Ideology,* 295.

abjures in a dispute over employment status. Rejecting its authority as employer leaves one legal pillar to support its authority—property.

This leads us to a second problem: traditional property rights are inadequate to the task of supporting this authority. That property rights could not support the vast prerogatives employers sought over the business enterprise was recognized in the first half of the 19th century.[63] The right to exclude *might* support some authority over the material organization of the plant and choice of technology to use in production. However, property rights could not support the authority the employer sought to coordinate a complex division of labour in production. What they sought was the authority to rationalize and discipline the extraction of energy from worker bodies (and these are the prerogatives that FedEx, Lyft, and Uber assert over the enterprise). Since property rights over the means of production appeared inadequate, 19th-century courts expanded the master's prerogatives over the individual servant under the traditional master-servant relationship to include a right to "exercise powers of detailed regulation in workplace relations for itself."[64]

Even if a conventional understanding of property rights could sustain some of the prerogatives the alleged employer claims in these disputes, there is yet another, fatal, problem with these arguments: there is no reason that the legal standards for employment status should cede to property rights.

Although referencing debates over the scope of collective bargaining under the NLRA, Neil Chamberlain's critique is an apropos response to courts that would use property rights to limit the scope of labour statutes in employment status disputes: "While property rights carry with them a power of disposition of goods, they do not carry an equal power to use those goods *if* the cooperation of others is necessary to that use."[65] Like any property owner, the employer-owner may need to secure the cooperation of others to realise the fruits of its property. Property rights over non-labour inputs to production and investment capital confer no absolute right to direct the enterprise without regard to the owner's need to bargain with others—including workers—to make the most of its property. The case against such a right is even stronger when legislation intervenes to boost workers' bargaining leverage, or, in the employment status context, to establish baseline

---

63 *Ibid.*
64 *Ibid.*, 284. This expansion of master-servant authority indicates that the discussion of the origin of the ambiguity in the first part is incomplete: the semblance between the employer's authority over the enterprise *qua* employer and its authority *qua* property owner was also a consequence of achieving, as a matter of legal facticity, the employer's "ownership" of the enterprise. Given the expansion of master-servant authority, for property rights to be a plausible doppelgänger, property rights had to expand as well. This chapter does not undertake a historical exposition of this process. However, it suggests that the recognition of "managerial prerogative" under the NLRA is part of the story. Dilating the employer's authority in its capacity as enterprise owner helped make possible the shifting rationalisations for employer authority seen in recent disputes over employment status.
65 Neil W. Chamberlain, *The Labor Sector: An Introduction to Labor in the American Economy* (New York: McGraw-Hill, 1965), 314–315.

terms for that cooperation, like requiring that employers pay a minimum wage. Private property rights do not confer a private right to manage the full social means of production.[66]

Not all decision makers accept either the distinction between employer authority and property rights or the premise that exercises of property rights should be unencumbered by labour regulation. The London tribunal directly confronted Uber's argument that it was controlling property, not labour, under a pointed subheading, "Instruction, management and control or preserving the integrity of the platform"? The judge explained:

> The Claimants' [drivers'] case was that, in a host of different ways, Uber instructs, manages and controls the drivers. The Respondents…stoutly deny doing so and say that, to the extent that the documentary evidence points to them guiding or directing drivers' behavior, it merely reflects their common interest in ensuring a satisfactory 'rider experience' and (to adopt a formula repeatedly employed by [Uber's counsel) "preserving the integrity of the platform."[67]

In another case, an appellate court rejected the trial court's suggestion that any control FedEx imposed on the drivers that reflected the company's pre-rogatives over its customer relationships were irrelevant: "Many general instructions set forth by FedEx are based on customer demands' and FedEx required 'that drivers meet these customer demands' which the court con-cluded involved 'the results of the drivers' work.' Of course, it is FedEx that decides what services are provided to its customers, and when."[68] Another court noted, "[A]t some level, all company control and supervision over its workers are geared toward satisfying its clients and customers."[69] Disagree-ment as to how to deal with appeals to the company's ownership preroga-tives reflects both the salience of the property/employment ambiguity in service work and speciousness of the assumption that labour legislation must cede to property rights.

---

66 See Atleson, *Values and Assumptions*, 114
67 *Aslam and Farrar v. Uber*, Case Nos 2202550/2015, at 13, para. 47 (London Employment Tribunal, Oct. 28, 2015), *aff'd Uber BV v Aslam*, [2017] No. UKEAT/0056/17/DA (London Emp't App. Trib., Nov. 10, 2017). In another case, Uber characterized its disciplin-ary policy of logging off drivers who reject three ride requests in a row, as "a system integrity measure since…a trip request is sent to only one Uber driver at any given time, and having drivers who do not intend to give rides Online slows down the process of connecting riders and drivers, and leads to a poorer user experience for riders." *Razak v. Uber Techs., Inc.*, No. CV 16-573, 2017 WL 4052417, at *5 (E.D. Pa. Sept. 13, 2017).
68 *Craig v. FedEx Ground Package Sys., Inc.*, 686 F.3d 423, 429 (7th Cir. 2012), certified ques-tion answered, 300 Kan. 788, 335 P.3d 66 (2014). See also *Craig v. FedEx Ground Package Sys., Inc.*, 335 P.3d 66, 89-90 (Kan. 2014).
69 *Hurst v. Buczek Enterprises, LLC*, 870 F. Supp. 2d 810, 826 (N.D. Cal. 2012).

Conclusions

Employment status disputes involving interactive service work and work subject to digitalised control require decision makers to confront the duality of employer contractual rights and property rights. By claiming the extent of the customer interaction as their product, and by embedding managerial controls in software, companies try to subject extended and deeper forms of labour control to their prerogatives as owners of the means of production. In redefining the direction of labour as the disposition and protection of property, they also seek to expand and entrench their factitious status as "owners" of the enterprise. At stake in these arguments is whether the law will enfold the rights of labour into the prerogatives of capital and augur the restoration of the master's property rights to the servant's labour.

Part II

The impact of new technologies in the employees' private life

7 Technological innovation and its impact on the employment contract: special reference to the video surveillance and the intervention of private detectives

María Carmen López Aniorte, Francisco Miguel Ortiz González-Conde and Antonio Megías-Bas

Introduction[1]

The fundamental rights and public freedoms of working people,[2] frequently, collide with freedom of enterprise (Article 38 CE), which may limit its exercise through the execution of business powers of surveillance and control. The Spanish Constitutional Court, with unequal fortune and through a not always uniform doctrine, has tried to strike a balance between conflicting rights.[3] Now, this doctrine will have to be nuanced after the recent rulings of the ECHR Bărbulescu II and López Ribalda, which require a rethinking of the theory of fundamental rights of working people in the Spanish labour legal system.[4]

The basis of fundamental rights is the "dignity of the person",[5] one of its most important derivations, the right to privacy.[6] In Spain, its legal regulation is contained in the Organic Laws 1/1982, of May 5, on Civil Protection of the Right to Honour, Privacy and the Image itself, and 15/1999, of December 13,

---

1 Main abbreviations used: ET (Royal Legislative Decree 1/1995, of March 24, approving the revised text of the Law on the Statute of Workers); LRJS (Law 36/2011, of 10 October, Regulatory of the Social Jurisdiction; CE (Spanish Constitution 1978), TC (Constitutional Court), TS (Supreme Court) STJ (Superior Court); SSTC (Constitutional Court Judgments), RTC (Constitutional Court Code), SSTS (Supreme Court Judgments), RJ (Repertoire of Jurisprudence), SSTSJ (Judgments of a Superior Court of Justice), AS (Aranzadi Social), FJ (Legal Basis), ECHR (European Court of Human Rights), article (article), and cit . (Cited).
2 For all, SSTC 57/1994, of February 28 (RTC 1994, 57), 143/1994, of May 9, and no. 98/2000 (RTC, 98, 2000).
3 SSTC 204/1997, of November 25, FJ 2; 1/1998, of January 12, FJ 3, 90/1999, of May 26, FJ 3, 98/2000, of April 10, FJ 7; y80/2001, of March 26, among others.
4 Maria Emilia Casas Baamonde "Informar antes de vigilar. ¿Tiene el Estado la obligación positiva de garantizar un mínimo de vida privada a los trabajadores en la empresa en la era digital? La necesaria intervención del legislador laboral", *Derecho de las Relaciones Laborales* (2018), 2, pp. 103–121.
5 Article 10.1 EC.
6 Article 18.1. EC.

on Protection of Personal Data, hereinafter LOPD (developed by RD 1720/2007, of December 21), regulations that must be completed with Instruction 1/2006, of November 8, issued by the Spanish Agency for Data Protection. Meanwhile, in the field of the European Union, reference standard Directive 95/46/EC of the European Parliament and of the Council of October 24, 1995, concerning the protection of natural persons with regard to the processing of personal data and the free circulation of these data. And, on the international front, the Council of Europe Convention for the Protection of Persons with Regard to the Automated Treatment of Personal Data, ratified by Spain on January 31, 1984.

The conflict between business management power and the right to privacy of working people

The managerial power of businesses is based on art. 38.1 CE, where the freedom of business is recognised within the framework of the market economy. At the legal level, this power is implicitly referenced in art. 1.1. ET; and reiterated in art. 5. c) ET, where it is established that it is a basic duty of the worker to comply with "the orders and instructions of the employer in the regular exercise of his managerial faculties", and in art. 20.1 ET, in which it states that "the worker shall be obliged to perform the work agreed upon under the direction of the employer or person delegated by him". Manifestations of managerial power are the functions of surveillance and control, referred to in art. 20.3 ET, where it is established that the employer may adopt "the measures deemed most appropriate for surveillance and control," in order to "verify compliance by the worker of their obligations and duties" and by adopting such measures a company must give "consideration due to its employees' human dignity".

In principle, there are no prohibited or excluded methods of control and a company may choose the one they deem the most appropriate to achieve their desired outcome.[7] As the only guarantee of respect for the rights of salaried persons, art. 64. 5.f) ET establishes that the worker's committee will have the right to issue a report, prior to the execution by the employer of the decisions adopted by the latter, regarding the implementation and revision of labour control systems. Guarantee that it is not always respected, and that is often insufficient. In any case, "no evidence that has its origin or that has been obtained, directly or indirectly, by means of procedures that violate fundamental rights or public liberties" will be admitted.[8]

---

7 María Carmen López Aniorte "Límites constitucionales al ejercicio del poder directivo empresarial mediante el uso de las TIC y otros medios de vigilancia y seguridad privada en el ordenamiento jurídico español", *Revista Policía y Seguridad Pública* (2014), 1, pp. 31–52.
8 Article 90.2 LRJS.

The expansion of forms of business control through new technologies

In recent times, the instruments for the control of work performance have been substantially expanded as a result of the use, for this purpose, of new information and communication technologies, the mechanisms of reproduction of images and sound and biometric or remote controls. These new forms of surveillance vastly expand the possibilities of control, rendering obsolete the traditional systems, while raising doubts of constitutionality by the possible affectation of the fundamental rights of working people to privacy, the ownership of the image and the secrecy of the communications and data protection.[9]

Due to the potential harmful nature of such rights, some of the business behaviours with the greatest media coverage in this area have related to the means by which images and/or sounds have been for the enforcement of compliance with the labour benefit, as well as the control of the use, by the worker, of the company's email.[10] And of the other computer tools that it puts at your disposal for the performance of your activity.[11]

The courts appear to be more inclined to accept the use of new technologies as a means for controlling the delivery of services by working people and considering them as an extension of a human body.[12] In this regard, the judicial doctrine has understood that control through video cameras can be as legitimate as exercised directly from the management company,[13] provided that the control is strictly for work related purposes and is limited in geographical proximity to the workplace premises, excluding toilets, changing rooms and rest rooms.

It possible to draw some general rules applicable to the activity monitoring and corporate control from the doctrine of TC, for the protection of fundamental rights of working people who here may conflict.[14] These rules make up the so-called proportionality trial, whose overcoming is configured as a guarantee of respect for those rights. However, it is doubtful that, in view of the recent ECHR doctrine, it can be considered a single guarantee.

The proportionality trial requires compliance with the following requirements:[15]

---

9 Aurelio Desdentado Bonete and Ana Belén Muñoz Ruiz, *Control informático, videovigilancia y protección de datos en el trabajo* (2012), Lex Nova, Spain.

10 Alejandra Selma Penalva "Los límites de la tolerancia en la utilización del ordenador de la empresa para fines personales", *Revista Doctrinal Aranzadi Social*, (2012), 11, pp. 55–61.

11 Francisca María Ferrando García "Vigilancia y control de los trabajadores y derecho a la intimidad en el contexto de las nuevas tecnologías", *Revista de Trabajo y Seguridad Social CEF* (2016), 399, pp. 38–68.

12 Javier Thibault Aranda, *El control multimedia de la actividad laboral* (2014), Tirant lo Blanch, Spain.

13 STSJ Galicia 21 April 1995 (AS 1514).

14 Among others, S STC 99/1994, 11-4-1994 (RTC 1994, 99), 98/2000, 10-4-2000 (RTC 2000, 98), and 186/2000, 10-7-2000 (RTC 2000, 186).

15 SSTC 186/2000, of July 10 (RTC 200, 186) and 170/2013, of October 7, 2013 (RTC 2013, 170).

1. It has to be treated of a justified measure, adopted, normally, in the presence of suspicions of irregular behaviour.
2. It will have to demonstrate its necessity, derived from the nonexistence of another more moderate measure to satisfy the business interest, with equal effectiveness, potentially less aggressive for the right of the worker.
3. Finally, a balance or proportionality between the benefit or benefit sought and the sacrifice required of the worker must be achieved.

Whether or not the results of the control exercise are recorded, stored or processed in automated files, said processes will be subject to the requirements regarding the protection of personal data contained in Organic Law 15/1999, of December 13, and in its development regulations, related above.

The control working people through electronic means of image capture

The pendular doctrine of the Constitutional Court

The SSTC 98/2000 and 186/2000: absence of transparency and legal uncertainty derived from the proportionality trial

We start this section by referring to an interesting sentence that deals with an assumption of business control by capturing sound (not the image). This is STC 98/2000, of 10 April, in which the following assumption is considered: in a casino, in order to control conversations between employed persons and customers in the areas of French roulette and box, it was decided to utilise one of the security systems that were already available – consisting of a closed circuit television – with the installation of microphones that would allow the Casino to collect and record conversations that could take place in the indicated sections of the casino. The company was interested in eavesdropping because it allowed them to resolve claims in the game and in the cash changes. No report was requested from the Works Committee, although the start-up of the recordings began after the communication to the Committee.

TC believes that the recordings violate the fundamental right to privacy of those persons recorded, although carried out in the workplace, with prior communication to their representatives – although without the mandatory report – and the existence of a business interest in the knowledge of the facts. The High Court resolves the conflict by applying the proportionality judgment, and as a result of it, concludes that, although the recording is not without utility, the mere utility does not justify the use of these means when there were other control mechanisms, in the understanding that the purpose pursued (give a surplus of security), is disproportionate to the sacrifice that implies the right to privacy of workers.

Meanwhile, the STC 186/2000, dated July 10, an appeal filed by an employee dismissed for irregularities in the management of the cash register, accredited by video surveillance cameras installed in the work place, which focused from the ceiling on the three cash registers in which irregularities had been detected, without notice to the affected employee, nor to the representatives of the workers. The TC concludes that filming and recording in this situation did not violate the right to privacy and/or the image of the worker, guaranteed by art. 18.1 CE, on the understanding that the measure exceeds the requirements of the proportionality trial. In this sense, it considers that the filming of the employee in the workplace would be a measure: 1) justified, by the suspicion of irregularities; 2) suitable for the purpose pursued by the company, which was to verify whether the worker actually committed the suspected irregularities; 3) necessary, since the filming serves as proof of the irregularities, 4) and balanced, given that the recording was limited to a specific area, near the cash register, and it was for a limited time duration.

The circumstance where the installation of the closed-circuit television was not previously placed at the discretion of the Company Committee or affected working people, lacks the judgment of the TC, from the perspective of constitutional significance, considering that it is "a matter of mere ordinary legality, completely alien to the subject of the protection resource".

According to jurisprudence and judicial doctrine after the SSTC 98/2000 and 186/2000, the capture of images or sounds for monitoring the work performance, in time and place of work, it may constitute an illegitimate interference with the worker's right to privacy, if the measure used does not exceed the proportionality judgment. The application of this doctrine has led to a prosecution of the different situations raised, case by case,[16] which, on occasion, has led to the adoption of contradictory solutions in identical cases. There are paradigmatic examples of the danger that the criterion of proportionality entails, the SSTSJ Galicia of November 30, 2001,[17] and of March 20, 2002,[18] regarding two cases of video-surveillance that captured the work activity of two night watchmen of the same museum. In both cases, the company had contracted with a private agency to provide an image recording service, by means of a micro-camera, in a room of the museum in which they provide security services, on night shift. The guards had not been previously informed that they would be captured on surveillance camera for the duration of their shifts. In both situations the video footage showed that both employees were in breach of their working/contractual obligations (they do not wear the regulatory uniform, they sleep, they surf the internet, and they receive visits...); nevertheless, the two cases had contradictory outcomes.

The judgment of November 30, 2001 concludes that the guard's right to privacy had been violated, because although it was admitted that the control measure could be suitable, the judicial body understands that it did not become necessary or balanced, and that shortcomings suppose a breach of the constitutional doctrine in the matter. It also emphasises that "the measure (...) was

16 Aurelio Desdentado Bonete and Ana Belén Muñoz Ruiz, *Control informático, videovigilancia y protección de datos en el trabajo* (2012), Lex Nova, Spain.
17 AS 390.
18 AS 3385.

installed surreptitiously, as it did not remain in view, was not communicated to the Museum's management and was not preceded by the report of the works council". For its part, the judgment of March 20, 2002 rejects the violation of the worker's right to privacy, relying, fundamentally, on three arguments: 1) the micro-camera was installed in the main workplace, and not in a space reserved for the safeguarding of that person's privacy (rest space, toilets…); 2) the measure was justified because it allowed the achievement of the proposed objective of verifying the behaviour of the worker; 3) there was no other more moderate business measure that could have achieved this purpose. Regarding the lack of information of the measure to the Works Committee and the workers affected, the judicial body stated that "this circumstance is not relevant from the constitutional perspective", and that, from the point of view of ordinary legality, "the knowledge of the recording would defeat the purpose of intended control."

Finally, opaque forms of video surveillance are accepted, usually by the use of hidden cameras, without prior information to the workers and their representatives. Numerous pronouncements insist on the need to overcome the proportionality trial, but do not attach importance to the previous information on the application of video surveillance, which they consider a mere matter of ordinary legality.[19]

The faltering road to transparency control mechanisms: SSTC 27/2013 and 39/2016

STC 29/2013 of 11 February is to start from the constitutional doctrine exposed above. The case settled was as follows: the University of Seville, before the suspicion of irregularities in the compliance of the working day by an employee of the Personnel of Administration and Services of said university, proceeded to supervise their working day through the images captured by the video surveillance cameras installed in the university campus, cameras that – according to statements made to the Data Protection Agency by the university – responded to a "public safety measure in such a place open to the public". After verifying, in this way, the irregularities committed, the appellant was punished by suspension of employment and salary, a penalty that, being imposed based on this single test, the TC declares null for violating art. 18.4 CE.

Unlike previous resolutions in the STC 29/2013, the fundamental right alleged is not art. 18.1 CE (right to honour, personal and family privacy and one's own image) but the art. 18.4 CE, which allows the High Court to focus on the solution of the case from a new perspective, that of the right to protection of

---

19 In this way, the STSJ Comunidad Valenciana 27–4–2004 (AS 3821), in a case of control by hidden camera of compliance with the working hours of the cleaning of a dental practice, resolves that the business measure was provided, not considering necessary justify the hidden nature of the control mechanism. In the same line, STSJ Galicia, of March 20, 2002 (AS 3385), cit.

data of working people. In this sense, the TC states that, in the case under trial, "the video-surveillance cameras installed in the university campus reproduced the image of the appellant and allowed the control of his working day; they therefore captured their image which is a personal data, and were used to monitor compliance with their contract"; the University of Seville used the described ends the recordings, "being the person in charge of the treatment of the data without having informed the worker on that utility of labour supervision associated to the captures of his image", violating "the art. 18.4 CE". Thus, "deprived the person of those powers of disposition and control over their personal data, it was also their fundamental right to data protection".

The TC considers that this conclusion does not counteract the existence of signage and notifications announcing the installation of cameras and the capture of images, or that the creation of the file had been notified to the Spanish Agency for Data Protection, because "it was also necessary to provide prior information in an express, precise, clear and unequivocal manner to the workers the purpose of control of the work activity to which this recruitment could be directed", (...) "explaining very particularly that they could be used for the imposition of disciplinary sanctions for breaches of the contract of work".

The pendulum line, the STC 39/2016, announced on March 3, assumes the recovery of business technological control lost, largely in the ruling of 2013, because, by a broad interpretation of the powers and rights of the company *ex* art. 20.3 ET, free to this one of the "previous and express, precise, clear and unequivocal information to the workers of the purpose of control of the labour activity to which that recruitment could be directed" demanded by the STC 29/2013.

This judgment resolves an appeal lodged by a worker of Bershka who was dismissed for appropriating cash from the cash register. This breach was verified by the installation of security cameras overlooking the cashier area. The worker filed an application for dismissal requesting the declaration of nullity for having violated his honour, privacy and dignity, and subsidiary the declaration of inadmissibility, based on the images obtained from a camera that was not installed for the sole purpose of employee surveillance and whose installation, for that purpose specific, the workers had not been warned. The company itself had placed the information badge required by Instruction 1/2006.

The novelty of the doctrine contained in this judgment, with respect to the previous one, is that it does not require workers to be warned that the video surveillance for security reasons could also be used for the control of work activity. The company would not need the express consent of the worker "for the treatment of images that have been obtained through the cameras installed in the company for the purpose of safety or labour control, since it is a measure aimed at controlling the employment relationship and is in accordance with art. 20.3" ET; it would need such consent if the purpose of the treatment of the images was not directly related to the maintenance, development or control of the contractual relationship. In short, "taking the worker information prior to the installation of video cameras surveillance through the corresponding informative badge and having treated the images captured for the control of the employment relationship, art. 18.4 CE."

For the rest, the installation of security cameras that control the cashier area would not violate the right to privacy enshrined in art. 18.1, when considered a justified measure, because there are suspicions of contractual breaches; suitable, for the purpose pursued by the company (verify irregularities and take disciplinary measures); necessary, since the recording would serve as proof of the irregularities; and balanced by limiting itself to the box area.

The doctrine of the STC 39/2016, of March 3, has been fully collected in the SSTS of January 31, 2017[20] and of February 2, 2017.[21]

A definitive point of inflection? The Judgment of the European Court of Human Rights of 9 January 2018; López Ribalda and others v Spain

In this judgment, the ECHR resolved, by six votes to one, that, in the case prosecuted, there was a violation of Article 8 of the European Convention on Human Rights, specifically respect for private and family life,[22] and unanimously, that art. 8 of the said Convention, on the right to a fair trial. The case related to five employees of a Spanish supermarket chain who were covertly recorded using both visible and hidden cameras who were alleged to have stolen money. The company notified its staff of the visible cameras but did not inform either the employees or the Works Committee of the hidden ones. The employees were dismissed based on the video recordings. The Spanish courts took the recordings as valid evidence and confirmed the dismissal decisions. The ECHR found that, according to Spanish legislation on data protection, the plaintiffs should have been informed that they were under video surveillance, which had not happened,[23] so that the national courts had not achieved a balance between the right to privacy of the workers and the property rights of the company. However, the Court considered that the process had been fair because the video material was not the only evidence on which the national courts relied when confirming the dismissal decisions and because the plaintiffs had been able to challenge the recordings.

---

20 Resolution No.: 77/2017.
21 Resolution No.: 96/2017.
22 Art. 8.1 the European Convention on Human Rights on the right to respect for private and family life, states: "1. Everyone has the right to respect for his private and family life, his home and his correspondence."
23 The ECHR notes that the situation differs from the *Köpke v. Germany*, since at the time the employer made the covert video surveillance following suspicion of theft, "the conditions under which an employer could resort to video surveillance of an employee to investigate a crime had not yet been established" in Germany. And it goes on to say: in the Spanish case, in a situation "where the right of each affected party to be informed of the existence, purpose and form of the covert surveillance was clearly regulated and protected by law, the claimants had reasonable expectations of privacy."

The ECHR emphasises the need for prior, express, specific and unequivocal information required by art. 5.1 LOPD,[24] a requirement that is reiterated in Instruction 1/2006, of November 8, of the Spanish Agency for Data Protection, and, at the international level, in the Recommendation of the Committee of Ministers of the Council Europe of 1 April 2015 on the processing of personal data in the workplace, which set as a major guarantee of transparency.

These requirements, as has been observed, have been overlooked by TC (with the exception of STC 29/2013), the TS and judicial doctrine. The ECHR ruling represents a turning point in the matter that will allow deepening transparency and the protection of the privacy and personal data of working people in an environment of intensification of the capacity of business control of labour activity through of new technologies. The change of tendency has already materialised, in the judicial doctrine, in the STSJ Castilla-La Mancha dated January 12, 2018,[25] which, following the judgment of the ECHR concluded that the installation of video surveillance cameras in the workplace without notice violates the right to privacy of the worker, even if there were reasonable grounds for believing breaches of the same. Likewise, the judicial body resolves that the foregoing does not lead to the nullity of the dismissal, but to the nullity of the evidence thus obtained, qualifying the dismissal as unfair.

The control of working people by private detectives

On private investigation services in the workplace

Sometimes, the company considers it necessary to have control beyond the limits of the workplace, which requires the use of private detective services.[26] This is the case when it comes to supervising the work activity that has to be developed outside the business establishment (trade representatives, home salesmen, transporters…); when it is suspected that the worker performs illicit competition activities; when it is necessary to verify the causes of alleged non-attendance or punctuality or to check breaches of work; and in cases in which it is a matter of supervising certain extra-labour behaviours, contrary to the duty of good faith, of those who are in a situation of contractual suspension (temporary disability, maternity, leave of absence with the right to reserve a job).

---

24 Cristóbal Molina Navarrete "De Bărbulescu II a López Ribalda: ¿qué hay de nuevo en la protección de datos de los trabajadores. Comentario a la Sentencia del Tribunal Europeo de Derechos Humanos de 9 de enero de 2018, caso *López Ribalda et alli vs. España* (Demandas acumuladas 1874/13 y 8567/13)", *Revista de Trabajo y Seguridad Social CEF* (2018), 419, pp. 125–135.

25 JUR\2018\33307.

26 José Manuel del Valle Villar "El derecho a la intimidad del trabajador durante la relación de trabajo" Actualidad Laboral (1991), 3, pp. 480–499, and Carolina San Martín Mazzucconi "Detectives, nuevas tecnología y derecho a la intimidad de los trabajadores", *Revista Aranzadi Social* (2007), 52, pp. 1346–1352.

Law 5/2014, of April 4, on Private Security, which aims to overcome the regulatory deficiencies of its immediate normative precedent, specifies the functions of the private detective and defines private investigation services. In this regard, it states that "private detectives will be responsible for the personal execution of private investigation services (…), by conducting inquiries in relation to individuals, facts and private conduct", being obliged to prepare investigation reports and ratify the content of the same before the judicial or police authorities when they are required to do so (Article 37).

The criterion of the judicial bodies before corporate control by private detectives

The intervention of detectives is considered a precedent for cameras and microphones as a surveillance mechanism. It is a particularly invasive means in the private life of working people, especially when it comes to using new information and communication technologies, the mechanisms of reproduction of an image and sound, or biometric or distance controls. As a general rule, the judicial bodies admit this way of corporate control, provided that their need is proven, compliance with constitutional limits and the impossibility of using other more confidential means.[27] It is also accepted the incorporation of detective reports in the labour process as a means of proof in relation to the demonstration of eventual contractual breaches of the worker, in the understanding that they have an exclusively testimonial nature.[28]

On this instrument of control, the Supreme Court has indicated that the testimony of private detectives has in favour of its veracity, not only the guarantee of professionalism presumed in a legally regulated profession, but also the one that provides "the precise and continued dedication to the object of the further testimony to be issued and the complementary graphic or sound accreditations that are usually accompanied."[29] Precisely, the increasing professionalism of private detectives, and the fact that their activity is not usually limited to the mere observation of what has been investigated but also uses technical contributions, could advise their use, not only as testimony, but also as an expert.[30]

There are many judgments of the Chambers of the Social of the Spanish Superior Courts of Justice that consider the surveillance activity of a private detective an adequate measure of control of the work activity, which does not violate the right to privacy of the worker subjected to the surveillance. In this regard, the judgment of the ECHR of May 27, 2014[31] has stated that a recording made by a private

---

27 STS June 14, 1990.
28 STSJ Madrid of April 21, 2008 (Num. Of appeal 419/2008).
29 STS November 6, 1990.
30 Salcedo, M.C. "Intervención de detectives en las relaciones laborales", *Revista de Trabajo y Seguridad Social CEF* (2013), 368, pp. 86–140.
31 TEDU 2014, 34, De la Flor Cabrera c. Spain.

detective of a person is not an illegitimate interference in their right to privacy, honour or image, as set out in Article 8 of the Europe Agreement on Human Rights, provided that such activity takes place in public. And all this despite the fact that the idea that the protection of private life cannot be limited, a priori, to the areas that make up the "inner circle" of intimacy is gaining ground.[32]

The STSJ of Asturias of March 30, 2017: towards the limitation of the detective report test?

A worker, employed as a forestry technician, who spends only part of his working hours in an office (he was obliged to inform the company of his activities on the remainder of his working hours) is sanctioned for very serious misconduct due to absences and not being punctual at work. Months before an assembly took place, outside the company's facilities, in which he held a critical position with the company it was agreed that he would be the spokesperson/workers representative for the Committees.

Shortly after, the company ordered a follow-up report from a private detective, who described details of their daily lives, mixing private aspects and work activities, and photographs were provided. Coinciding with the development of the detective report, he was elected a staff delegate. It is recorded as proved that the worker, during follow-up had not changed the way the company worked and had met the objectives fixed by the company.

The sentence declared the sanction unjustified and considered that the company had violated the fundamental right to honour, privacy, freedom of association and freedom of expression of the worker. The Court held that the mechanisms of supervision and control used by the company had been excessive: to hiring a detective, installing a GPS in the vehicle made available to the worker, monitoring their activity and making a video recording of the employee are measures that violated the employee's right to privacy, especially when, as in this case, there were no well-founded suspicions of any contractual wrongdoing.

The ruling is relevant because it puts limits on the detective test, a test that can be especially invasive in people's private lives and that should only be admitted in very specific cases;[33] it is not clear, however, what would have been the criterion of the judicial body if there had been, on the part of the company, well-founded suspicions of any irregularity being committed.

Today, this test should be analysed in the light of transparency requirements of the judgment of the ECHR López Ribalda. In this way, to the extent that

---

32 Diego Álvarez Alonso "Despido disciplinario, seguimiento por detective privado y derecho a la intimidad. STSJ País Vasco 9 abril 2013 (AS 2014, 1587)", *Nueva Revista Española de Derecho del Trabajo* (2014), 171, pp. 329–338.

33 Jaime Cabeza Pereiro, "Informe de detectives, intimidad y otras cuestiones en el entorno de la potestad disciplinaria del empresario: Comentario a la Sentencia del Tribunal de Justicia de Asturias de 30 de marzo de 2017, rec. núm. 2997/2016", *Revista de Trabajo y Seguridad Social CEF* (2017), 415, pp. 173–181.

who carries out private research makes use of the video surveillance – which is often ordinary working people who should be informed in advance – should be in accordance with the Spanish legislation on protecting data; which, no doubt, to a large extent, would remove a large majority of the traditional tasks of the private investigation services, according to art. 48 Law 5/2014, of April 4, on Private Security.

Conclusions

According to the doctrine of the TC, all means of corporate control, including those based on video surveillance and the hiring of detectives, must overcome the so-called "proportionality trial", as a guarantee for the protection of the fundamental rights of workers. However, the casuistic nature of the judgment of proportionality and the relative freedom of appreciation that allows the interpreter of the rule, generates legal uncertainty because it makes it possible for identical cases to be resolved in a contrary manner.

Moving away from the positions defended from the European Union, favourable to the transparency of the activity of the workers, in Spain, the courts have tolerated opaque forms of video surveillance, with the use of a hidden camera, without a prior report from the worker's committee, and no information provided to workers, in accordance with data protection regulations. The TC, except in S 27/2013, has not granted relevance to such lack of information, considering this omission a mere matter of ordinary legality that does not harm the right to privacy.

The ECHR Judgment of January 9, 2018, case of *López Ribalda and others v Spain* emphasises the need for prior, express, specific and unequivocal information required by the LOPD. This ruling will allow deepening transparency and the protection of privacy and personal data of workers in an environment of intensification of the capacity of business control of labour activity through new technologies. The judgment of the López Ribalda case has already been applied in the STSJ Castilla-La Mancha on January 12, 2018.

As a general rule, the judicial bodies admit the intervention of private detectives as a way to control compliance with labour duties, provided that their need is proved, compliance with the constitutional limits and the impossibility of using other more confidential means. These professionals currently have innovative devices that, while improving the effectiveness of their research, raise new questions of constitutionality, especially when they involve a disproportionate interference with the right to privacy of the subject to surveillance.

To this day, detective work must be analysed in light of the transparency requirements on the TEDH López Ribalda ruling/judgement. Thus, if those who perform the private investigation make use of video surveillance, the workers subjected to it must be informed, in accordance with the Data Protection Regulations.

8 New technologies and the employee's right to privacy

Artur Rycak

The concept of the right to privacy

The discussion concerning the precise determination of the concept of privacy or the right to privacy has lasted for over a hundred years, i.e. since the publication of a famous work of American lawyers V. Brandeis and E. Warren entitled "The Right to Privacy" published in the Harvard Law Review in 1890.[1] Countless things have already been written about the right to privacy in European legal thought, yet there are still no clear-cut views on the boundaries of this law in work relations.

The right to protection of private life is the subject of numerous regulations contained in the acts of international law, including the European Convention for the Protection of Human Rights and Fundamental Freedoms, the Charter of Fundamental Rights of the European Union and the International Covenant on Civil and Political Rights.

According to art. 8 sec. 1 of the European Convention on Human Rights (hereinafter "the Convention"), everyone has the right to respect for their private and family life, their home and their correspondence. According to art. 7 of the EU Charter of Fundamental Rights (hereinafter "CFR") everyone has the right to respect for private and family life, home and communication. According to art. 17 sec. 1st of the International Covenant on Civil and Political Rights none can be exposed to arbitrary or unlawful interference with their private life, family, home or correspondence, or against unlawful attacks on his honor and reputation. According to paragraph 2 of this article, everyone has the right to legal protection from such interference and attacks.

Art. 12 of the Universal Declaration of Human Rights also refers to the right to privacy, according to which one must not arbitrarily interfere in anyone's private, family, domestic life, or in their correspondence, or defame their honour or good name. Everyone has the right to legal protection against such interference or defamation.

In the Polish legal system, the right to privacy was distinguished as a separate subjective right in court judicature in the 1980s, whereas in the judicature of the Constitutional Court it derived from the principle of the democratic state of

---

1 V. Brandeis and E. Warren, "The Right to Privacy", *Harvard Law Review*, 1890, Vol. 4, s. 193.

law in the 1990s.[2] Currently, it is assumed that this is a non-transferable right, of a personal nature, subject only to such restrictions as the Constitution expressly provides. Its source is the dignity of man, and its legitimacy is in the autonomy of the individual.

In the European and Polish science of labour law, there is a lack of mutual views on the definition of the right to privacy. In Anglo-Saxon science a broad and narrow understanding of the term is distinguished. In broad terms, it is assumed that privacy is a state in which an individual makes decisions regarding himself without the interference of third parties.[3] In narrow terms, it is a state in which an individual decides about the scope and range of information shared and communicated to other people.

The most popular, as it seems, definition proposed in American science at the end of the nineteenth century by T. Codey, defines this right as "the right to be left alone, to live your own life" (right to be alone[4]). Its purpose is to protect the individual from arbitrary intervention of public authorities and against the community and other individuals.[5]

Similarly, the right to privacy is defined in the judicature of the European Court of Human Rights. Protection of the right to private life applies to both physical and mental integrity of the person[6] and the right to personal development and autonomy.[7] The Court at the same time takes up the position that there is neither the possibility nor the need for a precise definition of private life.[8]

The Court does not consider it possible or necessary to attempt an exhaustive definition of the notion of "private life". However, it would be too restrictive to limit the notion to an "inner circle" in which the individual may live his own personal life as he chooses and to exclude therefrom entirely the outside world not encompassed within that circle. Respect for private life must also comprise to a certain degree the right to establish and develop relationships with other human beings. There appears, furthermore, to be no reason of principle why this understanding of the notion of "private life" should be taken to exclude activities of a professional or business nature since it is, after all, in the course of their working lives that the majority of people have a significant, if not the greatest, opportunity of developing relationships with the outside world. "This view is supported by the fact that, as was rightly pointed

---

2 See the judgment of the Polish Constitutional Tribunal in case 21/96.
3 See J. Sobczak, in: *Karta Praw Podstawowych w Unii Europejskiej*, Komentarz pod red. A. Wróbla, Warszawa, C.H. Beck, 2013, p. 221.
4 See W. Sokolewicz, „Prawo do prywatności" in: L. Pastusiak (red.), *Prawa człowieka w Stanach Zjednoczonych*, Warszawa, Książka i Wiedza, 1985, p. 248.
5 More about determination of the concept of "privacy" and "a right to privacy" see J. Braciak, "Prawo do prywatności", Warszawa, Wydawnictwo Sejmowe, 2004, p. 28 and following; see also M. Wujczyk, *Prawo pracownika do ochrony prywatności*, Warszawa, Wolters Kluwer business, 2012, p. 69 and following.
6 *Judgment X and Y vs The Netherlands* of 26 March 1985, application no. 8978/80.
7 *Judgment Bensaid vs Great Britain* of 6 February 2001, application no. 44599/98.
8 As in the case of *Niemietz vs Germany*, see footnote no. 1.

out by the Commission, it is not always possible to distinguish clearly which of an individual's activities form part of his professional or business life and which do not. Thus, especially in the case of a person exercising a liberal profession, his work in that context may form part and parcel of his life to such a degree that it becomes impossible to know in what capacity he is acting at a given moment of time").

The very notion of private life is defined in the Court's judicature very broadly.[9]

From a philosophical perspective, it can be said that the sphere of private life embraces such circumstances as to which the individual's interest over the public interest or the interest of other people can be assumed.[10]

The right to protection of private life in employment relations

The concept of the right to privacy in employment relations, or more broadly in any work relationships also performed on the basis of civil law contracts, is extremely interesting, and the results of research on that issue are of great practical importance.

Analysis of the statements of both foreign and Polish legal doctrine as well as analysis of the views of the judicature allows to conclude that the right to privacy also includes professional life.[11]

In the judicature of the European Court of Human Rights, it is assumed that professional life permeates private life, therefore it is impossible to talk about the right to privacy only in the sphere of non-professional life. This position of the Court can be found in many cases.[12]

In its judicature, the Court recognises that private life "which encompasses the right for an individual to form and develop relationships with other human beings, including relationships of a professional or business nature".[13] Against the background of the interpretation of art. 8 of the Convention, the Court accepts that

---

9 The judgment of 19 April 2002 in the case of *Pretty vs The United Kingdom,* application no. 2346/02.

10 More about the notion of private life see: J. Rubenfeld, "The Right of Privacy", *Harvard Law Review*, 1989, Vol. 102, p. 737; O. De Schutter, „La vie privée entre droit de la personnalité et liberté", *Revue trimestrielle des droits de l'homme*, 1999, p. 827, P. Wachsmann, "Le droit au secret de la vie privé", in: *Le droit au respect de la vie privée au sens de la Convention européenne des droits de l'homme*, F. Sudre, Bruylant 2005, p. 119; i F. Rigaux, „La protection de la vie privée en Europe", in: *Le droit commun de l'Europe et l'avenir de l'enseignement juridique*, B. Witte, C. Forder, eds., Metro, Kluwer 1992, p. 185; M. Wild, in: *Konstytucja RP. Tom I. Komentarz – Art. 1-86*, ed. M. Safjan, L. Bosek, Warszawa, C.H. Beck, 2016, p. 1175.

11 See, for example, papers of the famous German lawyer H. Giesker, 1904.

12 The *Niemetz vs Germany* judgment of 16 December 1992, application no. 13710/88, § 29; the *Bigaeva vs Greece* judgment of 28 May 2009, application no. 26713/05, § 23; the Oleksandr *Volkov vs Ukraine* judgment of 9 January 2013, application no. 21722/11, § 165–167; The *Fernández Martínez vs Spain* judgment of 12 June 2014, application no. 56030/07, § 110; The *Lopez Ribalda and others vs Spain* judgment of 9 January 2018, complaint no 1874/13 and 8567/13.

13 *The C. vs Belgium* judgment of 7 August 1996, § 25, application no. 21794/93.

this provision also protects a right to personal development, and the right to establish and develop relationships with other human beings and the outside world.[14]

In the case *Niemietz vs Federal Republic of Germany* (1992), the Court assumed that "the notion of 'private life' should be taken to exclude activities of a professional or business nature." Even if the interference had a legitimate aim, namely preventing crime and protecting others, it was not proportionate to the aims claimed because "the search impinged on professional secrecy to an extent that appears disproportionate in the circumstances." The Court's judicature further recognises that any restrictions imposed on access to the profession have an impact on private life.[15]

In the case of *Özpınar vs Turkey*,[16] it was considered that under certain circumstances the removal from office constitutes an interference with the right to respect for private life.

In the following cases, the Court underlines that the majority of people build their social identity and enter into relationships with other people through their professional work.

In the judicature, the boundaries of the right to privacy in matters of people performing public functions are set differently. The case concerns the so-called information autonomy of these people. The right to keep confidential information concerning the professional life of a person performing a public function is in conflict with the right of the public to access information about the performance of public functions, in particular the value of transparency of public life.[17] Performing a public function means that the right to be forgotten is severely restricted. If the performance of a professional work consists mainly in the performance of a public function by a given person, the right to protect the private life of such a person must, by its very nature, be much narrower than the right of a person who does not perform a public function.

Areas of the right to privacy violation in work relations with the use of modern technologies

Violation of the employee's privacy rights may occur in many areas. It is impossible to discuss the extensive problem of this issue in this chapter. It is therefore

---

14 See, for example, Burghartz, cited above, opinion of the Commission, p. 37, § 47, and *Friedl vs Austria*, judgment of 31 January 1995, Series A no. 305B, opinion of the Commission, p. 20, § 45; the *Pretty vs the United Kingdom* Judgment of 29 July 2002, § 61, application no. 2346/02,; see also: *Friedl v. Austria*, judgment of 31 January 1995, Series A no. 305B, opinion of the Commission, p. 20, § 45.

15 Such as *Sidabras and Džiautas vs Lithuania* judgment of 27 July 2004, applications no. 55480/00 and 59330/00. Also in the Bigaeva against Greece judgment of 28 May 2009, application no. 26713/05.

16 Judgment of 19 October 2010 r., application no. 20999/04, §§ 43-48.

17 See the judgment of Polish Constitution Tribunal of 21 October 1998, K 24/09, OTK 1998, no. 6, poz. 97.

proposed to limit the discussion by indicating in which situations during the employment relationship it is possible to violate the employee's right to privacy, with particular emphasis on those that may result from using modern technologies by employers.

In the subject literature, the following areas are enumerated in which there may occur a breach of the employee's privacy rights[18] namely monitoring the employer's premises using cameras, monitoring the employee's e-mail and reading the content of letters, monitoring of internet connections, monitoring telephone connections and control of conversation contents, control of text messages from the employee's work telephone, checking the content of the computer's hard drive, control of copying files from a computer disk to storage devices, control of traditional correspondence addressed to the employee, control of entries to the employer's premises, using wiretaps, personal control, inspection of the employee's lockers, disclosure of the employee's remuneration, giving opinions on the employee, disclosure of personal data via information materials, marketing, on the website, etc. of the employer, processing of employee biometric data, outsourcing of services, requirements regarding the appearance and outfit, use of voice and image, obligation to disclose information on criminal records, determination of an employee's confession, sexual preferences and views, including political ones, control of the employee's working time, including the use of time off from work, using the GPS system to track the car or movement of the employee, obtaining information about the employee's family life, obtaining information about the state of health, obtaining information about pregnancy, obtaining information about the assets of an employee and his family, sobriety control, carrying out polygraph tests and conducting psychological tests.

Most of the above potential violations can take place by means of modern technologies. This applies mainly to e-mail monitoring, browsing the internet, telephone calls, text messages, computer disk contents, copying computer data, monitoring premises, using GPS geolocation (or other), biometric data processing or using entrance cards to enter rooms in the establishment.

As a rule, the use of modern technologies by the employer, just like traditional ones, can be justified for a number of reasons, including: protecting the employer's property, protecting the company's good reputation, preventing or detecting corporate secrets, detecting the violation of non-competition clause, increasing efficiency and quality of production, employee safety, prevention of employee claims against the employer.[19]

---

18 M. Wujczyk, *Prawo pracownika do ochrony prywatności*, Warszawa, Wolters Kluwer Business, 2012, pp. 227–332.

19 See: The Employment Practices Code, International Commissioner's Office, 2013, p. 3, availilable at: https://ico.org.uk/media/for-organisations/documents/1064/the_employment_practices_code.pdf.

The right to privacy under the ECHR judicature regarding the use of new technologies in the workplace

In its previous judicature, the European Court of Human Rights held a position on the subject of protection of the right to employee's privacy in the following four areas, namely in video monitoring, including hidden monitoring, monitoring and controlling of electronic communication (e-mail, telephone conversations, text messages), computer content control and use of drug detection tests.

Monitoring

Monitoring of the workplace and the work process is an employer's right as part of the process of supervision and control of the commissioned work, which determines the success of the business. It can serve several purposes, including the protection of the employer's property, as well as the protection of the employees' safety, controlling the work quality, controlling the employees' working time or controlling the confidentiality of the enterprise.

Monitoring can take on a continuous or occasional form. It may have a preventive and consequential character or an open or hidden character. The employer can monitor the workplace and work processes with the help of employees or by sub-contracting to external companies.

Monitoring violates the right to privacy, as well as the processing of personal data of an employee. The latter is regulated in detail by international law[20] and legal systems of individual countries. Observing the requirements regarding the legal processing of personal data in principle ensures that the right to employee privacy is preserved. On the other hand, in some situations the employer cannot formally breach the rules of the personal data processing, for instance in the event of a suspicion of theft by an employee, which does not mean, however, that there will always occur a breach of the employee's privacy. We will examine this issue in the presentation of ECHR judicature regarding the alleged violation of Article 8 of the Convention.

Video monitoring

The use of video monitoring by the employer may certainly interfere with the employee's private life. Sometimes, however, it is necessary by reason of protectig the employer's property or the employees' safety. On this topic, two important judgments of the Court relating to the use of video monitoring in enterprises – in particular hidden monitoring – should be noted.

---

20 For instance by Regulation (EU) 2016/679 of the European Parliament and of the Council of 27 April 2016 on the protection of natural persons with regard to the processing of personal data and on the free movement of such data, and repealing Directive 95/46/EC or Convention of Counsil of Europe no. 108 of 28 January 1981 for the Protection of Individuals with regard to Automatic Processing of Personal Data.

THE CASE OF *KÖPKE V GERMANY* (2010)[21]

Mrs. Karin Kopke was an assistant in a shop. Because the employer noticed the shortages of goods in the beverage department, where she worked, suspecting the employees of theft, he installed hidden cameras with the help of a detective agency. After reviewing the recordings, the agency prepared a report, which showed that the employee was stealing which resulted in her dismissal. The German labour courts considered the claim unfounded and held that the hidden recording of the employee was justified in this situation. The ECHR held that in respect of the balance struck between the two competing interests, that the domestic courts considered that there had not been any other equally effective means to protect the employer's property rights which would have interfered to a lesser extent with the applicant's right to respect for her private life. Having regard to the circumstances of the case ECHR agreed with this finding indicating that, "the stocktaking carried out in the drinks department could not clearly link the losses discovered to a particular employee. Surveillance by superiors or colleagues or open video surveillance did not have the same prospects of success in discovering a covert theft". The EUCJ concluded that "there was nothing to indicate that the domestic authorities failed to strike a fair balance, within their margin of appreciation, between the applicant's right to respect for her private life under Article 8 and both her employer's interest in the protection of its property rights and the public interest in the proper administration of justice." The Court observed, however, that the balance struck between the interests at issue by the domestic authorities did not appear to be the only possible way for them to comply with their obligations under the Convention. ECHR held that a state did not violate the right provided for by art. 8 of the Convention becouse there was a fair balance between interests of the employee and the employer.

THE CASE OF *LÓPEZ RIBALDA AND OTHERS V SPAIN* (2018)[22]

In the judgment of 9 January 2018, the ECHR held that the video monitoring of shop assistants in a Spanish supermarket without their knowledge violated the right to respect for employees' private lives. According to the facts of the case Isabel López Ribalda and another five Spanish nationals were cashiers employed in a supermarket. The employer – after the store manager noticed the differences in stock levels and suspected the theft of goods – installed cameras, but he only informed the employees about some of the cameras. He did not inform employees about recordings from hidden cameras. The recordings confirmed the theft. The employees were dismissed on disciplinary grounds. Two of them filed lawsuits against the employer to the labour court. The courts of first and second instance dismissed the claim, recognising that the recordings constituted legal evidence.

21 The judgment of 5 October 2010, application no. 420/07.
22 The judgment of 9 January 2018, complaint no. 1874/13 and 8567/13.

In its judgment of 9 January 2018, the ECHR held, by six votes to one, that there had been a violation of Article 8 of the Convention. The Chamber found in particular that under Spanish data protection legislation the applicants should have been informed that they could eventually be placed under surveillance, but they had not been. The ECHR noted that the legislation in force at the time of the facts of the case clearly established that every data collector had to inform the data subjects of the existence of a means of collecting and processing their personal data. In a situation where the right of every such subject to be informed of the existence, aim and manner of covert video surveillance was clearly regulated and protected by law, the applicants had had a reasonable expectation of privacy. The ECHR did not share the domestic courts' view on the proportionality of the measures taken by the employer with the legitimate aim of protecting the employer's interest in the protection of its property rights. The employer's rights could have been safeguarded by other means and it could have provided to the applicants at least with general information about the surveillance. The domestic courts had thus not struck a fair balance between the applicants' privacy rights and the employer's property rights. It should be noted that on 28 May 2018 the Grand Chamber Panel accepted the Government's request that the case be referred to the Grand Chamber.

Employee testing for drug use

One of the areas in which the right of the employee to privacy can be violated is testing employees for drug use. This issue was the subject of the case before the ECHR in 2004.

CASE OF *WRETLUND V SWEDEN* (2004)[23]

Inga-Lill Wretlund, was employed as an office cleaner at a nuclear power plant in Oskarshamn, Sweden. She was assigned to clean the offices at the plant and was not working in an area where she might be subjected to radioactivity, thus was not obliged to undergo any radiological examinations under the Swedish safety regulations for nuclear plants.

The sectoral collective agreement for the power plant sector (Kraftsverksavtalet) did not provide for drug or alcohol tests among the employees. In 1991, a drug policy programme was agreed upon between the employer and the four trade unions at the Oskarshamn plant. All job applicants were to undergo a drug test in connection with their health examination before they could be employed. In 1993, it was proposed that employees already in employment should also undergo tests. Her employer *OKG Aktiebolag* (hereinafter "OKG") and three of the four trade unions concluded a local agreement that introduced compulsory drug and alcohol tests for all the members of the three unions at the plant. OKG intended

23 The judgment of 9 March 2004, application no. 46210/99.

to conclude a similar agreement with the fourth union, the Electricians' Union. However in December 1993, this union declined to sign such a deal. The company nevertheless decided that all employees should undergo drug and alcohol tests. Ms Wretlund refused to be tested. The case did not refer to the question of dismissal becouse she was not dismissed by her employer as an effect of refusal to be tested.

In 1996, the Electricians' Union took OKG and the Energy Companies' Employers' Association to the Labour Court (Arbetsdomstolen) seeking a declaratory judgment that the applicant, Ms Wretlund, was not obliged to participate in the drug and alcohol tests at the nuclear plant. The union argued that the tests were in breach of Article 8 of the Convention, the collective agreement in force at the plant and the Secrecy Act.[24] The trade union argued, *inter alia*, that there was nothing mentioned in the employee's individual employment contract about drug tests, and that the union had not signed the local agreement on drug testing. Also, the union alleged that testing was unjustified with regard to the cleaner's tasks in the office at the nuclear plant.

The Swedish Labour Court stated that running a nuclear plant was subject to high safety and security standards imposed by the relevant public authorities. The Swedish Labour Court also noted that OKG was under an obligation to take measures preventing sickness and accidents at work under the Work Environment Act.[25] The Labour Court concluded that OKG had a strong justified interest in carrying out the tests in order to maintain a drug-free environment. Drug testing was conducted at all Swedish nuclear power plants.

Mrs Wetlund claimed that there was no Swedish legislation that gave employers the right to conduct drug tests on their employees and that Labour Court's judgement had no basis in law.

The ECHR noted that the applicant and other employees of OKG were informed of the drug policy programme, including the drug testing. It had not been claimed that the information given was insufficient. The obligation to submit to drug testing did not follow from legislation – however, the ECHR observed that, in accordance with a long-running Swedish tradition, the social partners mainly regulate employment-related issues through collective agreements. The employer's right to manage and organise the work was a principle agreed upon by the parties, and the Swedish Labour Court had established that this right constituted a general legal principle. According to the case law of the Swedish Labour Court, an employer may have the right to carry out control measures in relation to its employees, as part of the employer's right to manage and organise the work.

---

24 See the relevant page of the Swedish Parliament website: https://www.riksdagen.se/sv/doku ment-lagar/dokument/svensk-forfattningssamling/sekretesslag-1980100_sfs-1980-100.

25 See the relevant page of the Swedish Parliament website: https://www.riksdagen.se/sv/doku ment-lagar/dokument/svensk-forfattningssamling/arbetsmiljolag-19771160_sfs-1977-1160.

The ECHR found that the measure challenged by the applicant had a sufficient basis in Swedish law and thus was "in accordance with the law" within the meaning of Article 8.2.

That Court also noted that the tests performed at OKG were carried out in private; the test results were disclosed only to people involved in the drug policy programme; and the testing was performed on all employees at OKG. In the light of these circumstances, the ECHR found that operational considerations at OKG relating to the public safety and the protection of the rights and freedoms of others, in particular other employees, justified the control measure in question. The Court stated that Swedish Labour Court struck a fair balance between that interest and the applicant's interest of protecting her personal integrity. In sum, the ECHR considered that there was no evidence that could lead to the conclusion that the control measure or the way it was carried out was disproportionate. Accordingly, the assumed interference with the individual's rights in the case was "necessary in a democratic society" (as required by Article 8.2 of the Convention) for the abovementioned aims. The ECHR thus rejected the application as being manifestly ill founded.

Controlling of telephone connections

The control of the employee's working time by the employer can undoubtedly rely on the obligation to monitor and limit private telephone conversations while performing duties under the employment contract. The monitoring of telephone calls made from a business telephone after informing an employee in advance does not lead, in this author's opinion, to a violation of the employee's privacy rights. Working time should be devoted by the employee to the work for which he is paid. Otherwise, the employee would receive an unwarranted benefit.

Similarly, the control of telephone call bills from a company phone will not constitute a violation of the right to privacy, unless the employee has the employer's consent to use the office phone for private purposes.

A far more difficult issue is the question of tapping phone calls from a business phone. This was the subject of the case before the Court in 1997 in the case of *Halford v the United Kingdom*.

THE CASE OF *HALFORD V THE UNITED KINGDOM* (1997)[26]

In this case the ECHR stated that an employee has a right to privacy also while using business telephones while calling on private matters especially when the employer did not warn an employee that his/her calls would be monitored.

In May 1983 Ms. Halford was appointed to the rank of Assistant Chief Constable of the Merseyside police. She was provided with her own office and two telephones, one of which was for private use. These telephones were part of the Merseyside police internal telephone network, a telecommunications system outside

---

26 The judgment of 27 June 1997, application no. 20605/92.

the public network. No restrictions were placed on the use of these telephones and no guidance was given to her. In addition, since she was frequently "on call", a substantial part of her home telephone costs were paid by the Merseyside Police. Her home telephone consisted of a telephone apparatus connected, through the "network termination point", to the public telecommunications network.

On eight occasions during the following seven years, Ms. Halford applied unsuccessfully to be appointed to the rank of Deputy Chief Constable. In order to be considered for promotion to this rank, Home Office approval was required. However, according to the applicant, this was consistently withheld on the recommendation of the Chief Constable of the Merseyside police, who objected to her commitment to equality of treatment between men and women.

She alleged that calls made from her home and her office telephones were intercepted for the purposes of obtaining information to use against her in her discrimination proceedings. Thus she alleged that the interception of her telephone calls amounted to violations of Article 8 of the Convention.

In the ECHR's view, it was clear from its case law that telephone calls made from business premises as well as from the home may be covered by the notions of "private life" and "correspondence" within the meaning of Article 8 para. 1.[27]

The ECHR stressed that there was no evidence of any warning having been given to Ms. Halford, as a user of the internal telecommunications system operated at the Merseyside Police headquarters, that calls made on that system would be liable to interception. She would, the Court considered, have had a reasonable expectation of privacy for such calls. As Assistant Chief Constable she had sole use of her office where there were two telephones, one of which was specifically designated for her private use. Furthermore, she had been given the assurance, in response to a memorandum, that she could use her office telephones for the purposes of her sex-discrimination case. For all of the above reasons, the Court concluded that the conversations held by Ms. Halford on her office telephones fall within the scope of the notions of "private life" and "correspondence".

In that case, the Government accepted that if, contrary to their submission, the Court were to conclude that there had been an interference with the applicant's rights under Article 8 in relation to her office telephones, such interference was not "in accordance with the law" since domestic law did not provide any regulation of interceptions of calls made on telecommunications systems outside the public network. The Court noted that the 1985 Act did not apply to internal communications systems operated by public authorities, such as that at Merseyside Police headquarters, and that there was no other provision in domestic law to regulate interceptions of telephone calls made on such systems. It cannot therefore be said that the interference was "in accordance with the law" for the purposes of Article 8

---

27 See, for example, the *Klass and Others vs Germany* judgment of 6 September 1978, Series A no. 28, p. 21, para. 41; the *Huvig vs France* judgment of 24 April 1990, Series A no. 176-B, p. 41, para. 8, and p. 52, para. 25; the *Niemietz vs Germany* judgment of 16 December 1992, Series A no. 251-B; and the *A. vs France* judgment of 23 November 1993, Series A no. 277-B.

para. 2 of the Convention, since the domestic law did not provide adequate protection to Ms. Halford against interferences by the police with her right to respect for her private life and correspondence.

In conclusion, the Court stated that there had been a violation of Article 8 of the Convention in relation to calls made on the applicant's office telephone and that there was no violation of Article 8 in relation to calls made on the applicant's home telephone.

Monitoring of an employee's electronic communications (e-mail and internet connections)

Sending messages by electronic mail has become much more frequent than sending traditional letters. There is no doubt that the use of electronic mail should be subject to similar protection as traditional mail as far as the right to privacy and the confidentiality of correspondence is considered.

Employer monitoring of the private electronic mail of an employee is, in principle, prohibited and violates the secrecy of correspondence guaranteed in Article 8 sec. 1 of the Convention. A much more complicated matter is the issue of mail control, especially when the employer does not prohibit its use for private correspondence.

While in the internal regulations applicable at the employer or in the employment contract, there is a ban on using business mail for private correspondence, monitoring of the company mail by the employer, after informing the employee, is completely legal. Employers have the right to control the process of work, which takes place i.e. using modern means of communication. If such prohibition does not exist, then the employer cannot read the content of the employee's private correspondence sent through the company's mailbox.

The above remarks apply to the use of a company computer. This issue was the subject of the *Copland v The United Kingdom* case[28] examined by the ECHR in 1997 and a very interesting case of *Bărbulescu v Romania*, heard in the first Chamber in 2016 and the Great Chamber in 2017, in which the Court for the first time referred to the interference with the right to privacy and the confidentiality of correspondence by the employer in the private sector.

THE CASE OF *COPLAND V THE UNITED KINGDOM* (2007)[29]

In this case the employer knew that the employee was using telephone and the computer for private matters. In 1991 Ms Copland was employed by Carmarthenshire College ("the College"). The College was a statutory body administered by the State and possessing powers under sections 18 and 19 of the Further and Higher Education Act 1992 relating to the provision of further and higher education. In 1995 the

---

28 The judgment of 3 April 2007, application no. 62617/00.
29 See footnote no. 27.

applicant became the personal assistant to the College Principal ("CP") and from the end of 1995 she was required to work closely with the newly appointed Deputy Principal ("DP"). In about July 1998 the applicant visited another campus of the College with a male director. She subsequently became aware that the DP had contacted that campus to enquire about her visit and understood that DP was suggesting an improper relationship between her and the director.

During her employment, the applicant's telephone, e-mail and internet usage were subjected to monitoring at the DP's instigation. According to the Government, this monitoring took place in order to ascertain whether the applicant was making excessive use of College facilities for personal purposes. The Government stated that the monitoring of telephone usage consisted of an analysis of the college telephone bills showing telephone numbers called, the dates and times of the calls and their length and cost.

The applicant's internet usage was also monitored by the DP. The Government accepted that this monitoring took the form of analysing the web sites visited, the times and dates of the visits to the web sites and their duration and that this monitoring took place from October to November 1999.

The Government submitted that monitoring of e-mails took the form of an analysis of e-mail addresses and dates and times at which e-mails were sent and that the monitoring occurred for a few months. There was no policy in force at the College at the material time regarding the monitoring of telephone, e-mail or internet use by the employee.

At the relevant time there was no general right to privacy in English law. Since the implementation of the Human Rights Act 1998 on 2 October 2000, the courts have been required to read and give effect to primary legislation in a manner which is compatible with the Convention rights so far as possible. The Act also made it unlawful for any public authority, including a court, to act in a manner which is incompatible with a Convention right unless required to do so by primary legislation, thus providing for the development of the common law in accordance with Convention rights.

The Regulation of Investigatory Powers Act 2000 ("the 2000 Act") provided for the regulation of, inter alia, interception of communications. The Telecommunications (Lawful Business Practice) Regulations 2000 were promulgated under the 2000 Act and came into force on 24 October 2000. The Regulations set out the circumstances in which employers could record or monitor employees' communications (such as e-mail or telephone) without the consent of either the employee or the other party to the communication. Employers were required to take reasonable steps to inform employees that their communications might be intercepted.

At the time of the acts complained of by the applicant, the Data Protection Act 1984 ("the 1984 Act") regulated the manner in which people and organisations that held data, known as "data holders", processed or used that data. The 1984 Act has since been replaced by the Data Protection Act 1998.[30]

---

30 See http://www.legislation.gov.uk/ukpga/1998/29/contents. This Data Protection Act dated 1998 was updated by by The Data Protection Act 2018 (c 12), which is a United

According to the ECHR's case law, telephone calls from business premises are *prima facie* covered by the notions of "private life" and "correspondence" for the purposes of Article 8 § 1. It follows logically that e-mails sent from work should be similarly protected under Article 8, as should information derived from the monitoring of personal internet usage. It is important to stress that the employee had been given no warning that her calls would be liable to monitoring; therefore she had a reasonable expectation as to the privacy of calls made from her work telephone. The same expectation should apply in relation to the applicant's e-mail and internet usage.

The ECHR recalled, as in the case of Malone,[31] that the use of information relating to the date and length of telephone conversations and in particular the numbers dialled can give rise to an issue under Article 8 as such information constitutes an "integral element of the communications made by telephone". Moreover, the storing of personal data relating to the private life of an individual also falls within the application of Article 8 § 1.[32] Thus, it is irrelevant that the data held by the college were not disclosed or used against the applicant in disciplinary or other proceedings.

The ECHR stated that the collection and storage of personal information relating to the applicant's telephone, as well as to her e-mail and internet usage, without her knowledge, amounted to an interference with her right to respect for her private life and correspondence within the meaning of Article 8.

The ECHR recalled that it is well established in the case law that the term "in accordance with the law" implies – and this follows from the object and purpose of Article 8 – that there must be a measure of legal protection in domestic law against arbitrary interferences by public authorities with the rights safeguarded by Article 8 § 1. This is all the more so in areas such as the monitoring in question, in view of the lack of public scrutiny and the risk of misuse of power. This expression not only requires compliance with domestic law, but also relates to the quality of that law, requiring it to be compatible with the rule of law concept.[33] In order to fulfil the requirement of foreseeability, the law must be sufficiently clear in its terms to give individuals an adequate indication as to the circumstances in which and the conditions on which the authorities are empowered to resort to any such measures.[34]

There was no domestic law regulating monitoring at the relevant time, thus the interference in this case was not "in accordance with the law" as required by Article 8 § 2 of the Convention.

Kingdom Act of Parliament that updates data protection laws in the UK. It is a national law that complements the European Union's General Data Protection Regulation (GDPR).

31 *Malone v. the United Kingdom*, judgment of 2 August 1984, Series A, no. 82, § 84.
32 See *Amann v. Switzerland*, no. 27798/95, § 65.
33 See, inter alia, *Khan v. the United Kingdom*, judgment of 12 May 2000, Reports of Judgments and Decisions 2000-V, § 26; *P.G. and J.H. v. the United Kingdom*, § 44.
34 See *Halford vs the United Kingdom*, § 49 and Malone, § 67.

Finally, the ECHR found that there has been a violation of Article 8 of the Convention.

THE CASE OF *BĂRBULESCU VS ROMANIA* (2016–2017)[35]

Mr. Bărbulescu was employed in the Bucharest office of S. – a Romanian private company – as a sales engineer. At his employer's request, for the purpose of responding to customer's enquiries, he created an instant messaging account using Yahoo Messenger, an online chat service offering real-time text transmission over the internet. He already had another personal Yahoo Messenger account.

The employer's internal regulations prohibited the use of company resources by employees in the following terms: "any disturbance of order and discipline on company premises shall be strictly forbidden, in particular … personal use for computers, photocopiers, telephones or telex or fax machines."

The regulations did not contain any reference to the possibility of the employer monitoring employees' communication. The applicant had been informed of the employer's internal regulations and had signed a copy of them on 20 December 2006 after acquainting himself with their contents.

From 5 to 13 July 2007, the employer recorded the applicant's Yahoo Messenger communications in real time. On 13 July 2007, at 4.30 p.m., the applicant was summoned by his employer to give an explanation. In the relevant notice he was informed that his Yahoo Messenger communications had been monitored and that there was evidence that he had used the internet for personal purposes, in breach of the internal regulations. Charts were attached indicating that his internet activity was greater than that of his colleagues.

At that stage, he was not informed whether the monitoring of his communications had also included their content. The notice was worded as follows: "please explain why you are using a company resources (sic) for personal purposes during working hours, as shown by the attached charts".

On the same day, the applicant informed the employer in writing that he had used Yahoo Messenger for work-related purposes only. At 5.20 p.m., the employer again summoned him to give an explanation in a notice worded as follows: "Please explain why the entire correspondence you exchanged between 5 to 12 July 2007 using the S. Bucharest site ID had a private purpose, as shown by the attached forty-five pages." The forty-five pages mentioned in the notice consisted of a transcript of the messages that the applicant had exchanged with his brother and his fiancée during the period when he had been monitored; the messages related to personal matters and some were of an intimate nature. The transcript also included five messages that the applicant had exchanged with his fiancée using his personal Yahoo Messenger account; these messages did not contain any intimate information.

---

35 Judgment of Great Chamber of the Court of 5 September 2017, application no. 62617/00. See https://www.echr.coe.int/Documents/Press_Q_A_Barbulescu_ENG.PDF.

On 13 July, the applicant informed the employer in writing that in his view it had committed a criminal offence, namely breaching the secrecy of correspondence. On 1 August 2007 the employer terminated the applicant's contract of employment. On 12 January 2016, the Fourth Section of the ECHR, unanimously delivered a judgement and found, by six votes to one, that there had been no violation of Article 8 of the Convention. On 12 April 2016, Mr. Bărbulescu requested the referral of the case to the Grand Chamber in accordance with Article 43 of the Convention. In the judgement of Grand Chamber dated 5th September 2017, the court held – eleven votes to six – that there has been a violation of Article 8 of the Convention.

ECHR, delivering the judgment, listed a number of international laws, codes and politicies regarding collective personal data, including:

- Regulation (EU) 2016/679 of the European Parliament and of the Council of 27 April 2016 on the protection of natural persons with regard to the processing of personal data and on the free movement of such data.
- The Council of Europe Convention for the Protection of Individuals with regard to Automatic Processing of Personal Data (1981, ETS no. 108).
- The Code of Practice on the Protection of Workers Personal Data (1997).
- The Guidelines for the regulation of computerised personal data files, adopted by the United Nations General Assembly on 14 December 1990 in Resolution 45/95 (A/RES/45/95), which lay down the minimum guarantees that should be provided for in national legislation.
- The ECHR concluded that the Romanian courts failed to strike a fair balance between the interests at stake: namely Mr. Bărbulescu's right to respect for his private life and correspondence on the one hand, and his employer's right to take measures in order to ensure the smooth running of the company, on the other.

The ECHR found that the Romanian courts failed to determine whether Mr. Bărbulescu had received prior notice from his employer of the possibility that his communications might be monitored. They did not address the fact that he had not been informed of the nature or the extent of the monitoring, in particular the possibility that the employer might have access to the actual contents of his messages. The national courts also failed to determine, firstly, the specific reasons justifying the introduction of the monitoring measures; secondly, whether the employer could have used measures entailing less intrusion into Mr. Bărbulescu's private life and correspondence and thirdly, whether the communications might have been accessed without his knowledge.

The court stressed that it does not mean that employers cannot, under any circumstances, monitor employees' communications or that they cannot dismiss employees for using the internet at work for private purposes. However, the Court noted that States should ensure that, when an employer takes measures to monitor employees' communications, these measures are accompanied by adequate and sufficient safeguards against abuse.

The Court set up the list of a few criteria to be applied by the national authorities when assessing whether a given measure is proportionate to the aim pursued and whether the employee concerned is protected against arbitrariness. The Court declared that the authorities should determine the following ("ECHR standards of preventing violation of the employees right to privacy":

- Whether the employee has been notified of the possibility that the employer might take measures to monitor correspondence and other communications, and of the implementation of such measures. For the measures to be deemed compatible with the requirements of Article 8 of the Convention, the notification should be clear about the nature of the monitoring and be given in advance.
- The extent of the monitoring by the employer and the degree of intrusion into the employee's privacy. In this regard, a distinction should be made between monitoring of the flow of communications and of their content. Whether all communications or only part of them have been monitored should also be taken into account, as should the question whether the monitoring was limited in time and the number of people who had access to the results.
- Whether the employer has provided legitimate reasons to justify monitoring the communications and accessing their actual content. Since monitoring of the content of communications is a distinctly more invasive method, it requires weightier justification.
- Whether it would have been possible to establish a monitoring system based on less intrusive methods and measures than directly accessing the content of the employee's communications. There should be an assessment in the light of the particular circumstances of each case of whether the aim pursued by the employer could have been achieved without directly accessing the full contents of the employee's communications.
- The consequences of the monitoring for the employee concerned and the use made by the employer of the results of the monitoring operation, in particular whether the results were used to achieve the declared aim of the measure.
- Whether the employee has been provided with adequate safeguards, especially when the employer's monitoring operations are of an intrusive nature. Such safeguards should in particular ensure that the employer cannot access the actual content of the communications concerned unless the employee has been notified in advance of that eventuality.

Computer content control

The latest ruling of the ECHR, namely the case of *Libert v France* refers to the employer control of the content of a company computer of an employee employed in the public sphere.

THE CASE OF *LIBERT VS FRANCE* (2018)[36]

In this case, the ECHR in its judgement of 22 February 2018 held, by a majority, that there had been no violation of Article 8 of the Convention. The employer (SNCF: French national railway company) dismissed Mr. Libert after his superviser discovered in his computer the storage of pornographic files (films and images) and forged certificates drawn up for third persons. The empoyees's files had been opened on his work computer without his knowledge and in his absence.

The ECHR noted that the consultation of the files by Mr. Libert's employer had pursed a legitimate aim of protecting the rights of employers, who might legitimately wish to ensure that their employees were using the computer facilities that they had placed at their disposal in line with their contractual obligations and the applicable regulations. The Court observed that French law comprised a privacy protection mechanism allowing employers to open professional files, although they could not surreptitiously open files identified as being personal. They could only open the latter type of files in the employee's presence. The domestic courts had ruled that the said mechanism would not have prevented the employer from opening the files at issue since they had not been duly identified as being private. Lastly, the ECHR considered that the domestic courts had properly assessed the applicant's allegation of a violation of his right to respect for his private life, and that those courts' decisions had been based on relevant and sufficient grounds.

In this case, the French Court of Cassation stressed that files created by employees using computers provided by their employers are presumed to be professional in nature unless they are identified as "personal". The applicant complained that his employer had opened, in his absence, personal files stored on the hard drive of his work computer.

The EHCR stated that under certain circumstances, non-professional data, for example data clearly identified as private stored by an employee in a computer supplied by his employer in order to discharge his duties, might be deemed to relate to his "private life". It noted that the SNCF allowed its staff occasionally to use the computer facilities placed at their disposal for private purposes, subject to compliance with specific rules. The SNCF was a public-law entity supervised by the State. That case was therefore distinct from the case of *Bărbulescu v. Romania,* in which an employer had a status of private entity.

Since the interference in this case had been due to a public authority, the complaint had to be analysed from the angle not of the State's positive obligations but of its negative obligations. At the material time positive law had provided that employers could open files contained in employees' work computers unless such files had been identified as personal. French law comprised a mechanism to protect private life: although the employer could open any professional files stored in the hard drives of the computers with which he had supplied his employees in the exercise of their functions, he could not surreptitiously open files identified as

---

36 The judgment of 22 February 2018, application no. 588/13.

being personal "unless there was a serious risk or in exceptional circumstances"; he could only open such files in the presence of the employee concerned or after the latter had been duly informed. French courts have determined that the impugned photographs and videos had not been clearly identified as "private" by the employee. The French court of appeal also held that Mr. Libert's dismissal had not been disproportionate since he had committed a serious breach of the SNCF professional code of ethics and of the relevant internal guidelines.

The EHCR declared that the domestic authorities had not overstepped the margin of appreciation available to them, and there had therefore been no violation of Article 8 of the Convention.

Conclusion

The use of modern technologies while providing work as part of an employment relationship is linked with the threat of a violation by the employer of the right to privacy and the confidentiality of the employee's correspondence. In its previous judicature, the European Court of Human Rights has ruled that the right to privacy also embraces the sphere of employment within the framework of industrial relations, both in the public and private sectors. Simultaneously, in a few judgments, the Court determined the boundaries of the employer's interference with the employee's private sphere based on a number of international laws, in particular in the light of Art. 8 of the Convention and those regulating the principles of personal data protection. Especially in the case of *Bărbulescu v Romania* in 2017, the Court established minimum standards for the protection of the right to employee privacy and the secrecy of correspondence, which the governments of individual countries of the European Council must take into account in their legislative process.

These standards are also addressed to employers who, with the help of modern technologies, can monitor and control the work of employees using modern devices while working. It results from the Court's judicature that, to guarantee respect for an employee's right to privacy, it is not sufficient to inform about monitoring or control (the notification should be clear and be given in advance), which are in accordance with national law, but to adequately interfere with that privacy, including its purpose and compliance with the principle of proportionality. In each case, the extent of the monitoring by the employer and the degree of intrusion into the employee's privacy should be considered. Furthermore, since monitoring of the content of any communications used by an employee is more invasive than other methods, it requires stronger justification.

A condition for the legality of the employer activities in the light of Art. 8 of the Convention is to maintain the balance between employee's right to respect for his private life and correspondence, and employer's right to take measures in order to ensure the smooth running of the company.

9 Work-life balance and Industry 4.0 in the legal framework of the European Union

Tatsiana Ushakova

Introduction

Traditionally, the problem of conciliating of working life and private life has attracted a lot of attention from legal doctrine, particularly in Spain.[1] This interest may be explained by the close relationship between conciliation and other important matters in the field of labour law. In fact, it relates to such central issues as: labour rights, equality and non-discrimination, protection against dismissal, safety and health at work, the organisation of working time and new forms of work. In addition, work-life balance is a dynamic concept that has experienced and continues to experience the "great transformations" affecting the world of work at large. The new forms of life and business organisation make it extremely difficult to achieve a model that allows effective conciliation of responsibilities in both spheres, and this means that work-life balance is one of the greatest challenges facing society today. The lack of any such balance is becoming a new social risk, alongside atypical forms of employment, low labour qualifications and single-parent families.[2]

The reason for revisiting this issue within the European Unión legal framework is to be found in two brand new contexts: on the one hand, the European Pillar of Social Rights[3] and, on the other, Industry 4.0.[4]

---

1 See, among many others: Cabeza Pereiro, J., "Conciliación de vida privada y laboral", *Temas laborales* 103 (2010): 45–65; Mella Méndez, L., Serani, L., eds., *Work-Life Balance and the Economic Crisis. Some Insights from the Perspective of Comparative Law, Vol. II. The International Scenario*. ADAPT: Cambridge Scholars Publishing, 2015; Mella Méndez, L., "Nuevas tecnologías y nuevos retos para la conciliación y la salud de los trabajadores", *Trabajo y Derecho. Nueva Revista de actualidad y Relaciones laborales* 16 (2016): 30–52; Mella Méndez, L., Núñez-Cortés Contreras, P., dirs., Moreno Solana, A., coord., *Nuevas tecnologías y nuevas maneras de trabajar: estudios desde el Derecho español y comparado. Alemania, Reino Unido, Polonia, Portugal y Argentina,* Madrid: Dykinson, 2017; Núñez-Cortés Conteras, L., *Eficacia de las medidas de conciliación,* Madrid: Tecnos, 2016; Núñez-Cortés Contreras, L.; Lousada Arochena, J. F., *Jornada de trabajo y derechos de conciliación,* Madrid: Tecnos, 2015.
2 Taylor-Gooby, P., ed., *New risks, new welfare. The transformation of the European welfare state,* Oxford: Oxford University Press, 2004; Esping-Andersen, G., *Incomplete revolution: Adapting welfare states to women's new roles,* Cambridge: Polity Press, 2009.
3 Commission Recommendation (EU) 2017/761 on the *European Pillar of Social Rights, OJ* L 113, 29.04.2017.
4 See about Industry 4.0 at "Concepts" of this chapter.

Concepts

Work-life balance

It should be noted that there is no explicit mention of work-life balance in the European Union's founding treaties.[5] The legal sources providing the basis for the consolidation of the European Pillar of Social Rights contain the more general objectives, such as the promotion of the well-being of the peoples of the EU for the sustainable development of Europe, based on a highly competitive social market economy; the fight against social exclusion and discrimination; the promotion of social justice and protection, male-female equality, intergenerational solidarity and the protection of the rights of the child.[6] Likewise, in the definition and execution of its policies and activities, the EU takes into account the requirements related to the promotion of a high level of employment, the guarantee of adequate social protection, the fight against social exclusion, high educational and training levels and the protection of human health.[7] For its part, EU social policy[8] is based on the fundamental social rights of the European Social Charter of 1961 and on the Community Charter of the Fundamental Social Rights of Workers of 1989.

It must be emphasised that the EU Charter of Fundamental Rights of 2000[9] is of limited relevance to the consolidation of the European Pillar of Social Rights. It is cited in fifth place, after the founding treaties and other sources mentioned. Although its importance for the EU social model is acknowledged, its provisions are addressed to the institutions and bodies of the Union with due regard for the principle of subsidiarity, and to the Member States only when they are implementing EU law. In other words, the Charter does not establish any new power or task for the Union, or modify powers and tasks defined by the treaties. This limitation undermines the binding character bestowed upon it after the coming into force of the Treaty of Lisbon in 2009.

Taking into account that the right to conciliation is mentioned in Article 33 "Family and professional life" of the Charter for the first time in EU law, it should be analysed in the context of this study. The protection of the family is tied to the conciliatory measures and the specific rights in the following terms:

1. The family shall enjoy legal, economic and social protection.
2. To reconcile family and professional life, everyone shall have the right to protection from dismissal for a reason connected with maternity and the

---

5 See consolidated versions of Treaty of European Union (TEU) and Treaty of the Functioning of the European Union (TFEU), *OJ* C 202, 7.06.2016, and Treaty establishing the European Atomic Energy Community (EURATOM), *OJ* C 203, 7.06.2016.
6 Article 3 TEU.
7 Article 9 TFEU.
8 Articles 151-161 TFEU.
9 Charter of the Fundamental Rights of the European Union, *OJ* C 202, 7.06.2016, 391–407.

right to paid maternity leave and to parental leave following the birth or adoption of a child.

Accordingly, this Article should be considered as an explicit reference to work-life balance in the primary law of the EU and, therefore, the expression of the current concept in the legal framework of the Union.[10] The European legislator refers to conciliation as a series of measures to address the conflict between family life and professional life. In general, the protection of the family is guaranteed at legal, economic and social levels; more specifically, the guarantee is articulated, on the one hand, and in a prohibitive key, through protection against dismissal for causes related to maternity; and on the other, and in the key of positive action, through proclaiming the right to paid maternity or parental leave on the birth or adoption of a child. As can be seen, there is no complete recognition of the right to conciliation, but rather a very specific development of what the guarantee of family protection should entail in the three announced plans. In this sense, Article 16 of the European Social Charter,[11] which is the inspiration for Article 33 of the EU Charter of Fundamental Rights, is much more comprehensive and generous in including the commitment of States to promote the economic, legal and social protection of family life by social and family benefits, fiscal arrangements, provision of family housing, benefits for the newly married and other appropriate means.

In this piecemeal and incomplete legal framework, which is also reflected in EU case-law, the conciliation of working life and private life (work-life balance) has not yet been fully, or even literally, accomplished given that the core foundations of the guarantee lies in the protection of family (and not private) life.

From the perspective of equality, and especially gender equality, the conciliation of family and working lives is understood not to be a problem exclusive to women.[12] Thus, the fact that some men take on responsibility for

---

10 See, among others, about the concept of work-life balance in the EU Law: Cruz Villalón, J. "Elementos condicionantes para la efectividad de la conciliación laboral en España", in Mella Méndez, L., dir., *Conciliación de la vida laboral y familiar y crisis económica. Estudios desde el Derecho internacional y comparado,* Madrid: Delta, 2015: 12–14; Ushakova, T., "De la conciliación a la desconexión tecnológica. Apuntes para el debate", *Nueva Revista Española de Derecho del Trabajo,* 192 (2016):117–138, and "Del *work-life balance* al *work-career blend:* apuntes para el debate", in Mella Méndez, L., Nuñez-Cortés Contreras, P., dirs., Moreno Solana, A., coord., *Nuevas tecnologías y nuevas maneras de trabajar: estudios desde el Derecho español y comparado. Alemania, Reino Unido, Polonia, Portugal y Argentina,* E-book, Madrid: Dykinson, 2017.

11 Article 16 was drafted identically in the European Social Charter, *ETS,* n° 35, 18.10.1961, and in the European Social Charter (Revised), *ETS,* n° 163, 3.05.1996.

12 "In 2015, the female employment rate reached an all-time high of 64.5%. This rate is however well below the male employment rate (75.6%) and women are still more likely than men to work part-time or to be inactive. On average in the EU, the gender employment gap is 11.6 percentage points (pp), but this gap ranges considerably between Member States, from 1.9 pp to 28.4 pp". *Towards the European Pillar of Social Rights,* "Gender equality and work-life balance", available at: https://ec.europa.eu/commission/sites/beta-political/files/gender-equality-work-life-balance_en.pdf, accessed June 2, 2018.

some family tasks extends the possibility of work-life balance to all workers. Yet this formal hypothesis notwithstanding, it must be recognised that, nowadays, women continue to assume most family responsibilities. Taking into account their biological conditions, they also suffer less favourable treatment when looking for employment and are forced to accept worse working conditions. In this way, the correlative settlement of anti-discrimination theory allows conciliatory formulas to be introduced and offers protection against discriminatory treatment, whether direct or indirect, based on sex or gender.[13] The guarantee of male-female equality in all areas, including employment, does not militate against maintaining or adopting measures that bring real advantages to the less represented sex. In this connection, it should be remembered that one of the elements in Article 33, namely, protection from dismissal for a reason relating to maternity and the right to paid maternity leave, has also been provided for as a guarantee against discrimination pursuant Article 2.2 (c) of Directive 2006/54/EC. For the purposes of this Directive, discrimination includes "…any less favorable treatment of a woman related to pregnancy or maternity leave within the meaning of Directive 92/85/EEC."[14]

This relevance of gender equality to the concept of conciliation is also emphasised in the initial proposal for the European Pillar of Social Rights of 2016, where the respective principle no. 5 entitled "Gender equality and work-life balance" is to be found in Chapter I "Equality of opportunities and access to the labour market".[15]

However, between the adoption of the Charter of the Fundamental Rights and the European Pillar proposal, another instrument is worth mentioning,

---

13 Directive 2006/54/EC of the European Parliament and the Council, of 5 July 2006, on the implementation of the principle of equal opportunities and equal treatment of men and women in matters of employment and occupation (recast), *OJ* L 204, 26.7.2006, endorsed the definitions of direct and indirect discrimination mentioned in earlier instruments, in particular in Directive 2002/73/EC.

   Recital 10 of the Directive 2002/73/EC of the European Parliament and the Council, of September 23, 2002, amending Council Directive 76/207/EEC on the implementation of the principle of equal treatment for men and women as regards access to employment, vocational training and promotion, and working conditions, *OJ* L 269, 5.10.2002, states that "[t]he appreciation of the facts from which it may be inferred that there has been direct or indirect discrimination is a matter for national judicial or other competent bodies, in accordance with rules of national law or practice. Such rules may provide in particular for indirect discrimination to be established by any means including on the basis of statistical evidence. According to the case-law of the Court of Justice, discrimination involves the application of different rules to a comparable situation or the application of the same rule to different situations."

14 Council Directive 92/85/EEC of October 19, 1992 on the introduction of measures to encourage improvements in the safety and health at work of pregnant workers and workers who have recently given birth or are breastfeeding, *OJ* L 348, 28.11.1992.

15 See Annex to the Communication from the Commission to the European Parliament, the Council, the European Economic and Social Committee and the Committee of the Regions, "Launching a consultation on a European Pillar of Social Rights", COM (2016) 127 final, 8.03.2016.

namely the Commission's Communication on "Better work life balance: stronger support for reconciling professional, private and family life" of 2008.[16] The title shows how the concept of conciliation has evolved from the Charter's formula "conciliation of professional and family life", through a longer statement on "conciliation of professional, private and family life", to the Social Pillar's recent "work-life balance".

The importance of the "personal" dimension is announced in the first lines of the Communication which affirm that "[t]he choices which men and women make in combining the professional, private and family aspects of their lives are primarily personal".[17] However, the way in which people combine these obligations has consequences for public policies by influencing, for example, labour-market participation and fertility rates. At the same time, public policy in turn influences these choices, for instance by establishing legal rights to family-related leave or by affecting other factors, such as shop opening hours or the length of the school day. The Communication also recognises that "[c]hildcare facilities, leave entitlement and flexible working time arrangements are core components of the policy mix, while the powers are spread between European, national and local levels and between social partners at European, national and sectoral levels."[18]

As for the EU's role in this field, it is defined as "relatively limited".[19] However, the success of conciliation policies has repercussions for achieving important EU objectives, none more so than the creation of more and better jobs. Several directives provide minimum standards for work-life balance.[20] There is, then, a need to continue developing the legislative framework.

Thus, the principle no. 9 of the European Pillar of Social Rights insists on permits, which is undoubtedly the central axis of the concept of conciliation in EU Law: parents and people with caring responsibilities have the right to suitable leave, flexible working arrangements and access to care services. Women and men shall have equal access to special leaves of absence in order to fulfil their caring responsibilities and be encouraged to use them in a balanced way.[21]

As is clear, the aspiration for a more balanced and comprehensive approach underlies the references to flexible working conditions and care services. The very fact that work-life balance is set among principles of Chapter II "Fair working conditions" ensures a more holistic treatment. That is why one of the Pillar's "deliverables" is the idea of tackling the conciliation of work and private life of workers who assume the responsibilities of caring for their children or other members of their family or relatives in need regardless of those workers' sex.

16 COM (2008) 635 final, 3.10.2008.
17 COM (2008) 635 final, 2.
18 *Ibid.*
19 *Ibid.*
20 Among them, directives 92/85, 2010/41, 2010/18 and 2003/88 can be mentioned.
21 Commission Recommandation (EU) 2017/761, *JO* L 113/60.

Moreover, the European Commission takes into account technological progress, pointing out the radical transformation of working life. It highlights that, for some, these changes represent opportunities for more flexible forms of work thanks to the use of digital tools, but for others, they are a source of insecurity. Many of these changes have begun to take shape under the aegis of Industry 4.0.

Industry 4.0

While the European Pillar of Social Rights provides a new "strategical" framework, Industry 4.0 offers a new "technological" one for the conceptualisation of work-life balance.

Industry 4.0 is assimilated with the Fourth Industrial Revolution, the successor of the three preceding ones.[22] Nevertheless, the Fourth Industrial Revolution is fundamentally different in that it is characterised by a range of new technologies that are fusing the physical, digital and biological worlds, impacting all disciplines, economies and industries, and even challenging ideas about what it means to be human.[23]

The origin of the term refers to the high-tech strategy of the German Federal Government and describes "rapid transformations in the design, manufacture, operation and service of manufacturing systems and products."[24] In 2011, this strategy was made known to a wide audience at the *Hannover Messe*, Germany's most important industrial fair.[25] In the words of German Chancellor Angela Merkel, Industry 4.0 is "the comprehensive transformation of the whole sphere of industrial production through the merging of digital technology and the internet with conventional industry."[26]

Despite its terminological roots in Germany, the phenomenon itself is known in many other EU countries under the names of *smart factories, the Industrial Internet of Things, smart industry* or *advanced manufacturing*. Several States have developed and implemented initiatives related to Industry 4.0.

---

22 Schwab, K., *The Fourth Industrial Revolution,* Geneva: World Economic Forum, 2016. At the website of *World Economic Forum* [https://www.weforum.org, accessed June 2, 2018] it is explained that "[t]he First Industrial Revolution used water and steam power to mechanize production. The Second used electric power to create mass production. The Third used electronics and information technology to automate production. Now a Fourth Industrial Revolution is building on the Third, the digital revolution that has been occurring since the middle of the last century. It is characterized by a fusion of technologies that is blurring the lines between the physical, digital, and biological spheres."
23 *Ibid.*
24 European Parliamentary Research Service (EPRS), Davies, R., "Industry 4.0. Digitalisation for productivity and growth, Briefing", September 2015, 2.
25 See: http://www.hannovermesse.de/de/news/top-themen/industrie-4.0/, accessed June 2, 2018. See also Pfeiffer, S., "The Vision of 'Industrie 4.0' in the Making – a Case of Future Told, Tamed, and Traded", *Nanoethics,* 11 (2017), 1: 107 ff.
26 EPRS, Davies, *Industry 4.0,* 2.

At EU level, the aforementioned initiatives and plans are part of the *Digital Single Market.*[27] Among the strategic lines drawn up by the Commission, there is a drive toward "boosting competitiveness through interoperability and standardisation".[28] This Communication states that in the digital economy, interoperability means ensuring effective communication between digital components such as devices, networks or databases. In the same way, it means better connectivity throughout the supply chain and between industry and service sectors. There is currently consensus among the Member States on the basic requirements for achieving interoperability, based on the *European Interoperability Framework*, presented by the European Commission in 2010. Through the *Digital Single Market Strategy*, it is proposed to update and expand this framework. Industry 4.0 is listed as one of new technological tools (together with 5G wireless communications, data-based services, cloud services, cybersecurity, health and electronic transport and mobile payments) that should play an essential role in increasing interoperability in the digital single market.

In the inclusive e-society, citizens and businesses are supposed to have the necessary skills and be able to benefit from e-services, e-justice, e-health, e-energy or e-transport. Digital skills and expertise require digitally skilled employees. The EU has seen improvements in the basic digital skills of its citizens (increasing from 55% to 59% of the population), but still has a long way to go.[29] Digital skill levels also need to be raised among employees in all economic sectors and among job seekers to improve their employability. Change is required in education and training systems to help them to adapt to the digital revolution.

However, for the purposes of this study, what is significant is the need to adapt the welfare state to technological change.[30] The digitalisation of the economy offers new opportunities and increases the prospect of self-employment and new forms of employment by multiplying work models. Nevertheless, it also creates new "grey areas" in terms of labour rights and access to social care. Technological advance implies that the working life will become longer and less stable, with numerous transitions between jobs and professions and alterations in the work cycle to attend to family needs or to access re-training opportunities. Due to digitalisation, the very concept of work is undergoing inevitable change and the pre-established constituents of the "classic" labour relationship are becoming a thing of the past. All this requires the modernisation of Welfare States if they are to face the new challenges.

---

27 Communication from the Commission to the European Parliament, the Council, the European Economic and Social Committee and the Committee of the Regions, *A Strategy for the Digital Single Market in Europe*, COM (2015) 192 final, 6.05.2015, and the later documents.
28 COM (2015) 192 final, 15–16.
29 COM (2015) 192 final, 16.
30 European Commission, *Key economic, employment and social trends behind a European Pillar of Social Rights*, Staff Working Document of 8 March 2016, SWD (2016) 51, 3–4.

Scenarios

"Realistic" scenarios

Teleworking (telecommuting)

The first conciliation initiatives in the context of technological development are linked to the concept of "telework" ("telecommuting").[31] It should be remembered that the idea has national origin and, far from being legal, is economic in nature. The term was coined in 1973 by a group of American scientists from the University of Southern California, which was carrying on under the leadership of physicist Jack Nilles, known as the "father of telework".[32] Nilles and his group conducted studies on the application of computer technologies to improve corporate profits by reducing or eliminating workers' commuting and its substitution by transferring information required for the purposes of their work to their homes or the closest work centre. After analysing the first cases in 1973–1974, the idea was put forward of "moving the work to the workers instead of moving the workers to work".[33] Afterwards, the multiple impacts of its application were made known: on the organisation of work, productivity, costs and benefits, energy saving, public policies and, finally, on work-life balance.

In EU Law, the European Framework Agreement on Telework was adopted in 2002.[34] The social partners negotiated and signed the Agreement on the

31 About the concepts of telework, distance work and homework, see, among others: Ushakova, T., "El teletrabajo en el Derecho de la OIT", *Revista de información laboral* 9 (2015): 55–75; "El Derecho de la OIT para el trabajo a distancia: ¿una regulación superada o todavía aplicable?", *Revista Internacional y Comparada de Relaciones Laborales y Derecho del Empleo* 3, 4 (2015): 1–19, and "Los modelos de la acción normativa de la OIT para regular el trabajo a distancia", en *El futuro del trabajo que queremos*, Vol. II, OIT, Madrid: Gobierno de España, Ministerio de Empleo y de la Seguridad Social, 2017: 445–459.

32 See the first works of Nilles published in 1976 and reprinted afterwards: Nilles, J. M. et al., *The Telecommunications-Transportation Tradeoff: Options for Tomorrow*, New York: Wiley, 1976,, and Nilles, J. M., *Making Telecommuting Happen: A Guide for Telemanagers and Telecommuters*, New York: Van Nostrand Reinhold, 1994.

33 This statement opens the presentation of the Nilles's book: Nilles et al., *The Telecommunications-Transportation Tradeoff*.

34 Framework Agreement on Telework was signed on 16 July 2002, by the European Trade Union Confederation (ETUC), the Union of Industrial and Employers' Confederations of Europe/the European Union of Crafts and Small and Medium-Sized Enterprises (UNICE/UEAPME), and the Centre of Enterprises with Public Participation (ECPE). It aims at ensuring greater security for teleworkers employed in the EU. This agreement is of particular importance because it is the first European agreement put in place by the social partners themselves.

See, among the most outstanding Spanish contribution on telework: García Romero, B., *El Teletrabajo*, Cizur Menor: Civitas, 2012; Pérez Pérez, M., *El teletrabajo: efectos en la conciliación de la vida familiar y laboral*, Zaragoza: Fundación Economía Aragonesa, 2008; Sempere Navarro, A. V.; Kahale Carrillo, D. T., *Teletrabajo*, Madrid: Colección Claves prácticas Francis Lefebvre 1, 2013; Sierra Benítez, M., *El contenido de la relación laboral en el*

understanding that its provisions should serve to modernise companies and public service organisations, but also contribute to the conciliation of work and personal life by making available the benefits of greater time flexibility and autonomy in the fulfilment of tasks.

The Agreement contributes to the strategy defined at the Lisbon European Council meeting as it supports a knowledge-based economy and society. Its main objectives consist in developing a general framework for the working conditions of teleworkers at European level and in balancing both workers' and employers' needs of flexibility and security. However, it amounts to a non-binding instrument,[35] whose implementation is carried out according to the procedures and practices of the social partners and the Member States.[36] Hence, the Agreement's legal nature has come in for criticism since it impedes its effective implementation in national legal systems. In the future, it would be advisable for it to take the form of a European Directive, as in the cases of agreements of a similar kind concerning parental leave, part-time work and fixed-term work.

In conformity with the agreed provisions, telework is defined as "a form of organising and/or performing work, using information technology, in the context of an employment contract/relationship, where work, which could also be performed at the employer's premises, is carried out away from those premises on a regular basis." In this sense, the Agreement has been limited to the regulation of a traditional labour relationship and has not adequately contemplated the diversity of forms of work, especially self-employment. However, this type of work is characterised by a considerable degree of employee autonomy, since the teleworker manages the organisation of her/his working time.

For the rest, the Framework Agreement tries to ensure that teleworkers enjoy the same rights as counterparts working on the employer's premises. This is actually the case with regard to employment conditions, account taking of all the particularities of teleworking; collective rights; providing the necessary equipment; disciplinary responsibility; the protection of health and safety at work and training.

Some peculiarities are foreseen in relation to data protection and teleworker privacy. In order to verify the correct application of health and safety conditions, the employer, the workers' representatives and/or the competent authorities can have access to the place of teleworking, within the limits established in the national laws and collective agreements. If the task is performed at home, teleworkers should be notified beforehand and asked for their consent. Teleworkers are also entitled to request inspection visits.

Undoubtedly, this form of work is the most opportune way of balancing work and private life, and the EU continues to bet on its future development and promotion.

---

teletrabajo, Sevilla: Consejo Económico y Social, 2011; Thibault Aranda, J., *El Teletrabajo: Análisis jurídico-laboral*, Madrid: CES, 2000.

35 This instrument was adopted pursuant Article 138 TEC (current Article 154 TFEU).

36 Article 139.1 TEC (currently, Article 155.2 TFEU).

Blending

Based on the premise of the greater worker's autonomy, introduced by telework (distance work and home work), a new conception of well-being is emerging with the name "blending".[37] Its distinctive feature lies in the univocal meaning of work and private life, but with a greater emphasis, if possible, on the unity of both. The term has been introduced by managers as being in their interest and embraced by workers as being in theirs.

To illustrate the business approach, there is no better place to start than a book entitled *We: How to Increase Performance and Profits through Full Engagement?*[38] As long as decades ago new technologies led to the implementation in the legal field of the concept of telecommuting, which was designed to increase the productivity of companies by saving on transport costs, the concept of blending was introduced from the employer's point of view and for a similar purpose. It has been linked to the business project's insistence on motivating workers "to run extra kilometres" and achieve the goals proposed by the company. Karsan, one of the authors of the book, argues that, in our cultural environment, smartphones and the internet have ended the notion of working time. Reality itself invites us to abandon the idea of work-life balance and to address the situation instead through the career-life blend. This vision obliges the employer to "take note" and keep in mind that employees often bring their family and personal problems to work, and this affects their performance.[39] Moreover, workers tend to gauge the compatibility between their company's philosophy and their own priorities, flexible hours and telecommuting, among them.

This approach is not completely new. For years, it has been noticed how models of flexible working time can contribute to better conciliation of work, family and private life.[40] In this respect, it is worth mentioning flexi-time programmes and "time-banking" arrangements, which allow workers to accumulate extra hours and use them to obtain a few free days or free hours. So long as companies administer work schedules properly, these programmes acknowledge that working hours may vary according to the concrete situation of the family and private needs. In addition, telecommuting from home makes it possible to combine work and family life on a daily basis. However, care must be taken to ensure that overwork does not "burn" the boundaries between work and rest. It is interesting to note that in his discussion on this subject paragraph, Messenger turns to the verb "to blend" in the positive sense of "to

---

37 About the concept of "blending", see Ushakova, "Del *work-life balance* al *work-career blend: apuntes para el debate*", *Nueva Revista Española de Derecho del Trabajo,* 192 (2016), 117–138.

38 Karsan, R.; Kruse, K., *We: How to Increase Performance and Profits through Full Engagement,* New Jersey: Hoboken, 2011.

39 Karsan, Kruse, *op. cit.*

40 Messenger, J.C., "Towards decent working time", in Boulin, J-Y. et al. eds., *Decent working time. New trends, new issues,* Geneva: ILO, 2006, 426.

melt", in opposition to that of "to blur" in the negative sense of "to erase" or "to eliminate borders".[41]

In line with business beliefs, in today's blogs and websites workers say that they are likely to forget about a working day ending at 5:00 p.m., and to proclaim: "Work and home no longer balance, they blend."[42] In this sense, we are facing the creation and implementation of a business and cultural model, rather than a legal one.

Thus, from the business perspective, the goal of achieving complete commitment is at the centre of human resources policies. To do so, workers have to identify with the company, in some way, to melt with it, fully associating with its culture and turning work into life and life into work. It could be argued that the intention is to arrive at the total work system through a much more capillary penetration, which reaches all an individual's vital areas.[43] The paradox is that instead of brining workers advantages, the flexible management of working time breaks down the last limits and transforms them into a single and flexible instrument of production.[44]

In this connection, the question arises: how could it be possible to prevent a worker from assuming greater involvement with the company and fulfilling her/himself professionally and personally? Both employers and workers defend this new form of well-being: the former because it increases workers' productivity and performance by creating emotional links of identification with the company; the latter, because it permits them to achieve personal well-being through their full self-realisation by abolishing borders and eliminating the conflict between work and private life.

"Idealistic" scenarios

Smart-working

In recent years, a new work model has emerged that, according to some doctrinal opinions, is considered a step forward with respect to teleworking, namely, the new productive model called "smart work".[45] In relation to the factor of distance

---

41 "[O]ffering workers the possibility of 'telecommuting' to their jobs by working from home can also provide them with the ability to blend work and family responsibilities on a daily basis, although care must be taken that this does not lead to excessive hours due to the inevitable blurring of the boundaries between paid work and personal life." *Ibid.* (emphasis added).

42 Available at: http://www.forbes.com/sites/ronashkenas/2012/10/19/forget-work-life-bal ance-its-time-for-work-life-blend/#676033fa3e2f, and at: http://www.success.com/article/ why-we-need-work-life-blending-not-balance, accessed April 2, 2018.

43 Gómez Villar, A., "El trabajador precario y la construcción del precariado como sujeto del cambio", *Astrolabio. Revista internacional de filosofía*, 11 (2010), 210.

44 Gómez Villar, "El trabajador precario...", 211.

45 Boorsma, B., Mitchell, Sh., "Work-Life Innovation. Smart Work – A Paradigm Shift Transforming. How, Where, and When Work Gets Done", September 2011, Cisco Internet Business Solution Group (IBSG), 2011. See also one of the first sources concerning smart work:

from a company's central office, there is an evolution from carrying out work activity usually at home and in isolation to performing work in remote workplaces, satellite offices and remote connection spaces. Although teleworking still retains features of the previous "centralist" model it contains the embryo of the co-working (collaborative work) of the future. Its achievement consists in allowing new technologies not only to optimise productivity, as was the case before, but also to create new ways of working. Connection (networking) in its pure state is established as a working model *par excellence*, in which the public and private environments are "interconnected", while physical and virtual states are "interposed". The "peer-to-peer" and "wiki-style" models are postulated as advanced and institutionalised modes of collaboration and decision-making. The worker per se is "service-centric", in other words, has access to connection centres.

Despite the undoubted technological advance it represents, the message conveyed by this model in terms of work-life is similar to the one transmitted by blending.

Consequently, in its conceptual approach to smart working the European Parliament categorically rejects the change from a culture of presence to a culture of permanent availability. In the relevant parliamentary Resolution, "smart working" is defined as an approach to organising work through a combination of flexibility, autonomy and collaboration, which does not necessarily require the worker to be present in the workplace or in any pre-defined place and enables them to manage their own working hours, while nevertheless ensuring consistency with the maximum daily and weekly working hours laid down by law and collective agreements.[46]

Emphasis is placed on the potential of "smart work" for a better work-life balance, especially for parents returning to or joining the labour market maternity or parental leave. The emphasis on leaves is a reprise of the well-known concept of conciliation according to Article 33 of the EU Charter of Fundamental Rights. In this regard, the Commission is called on to propose well-grounded and coherent initiatives about a paternity leave directive with a minimum of compulsory two-week fully paid leave; a careers' leave directive which supplements the provision of professional care enables workers to care for dependents and offers the career adequate remuneration and social protection; employee-driven flexibility and sufficient incentives for men to take up careers' leave; and minimum standards applicable in all Member States to address the specific needs of adoptive parents and children and to establish the same rights as for natural parents.[47]

The Smart Working Handbook. How to reduce costs and improve business performance through new ways of working. A practical guide, June 2011, and its 2nd edition, September 2015, more information available at: www.flexibility.co.uk, accessed April 2, 2018.

46 European Parliament Resolution of 13 September 2016, on *Creating labour market conditions favourable for work-life balance,* 2016/2017(INI), para. 48.

47 2016/2017(INI), para. 33.

It is here that the 2017 Proposal for a Directive on Reconciliation of 2017 entered into the picture.[48] Article 9 of the Proposal provided for the adoption of measures to ensure that workers with children up to a certain age (at least twelve) and caregivers have the right to request flexible working methods to help cater to their family obligations; those methods must be valid for a reasonable period of time. As can be seen, the idea is to increase work flexibility for parents who return after parental leave, and although the Directive on the aforementioned permit already contemplates the possibility of requesting two types of flexible work formulas (flexible work schedules and reduction of working hours), the proposal adds a third (distance working), while extending the scope of the personal application of these rights to all caregivers, as well as workers with children up to a certain minimum age marking the transition from childhood to adolescence.[49]

The Directive on work-life balance for parents and carers was finally adopted in June, 2019.[50] Its Article 9 on flexible working arrangements states:

1. Member States shall take the necessary measures to ensure that workers with children up to a specified age, which shall be at least eight years, and carers, have the right to request flexible working arrangements for caring purposes. The duration of such flexible working arrangements may be subject to a reasonable limitation.
2. Employers shall consider and respond to requests for flexible working arrangements as referred to in paragraph 1 within a reasonable period of time, taking into account the needs of both the employer and the worker. Employers shall provide reasons for any refusal of such a request or for any postponement of such arrangements.
3. When flexible working arrangements as referred to in paragraph 1 are limited in duration, the worker shall have the right to return to the original working pattern at the end of the agreed period. The worker shall also have the right to request to return to the original working pattern before the end of the agreed period where justified on the basis of a change of circumstances. The employer shall consider and respond to a request for an early return to the original working pattern, taking into account the needs of both the employer and the worker.

48 Proposal for a Directive of the European Parliament and of the Council on the reconciliation of family life and professional life of parents and carers, and repealing Council Directive 2010/18/EU of 26 April 2017, COM (2017) 253 final. In relation to the Proposal of Directive, see, for all: Mella Méndez, L. (2017), "El trabajo a distancia como medida de flexibilidad y conciliación laboral", *IUSlabor* 2 (2017), 4, available at: https://www.upf.edu/web/iuslabor/2/2017, accessed March 8, 2018.
49 COM (2017) 253 final, Mella Méndez, "El trabajo a distancia...", 1.
50 Directive (EU) 2019/1158 of European Parliament and of the Council of 20 June 2019, on work-life balance for parents and carers and repealing Council Directive 2010/18/EU, *OJ* L 188, 12.7.2019.

4. Member States may make the right to request flexible working arrangements subject to a period of work qualification or to a length of service
   qualification, which shall not exceed six months. In the case of succes-
   sive fixed-term contracts within the meaning of Directive 1999/70/EC
   with the same employer, the sum of those contracts shall be taken into
   account for the purpose of calculating the qualifying period.

As it shows, the needs of employers and workers must be considered. Therefore,
it is necessary to offer States the possibility of limiting the duration of flexible
working formulas, a point of special importance in the case of part-time work.

In this context, there is concern about the increase in non-voluntary part-time
work, particularly among women with family responsibilities, for this increases the
risk of in-work poverty. To avoid that, in the case of part-time work, the quality
of employment and non-discrimination with respect to full-time workers should
be guaranteed in accordance with the Part-time Work Directive. It is vitally
important to provide for the right of access to an adequate, non-discriminatory
pension scheme for part-time workers, workers with a discontinuous working life
and workers who have had interruptions in their working life.

Making the most of the potential advantages offered by technology, such as
digital information, high-speed internet and audio-visual technology, for
"smart" (tele) work methods implies taking into account all aspects of working
time regulation established in EU law in general by Directive 2003/88/EC.[51]
It is worth remembering that the European definition of smart-working insists
on respect for the maximum limits of daily and weekly work time laid down in
legislation and collective agreements.

When the EU adopts the concepts of "Industry 4.0", borrowed from the
German national initiative, and "smart work", inspired by the method of the
collaborative economy, workers' protection systems will have to be introduced
which are appropriate for the new forms of work. Once again, an initiative from
the national sphere, in particular, French Law's right to disconnect could be
considered. Section 7 of Article L.2242-8 of the French Labour Code establishes
that the annual negotiation on professional equality between women and men
and the quality of life at work should include the modalities of full exercise by
workers of their right to disconnect.[52]

51 Directive 2003/88/EC of the European Parliament and of the Council of 4 November 2003
    on certain aspects of the organization of working time, *OJ* L 299, 18.11.2003. See, among
    others: Mella Méndez, "Nuevas tecnologías y nuevos retos...", 30–52, and Ushakova, T.,
    "Algunos aspectos de la ordenación del tiempo de trabajo en el Derecho de la Unión Europea",
    Revue Europeénne du droit social XXXIII (2017), 4, 95–112.
52 *Loi nº 2016-1088 du 8 août 2016 relative au travail, á la modernisation du dialogue social et
    á la sécurisation des parcours professionnels, JORF* nº 0184 du 9 août 2016, available at:
    https://www.legifrance.gouv.fr/affichTexte.do?cidTexte=JORFTEXT000032983213&cate
    gorieLien=id#JORFARTI000032984268, accessed April 2, 2018. See about the right to

The Directive does not include this right, given that its starting point, as well as the corresponding principle of the European Pillar of Social Rights, is not the organisation of working time in the technological context, but the extension of the permits of parents and caregivers, that is, the traditional view of conciliation of work and family life. Indeed, it must be recognised that EU strategy in this respect, that is to say, its "quantitative" approach, seems to be more feasible than the holistic one required by the concept of "smart work".

The future without work

If Chesterton's definition of technology as "a set of knowledge that reduces the number of workers ... and owners"[53] were to be accepted, Industry 4.0 would seem to inaugurate the somewhat futuristic scenario of the many times announced world without jobs.

As the twentieth century came to end, there was still general consensus over the division between human and digital work. In that view, workers were supposed to focus on the most creative tasks, those that could not be reduced to the mere execution of orders or the application of the algorithms, while machines were earmarked for carrying out routine tasks like data processing. However, today, technological progress makes it possible to automate even the most complex and non-routine tasks.[54] In fact, not a few studies warn about the increasing substitution of cognitive tasks by computers.[55] Moreover, substitution and, consequently, the destruction of jobs are outstripping the creation of new ones.[56] Not in vain, the involvement of new technologies in the workplace is one of the most burning issues in the debate on the "Future of Work".[57] "Will it be different this time round?" many scholars wonder.[58]

disconnect: Mercader Uguina, R. J. (2017), *El futuro del trabajo en la era de la digitalización y la robótica,* valencia: Tirant lo Blanch, 2017, 160–163.

53 Quoted by Sagardoy, I.; Mercader Uguina, R. J., in *El futuro del trabajo que queremos,* Vol. II, Madrid: OIT, Gobierno de España, Ministerio de Empleo y de la Seguridad Social, 2017, 131.

54 UN, DESA/DPAD, in collaboration with UNDP, ILO and UN Women (2017), *The impact of technological revolution on labour markets and income distribution,* 31 July 2017, 3 ff. This study was conducted in response to a request by the Secretary-General's Executive Committee Decision No. 2017/43 of 23 March 2017.

55 Benedikt Frey, C. et al, *Technology at work v 2.0: The future is not what it used to be,* Oxford: Oxford Martin Institute and Citi, 2016, 11; UN, ECOSOC, *Foresight for digital development,* Report of the Secretary-General, 29 February 2016, UN Doc E/CN.16/2016/3, p. 10.

56 Brynjolfsson, E. and McAfee, A., *The Second Machine Age: Work, Progress, and Prosperity in a Time of Brilliant Technologies,* New York: W. W. Norton & Company Inc. Publishers, 2014.

57 ILO, *Technological Changes and work in the future: Making technology work for all,* The Future of Work Century Initiatives, Issue Notes Series, n° 1 note series, Geneva: International Labour Office, 2017, available at: http://www.ilo.org/wcmsp5/groups/public/—dgreports/—dcomm/documents/publication/wcms_534201.pdf, accessed April 2, 2018.

58 ILO *Technological Changes...,* 4.

Firstly, European regulation on "technological dismissal" should be proposed to establish effective protection measures. However, there is simply no harmonised concept of dismissal in the EU Law.[59] Considering the Framework Agreement on Telework, the general purpose of promoting the equal rights of teleworkers and other workers can be deduced. Nevertheless, the peculiarities of teleworking may require a tailored approach, above all, with regard to health and safety at work or personal data protection.

Secondly, in the framework of the ILO's initiative on the "Future of Work", two proposals are discernible: one tackles the "taxing of new technologies", i.e. imposing "tax on robots" which replace human work, the other address the creation of a fund with income from this tax to finance the training of the most affected workers.

Within this scenario, the possibility of a universal basic income should be considered, but not in the sense proposed by the European Pillar of a minimum threshold of protection to ensure the dignity of existence; rather it should be not linked to the level of income and granted by virtue of the mere fact of the existence of a human being.[60]

In the same scenario, the idea of putting technology at the service of society (those intelligent robots that take care of elderly and play with children) can be approached, and indeed already has been in some countries, like Japan, with considerable economic development and demographic problems. The European Parliament pronounced against this proposal since it considered that the European tradition could not countenance care by robots.[61] Nevertheless, as with the over-ambitious legal package on work-life balance, the rejection of technology at the service of society seems to be unrealistic and hardly in keeping with current trends and needs.

Conclusions

The European Pillar includes a correct and comprehensive approach to the work-life balance. However, the European Pillar itself is a vague proposal in terms of its

---

59 In this regard, it should be remembered that the workers' protection in the event of termination of the labor contract [Article 153.1 (b) TFEU] requires a special legislative procedure by the Council's unanimous decision [Article 153.2 (b)]. In general, protection against unjustified dismissal is guaranteed by Article 30 of the Charter, which is connected with the Directives 2001/23/EC on the rights of workers in the cases of transfers and undertaking of companies and the Directive 2008/94/CE on insolvency of the employer. Two directives refer to dismissal at EU level: Directive 98/59/EC on collective redundancies, and Directive 92/85/EEC, which includes the prohibition of dismissal for reasons of pregnancy or motherhood (Article 10).

60 See the definition by the *Basic Income European Network (BIEN)*, available at: https://basicincome.org, accessed June 2, 2018, and the Standing's one, at: Standing, G., *Basic Income: And How We Can Make It Happen?* New York: Penguin Books, 2017. According to Standing, "a basic income can be defined as a modest amount of money paid unconditionally to individuals on a regular basis."

61 Draft Report with recommendations to the Commission on *Civil Law Rules on Robotics*, Committee on Legal Affairs, Rapporteur: Mady Delvaux, 2015/2103 (INL), PR\1095387EN.doc, 4–5 and 9.

legal nature and effectiveness. With respect to relevant EU Law, neither the Charter of Fundamental Rights nor the directives seem coherent or adequate to ensure conciliation in the context of Industry 4.0. Even conceptually, EU Law still retains the traditional vision of the conciliation of work and family life.

In this sense, as already proposed by the European Parliament, the recognition of the fundamental right to work-life balance should be considered, including a set of measures required to ensure this balance using traditional techniques, such as the organisation of working time, protection against discrimination and the introduction of positive protection measures.

In particular, and on the basis of the 2002 Agreement on Telework and existing directives, a Framework Directive with a comprehensive approach and striking a genuine balance between organisational and technological aspects and negative and positive protection should be devised. In any case, the organisation of working time should be the starting point when conceiving the future regulation of the work-live balance in the new technological context. This may seem to be an inevitable proposal, but to what extent it is realistic is another question.

Bibliography

Anderson, K. M., *Social Policy in the European Union*, The European Union Series (London: Palgrave, 2015).

Boorsma, B. & Mitchell, Sh., "Work-Life Innovation. Smart Work – A Paradigm Shift Transforming. How, Where, and When Work Gets Done", September 2011, Cisco Internet Business Solution Group (IBSG),2011.

Cabeza Pereiro, J., "Conciliación de vida privada y laboral", *Temas laborales* 103 (2010): 45–65.

Cruz Villalón, J., "Elementos condicionantes para la efectividad de la conciliación laboral en España", in Mella Méndez, L., dir., *Conciliación de la vida laboral y familiar y crisis económica. Estudios desde el Derecho internacional y comparado* (Madrid: Delta, 2015) 5–26.

Benedikt Frey, C., Osborne, M. A. & Holmes, C., *Technology at work v 2.0: The future is not what it used to be* (Oxford: Oxford Martin Institute and Citi, 2016).

Brynjolfsson, E. & McAfee, A., *The Second Machine Age: Work, Progress, and Prosperity in a Time of Brilliant Technologies* (New York: W. W. Norton & Company Inc. Publishers, 2014).

EPRS, Davies, R., "Industry 4.0. Digitalisation for productivity and growth", Briefing, September 2015.

Esping-Andersen, G., *Incomplete revolution: Adapting welfare states to women's new roles* (Cambridge: Polity Press, 2009).

García Romero, B., *El Teletrabajo* (Cizur Menor: ed. Civitas, 2012).

Gómez Villar, A. (2010), "El trabajador precario y la construcción del precariado como sujeto del cambio", *Astrolabio. Revista internacional de filosofía*, 11 (2001): 209–217.

Karsan, R. & Kruse, K., *We: How to Increase Performance and Profits through Full Engagement* (New Jersey: Hoboken, 2011).

Mella Méndez, L. & Serrani, L., eds., *Work-Life Balance and the Economic Crisis. Some Insights from the Perspective of Comparative Law*, Vols. I and II (ADAPT: Cambridge Scholars Publishing, 2015).

Mella Méndez, L., "Nuevas tecnologías y nuevos retos para la conciliación y la salud de los trabajadores", *Trabajo y Derecho. Nueva Revista de actualidad y Relaciones laborales*, 16 (2016): 30–52.

Mella Méndez, L., "El trabajo a distancia como medida de flexibilidad y conciliación laboral", *IUSlabor* 2 (2017), available at: https://www.upf.edu/web/iuslabor/2/2017.

Mella Méndez, L. & Núñez-Cortés Contreras, P., dirs., Moreno Solana, A., coord., *Nuevas tecnologías y nuevas maneras de trabajar: estudios desde el Derecho español y comparado. Alemania, Reino Unido, Polonia, Portugal y Argentina*, E-book (Madrid: Dykinson, 2017).

Mercader Uguina, R.J., *El futuro del trabajo en la era de la digitalización y la robótica* (Valencia: Tirant lo Blanch, 2017).

Messenger, J.C., "Towards decent working time", in Boulin, J.-Y. et al; Lallement, M.; Messenger, J.C. and Michon, F., eds, *Decent working time. New trends, new issue*, (Geneva: ILO, 2006).

Núñez-Cortés Contreras, L., *Eficacia de las medidas de conciliació*, (Madrid: Tecnos, 2016).

Núñez-Cortés Contreras, L. & Lousada Arochena, J.F. (2015), *Jornada de trabajo y derechos de conciliación* (Madrid: Tecnos, 2015).

Pérez Pérez, M., dir *El teletrabajo: efectos en la conciliación de la vida familiar y laboral* (Zaragoza: Ed. Fundear, 2008).

Pfeiffer, S., "The Vision of 'Industrie 4.0' in the Making – a Case of Future Told, Tamed, and Traded", *Nanoethics* 11 (2017) 1: 107–121.

Sagardoy, I. & Mercader Uguina, R.J. in *El futuro del trabajo que queremos*, Vol. II (Madrid: OIT, Gobierno de España, Ministerio de Empleo y de la Seguridad Social, 2017): 123–131.

Schwab, K., *The Fourth Industrial Revolution* (Geneva: World Economic Forum, 2016).

Sempere Navarro, A. V. & Kahale Carrillo, D. T., *Teletrabajo* (Madrid: Colección Claves prácticas Francis Lefebvre 1, 2013).

Sierra Benítez, M., *El contenido de la relación laboral en el teletrabajo* (Sevilla: Consejo Económico y Social, 2011).

Standing, G., *Basic Income: And How We Can Make It Happen?* (New York: Penguin Books, 2017).

Taylor-Gooby, P., ed., *New risks, new welfare. The transformation of the European welfare state* (Oxford: Oxford University Press, 2004).

Thibault Aranda, J., *El Teletrabajo: Análisis jurídico-laboral* (Madrid: CES, 2000).

Ushakova, T. (2015), "Protecting the Pregnant Women against Dismissal: Subjective and Objective Components in EU Law", in Mella Méndez, L. & Serani, L., eds, *Work-Life Balance and the Economic Crisis. Some Insights from the Perspective of Comparative Law*, Vol. II (ADAPT: Cambridge Scholars Publishing, 2015), 93–121.

Ushakova, T., "El teletrabajo en el Derecho de la OIT", *Revista de información laboral* 9 (2015): 55–75.

Ushakova, T., "El Derecho de la OIT para el trabajo a distancia: ¿una regulación superada o todavía aplicable?", *Revista Internacional y Comparada de Relaciones Laborales y Derecho del Empleo* 3 (2015) 4: 1–19.

Ushakova, T., "De la conciliación a la desconexión tecnológica. Apuntes para el debate", *Nueva Revista Española de Derecho del Trabajo* 192 (2016): 117–138.

Ushakova, T., "Algunos aspectos de la ordenación del tiempo de trabajo en el Derecho de la Unión Europea", *Revue Européenne du droit social*, Vol. XXXIII (2016) 4: 95–112.

Ushakova, T., "Del *work-life balance* al *work-career blend*: apuntes para el debate", in Mella Méndez, L., Núñez-Cortés Contreras, P., dirs, Moreno Solana, A., coord., *Nuevas tecnologías y nuevas maneras de trabajar: estudios desde el Derecho español y comparado.*

Alemania, Reino Unido, Polonia, Portugal y Argentina, E-book (Madrid: Dykinson, 2017).

Ushakova, T., "Los modelos de la acción normativa de la OIT para regular el trabajo a distancia", in *El futuro del trabajo que queremos*, Vol. II (Madrid: OIT, Gobierno de España, Ministerio de Empleo y de la Seguridad Social, 2017), 445–459.

Ushakova, T., "De la máquina al trabajador y viceversa. Un ensayo sobre la implicación de las nuevas tecnologías en el mundo laboral", *Revista Internacional y Comparada de Relaciones Laborales y Derecho del Empleo* 6 (2018) 1: 114–137.

10 Digital disconnection as a limit to corporate control of working time

Sarai Rodríguez González

Introduction

In today's society, the constant need for corporations to boost productivity and satisfy demand has, in many instances, occasioned an organisation of working time which can have serious impacts on workers' occupational well-being, perception of satisfaction and psychosocial health, and present significant obstacles to achieving a suitable work/life balance.[1] In addition, the most recent labour reforms have introduced a reframing of the Right to Work that favours the value of productivity and the principle of performance, wherein new Information and Communications Technology (ICT) is seen as a fundamental tool for enhancing efficiency, thus giving rise to a new paradigm which has come to be known as Industry 4.0 or the Fourth Industrial Revolution.[2] This new labour landscape is characterised by the flexibilisation of working time and the inadequate management of technology, factors whose growth is accompanied in equal measure by the presentation of substantial psychosocial risks.[3]

The image projected by the current environment wherein services are rendered in a labour market that calls for increasingly flexible employees capable of enabling companies to adapt more readily to market needs while still lowering production costs, is worthy of an analysis from the optics of the conventional concerns of the International Labour Organization (ILO), with respect to the requirement to provide safe and secure working time. These new means and formats of service provision bring substantial instability, with higher workloads, anti-social hours, night work, and an overall vulnerability, prompting a new reality that leads to great difficulties in reconciling work and family, and generating conditions which can negatively impact the quality of life and personal health of working persons, resulting in health problems, disincentivisation, frequent absenteeism or tardiness, and other occupational issues that ultimately hamper a company's overall productivity.[4]

---

1 Cladellas, 2008: 237 et seq.
2 Mercader, 2017: 24–33.
3 Dans, 2017: 63–66.
4 Spurgeon, 2003; Fagan, 2004; 108 et. seq.

Among the objectives of the ILO is to promote the attainment of 'decent work', a concept that denotes the provision of 'opportunities for women and men to obtain decent and productive work, in conditions of freedom, equity, security and human dignity'.[5] The application of such a premise to the structural aspects of working time implies starting our analysis from the presumption that all corporate policies on time management are inspired by the will to provide the said 'decent working time').[6] It is clear that in order to develop a supply of labour which satisfies the five dimensions by which this concept is characterised, it becomes necessary to establish working time policies that entail the collective reduction of working time, advances with respect to distributing working time in structures featuring continuous workdays, personalised and flexible schedules, compressed work weeks, etc., broadening the uses of so-called *flexitime*, or promoting high-quality part-time work. It becomes still more complicated when we attempt to apply these same considerations to the types of work shifts which have resulted from the widespread incorporation of ICT into service provision, giving rise to even more novel work formats, known alternatively as 'third time', 'work contact time', or 'technological connectivity time'. To that end, this analysis explores the question of whether the so-called 'technological connectivity time' is capable of satisfying the five dimensions denoted by the concept of 'decent working time'.

Working time and ICT: implications for occupational health

The emergence and ubiquity of ICT has permeated people's living spaces and personal time, introducing major changes in workers' social, family, and especially professional lives;[7] at the same time, it has given rise to a new paradigm characterised by the digitisation or virtualisation of work, whose nature is typically informational, global, fluid, liquid, and habitually produced at a marginal cost of zero.[8]

While the incorporation of ICT has brought numerous advantages in terms of productivity, and notwithstanding the myriad ways in which constant connectivity opens up enormous possibilities for more flexible and interactive modes of work,[9] it has also incited the emergence of psychosocial risks closely linked to the accompanying transformations observed in the organisation, pace, and intensification of work, the high degree of uninterrupted communication and connectivity, work autonomy, the need to constantly update and refresh one's skills and knowledge, the rapid accumulation of information – much of it unwanted or gratuitous (also dubbed information overload or 'infoxication')[10] –

5 Reich, 2007: 153–163; Messenger, 2004; Boulin, Lallement, Messenger and Michon, 2006: 20 et seq.
6 ILO, *Reducing the Decent Work Deficit: A Global Challenge*, International Labour Conference, 89th Session 2001, Geneva. Rodríguez González, 2017: 102.
7 Mercader, 2002: 107; Cardona, 2003: 158; Aguilera and Cristóbal, 2017: 334.
8 Alemán, 2017b.
9 Mella, 2016: 31.
10 Alemán, 2017a: 17; Alemán, 2017b: 406.

not to mention untimely phone calls, excessive workloads, disorientation, work addiction, etc.[11] In addition to all this comes the paradox of smart devices enabled with geolocation technology, which may in some instances help to facilitate the attainment of work/life balance by giving workers a higher margin of autonomy, but which at the same time impede personal rest time by compelling them to stay ever-attentive to their devices, even after the conclusion of the work day.[12]

Within this new labour environment, a pattern of habitual behaviour is assumed wherein which professional matters accompany the worker beyond and outside of the daily work shift, causing employees to use their rest time to answer e-mails, take phone calls, or respond to WhatsApp messages. This perceived 'requirement' may be implicit in the company's organisational culture, or it may be the fruit of a self-imposed pressure exerted as a result of work addiction. Aside from this, we must not forget that the incorporation of ICT, and moreover its inadequate management and potential abuse[13] may indeed be a reason for which the worker is unable to observe firm boundaries between private life and the professional sphere, as these areas overlap with one another with increasing frequency.[14] It is precisely this aspect that demonstrates that the proliferation of these new communication tools has come to be perceived as a factor which actually degrades quality of life, by blurring or altogether obliterating the boundaries between workers' personal and professional lives, thereby 'liquefying' certain borders which were perfectly evident and static within a traditional format of service provision.[15] This blurring or removal of boundaries only intensifies as workloads grow heavier, and increasingly corrupts or interferes with rest time, ultimately harming workers' mental health[16] to the extent that in extreme cases, the blurred lines in-between working time and rest time can turn the worker into a '24-hour' or perennially 'on-call' employee, remaining at the company's continuous and uninterrupted disposition. For this very reason, such a mode of work fails to meet the criteria exacted by the concept of 'decent work'. The situation constitutes an excess of labour, wherein the unlimited extension of working hours begins to adversely affect the safety and security of individuals, families, organisations, and the general public, even in cases in which workers engage in these activities voluntarily or of their own volition.[17]

In addition to all this, we must not forget the potential psychosocial risks associated with the pressure deriving from the fact that retaining a professional post might very well depend upon maintaining permanent availability, presupposing a 'duty' to check and answer e-mail on a constant basis, or triggering an 'anticipatory stress', whereby the very expectation of an e-mail arriving in the inbox

---

11 Eurofound and ILO, 2017; Vallecillo, 2017: 170; Pinilla: 2016.
12 González, 2015: 35; González, 2016: 266.
13 Falguera, 2016: 35.
14 Martínez Fons, 2002; González Cobaleda 2016: 263.
15 Vallecillo, 2017: 170.
16 Triclin, 2016: 314.
17 Mella, 2016: 32.

after-hours impedes the worker's personal rest time or prevents him or her from achieving technological disconnection.[18] According to figures cited in a study by the human resources firm Randstad (2015), 67% of Spanish workers say they use e-mail or other professional tools outside of their normal working hours when they consider it to be advisable or important, and more than half admit to responding to said correspondence on an immediate basis; while 41% of workers say they feel pressured to answer calls and e-mails even while on vacation.

This pervasiveness of this situation has also been demonstrated in reports recently released by the ILO within the European Union, which highlight the importance of recognising the impact that emerging technologies and new methods of production can have on occupational health.[19] Specifically, this phenomenon is documented in *EU Occupational Safety and Health Strategic Framework 2014–2020*, which notes that the 'effective prevention of work-related diseases requires anticipating potential negative effects of new technologies on workers' health and safety'.[20]

Working time and rest time: the risk of permanent connectivity

It is within this digital era, marked by the blurring of lines between professional and personal life, and the legitimate risk factors induced by such blurring, that the debate on the right-vs.-need to disconnect plays out, in an attempt to guarantee recognition in favour of a specific cohort of workers, also known as 'always connected workers', at a moment in which the ubiquity of technology and computer resources can heavily impact the worker's psychophysical integrity and jeopardise the very enjoyment of human rights.[21]

The question then becomes one of how to effectively respond to the myriad quandaries derived from the fact that workers find themselves wholly 'absorbed' by technology both within and outside of standard working hours, causing them to experience stress, techno-stress, techno-addiction, techno-anxiety, information overload, etc.[22] In fact, it has been shown that when workers finish their formal work shift but still feel compelled to remain involved or concerned with professional matters, or are forced, either directly or indirectly, to stay in contact with the company, they enter into a *sui generis* time, or 'third time', which may present itself as a prolonged period of 'technological availability' (Mella, 2016: 32). This 'work contact time' is not formally considered to be working time, and is therefore not remunerated, despite that this period is marked by the sensation of feeling distinctly under another's employ.[23]

18 Belkin, Becker and Conroy, 2016.
19 ILO, 2016; EU-OSHA, 2014.
20 COM (2014) 332 final, p. 7.
21 Rota, 2016: 289.
22 Dans, 2017: 73–83.
23 Mella, 2016: 33.

Such circumstances were observed in the *Mettling Report, for adapting labour to the digital transformation*, released on 15 September 2015, which proposes 36 methods for correcting the negative effects that new technologies can have on occupational health. One such technique for assuring workers' quality of life in favour of better work/life balance is by recognising a right and a duty to disconnect. This right is expressed as 'a joint responsibility of the worker and the employer' that incorporates both company regulation and individual education.[24]

In recent years, multiple European countries (predominantly Sweden, Germany and France) have laid out ways to incorporate professionally established methods – best practices – for ensuring the firm distinction between working time and personal time through technological disconnection.[25] To that effect, in 2014, Germany discussed passing, as part of an anti-stress law, a regulation by which companies were prohibited from contacting workers at certain hours of the day (Vallecillo, 2016: 172; Rota, 2016: 291–294).

The incorporation of the right to disconnect in the French law 2016-1088 of 8 August – *Loi n° 2016-1088 du 8 août 2016 relative au travail, á la modernisation du dialogue social et à la sécurisation des percours prodessionnels*, known as the 'Loi Travail' or the 'Loi El Khormri' – served somewhat as a wake-up call by adding a seventh point to article L.2242-8 of the French Labour Code.[26] This legislation captures the approach foreseen by extra-legislative regulations and by the Triclin precedent,[27] by presenting a model of the right to disconnect based on an approach that establishes legal safeguards for workers. That said, the French regulation suffers from a lack of precision, in that it fails to define the concept or the content of the right to disconnect – leaving the matter up to collective bargaining, or, failing this, to the agreement arrived at with the employer in question – nor does it expound upon the consequences of noncompliance with the criteria as established. With respect to the literal content, it simply calls for 'the implementation of training and awareness-raising activities on the reasonable use of digital devices, directed at workers, middle management, and executives'; a rather abstract formulation whose actual extent is left to collective bargaining.

While at first it may seem as though the right to technologically disconnect is reduced to a programmatic policy regulating training and awareness-raising

---

24 Mettling, 2016: 136.
25 González Cobaleda, 2015: 17–42.
26 This seventh section establishes that 'the annual negotiations on gender equality in the workplace and quality of life at work must also address: The terms and conditions in which the employee can fully exercise his/her right to disconnect and the implementation by the company of mechanisms to regulate the use of digital tools, to ensure compliance with rest periods and vacation time and respect personal and family life. If no agreement is reached, the employer must also draw up a charter, after seeking the opinion of the works council, or in the absence of a works council, of the staff representatives. This charter must set forth the terms and conditions in which employees can exercise their right to disconnect and provide for the implementation of training and awareness programmes on the reasonable use of digital tools for the employees and management staff'.
27 Triclin, 2016: 321–324.

measures on the correct use of new technologies,[28] the French law not only recognises the worker's right to disconnect, but also imposes a corporate requirement to disconnect by stipulating that companies establish an oversight policy based on a business model – preferably negotiated – for responding to possible instances of noncompliance which could negatively affect workers' health. As a result, collective bargaining – or, in its absence, the business owner, following a hearing by the works council or the staff representatives – must draw up an 'action policy' (*Charter*) on the modalities of exercising the right to disconnect, regardless of the size of the company, and the implementation, on the part of the company, of regulatory measures guiding the use of digital devices. In this sense, the means and methods that have been enacted in recent years which have typically been included in the contents of the negotiated right to disconnect comprise: partially replacing the use of e-mail with engagement with the company's social networks, promoting the principle of exemplariness among management, as well as efforts towards raising awareness and taking precautions with respect to the configuration settings of mobile devices (network blackouts, remote access interruptions, installation of *call-door* tools, email-free days, restriction of *reply-all* responses, etc.).[29]

Digital disconnect in Spain: recommendations for regulation

In our country, the debate sparked in the wake of the adoption of the French law establishing the 'right to disconnect' revolves around the question of whether the proper approach to the suite of problems workers experience as a result of hyperconnectivity calls for the recognition of a new right, or is indeed a matter of better securing a pre-existing right (the right to rest) through the adequate management of the use of ICT. Despite the fact that the Spanish legislature has not yet tackled the regulation of digital disconnection, various judicial decisions have been oriented around the recognition of this right.[30] Of particular relevance is the National High Court Ruling of 17 July 1997, which declares null the corporate regulations requiring the worker to maintain uninterrupted connectivity with the company and its clients through mobile devices upon the conclusion of working time. This judicial approach maintains, spells out, and broadens the theoretical-conceptual recommendation which conceives of the right to disconnect as a right of reversal that confers upon the workers themselves the ability to determine, on either a temporary or permanent basis, the nature of their technological availability through digital devices, respecting basic social rights and integrating, as appropriate, the conditions that may apply on an individual or collective basis.[31]

28 Alemán, 2017b: 408.
29 Mella, 2016: 45 et seq.
30 Aguilera and Cristóbal, 2017: 337.
31 Alemán, 2017a: 31.

In Spain, working time is regulated by the working day (as established in Article 34 of the Workers' Statute), which suggests that once this period has ended, we find ourselves within temporospatial circumstances of complementary or extraordinary hours, whose management and delimitation are also regulated. Notwithstanding, the concept of 'work availability' also fits into our labour laws, as legal regulations admit judicial mechanisms that may incorporate into service provision a worker's obligation to remain available to the company in certain cases, either by way of inclusion in certain clauses of the labour contract, by conventional regulations, or by explicit agreement.[32] If we are to consider the potential equivalency of work availability and 'digital work connectivity', we might highlight that the latter term entails an authorisation for the company to invade the rest period of the worker with the objective of ensuring that said worker be at the company's disposition, when necessary. The question would then centre around the need to regulate these 'temporary periods of technological connectivity' upon the basis of two fundamental prerequisites: firstly, they must be causal, that is, founded upon the needs or demands germane to certain predetermined services which specially call for a period of technological connectivity in order to guarantee the proper operation of the company's function;[33] and, secondly, they must be remunerated, that is, economically compensated through supplementary payments in a manner specified for the provision of technological availability as it reverts to the effective provision of labour, not excluding the possible remuneration for the very availability itself, understood as a quantification in economic terms of the inconvenience, additional efforts exerted, or possible harm which this might incur upon the worker,[34] nor partial access to the resource of compensatory rest periods granted. In the case of the latter, the regulation that is enforced must precisely delimit the form of application – and, where necessary, any exceptions thereto – of the rule of quantitative equivalency between periods of technological connectivity and compensatory rest periods.[35]

The said regulation would, concretely, equalise periods of digital work connectivity with periods of 'on-call work', in that both modes present scenarios in which workers find themselves outside of their standard time and place of work and not formally carrying out their work functions, but are still connected with the company, and maintain a situation of ready availability at the disposition of same,[36] such that in the event that the company requires their services, they may perform their functions from wherever they presently are. Therefore, the regulation of periods of digital connectivity would imply the interruption of time periods in which workers are independently and freely managing their periods of rest, with the sole condition that those workers may be potentially connected to their

32 Basterra, 2017: 51–62.
33 Martínez, 2011: 215.
34 Martínez, 2011: 411–412.
35 Martínez, 2011: 371.
36 Martínez, 2011: 55.

professional sphere, in such a way that if their services are required, those services may be rendered within the parameters as previously accorded. Therefore, applying by analogy the criterion established for 'on-call work' by the CJEU, only the actual rendering of services, and not the mere situation of availability itself,[37] would be considered as work time effective *ex* Directive 2003/88/EC, a position that the Supreme Court of Spain similarly upholds.[38] Nonetheless, the equal treatment of periods of digital work connectivity and periods of 'on-call work' may not be applied automatically, given that the complexity of the former requires the consideration of other unique circumstances which may be relevant on a case-by-case basis, such as the technological means substantiating the digital connectivity (whether this be via WhatsApp, e-mail, phone calls, or other communication tools).

Notwithstanding the above, it may be understood *a contrario sensu* that any and all technological connectivity undertaken by the worker outside of the formal working period and embarked upon during personal rest time falls within the frame and context of said worker's own volition. If this were the case, we would then need to ask ourselves if such connectivity, even when engaged in voluntarily, and not remunerated economically, would be subject to some kind of regulation or maximum allowance. The answer to this question should be in the affirmative, if we recall that the legal right protected throughout the time in which the technological connectivity is maintained is, as a matter of fact, a social right as fundamental in nature as is the right to rest.

At this juncture it is proposed to share the arguments defended by a public opinion sector which considers that the right to disconnect, to be inaccessible, or to be out of touch, only makes more explicit a right which is already held by workers, namely, the fundamental social right to rest (namely Article 40 EC and ILO Convention no. 132)[39] whose enforcement has been put at risk by a society inundated by ICT and by the pressures of work deriving from maximum labour availability.[40] From this point of view, if we understand that the right to technologically disconnect is not accompanied by any additional content that protects the right to rest, its express recognition would only make sense if made in order to demand effective action policies designed to prevent real psychosocial risks, and which go beyond well-meant awareness-raising or training programmes, thereby correcting the lapses and deficiencies of the French legislation discussed earlier. In the absence of said provisions, the alternative would be to fortify the current regulation[41], by including measures to disincentivise or penalise abuse, fostering a new adaptation of the meaning of the regulations by updating same to current labour environments and thereby firmly guaranteeing the fundamental

---

37 Among others, STJUE Judgment of the Court of 3 October 2000 (case C-2000/234, *SIMAP*), and STUE of 9 September 2003 (case C-151/02, *Norbert Jaeger*).

38 Most meaningfully in STS of 29 November 1994 (RJ 2005, 1589), and STS of 7 February 2001 (RJ 2001, 2148), among others.

39 Molina, 2015: 5–10.

40 Mella, 2017: 42.

41 Article 14 of the Labour Risk Prevention Law LRPL and Article 20 of the Workers' Statute.

social right to rest while reinforcing the labour culture of decent work and buttressing the paradigm of high-quality employment.[42]

In this sense, it is supposed that technological disconnection – as a discrete component of the right to rest – is expressly recognised in Article 34 of the Workers' Statute and that its guarantee is articulated by the fact of its inclusion into the minimal contents of the collective bargaining agreement as per Article 85.3 of that Statute, in such a way that establishes a duty to regulate, during the collective bargaining process at or above the company level, those concrete measures and formal actions which by protocol are undertaken to promote and guarantee the negotiated regulation of the technological disconnection which duly defines its effects and the conditions of its provision.[43] With respect to the structure of the collective bargaining, it is reasonable to take to understand that the regulation of the systems of technological connectivity is developed during the collective bargaining process at the company level, as it will be concretely within this specific environment that the particular circumstances germane to each activity will justify the motives permitting the recourse to a certain mode of technological availability. In addition to anticipating the causes that might engender timeframes of digital connectivity, the collective bargaining process must also concretely specify and determine the terms by which these periods of availability are compensated (be this by economic remuneration or the earning of compensatory rest periods), as well as firm limits on the means of corporate control, and protective measures put in place for the worker's safety and security (particularly with regard to the high degree of exposure to psychosocial risk factors); the process should also explicitly define the possible impacts on Social Security (contributions, access to loans by way of occupational contingencies, etc.). We must also not neglect that similarly, in order to guarantee the effectiveness of digital disconnection, appropriate precautions should accompany any corresponding infractions – in accordance with that which is stipulated by Royal Legislative Decree 5/2000 of 4 August, which approves the revision to the Law on Social Infractions and Sanctions in the Social Order – for those companies that do not carry out the measures designed to prevent workers from suffering the psychosocial risks mentioned earlier (predominantly, burnout) and deriving from lack of rest or the inability to disconnect from work.

As a result, such precautions would force negotiators to introduce into the conventional regulation an explicit definition of the systems which qualify scheduled times of technological connectivity, thereby putting their control in the hands of the workers' representatives or, where applicable, at the discretion of the courts. The need to favour the control of this time of digital connectivity is indispensable, given that this 'third time' is oriented towards company interests and not for the benefit of the workers, making it necessary to establish patterns

---

42 Vallecillo, 2017: 177–178.
43 Alemán, 2017a: 33.

that help to limit and control the power conferred to the business owner, so as to inhibit its abuse or excess.[44]

Additionally, it would be suitable for the right and duty to digitally disconnect to be accompanied by a global company policy adopted to assist workers and raise awareness throughout company hierarchies in order to overcome the barriers imposed by corporate cultures which might interpret the said measures as an obstacle to business activity rather than as an opportunity to reassess productive processes and design new strategies that actually boost efficiency.[45]

To that effect, it is worth noting that periods of technological disconnection enacted in Spain have followed the example modelled by companies like Volkswagen, which since 2012 has blocked access to company e-mail from 18:15 to 7:00 the following morning; Porsche, which established in negotiation with the Work Council a mechanism to automatically return to sender any e-mails which are received by company employees at inopportune hours; BMW, Daimler Benz, or Bosch, which have introduced criteria regulating 'networked mobile work',[46] or Atos, which established a Zero Email™ programme.[47]

To date, there have been some initiatives towards passing regulations on digital disconnection in Spain. In March of 2017, the coalition *Podemos-En Comú Podem En-Marea* presented a non-legislative motion on the right to disconnect after the conclusion of the work shift, calling for the elaboration of a plan to guide usage of ICT, the creation of tools to measure work-related stress levels on the part of the INE, and the elaboration of a study on the repercussions of ICT on workers' psychosocial health.[48] Related efforts, though of a different scope, were seen on 7 April of the same year, when the Socialist Parliamentary Group proposed a non-legislative motion that would protect the citizens' digital rights, constitutionalising these rights as well as their legislative treatment.[49] For its part, in January 2018, the Government announced that it would include digital disconnection in a future conciliation agreement. More recently, the Socialist Group once again underscored the importance of the right of workers to digitally disconnect during rest times, 'in function of the nature and the object of work', as well as the need for companies to develop means to avoid the risks of 'information fatigue', in the partial amendments the Organic Law on the Protection of Personal Data registered on 3 April 2018.

However, the only initiatives to have really taken root in Spain thus far have been in Catalonia, when in 2016, more than 100 municipalities in that region joined the initiative known as the *Network of Cities and Towns for Schedule Reform*, founded to promote reforms that would 'humanise' work schedules with the objective of

---

44 Martínez, 2011: 215.
45 Rota, 2016: 287–310.
46 *Vernetzte Mobilarbeit.*
47 Aguilera and Cristóbal, 2017: 336–337.
48 Official Bulletin of the General Courts (22 March 2017, pp. 52–54).
49 Official Bulletin of the General Courts (7 April 2017, pp. 4–7).

boosting productivity, improving health, and promoting the attainment of work/ life balance – in short, aspiring to the principles behind 'decent work' – and entailing such measures as prohibiting holding meetings later than 16:00 or sending e-mails after 18:00. It's also worth noting that the right to disconnect was included in Axa Group's Collective agreement for 2017–2020,[50] framing it within the company's reconciliation and flexibility policy, and formally recognising the right to ignore e-mails or work-related messages received outside of working time, 'except in cases of force majeure or exceptional circumstances'. Although this pioneering measure is constructive and valuable, it still treats digital disconnection as a voluntary option for workers, unaccompanied by a regulatory measure which could afford greater legal security; nor does it clarify the precise meaning of 'force majeure' or 'exceptional circumstances', legally undefined concepts whose interpretation may fall to the hands of the business owner, along with any associated risks.

Conclusions

The incorporation of ICT into the work sphere has engendered a corporate culture that favours high performance on a continuous basis, and counts on the uninterrupted availability of workers for indefinite periods of time outside traditional working hours, significantly blurring the lines between working time and the time for rest, and even creating a new kind of working time, known alternatively as 'third time', 'work contact time,' or 'technological connectivity time'.

In an analysis of the said periods of 'technological availability' made with the assumption that all company policies with respect to the organisation of working time must ultimately be motivated by the will to provide 'decent working time' (ILO), it becomes evident that the adverse effects of the poor regulation, insufficient control, or mismanagement of ICT can lead to major problems in terms of workers' psychosocial health, well-being, and attainment of work/life balance.

In this regard, and with respect to the regulation of the right to disconnect as enforced in France, we may conclude that within our judicial framework, technological disconnection need not be incorporated as a novel right, but may instead be simply upheld as a specific subset of the established 'right to rest', whose emergence is occasioned by the ubiquitous incorporation and proliferation of ICT into the work sphere. To that end, a modification of Articles 34 and 85.3 of the Workers' Statute in Spain is recommended, in order that the notion of technological disconnection is duly and sufficiently upheld and considered as part of collective bargaining, and so that the right and duty to disconnect is accompanied by global company policies implemented to assist workers and raise awareness of this issue throughout and across corporate hierarchies.

50 Resolution of 21 September 2017, of the Directorate General of Employment (DGE), by which the Collective Agreement of the Axa Group is registered and published (BOE of 10).

Outside of the specific proposals put forth in this paper, the future of the incorporation of the right to disconnect, as it is interpreted in Spain, will depend on the positions of the institutional actors and the awareness of social representatives; but no matter the nuances of these conditions, it must first overcome the barriers presented by a widespread corporate culture which interprets disconnection as an obstacle to company operation and not as an opportunity to restructure and refresh systems of production and foster new strategies that actually boost and support productivity.

Bibliography

Aguilera Izquierdo, R. & Cristóbal Roncero, R. (2017). 'Nuevas tecnologías y tiempo de trabajo: el derecho a la desconexión tecnológica'. *El futuro del trabajo que queremos. Conferencia Nacional tripartita.* Madrid, MESS, 331–341.

Alemán Páez, F. (2017a). 'El derecho de desconexión digital. Una aproximación conceptual, crítica y contextualizadora al hilo de la "Loi Travail N° 2016-1088"'. *Trabajo y Derecho*, no. 30, 12–33.

Alemán Páez, F. (2017b). 'Digitalización del trabajo, poder de control empresarial y derechos fundamentales de los trabajadores'. *Los actuales cambios sociales y laborales: nuevos retos para el mundo del trabajo. Cambios tecnológicos y nuevos retos para el mundo del trabajo (Portugal, España, Colombia, Italia y Francia)* [Serrani, L. coord.], Switzerland, Peter Lang, 385–431.

EU-OSHA (2014). *La estimación del coste del estrés y los riesgos psicosociales relacionados con el trabajo.* Luxemburgo, EU-OSHA.

Basterra Hernández, M. (2017). *Tiempo de trabajo y tiempo de descanso.* Valencia, Tirant lo Blanch.

Boulin, J.-Y., Lallement, M., & Michon, F. (2006). 'Decent working time in industrialized countries: Issues, scopes and paradoxes'. *Decent Working Time. New trends, new issues* (Boulin, J.-Y., Lallement, M., Messenger, J.C., & Michon, F. eds), Ginebra, OIT, 13–40.

Cardona Rubert, M.B. (2003). 'Las relaciones laborales y el uso de las tecnologías informáticas'. *Lan Harremanak: revista de relaciones laborales*, no. Extra 1.

Cladellas, R. (2008). 'La ausencia de gestión de tiempo como factor de riesgo psicosociales en el trabajo'. *Intangible Capital*, no. 4, 237–254.

Dans Álvarez de Sotomayor, L. (2017) 'Incidencia de las tecnologías digitales en la salud psicosocial de los trabajadores'. *Riesgos psicosociales y organización en la empresa* (Ramos Quintana, M.I., coord.), Navarra, Aranzadi, 63–95.

Eurofound and OIT (2017). *Working anytime, anywhere: The effects on the world of work. Geneva, Publications Office of the European Union,* Luxembourg, and the International Labour Office.

Fagan, C. (2004). 'Gender and working time in industrialized countries'. *Working time and workers' preferences in Industrialized countries: finding the Balance* (J.C. Messenger, ed.), London, New York, Routledge, 108–146.

Falguera Barò, M.A. (2016). 'Nuevas Tecnologías y trabajo (I): perspectiva contractual' *Trabajo y derecho: Nueva revista de actualidad y relaciones laborales*, no.19–20, 31–45.

Gonzáles Cobaleda, E. (2015). 'Riesgos psicosociales, derechos fundamentales y NTIC: una perspectiva de protección diferente', *RTSS.CEF*, no. 387, 17–42.

González Cobaleda, E. (2016). 'Nuevas tecnologías, tiempo de trabajo y la prevención de riesgos psicosociales'. *Anuario Internacional sobre la prevención de Riesgos Psicosociales y calidad de vida en el trabajo: Nuevas Tecnologías de la Información y de la Comunicación* y *Riesgos psicosociales en el trabajo*. Madrid: Secretaría de Salud Laboral y Medio Ambiente UGT-CEC, 261–286.

Martínez Fons, D. (2002). 'Uso y control de las tecnologías de la información y comunicación en la empresa'. *Relaciones laborales: Revista crítica de teoría y práctica*, no.2, 1311–1344.

Martínez Yañez, N.M. (2011). *El régimen jurídico de la disponibilidad horaria*. Navarra, Aranzadi.

Mella Méndez, L. (2016). 'Nuevas tecnologías y nuevos retos para la conciliación y la salud de los trabajadores'. *Trabajo y Derecho*, no. 16, 30–52.

Mercader Uguina, J. (2017). *El futuro del trabajo en la era de la digitalización y la robótica*, Tirant lo Blanch: Valencia.

Mercader Uguina, J.R. (2002). *Derecho del Trabajo, Nuevas Tecnologías y sociedad de la información*. Valladolid: Lex Nova.

Messenger, J. (2004). *Finding the balance: working time and workers' needs and preferences in industrialized countries*. A summary of the Report and its implications for Working Time Policies, Paper presented at the 9th International Symposium in Working time.

Metling, B. (2015). 'Informe Mettling, para adaptar el trabajo a la transformación digital'. *MESS, Revista de actualidad Internacional Sociolaboral*, no.194.

Molina Navarrete, C. (2015). '(In)culturas laborales y vida privada: El sentido del límite'. *RTSS.CEF*, no. 381, 5–10.

OIT (2016). 'El estrés en el trabajo: un reto colectivo'. Ginebra.

Pinilla García, F.J. (2016). 'Riesgos psicosociales de los usuarios intensivos de las TIC's. Análisis a partir de los datos de la VII Encuesta Nacional de Condiciones de Trabajo'. *Anuario Internacional sobre la prevención de Riesgos Psicosociales y calidad de vida en el trabajo: Nuevas Tecnologías de la Información y de la Comunicación y Riesgos psicosociales en el trabajo*. Madrid: Secretaría de Salud Laboral y Medio Ambiente UGT-CEC, 57–82.

Randstad Workmonitor (2015). 'Desconectar en vacaciones'. Madrid, 27 July.

Reich. R.B. (2007). 'El reto del trabajo decente'. *Trabajar por tiempos mejores: Repensar el trabajo en el siglo XXI* (Servais, J-M., Bollé, P., Lansky, M., & Smith, C.L., dirs.), Madrid, MTAS, 153–163.

Rodríguez González, S. (2017). 'Trabajo decente y riesgos psicosociales: la organización del tiempo de trabajo'. *Riesgos psicosociales y organización en la empresa* (Ramos Quintana, M.I., coord.) Navarra, Aranzadi, 97–144.

Rota, A. (2016) 'El debate europeo sobre el derecho a la desconexión en las relaciones de trabajo'. *Anuario Internacional sobre la prevención de Riesgos Psicosociales y calidad de vida en el trabajo: Nuevas Tecnologías de la Información y de la Comunicación y Riesgos psicosociales en el trabajo*. Madrid: Secretaría de Salud Laboral y Medio Ambiente UGT-CEC, 287–310.

Spurgeon, A. (2003). *Working time: Its impacts on safety and health*. Seúl: OIT and Korea Occupational Safety and Health Research Institute.

Triclin, A. (2016). 'La experiencia francesa del derecho a la desconexión'. *Anuario Internacional sobre la prevención de Riesgos Psicosociales y calidad de vida en el trabajo: Nuevas Tecnologías de la Información y de la Comunicación y Riesgos psicosociales en el trabajo*. Madrid: Secretaría de Salud Laboral y Medio Ambiente UGT-CEC, 311–340.

Vallecillo Gámez, M.R. (2017). 'El derecho a la desconexión: ¿"Novedad digital" o esnobismo del "viejo" derecho al descanso?'. *RTSS. CEF*, no. 408, 167–178.

11 The right to disconnect from the workplace: strengths and weaknesses of the French legal framework

Loïc Lerouge

Introduction

In modern times information and communications technologies (ICTs) have overwhelmed the workplace and contribute a great deal to the changing world of work. They increase productivity, but at the same time they cause work intensification. They also accelerate the balance between workplace and personal life. Speaking about a "right to disconnect" from the workplace means to allow employees and executives to be disconnected outside the workplace.

France is currently experimenting, since January 2017, the "right to disconnect" which has been inserted in that country's Labour Code. The aim is the ability to suggest a sort of regulation of digital tools. The objective is also to promote the respect of rest periods (consecutive 11 hours rest is required between two working days, 35 hours rest per week according to the article L. 3131-1 of the Labour Code) and the balance between professional life and personal life, undermined by the use of ICTs. The right to disconnect has to be combined with the employer's obligation to ensure health and safety at work and to implement a general obligation of prevention through collective bargaining.

The Mettling report[1] handed to the Minister of Labour Myriam El Khomri on September 15, 2015 underlined the importance of finding solutions regarding the real danger for health in the workplace constituted by the permanent connection and information overload. The other risk is to get employees "illiterate" in terms of use of digital tools, that is to say they are incapable of mastering the basic tools in the digital field. This could generate a form of exclusion that could have radical effects.

The right to disconnect raises issues of conflicts of obligations. For instance, in the same workplace, it is necessary to take into consideration and to accept the employer's managerial powers at the same time as the obligation to respect private life. This is the same with regard to the employer's obligation to ensure

---

1 Mettling B., "Transformation numérique et vie au travail", report sent to Minister of Labour Myriam El Khomri, September 2015, p. 69; available at: http://www.ladocumentationfran caise.fr/var/storage/rapports-publics/154000646.pdf.

the right to health and the individual freedom to manage personal time. The right to disconnect also raises issues around the obligation to execute the employment contract in good faith, the bullying legal framework, the actions proportionate to the desired objective.

Through the right to disconnect, the aim is to attain wellbeing at work and to accord with the definition of mental health by the World Health Organisation (WHO), which states: "Mental health is more than just the absence of mental disorders or disabilities. Mental health is a state of well-being in which an individual realises his or her own abilities, can cope with the normal stresses of life, can work productively and is able to make a contribution to his or her community."[2] This definition is certainly applicable to life in the workplace and shows how necessary it is today to have a workplace that provides a good health balance.

The goal is to respond to the question of the objective of legal recognition of the right to disconnect from the workplace. In other words, how to legally respond to the respect of the work-life balance? Can we regulate digital tools in the workplace? How do we tackle work overload and to deal with work intensification?

Having presented the French right to disconnect legal framework and how it is enforced, the issues to be considered in this chapter will focus on its strengths and weaknesses. Through the strengths, the aim will be to analyse which content the right to disconnect deals with according to the kind of employees to include in its field (i.e. employees, executive managers, teleworkers) or life quality in the workplace policies. Employers have to bear in mind that continually soliciting employees without even respecting the border with their personal life is likely to be recognised by the courts as bullying or psychological harassment. Nevertheless, the main advantage is to enable employees not to response to employer requests during rest periods without any risk of penalties.

But even if the idea and the philosophy sound good, in some way we can have doubts regarding the effectiveness and the efficiency of this new right, especially the weaknesses of exploring the limits of the right to disconnect. The working conditions and the labour situations are so different from one company to another or between business activities that it is impossible to implement the identical right to disconnect. The range of issues makes the implementation of this right very complicated.

Legal framework and content of the right to disconnect

Right to disconnect framework

The right to disconnect was introduced in the French Labour Code by Law n° 2016-1088 enacted on August, 8th 2016 entitled "El Khomri" which is the name of the Labour Minister at that time. The arrangements for the exercise of this right by the employees are defined through collective bargaining which

---

2 See WHO webpage: http://www.who.int/mediacentre/factsheets/fs220/en/.

must be implemented by the companies having at least 50 employees and a trade union representative at the time of the annual negotiation on the professional equality between women and men and the quality of life at work (Article L. 2242-8 of the Labour Code). However, the employer is not compelled to reach an agreement.

If companies do not have any union representative or if bargaining does not succeed, the law provides that the employer must still implement the right to disconnect. This will be under the form of a charter relating to employees and executives. The text will cover training and awareness-raising actions on the "reasonable use" of ICTs and will be submitted for the opinion of the company's social and economic committee. Failing this, in companies with fewer than 20 employees, the text will be submitted to the employees' representatives. The employer is still the master of the decision; he is not bound by the opinion of the employees' representatives. Moreover, the absence of a "charter" is not sanctioned whereas the obligation to negotiate is punishable with one year in prison and a fine of € 3,750 according to article L. 2242-8 of the Labour Code.

Right to disconnect content

The meaning of the text is, first of all, that an employee cannot be punished, or suffer the reproaches from his employer if he/she refused to answer an e-mail or a telephone call outside his/her working hours. Article L. 3121-64 of the Labour Code states that the procedures for ensuring the right to disconnect are determined by collective agreement. However, in the absence of a contractual provision, these procedures for exercising the employee's right to disconnect are defined by the employer and communicated by whatever means to the employees concerned (article L. 3121-65 of the French Labour Code). In addition, if under Article L. 3111-2 of the Labour Code senior executives are not subject to working time regulations, they nevertheless must respect the right to disconnect of their subordinates.

Employees must have a daily rest of at least 11 consecutive hours and 35 hours per week. During the employee's rest, but also during his/her leave (namely, sick leave, holidays, maternity, etc.), it will be up to the employer to ask him/her to avoid, as far as possible, sending e-mails or use his/her smartphone for business purposes. The extreme cases of continually soliciting employees without even respecting the border between his/her personal life are likely to be interpreted by judges as workplace harassment or psychological harassment.

The French jurisprudence is indeed very strict. On November 10th, 2009 the French Supreme Court recognised psychological harassment without malice.[3] That means the conduct of an employee can be characterised as psychological harassment without the will to hurt the employee concerned. The same day, the Supreme Court also considered that management methods implemented by

---

3 Cass. soc. 10 nov. 2009 n° 08-41.497.

a supervisor towards an employee in particular could constitute acts of moral harassment, thus highlighting the notion of "managerial harassment".[4] For instance, sending multiple emails every day for two years to the same employee in order to ask him/her to accelerate the pace of work is characterised as psychological harassment. If the intention of the supervisor was to put the pressure to his/her subordinate in order to get from him/her better productivity, the aim of its conduct was not to hurt him/her. The Supreme Court judgements have, however, subsequently evolved. It is now possible for the employer to exonerate himself from his responsibility by proving that all preventive measures have been taken to discourage bullying.[5]

Some companies have also thought of setting up an alert system to identify employees connected outside working hours or who do not respect the rest period of 11 hours daily. This is a response from some employers related to their health and safety obligation[6] which obliges them to implement the general principles of prevention under penalty of incurring their responsibility.[7] But these kinds of alert systems are not a true response to connection overload issues. The employer will not be exempt from liability either in case of occupational accident because of work overload. This is just a way for warning the employee how much he is connected.

In order to assist employers during the bargaining process, the national inter-professional agreement of June 19, 2013 on work-life quality suggests four principles to follow that could apply to the negotiation regarding the right to disconnect: First, to establish a preliminary diagnosis; second, to define company-specific indicators; third, to accompany the management and management teams; fourth, to promote intelligent management of information and communication technologies in the service of business competitiveness, respecting the privacy of employees.

Regarding teleworkers, the employer must provide provisions governing their right to disconnect. In addition, article L. 1222-10 of the Labour Code requires the employer to organise an interview each year concerning, in particular, employees' working conditions and their workload. In consultation with the teleworker employee, he must also fix the time slots during which he/she can usually contact him/her. During the course of a year, many things can change. The solution of organising an interview each year is clearly insufficient to guarantee the respect of the time connection of the teleworker. The question is also how to control the time connection of the teleworker. Technically speaking it is possible to control the time when he/she is connected, but some teleworkers could be clever

---

4 Cass. soc. 10 nov. 2009 n° 07-45.321.
5 Cass. soc. 1ᵉʳ juin 2016, n° 14-19.702: "l'employeur qui justifie avoir pris toutes les mesures de prévention prévues par les articles L. 4121-1 et L. 4121-2 du Code du travail et qui, informé de l'existence de faits susceptibles de constituer un harcèlement moral, a pris les mesures immédiates propres à le faire cesser".
6 Article L. 4121-1 of the Labour Code.
7 Article L. 4121-2 of the Labour Code.

enough to bypass those limitations. Some careful thought has to be given on how to take into account the realities of the work of teleworkers according to their digital connection/disconnection and the respect of their private life parameters.

It should be noted that the Mettling report suggested a duty to disconnect from the employee in order to consider co-responsibility of the employee and the employer. The idea was to take over the security obligation of the employee from the article L. 4122-1 of the Labour Code in the light of the disconnection. Indeed, it is the responsibility of each employee to take as much care as possible of their own safety and health and that of other persons affected by their acts or omissions at work in accordance with the training and the instructions given by their employer. Behind this approach lies the issue of educating the employee to disconnect. Because of his own working habits, he/she has not to oblige his/her colleagues to be connected because of his own connection.

Weaknesses and limits of the right to disconnect from the workplace

One of the first limits is the scope of application. Indeed, the "El Khomri" Act included a right to disconnect only in the Labour Code. That means the public service is not directly concerned and that creates an unbalance in terms of this right between the private sector and the public service. In order to implement the right to disconnect, the public service has to bargain and conclude an agreement. In other words, the public service has to take up this issue in the collective bargaining without any legal incentives.

A second limit is related to the competent bodies. The Health and Safety Committee (since September 2017, the HSC is included in the Social and Economic Committee which gathers all the representative bodies into one[8]) is not expressly associated with the implementation of the right to disconnect or even for the arrangements for the exercise. The disconnection concerns the employees' physical and mental health and is naturally part of the HSC's competences. That shows that the legislator did not give all possible bodies the power to implement the right to disconnect. It would appear that the legislator remained cautious. The reason seems not to give to these bodies too much control on employer's management methods. It is submitted that sometimes it is better to start small and to learn from experience and build up the scope of the right to disconnect concept.

Thirdly, what about small companies? In accordance with the obligation of the employer to ensure health and safety in the workplace, whatever the size of the company, the same level of occupational health protection has to be provided to the employees. But, legally speaking, companies with at least 11 employees do not have to have any employees' representatives who are in charge of bargaining. Thus, small companies do not have the resources for bargaining and consequently for guaranteeing a right to disconnect.

---

8 See the "Macron Ordinance", on the reform of French Labour Law, September 22, 2018.

We can also question the effectiveness of a charter which constitutes "soft law". How can the company be able to guarantee the implementation of the right to disconnect by concrete and binding measures where the negotiations have not proved to have been successful or the size of the company does not allow for such negotiation? It might have not proved to have been more consistent to amend directly the rules of procedure resulting from the unilateral power and management of the employer. It will be subject to the supervision of the labour inspectorate or the labour judge in the event of a dispute concerning its application.

With respect to the right to disconnect, the stake is to guarantee to the employee the right to no longer respond to the solicitations of his employer when he is no longer under his subordination.[9] However, the right to disconnect comes up against certain realities such as the employee who has scruples about disconnecting from work or of companies working internationally and/or having a continuous activity preventing the cutting of servers or finally the culture of certain jobs where a disconnection out of work time is culturally frowned upon. The employer will finally have little control over the personal freedom of employees whose will is to connect whatever happens. On the other hand, the benevolent employer would be able to adapt the objectives of the employee and to give him/her the means adapted to their achievements in order to allow this employee to be disconnected out of working time. The possibility of disconnecting is thus strongly correlated with the workload, assigning a strict character in this context otherwise the right to disconnect from the workplace would be meaningless.

So as to deal with the right to disconnect from the workplace, the employer can use the national inter-professional agreement of June 19, 2013 on the quality of life at work. This agreement provides four principles that could be followed in order to begin collective bargaining on the right to disconnect:

- establishing a preliminary diagnosis (risks assessment and identification);
- defining company-specific indicators;
- accompanying executive managers and management teams;
- promoting intelligent management of ICTs in business competitiveness and at the same time respecting the privacy of employees.

The issue of connection and disconnection is now well known. Its enforcement constitutes a matter of will from the employers, as well as from employees and executives.

Conclusion and challenges

The aim of this chapter is to treat the right to disconnect issues and to approach challenges that the right to disconnect has to face. One of the major issues is to tackle work overload and manage it in accordance with the right to disconnect.

---

9 See Ray J.-E., "Grande accélération et droit à la déconnexion", *Droit social*, 2016, p. 912.

Another challenge is to combine the right to disconnect and respect of the individual liberty to enjoy our private life as we wish. Finally, can we expect a sort of co-responsibility between employer and employees? Each stakeholder and actor in the company is responsible for his/her acts and their effect on the others in the workplace.

These challenges (combatting work overload and being responsible for our attitudes towards others) result in the issue of ethics in the workplace and in the implementation of the work organisations. Promoting ethics in the workplace means promoting humanisation of work, taking into account the human factor as well as technical and economic factors. We have lost sight of that work which provides dignity and good health. The use of ICTs contributes to this loss of meaning of work.

It should be borne in mind that health at work and management of occupational health should be a concern of all, not only experts and managers. This is true through the use of ICTs. Each player/operator (the manager or the worker), each at his or her level of empowerment, must have the opportunity to participate in the development of a work organisation promoting health, based on the values of cooperation and justice. The recognition of a right to disconnect is one of the responses for reaching this goal. This approach leads us to consider a new way of working life, work environment and how to build up individual and collective relationships. Everyone's responsibility is questioned within a collective work.

Hence, in this context, the role of the law is to focus on the proper way to tackle the right to disconnect. The law establishes a framework within which the relations to the rule will be expressed: what is to be promoted, what are the limits. These limits can be expressed in terms of responsibility or behaviour while guaranteeing the exercise of the freedom of each. The law can also be perceived as an instrument that is able to promote health at work. The issues related to the "right to disconnect", shows how the law can promote the empowerment of workers in order to allow them to take control of their own health and to improve it. In this instance, occupational health promotion has to be encouraged.

The aim is to address psychosocial dimensions of occupational health from an educational approach in order to equip future players in the business world with the necessary awareness of occupational health issues. Occupational health education could be a lever for improving what can be practised today, in the logic of being able to act individually and collectively, for instance in terms of connection or disconnection. But we do not have to be naïve. To be enforced, it is necessary to show to the employer that his power of management will not be weakened. This is contrary to the right to disconnect which allows the employer to get employees in better shape. Productivity is not always linked to being present at work; productivity is also a question of working conditions that respect employees' physical and mental health.

According to the analysis of the agreements concluded on the quality of life at work in France, the right to disconnect is more focused on a technical and organisational approach rather than on an approach based on health at work.[10] Recognising legally a right to disconnect from the workplace is related not only to the employer's management power, but also to questions of health and psychological harassment generated by some manner of managing employees. The link has been recognised in France by the Court of Cassation.[11] But up to now, the judges did not make the link between the obligation of the employee to be most of the time connected with his work for fear of reprisal and because his/her employer permanently enjoins him/her to work harder including a situation of psychological harassment. At least, this is an opportunity to debate in labour law on work overload and the protection of the employees' physical and mental health.

10 Analysis of 155 agreements on quality of life at work in France from the MaRiSa research Project funded by the French National Agency for Research, available at: http://www.agence-nationale-recherche.fr/projet-anr/?tx_lwmsuivibilan_pi2[CODE]=ANR-17-CE26-0018.
11 See Cass. soc. 10 November 2009 n° 07-45.321.

Part III

The impact of new technologies on the labour process

12 The digital evidence in the labour process and the fundamental rights of the employee[1]

Lourdes Mella Méndez

Introduction

One of the new information and communication technologies which has become an essential work tool is the personal computer and its different applications, such as electronic mail or instant messaging, which enjoy wide-ranging labour and personal use in a company. One of the most interesting aspects of email, as well as other computer applications, such as instant messaging (WhatsApp type messages) or social networks, blogs and others, is that they serve to transmit and store information (written text, images, sounds) that can be provided to the prosecution as evidence of a particular claim against one of the parties. Thus, Art. 90.1 Law 36/2011, of 10 October 2011, regulating the social jurisdiction (LSJ), admits that the parties can use as many means of evidence as are regulated in the law to accredit the facts at issue, 'including the procedures of reproduction of the word, image and sound or archiving and reproduction of data, which must be provided by means of adequate support and making available to the court the means necessary for its reproduction and subsequent record in the case file'. In more detail, Arts. 299.2 and 384 Law 1/2000, of 7 January 2000, regulating Civil Procedure (LCP), also refer to the instruments which permit the access to, and archiving or reproduction of, the relevant data for the process (for example, recording instruments, filming and similar items). The use of these instruments results in a separate form of evidence, apart from documentary evidence, *digital evidence,* also known as the evidence 'of support' or 'instruments'.[2] However, this does not prevent the interested party from also transcribing the content of these instruments in the most appropriate and relevant form (e.g., documents), as well as verifying the veracity of that content (expert report).

1 This chapter is one of many results of the National Research Project carried out by MINECO (Spain), entitled 'New (newest) information and communication technologies and their impact on the labour market: emerging aspects at the national and international level' (DER2016-75376-R), led by Prof. Lourdes Mella.
2 The LCP treats documentary evidence (Articles 317 to 334) and digital evidence separately (Articles 382 to 384). However, in the criminal sphere, these means are both considered to be documentary evidence (Article 26 Penal Code).

An important difference between instrument evidence and documentary evidence is that, for the purpose of the review of proven facts, only documentary and expert evidence heard in the court are valid [Art. 193.b) LSJ]. The suitability of digital evidence for that purpose relates to the extraordinary nature of the appeal for reversal (*recurso de suplicación*), which requires a necessarily restrictive interpretation of the concept of documentary evidence.

On its probative value: authenticity and integrity

When digital evidence is submitted in the proceedings, the parties against whom the evidence is submitted may try to defend themselves by challenging its authenticity or integrity or alleging violation of their fundamental rights when obtaining that evidence.

Regarding the first aspect, it should be clarified that, once admitted as a valid means of proof, digital evidence does not have a superior probative value to that of other kinds of evidence, that is, its content should not necessarily be considered as true (especially when it can be easily manipulated) but it follows the general regime of assessment of the evidence. The accreditation of the authenticity (veracity) and integrity (accuracy) of this type of evidence appears, then, as a fundamental aspect of it. At first, the veracity and accuracy of the emails will depend on several circumstances, such as their nature, public or private, or the fact that they are digitally signed; something that, in the first case, must always be carried out by an official with the power to attest,[3] but that, in the second case, may either exist or not. In fact, in the workplace, in the majority of lawsuits in which the emails of one of the parties, usually of the employee, are provided as proof of their guilty conduct, lack a signature.[4] The contribution of these emails to the judicial process is made by delivering the original, or a copy authenticated by the competent public official, as a document printed on paper or an electronic document (contained on a data storage device, for example, USB or CD). After being submitted as evidence or providing testimony, the documents (original or authenticated copy) can be returned to the interested parties on their request.[5]

The party or parties harmed by the use of emails as evidence (for example, the employee(s)), especially if they lack a digital signature, can debate their authorship and the veracity of their content. To do this, that party or parties

---

3 Art. 3.6 Law 59/2003, of 19 December, of electronic signature.
4 With a critical position regarding the acceptance of these emails, see Falguera Baró, M.A.: 'Nuevas tecnologías y trabajo (III): perspectiva procesal', *Trabajo y Derecho*, 2016, n° 22 (Law 7161/2016), p. 11. The author cites the Judgment of the High Court (JHC) (Second Chamber) of 19 May 2015 (appeal n° 2387/2014), which only supports virtual transcription of messages if accompanied by further evidence (public document, expert, testimonial, judicial recognition, interrogation of part or instrument of reproduction of the word, sound or image).
5 Art. 268.1 LCP.

must provide sufficient and objective evidence, and must justify the challenge on well-founded grounds, as mere protest is not, logically, enough.[6] From that point, the party who initially submitted the e-mails as evidence (generally, the applicant) will be the one who will have to justify, with new evidence, that the emails are genuine and eliminate any doubt of fraud or alteration of their authorship or content. An effective way to eliminate possible doubts is through the submission, for their direct examination, of the original electronic devices or supporting devices (fixed or mobile) through which the act of communication or information was carried out in each situation. More specifically, in the case of an e-mail sent, a copy should be provided (made before a notary public) of the hard disc of the computer device from which it was sent, and in which a copy of the sent email is usually kept; and in the case of the received emails, the copy should be from the hard disc of the server in which the email was received before its delivery to its final recipient, in order to find the original email and compare it with the one provided in the process by its recipient. If the original email was not kept on the server (which is usually the case), it may be possible to retrieve some useful information such as the sender and recipient and the dates of receipt and delivery.

To be particularly noted is the fact that, after the submission of the hard disc copy of the computer device as evidence, it would advisable and even necessary to involve a computer expert to examine both copies and determine whether or not there has been manipulation of the evidence provided by the party to the labour process (expert evidence), with the consequent ratification in the trial.[7] Finally, the court will have to resolve the case in accordance with the new evidence, proceedings carried out and the rules of sound criticism.[8]

Unlawfulness of the evidence obtained with violation of fundamental rights

General issues

Even if the email is authentic and truthful, the party harmed by its contribution to the process may still try to challenge it, alleging a violation of their fundamental rights during the procedure for preparing such evidence. Thus, it is clear that a traditionally important issue is the *illegality* of the evidence obtained (whatever it may be) involving a violation of the fundamental rights of the employee and its

---

6 Judgment of High Court of Madrid of 18 April 2016 (appeal n° 156/2016). In the doctrine, Barrios Baudor, G.: 'La integridad y/o autenticidad de los medios de prueba digital en el proceso laboral: una aproximación al tema a propósito de los correos electrónicos', *RTSS, CEF,* 2017, n° 415, p. 36.
7 Delgado Martin, J.: *Investigación tecnológica y prueba digital en todas las jurisdicciones* (Madrid, 2016), p. 170.
8 Art. 384.3 LCP.

subsequent consequences (Article 11.1 Judicial Power Organic Law (JPOL)[9]).[10] In this sense, the current Art. 90.2 LSJ, establishes that 'no evidence will be admitted which has its origin or has been obtained, directly or indirectly, by means of procedures which violate fundamental rights or civil liberties'. Such evidence is null and void, thus it lacks evidentiary value and cannot be submitted, or, if it had already been submitted, it cannot be considered valid. In addition, such evidence cannot be corrected or validated later in any way. This qualification (nullity), on the one hand, seeks to sanction violations of fundamental rights and preventing the author from procedurally taking advantage of the evidence that is obtained illegally. On the other hand, it is necessary to avoid the commission of future behaviours that violate such rights. Only knowing in advance that those behaviours will not produce any effect, attempts to violate fundamental rights of the other party (in order to obtain evidence against him) can thus be discouraged.[11] Undoubtedly, this is very important in the labour relationship between the parties, which is unequal and hierarchical in nature, because this prohibition of illegal evidence acts as a compensating element 'for inequality and prevention of abuses' by the employer in respect to the employee.[12]

Thus, when first proposing the evidence, the court of first instance must assess this aspect (even superficially), rule on the legality or illegality of the evidence, and decide on its admissibility. If the illegality of the evidence is clear at that stage, the court must reject it, without prejudice to the timely protest of the interested party, for the purposes of the subsequent filing of the corresponding appeal against the decision. The failure to protest by the interested party at this stage prevents any subsequent allegation of wrongfulness for that reason in the course of appeal. If there are doubts as to the legality of the evidence, the reasonable thing to do is to provisionally admit the evidence, in order to guarantee the fundamental right to it, provided in Art. 24 Constitution (regardless of the timely protest, here too, against admission). If proved later that there has been a violation of the fundamental rights of the counterpart, the initial judicial decision of admission of the evidence will be annulled by the court itself before ending the process, either *ex officio* or at the request of a party;[13] in both cases, such a declaration of nullity requires the prior hearing of both parties.[14] Logically, in the case of annulment, the judge will not

9 'In all kinds of procedures, the rules of good faith should be respected. The evidence obtained will not be effective if it violates fundamental rights or freedoms'.
10 One of the first judgements to analyse the validity of the evidence that violates fundamental rights was the Judgment of the Constitutional Court (JCC) 114/1984, of 29 November, relating to a labour process in which a conversation had been recorded without the consent of the other interlocutor.
11 Del Rey Guanter, S.: 'Nuevas técnicas probatorias, obtención de prueba ilícita y derechos fundamentales en el proceso laboral', *Revista Española de Derecho del Trabajo*, 1989, n° 37, pp. 65 *et seq.* and Lousada Arochena, F.: 'La prueba ilícita en el proceso laboral', *Revista Doctrinal Aranzadi Social,* 2006, n° 11 (BIB 2006/1250), p. 3.
12 Lousada Arochena, F., *op. et loc. cit.*
13 Art. 240.2 JPOL.
14 Art. 90.2 LSJ.

take into account the evidence when making a ruling. Otherwise, if the judicial body would take the unlawful evidence into account, it would always be appropriate to challenge that evidence again in the corresponding appeal against the judgment.[15]

On the other hand, Art. 90.4 LSJ introduced the possibility of accessing, as part of a process and with prior judicial authorisation, documents or files (in any device), despite the fact that such access would affect 'personal privacy or another fundamental right'.[16] In these cases, the authorisation of the judge or court of such action, by means of an order, is subject to the following conditions: namely, 1) that there is no alternative means of evidence; 2) that it is necessary for the purposes of the process; and 3) a previous weighing up of the affected interests has been carried out applying proportionality principles and with the minimum sacrifice, determining the access conditions, guarantees of conservation and contribution to the process, obtaining and receiving delivery of copies and involving the parties or their representatives and experts, if applicable. This judicial authorisation is a guarantee prior to the trial itself, with the purpose of protecting the affected employee, as he/she has the right to know that the employer will provide the court with key and unique evidence which may disturb his or her privacy and adopt, then, the measures that it deems necessary. However, this possibility seems to be limited through practical application, on the one hand, by the subjection of this judicial action to the aforementioned cumulative requirements, which may result in a slow process which does not prevent the illicit destruction, concealment or modification of evidence; and, on the other hand, by the proliferation of so-called computer codes of conduct. More clearly, the code of this nature regulates the use that employees can make of company's computer tools, delimiting their private or purely professional use. In this case, especially when only professional use is allowed, the employee does not enjoy a reasonable expectation of privacy that could be violated. Therefore, this expectation and the application of the aforementioned procedural precept seems to be reserved to cases in which the company does not have a code of conduct which provides clear and precise guidelines for the use of computer tools.[17]

Finally, another complex aspect is the objective dimension or scope of the nullity of the unlawful evidence, especially when it is connected to another derived or

---

15 Arts. 193.a) and 207.c) LSJ (appeals for appeal and cassation, respectively). If these appeals are brought for this reason, the court *ad quem* may agree on the nullity of proceedings from the moment of denial or, where appropriate, admission of the evidence.

16 Art. 76.4 LSJ, which refers to that other provision, contemplates a partially different case of judicial authorisation, related to obtaining the evidence (preparatory acts and preliminary proceedings by the party claiming to sue). But it does not derive the need for the employer to request such judicial authorisation when it intends to monitor the computer or install video surveillance cameras.

17 In a similar sense, Gil Plana, J.: 'El uso particular por los trabajadores de las nuevas tecnologías empresariales en los códigos de conducta', *Revista Española de Derecho del Trabajo*, 2012, n° 155 (BIB 2012/2800), p. 49.

reflected piece of evidence. In such a case, it is understood that, if there is a natural connection between the two pieces of evidence, the general rule is that the declaration of nullity extends to both (in the criminal field, this position is called the doctrine of the fruit of the poisoned tree). However, if that natural connection is missing, or, even existing, and there is no specific connection of illegality between them, the evidence may be admitted. In making this judicial decision, which may end up limiting the effects of nullity, the court must assess, with some discretion, all the concurrent circumstances (for example, the type of fundamental right and all the details of its violation).[18]

Effects of the unlawfulness of the evidence on the qualification of the dismissal

Traditional positions of extreme character

Another issue of interest directly related to the nullity of the unlawful evidence, and much discussed in doctrine and jurisprudence, is the qualification of the consequences of the employer's decision taken from the information obtained from the evidence. Certainly, the cases in which the employer violates the fundamental rights of the employee – in line with the registration of the computer equipment used by him – are linked to disciplinary decision-making processes. In other words, the employer imposes a disciplinary sanction based on the information obtained with the illegal registration of the computer instrument or email. In such a case, the illegality of the evidence also entails the unlawfulness of the sanction affected, although it is disputed whether that illegality should be qualified as a nullity ('*nulidad*') or unfairness ('*improcedencia*').

A first doctrinal and jurisprudential position – which seems to be the majority position – holds that the nullity of the evidence for the violation of fundamental rights also implies the nullity of the disciplinary sanction based on it.[19] This position 'of irradiation' (as soon as the nullity of the evidence radiates its effects onto the disciplinary dismissal on which it is founded) considers applicable to the social process the doctrine of the fruit of the poisoned tree or, in the words of a ruling, 'the theory of the fruit of the rotten tree'.[20] Thus, the courts that share this position understand that when evidence is obtained in violation of these fundamental rights, not only is it absolutely ineffective, but that nullity also extends

---

18 JCC 471/2015, of 2 June, which analyses, in the criminal sphere, the connection of illegality in cases of breach of the secrecy of communications.

19 Colás Neila, E.: 'Nuevas tecnologías, obtención de pruebas y derechos fundamentales. Sentencia comentada: STSJ Madrid de 31 enero 2002', *Aranzadi Social*, 2002, n° 5, p. 6: 'while the evidence is instrumented to the achievement of a specific purpose, which is the accreditation of a just cause to dismiss', the violation of fundamental rights in obtaining it, which implies its illegality, 'must vitiate nullity, also, the legal institute to which it is linked'.

20 Judgement of High Court of Galicia of 2 March 2008 (appeal n° 6219/2007).

to all acts and decisions that are adopted based upon it.[21] For this position, the nullity of the disciplinary dismissal derived from the unlawful evidence is based on a double foundation: legal and jurisprudential. Indeed, on the one hand, this is found in Arts. 55.5 WS and 108.2 LSJ, according to which it is necessary to declare null and void a disciplinary dismissal based on 'an alleged imputation on evidence against fundamental rights and public freedoms'. In addition, 'the qualification of the dismissal as null or unfair' is not an issue that can be left to 'the discretion of the parties' because, being necessary, we must respect the conclusion legally established in the aforementioned statutory provision.[22] In the words of a ruling, it is specified that, according to 'grammatical, finalists and respect-to-the-Constitution criteria', 'in the aforementioned provisions' are included 'not only the cases where the cessation occurs as a result of the legitimate exercise of a fundamental right by the employee, but also those others in which the facts that support it have been known by the employer through methods which violate the fundamental rights of the affected person'.[23]

On the other hand, a constitutional basis is also alleged, which is implicitly understood to be established in the Judgment of the Constitutional Court (CC) 196/2004, of 15 November. In this Judgment, the violation of the worker's right to privacy was declared after a medical examination in which the consumption of narcotics was verified and, consequently, the contract produced during the trial period was terminated. For the CC, the violation of the aforementioned fundamental right through such medical evidence entails its nullity and, in addition, 'the absolute elimination' of all its effects, that is, the nullity of the subsequent dismissal.[24] Similarly, more recently, JCC 29/2013, of 11 February, held that 'sanctions imposed' based on a single piece of evidence that is detrimental to a fundamental right must be declared 'null'. In the face of such non-compliance, the TC annulled the judicial decisions and the employer decision that had imposed 'the sanctions of suspension of employment and salary' on the appellant employee.

This position considers that the ruling of the Judgment of the High Court (*Tribunal Supremo*) of 26 September 2007[25] sustaining the inadmissibility of the

---

21 JHC of Galicia of 30 November 2001 (appeal n° 5319/2001). According to the JHC of Basque Country of 12 September 2006 (appeal n° 1270/2006), when the computer records do not pass the necessity judgment, it must be considered that this evidence is null and void for violating Art. 18 Constitution and Art. 90.1 Law of labour procedure, the effect provided in Art. 11.1 JPOL: 'indicated nullity'. Also, more recently, the High Court of Madrid (two) judgments of 18 December 2014 (appeal n° 761/2014) (nullity of the dismissal is declared based on the 'illegitimate use of means of control of the activity of the employee', contravening of the fundamental right to control the personal data of them) and 13 May 2016, cited (if the information in the emails 'was obtained unlawfully, it would radically deprive any probative validity' of these). Likewise, Judgment of the Social Court (*Juzgado de lo Social*), n° 19 Madrid of 17 November 2017 (n° 453/2017).

22 Judgment of High Court of Galicia of 3 March 2008 already cited.

23 JHC of Basque Country of 10 May 2011 (appeal n° 644/2011).

24 JHC of Galicia of 3 March 2008, already cited.

25 Appeal n° 966/2006.

sanction is incorrect, since, in reality, such a pronouncement 'does not establish this criterion', limiting itself, in this point, to dismissing the appeal lodged by the company and in this way confirming the inadmissibility of the dismissal declared in the court of first instance and subsequently ratified by the Chamber. What this ruling really analyses are 'the guarantees applicable to the employer's control of the various computer tools made available to its employees'. It is asserted, then, that such a sentence does not deal with 'the qualification of the dismissal in case of the illicit obtaining of evidence with the violation of fundamental rights to accredit the facts contained in the extinctive communication'.[26]

This maximally protective position, which holds that the illegality of the evidence for the violation of fundamental rights also leads to the nullity of the dismissal, can have other consequences. More clearly, from the moment in which it is accepted that this sanction is null, this nullity can also derive *a compensatory liability for the employer*, in accordance with the provisions of procedural law. In effect, when declaring the existence of a violation of a fundamental right of the employee (here, generally, the privacy and secrecy of communications in obtaining evidence), it should be noted that Art. 183.1 LSJ establishes that 'the judge must rule on the amount of *compensation* that, if applicable, corresponds to the plaintiff' for having suffered the violation of 'his fundamental rights and public liberties, depending on the moral damage attached to the violation of the fundamental right, as well as of the additional damages and losses derived'. The purpose of this compensation is twofold, on the one hand, to compensate for the damage caused, both material and moral, and, on the other, to prevent the recurrence of a similar violation.

In the case of a disciplinary dismissal being held to be null and void, the material damage is made up of the loss of profit that results from the loss of the job and its consequences, something that is already remedied with the judicial order to reinstate the dismissed employee and to pay the salaries owed. Therefore, this specific compensation should be focused on the *moral damage* that is not completely satisfied with that sentence. This emerging damage is very difficult to assess from an economic point of view as it depends on very different factors, some purely subjective, such as 'strength of mind', of 'complicated accreditation'. For these cases where proof of the exact extent of moral damage result too difficult or expensive to deliver, paragraph 2 of Art. 183 LSJ provides that the court will decide on the amount of the damage, determining it 'prudentially', in order to comply with the two purposes of the compensation. A criterion that can serve as a reference for this prudential determination is the amount of the corresponding administrative sanction established for the infraction of the fundamental right violated by the employer in the Law of Infractions and Sanctions of the Social Order (LISSO).[27] Indeed, in one specific case, the amount of 6,251 EUR was

26 JHC of Madrid of 13 May 2016, cited.
27 Consolidated text approved by Royal Legislative Decree 5/2000, of 4 August. Cf. Judgement of High Court of 5 February 2013, cited by the Judgment of the Social Court (*Juzgado de lo Social*) n° 19 of Madrid of 17 November 2017, cited.

agreed, which corresponds to the very serious infringement – in its minimum amount – provided for in Art. 40.1.c) of the aforementioned LISSO.[28]

In short, this compensation for damages will be compatible, where appropriate, with that which might correspond to the employee due to the termination of the employment contract or in other cases established in the Workers' Statute and other labour regulations (Article 183.3 LSJ).

Faced with this position, another one emerges – more favourable to the interests of the employer – which argues that, in this type of unlawful evidence situation, what is appropriate is the qualification of *unfair* dismissal. The main arguments of those holding this position are the following. First, nullity is a category of inefficiency that must be interpreted *restrictively*, so the nullity of the evidence obtained with a violation of fundamental rights is one thing (nullity based on adjective or procedural rules: Article 90 LSJ), and the nullity (additional and cascading) of the disciplinary decisions based on that is another. This spreading of the nullity of the evidence to the final employer decision is not accepted, insofar as the aforementioned doctrine of the fruit of the poisoned tree it is not applicable, which is characteristic of the criminal process.[29] Thus it is specified that the meaning of this doctrine is to deny effectiveness, apart from the illicit evidence obtained directly in violation of a fundamental right, to other evidence that, even if obtained lawfully, has a link with the former because it has been obtained thanks to the knowledge provided by the evidence. In any case, it is a contagion of the nullity between evidences, from one to another, which does not happen in the labour process. In fact, it is criticised that the application of this doctrine to the labour sphere would mean an extension of its natural application, because, if the criminal law reaches the derived or reflected evidence, in the social field it would extend to the employer consequences based on the evidence, which is not exactly the same thing.[30]

Secondly, in the labour realm, and continuing with this restrictive approach, the *nullity* of dismissal is always based on rules of *material law* (Article 55 WS), and it is the act of dismissal itself that violates the employee's fundamental rights or implies discrimination against them. There is, therefore, a direct cause or relationship between the grounds for dismissal and the violation of the fundamental right, which is why it is declared null and void. In the words of a ruling, 'for the

---

28 Cf. Judgment of the Social Court *(Juzgado de lo Social)* nº 19 of Madrid of 17 November 2017, cited.
   JHC of Madrid of 5 November 2008 (appeal nº 4747/2008). This doctrine was reiterated by the same Court in the judgments of 17 July 2009 and 30 May 2011.
29 In this sense, JHC of Andalusia (Seville) of 9 March 2001 (appeal nº 4256/2001), for which the application of such doctrine in the social process is inadequate.
30 Gil Plana, J., *op. cit.,* p. 54. Also BAVIERA PUIG, I.: 'Sobre la calificación del despido basado en pruebas ilícitas', *Aranzadi Social,* 2008, nº 12 (BIB 2008/2159): in Criminal Law, the presumption of innocence of a constitutional nature governs, which requires a minimum of evidence to condemn, but in the labour sphere only a presumption of innocence of ordinary legality governs, so that the dismissal without cause must be declared unfair, not null.

dismissal to be null and void, it must occur for a cause outside the contract, directly threatening' a fundamental right of the employee and must be the 'true motive of the dismissal of the employer'.[31] More abundantly, it is the act of dismissal itself that violates the fundamental rights of the affected subject, for example, by relying on the legitimate exercise of their freedom of expression or being discriminatory of it, as happens when it is based on their race or gender.[32]

Third, in the case analysed, the unlawfulness of the evidence and the consequent unlawfulness of the dismissal have *different causes:* in the first situation, the ground is related to the violation of fundamental rights (hence, its nullity), and in the second case of dismissal the cause is the lack of evidence. More clearly, dismissal is always based on a specific contractual breach of the employee, which, if not proved, determines its illegality, materialised in the unfairness.[33] Thus, if the evidence is declared null, what happens is that the employer is left without this means of proof to prove the aforementioned breach, so it is most appropriate to qualify such disciplinary dismissal as inappropriate or unfair. In the words of some authors, the violation of fundamental rights in obtaining the evidence implies 'its inefficiency, and a without-cause dismissal (when the cause disappears) is not, in itself, discriminatory'.[34] Or, in other words, the declaration of unlawfulness of a source of evidence 'does not imply, at first, the qualification of nullity of a dismissal', a different issue is that such declaration of illegality may affect the latter, in the sense of making depend on it 'its fairness or unfairness'.[35] The violation of the fundamental right occurs in the field of obtaining evidence, and not in the area of motivation of dismissal, therefore, there is no direct or sufficient connection between both acts.

Fourth, the doctrine – even referring to criminal proceedings – of the Constitutional Court 'that the known facts do not cease to exist as a consequence of the fact that the method of discovering them is illegal' is also invoked here in favour of this position; a different issue is that 'these facts cannot be taken by judicially accredited to found a conviction, but by evidence of charge obtained with all the guarantees'.[36] In the labour field, in a correlative way, there is the opinion

---

31 JHC of Madrid of 5 November 2008 (appeal n° 4747/2008). This doctrine is reiterated by the same Court in the judgments of 17 July 2009 and 30 May 2011.

32 JHC of Galicia of 6 November 2008 (appeal n° 4148/2008). Also JHC of Catalonia of 5 September 2000 (appeal n° 2890/2000): 'the qualification of the dismissal must be linked to the mobile that determines it or to the violation of the rights and freedoms referred to in art. 55.5 WS, and not the illegality of any of the evidences incorporated into the process'.

33 JHC of Andalusia (Seville) of 9 March 2001, cited. Also JHC of Castile-La Mancha of 17 June 2014 (appeal request 1162/201): 'illegitimately obtained the evidence, its effectiveness lapses due to the pre-eminence of the protected constitutional interest' and it must be considered 'as not accredited the imputation made and as a consequence, in accordance with art. 55.4 WS', the dismissal 'must be declared unfair'.

34 Sempere Navarro, A.V. and San Martín Mazzucconi, C.: *Nuevas tecnologías y relaciones laborales* (Pamplona, 2002), p. 57.

35 Gil Plana, J., *op. cit.,* p. 51.

36 JCC 161/1999, of 27 September.

that the infringement or violation of fundamental rights does not change or cease to exist due to the fact that illegal evidence is used as proof, but this evidence cannot be admitted and it determines the fairness or unfairness of that dismissal, according to whether or not other legal and valid evidence of charge concurs.[37]

Fifth, the ruling of the Spanish High Court of 26 September 2007, already cited, is regarded as being in favour of this position, as it is understood that it ruled that the unlawfulness of the evidence that sustain the accusations made against the employee in the written communication of dismissal determine the unfairness, and not the nullity, of the latter.[38]

Finally, in the sixth instance, it is suggested that the thesis of the irradiation of the nullity of the illegal evidence to the qualification of the dismissal – as it is something very relevant and serious – could encourage fraudulent behaviour by the employer. Indeed, it is asserted that, before risking trying to prove the cause of dismissal (by obtaining evidence that may end up making that decision null and void), the employer may decide to dismiss the employee without providing any evidence or even without citing a cause, as in either case the employer would be in a better situation than when he risks producing illegal evidence, because the court would limit itself to declaring the dismissal inappropriate and unfair.[39]

Intermediate position

Facing these two extreme positions, which opt for the nullity or unfairness of the disciplinary sanction as a common solution for all cases of illegal evidence, there is no shortage of arguments to defend a *third mixed position*, which, in this author's opinion, is the fairest and most adequate. This position is more detailed and takes into account, on the one hand, the direct, causal and temporal relationship that exists between the violation of the fundamental right of the employee and the cause of his dismissal; and, on the other hand, the number of existing pieces of evidence to prove the contractual breach justifying the latter. Regarding the causal and temporal relationship of the two aforementioned aspects (violation of fundamental right and cause dismissal), it is reasoned that, in the situation in which the employer conduct which amounts to a violation of the employee's fundamental rights first occurs (for example, hidden surveillance with cameras in prohibited areas of the workplace, such as changing rooms) and, afterwards, as a consequence of that surveillance, a breach of contract is discovered (for example, theft), it is logical that the unlawfulness of that employer conduct (surveillance) and, consequently, the nullity of the technological evidence, also implies the nullity of the subsequent dismissal. The latter would not exist if the conduct that violates the fundamental right of the employee had not previously

---

37 Gil Plana, J., *op. cit.*, p. 52.
38 See, with respect to this claim, the thirty-fourth right basis of the Judgement of High Court of Madrid of 14 May 2016 (appeal n° 282/2016).
39 Gil Plana, J., *op. cit.*, p. 55.

been carried out, that is, the dismissal brings cause or proceeds from this unlawful conduct. The employer acquires knowledge of the contractual breach of the employee as a result of his own irregular conduct, so that this affects his subsequent termination decision.

However, the situation is very different when the employer, first, has some knowledge or a well-founded suspicion of an employee's breach of contract and, in order to prove it, decides to perform a surveillance to obtain objective evidence to contribute to the process. In this case, if that surveillance violates fundamental rights, it will be qualified as null and will not have any effect on its own, but the extension of the nullity to the termination decision of the employer may be excessive, which, finally, cannot be proved. Certainly, it is not exactly the same substantive situation of Art. 55.5 WS, as there is no dismissal decision that is based on a violation of fundamental rights, there is only one procedure to obtain the evidence that is illegal and, therefore, it cannot be taken into account. In the words of a specially qualified author (in so far as he is also a magistrate of the social jurisdiction), when the behaviour that violates fundamental rights is not the cause of the contractual termination, but merely a means of proving labour breach, and this one 'could have been accredited in other ways', the verdict on that termination must be 'unfairness and not nullity'.[40] In a similar sense, another prestigious magistrate said that the nullity of the disciplinary dismissal 'is not an inexorably linked consequence to the illegality of the evidence, but only when, putting the unlawful proof in parentheses, an absolute absence of factual data' is observed, and that situation reasonably allows concluding that, 'if the illicit evidence had not existed, the employer would not have fired' the employee.[41]

These arguments point to an important element since in the judgements that declare the illegality of the evidence and, consequently, also the unlawfulness of the dismissal, the phenomenon of *single evidence* is detected. More clearly, the evidence that proves the breach of contract is the only one contributed to the process, so its illegality directly leads to the illegality of the decision to dismiss, too. The contagion of the illicitness is especially clear in the case of nullity or, at least, it stands out more in the judgments that follow the doctrine of the fruit of the poisoned tree.[42] Thus, for example, it is stated that 'in view of what is reasoned in the legal basis of the judgment' the unlawful recording was the only evidence on which the trial judge relied to declare the facts proved (which were imputed to the employee to justify the dismissal). Therefore, 'the dismissal must be considered null' because in obtaining evidence of the only fact that is charged in the written communication of the dismissal, the right to privacy of Art. 18.4 Constitution was violated.[43] Or, similarly, it is also indicated when the decision to terminate the employment contract of the plaintiff for disciplinary

---

40 Falguera Baró, M.A, *op. cit.,* p. 8.
41 Lousada Arochena, F., *op. cit.,* p. 7.
42 JCC 29/2013, cit. Also JHC of Basque Country of 10 May 2011, cit.
43 JHC of Extremadura of 30 July 2014 (appeal n° 284/2014).

reasons was based exclusively on the conclusions that the company (after the report of a firm dedicated to the management of electronic evidence) extracted from the private email account of the employee and those conclusions were obtained illegally, a violation of constitutional rights occurs. In this case, we are not only in a situation of absolute ineffectiveness of such evidence, which is null but of nullity of all acts and measures that bring cause of it, so that the dismissal has to be qualified as null, too.[44]

Thus, it seems advisable that, apart from the instruments evidence, the employer should always provide other additional evidence (e.g., questioning or testifying), then if one is declared unlawful, the contractual breach could still be proved with the remaining evidence without immediately becoming 'infected' with that illegality.[45] In any case, it is important that these other pieces of evidence have no direct or indirect connection with the violation of fundamental rights. In this regard, it should be remembered that Art. 11.1 JPOL rejects the validity of the evidence that, even indirectly, is causally connected to direct illicit evidence. This rule is another example of application of the doctrine of the fruit of the poisoned tree, although applied to the plurality of evidence.

Conclusions

The main conclusions of this work are the following.

The new information and communication technologies, in the form of computing tools that allow filing, accessing or reproducing the relevant data of the different communications of the employees, result in a separate form of evidence, apart from the documentary evidence, *digital evidence*, also known as the evidence 'of support' or 'instruments'. However, the interested party must facilitate the possibility of transcribing the content of it in the most appropriate and relevant form (e.g. documents), as well as verifying the content's veracity (expert report).

When digital evidence is submitted in proceedings, the party against whom the evidence is submitted may try to defend themselves by challenging its authenticity (veracity) and integrity (accuracy). At first, the veracity and accuracy of the emails will depend on several circumstances. The party against whom the email evidence is submitted (for example, the employee) can contest their authorship and the veracity of their content, especially if they lack a digital signature. To do this, that party must provide sufficient and objective evidence, and must justify the challenge on well-founded grounds, as a mere protest is not enough. After that, the party who initially submitted the emails (generally, the applicant) will be the one who will have to justify, with new evidence, that

---

44 JHC of Madrid of 13 May 2016, cit.
45 Lousada Arochena, F., *op. et loc. cit.:* when 'there is factual data that is sufficient (or not) to justify a disciplinary dismissal', the nullity of this one is excluded 'by unlawfulness of the evidence'.

they are genuine and reflect the situation, eliminating any doubt of fraud or alteration of in terms of authorship or content.

When evidence is obtained through the violation of fundamental rights, the effects of its illegality on the sanction imposed by the employer on the employee (as a result of the information obtained with that) are discussed. On this point, there are two classic positions: one, maximalist, which, following the doctrine of 'the fruit of the poisoned tree' backs extending the nullity of the evidence to the employer decision, with its legal basis in Arts. 55.5 WS and 108.2 LSJ, and in an important judgment of the Constitutional Court. This position is especially protective of the employee, who may even be entitled to compensation for moral damages. Faced with this, the second theory is more protective of the interests of the company, insofar as it defends the inadmissibility of the sanction imposed. The main cause is the literal restrictive interpretation of Art. 55 WS, which limits the nullity of the dismissal to the existence of substantive reasons, something that does not happen in the case examined (illegality derived from the nullity of the evidence).

In view of the extreme positions, the intermediate or mixed position seems more appropriate, which makes reference to the causal and temporal relationship that exists between the violation of the fundamental right and the cause of dismissal. Thus, in that situation in which first an employer violates the fundamental rights of the employee and, later on, a contractual breach of the employee is discovered, it is logical that the illegality of that employer surveillance and, consequently, the nullity of the technological evidence, also implies the nullity of the subsequent dismissal. This one brings the cause of that unlawful conduct, that is, the employer acquires knowledge of the contractual breach of the employee as a result of his own irregular conduct, so that this affects his subsequent termination decision.

However, the situation is very different when the employer has certain knowledge or a well-founded suspicion of an employee's non-compliance and, in order to prove it, decides to perform surveillance behaviour to have objective evidence to submit to the proceedings. In this case, if that surveillance violates fundamental rights, it will be qualified as null and will not have any effect on its own, but the extension of the nullity to the employer's decision to dismiss may be excessive, but this one, finally, cannot be proven.

13 The probative value and effectiveness of the evidence obtained through email and messaging in the control of the workplace activity[1]

Francisca Ferrando García, Monserrate Rodríguez Egio and Antonio Megías-Bas

Introduction

The introduction of new technologies in the business sector at the service of the powers of management and control of the employer's work activity is increasingly frequent inside and outside the workplace. Specifically, the use of electronic mail in the workplace has become a common means of work activity not only as an instrument for developing work activity but also as a means of monitoring and controlling workers, so that often the content of the electronic mail is provided in a court hearing as proof of labour violations and to justify the sanction imposed. However, it is necessary to take into account the possibility of handling electronic mail along with the need to respect the fundamental rights of workers when obtaining information of or about a worker through email. In this sense, the violation of fundamental rights in obtaining evidence would call for the evidence to be classified as illicit evidence. In these cases, it is necessary to know the effects that illegal evidence obtained through email would have on the classification of the sanction imposed on a worker, and ultimately, whether there were grounds for dismissal.

This chapter deals with the use of new technologies in the development of work activity, specifically, electronic mail, as a means of controlling work activity, which requires on the one hand the analysis of the compatibility of this means of surveillance and supervision of the labour activity with the right to privacy recognised in Spanish Constitution (SC), in order to verify the legality or illegality of the evidence obtained and, on the other hand, the probative value of the

1 This chapter has been carried out within the framework of the Research Project DER2016-78123-R, on Procedural Implications of the Labor Market Reform ("Implicaciones procesales de la reforma del mercado de trabajo"), financed by the Ministry of Economy, Industry and Competitiveness, and included in the 2016 Call -Projects I + D-State Program for the Promotion of Scientific and Technical Research of Excellence, State Subprogram for the Generation of Knowledge.

information obtained and how it is incorporated into the labour process, normally, in order to support the disciplinary action.

Limits to business control through new technologies

Article 20.3 of Royal Legislative Decree 2/2015, of 23 October, which approves the revised text of the Workers' Statute Act (WS) allows the employer to resort to the measures it deems most appropriate to supervise the development of the activity, but must respect human dignity, of which one of the most important derivatives is the right to privacy.

As has been noted, corporate control can materialise through various means, generically alluded to in Article 20.3 of the WS, which are currently thought to be through personal supervision of the professional activity developed at the time and in the place of work, either by the employer himself or by workers of the company, or outside it, by private detectives, or by means of various indirect supervision formulas such as the use of audio-visual media, the control of the use of the internet or even through the information coming from of social networks.

Business control must be based on work activity in time and place of work. Therefore, business control that exceeds the limits of the provision of services to interfere illicitly in the worker's intimate life is considered abusive.[2] For this reason, even when the worker is in the workplace, business controls are rejected on the worker's activities totally unrelated to his labour service provision, as is the case with the means of recording sound or image located in common areas or places of transit, such as corridors, toilets, dining rooms, etc. However, supervision and business control outside the working day and place is admitted in very exceptional cases, in which it is considered that the behaviour followed by the worker outside of his working day, taking into account the specific characteristics of the contracted labour benefit or the specific obligations to which the worker is subject, is also relevant in the employment relationship, either for reasons of safety in people or things, or because it can negatively affect the worker's performance or because his or her private conduct may be considered as an attempt against contractual good faith or involve an abuse of business confidence.

In addition, jurisprudence has admitted the employer's control of situations in temporary disability, or in cases in which the worker's extra-work activity may imply a breach of their work obligations (e.g. unfair competition, breach of exclusive-use pacts etc.). The implementation of means of control by the employer requires prior information of their implementation and their existence being given out. Given the expectation of privacy that a worker can have in their daily lives, the use of means of control that may affect his or her rights requires the company to inform them previously of the existence of these means of control.

---

2 María C. López Aniorte, "Límites constitucionales al ejercicio del poder directivo empresarial mediante el uso de las TIC y otros medios de vigilancia y seguridad privada en el ordenamiento jurídico español". *Revista Policía y seguridad pública* 1 (2014): 31–52.

The Constitutional Court (CC) noted in the STC 29/2013, of 11 February, the need for "informing workers prior, expressly, accurately, clearly and unequivocally of the purpose of control of the work activity to which that means could be directed. Any information that should specify the characteristics and scope of the data processing to be carried out, that is, in which cases the recordings could be examined, for how long and for what purposes, explaining very particularly that they could be used for the imposition of sanctions, disciplinary proceedings for breach of the employment contract" (FJ 8). At the same time, on the level of ordinary legality, Article 64.5 of the WS requires the company to obtain a report, which is not binding, from the representatives of the workers prior to the implementation and revision of the work control system. However, the CC itself has corrected the doctrine expressed in the aforementioned STC 29/2013. Thus, STC 39/2016, of 3 March, has concluded that companies can use the images captured by surveillance cameras to verify compliance with work obligations when workers have knowledge of their installation through the corresponding informative document or sign which is located in the business in clear view for everyone to see. On the other hand, STC 170/2013, of 7 October, considers that it is not necessary to inform the workers that they will proceed to control the use of computers and equipment owned by the company, when there are guidelines on the prohibition of its use, to prevent generating the expectation of confidentiality in its use.

The rights to personal privacy included in Article 18 of the SC which encompasses fundamental right, together with the right to the personal dignity[3] which derives from the previously mentioned article, and which in turn implies "the existence of a personal and reserved space acting separately of the action and the knowledge of others, according to the guidelines of the Spanish culture, to maintain a minimum quality of human life".[4] This acts as a limit to the business possibility of surveillance and control of work activity. Their respect marks the dividing line between the legal or illegally obtained evidence and the possibilities of asserting the information obtained with the said measures in a possible judicial process in the event of objection against the businesses decision. In the workplace, Article 4.2.c) of the WS expressly includes the right of workers to have their privacy respected. However, the right to privacy is not an absolute right; it is possible to introduce limits to this right based on constitutionally relevant interests, provided that a legitimate purpose is achieved and that there is proportionality to the measure.[5]

The worker's right to privacy may come into conflict with the business interest of controlling compliance with labour obligations, which will be carried out by virtue of the managerial powers available to management personnel under the freedom of business, recognised in Article 38 of the SC. The sacrifice

---

3 Article 10.1 SC.
4 Vid. STC 98/2000.
5 SSTC 57/1994 and 443/1994.

of the right to privacy is not allowed, but a reciprocal modulation of the concurrent rights can be achieved. Jurisprudence has been deliberating the grounds for the validity of these means of control so that the legality of the control measure will depend on respect for the privacy of the worker. In this sense, the Constitutional Court warns that "the right to privacy is not absolute, as none of the fundamental rights are, and it may yield to constitutionally relevant interests, provided that the cutbacks these experienced and suffered is seen as necessary for the achievement of legitimacy, proportionate to achieving this and, in any case, be respectful of the essential content of the right".[6] It should be noted that the constitutional doctrine does not admit "the sacrifice of the privacy of workers in order to ensure the proper development of the employment relationship, but a proportional and reciprocal tempering of the rights of both parties to overall benefit the employment relationship".[7] Not in vain, the aforementioned Article 20.3 of the WS states that for the adoption and application of surveillance and control measures to verify compliance by the worker of their obligations and duties, the employer must "take into due consideration the dignity of the workers."

The compatibility of the exercise of the powers of control of the work activity with the privacy of the affected workers requires assessing, in each specific case, if the measures adopted by the employer exceed the so-called "proportionality trial", composed of a triple test, by virtue of which it is proven if that measure is capable of achieving the proposed objective (judgment of suitability); that there is no other more moderate measure for the achievement of such purpose (necessity judgment); and, finally, that it is balanced or proportional in accordance with the goods or values in conflict (proportionality trial in the strict sense).[8]

In the assessment of the control measure, special consideration is given to the existence of well-founded suspicions or indications of non-compliance on the part of the worker, and to the possibility of checking its veracity by other means.[9]

---

6 For all, SSTC 57/1994 and 143/1994.
7 Alejandra Selma Penalva, "La información reflejada en las redes sociales y su valor como prueba en el proceso laboral. Análisis de los últimos criterios jurisprudenciales". *Revista General de Derecho del Trabajo y de la Seguridad Social* 39 (2014): 362.
8 Vid. SSTC 57/1994, of 28 February, and 143/1994, of 9 May. And more recently, the SSTC 96/2012, of 7 May 241/2012, of 17 December, 170/2013, of 7 October, and 39/2016, of 3 March.
9 In this case it refers to the «Principal of indicated intervention», which justifies the adoption of the means of control on behalf of the employer when relevant indicators are accredited to an irregular action on the workers' part. In this sense, C.E. Morales Vállez, "El control de los medios tecnológicos por el empresario a la luz de la sentencia del TEDH de 12 de enero de 2016". *CEF. Laboral Social* 399 (2016), and Cristóbal Molina Navarrete, "'Expectativa razonable de privacidad' y poder de vigilancia empresarial: ¿'quo vadis justicia laboral?'" (Comentario a la sentencia del TEDH de 12 de enero de 2016, asunto Barbulescu c. Rumanía, demanda núm. 61496/2008). *Revista de Trabajo y Seguridad Social. CEF* 399 (2016): 171–180.

Nature and effectiveness of the means of proof obtained through email and messaging

In the described context, the nature and effectiveness of the evidence obtained will depend on the medium by which it was obtained and on the compliance with the requirements of the law established in each case. That is, it will depend on whether the evidence was obtained through other means, i.e., through private detectives, video surveillance, audio recordings, through social networks or through the control of electronic mail and messaging.[10] Among the means of control of work activity available to the employer, this chapter focuses on the study of the evidence obtained through computerised means, particularly through emails and messaging.

One of the most common problems related to the use of computer equipment provided by the company as a work tool is the limits of tolerance of its use for personal purposes during the day (e.g. access to the Internet, use of electronic mail), and the powers of control of the activity imposed on the worker at work.

In order to assess this equipment's correct use, the employer needs to find out if a possible rule breaking action has been performed during the course of the day to the detriment of work performance, which in turn requires determining if it was a punctual or abusive action, and even if the content of the files and messages is related to the work activity. Regarding the use of the computer provided to the worker by the employer, the STS of 26 September 2007[11] has indicated that the registration of such equipment is not regulated by Article 18 of the WS,[12] but by Article 20.3 of the same legal text, since the legitimacy of this control is not justified by the need to protect corporate assets, but derives from the character of an instrument of production of the object on which it falls. The aforementioned decision rejects the comparison between the existing lockers in the workplace for the worker to deposit their personal items and virtual folders with personal information, included in the memory of a computer that is used for the development of the work activity. Hence, the information contained in computer files and folders cannot benefit from the precautions provided in Article 18 of the WS, which, as is known, requires that the registration be made in the place and time of work, in the presence of a representative of the worker/s or, in his absence from the workplace, of another worker of the company, whenever possible.

However, this distinction is made at the level of ordinary legality, and, as stated in the aforesaid Decision, does not affect the dignity of the worker (Article 20.3

---

10 Recently, in the ECHR Decision of 9 January 2018, the case of López Ribalda and others against Spain (demands 1874/13 y 8567/13), the ECHR resolved that, in the case concerning video surveillance in was seen that, corresponding to present Spanish legislation at the time related to data protection, the defendants should have been informed that they were under video surveillance, resulting in the breach of Article 8 of the Human Rights European Convention, in relation to general respect to privacy, upon not being informed of this.
11 Rec. n. 966/2006.
12 See also STSJ Asturias, n. 2144/2013, of 15 November 2013.

WS) and, therefore, the application of the guarantee to the right to privacy (Article 18.1 SC) both to the personal files of the worker that are in the computer, as well as to the browsing history on the internet. And it is that this work of supervision that can affect the rights to privacy of the worker (Article 18.1 SC), the protection of personal data (Article 18.4 SC), and the secrecy of communications (Article 18.3 SC),[13] when it comes to controlling emails and other channels of instant messaging (Skype, Messenger, WhatsApp, Line, etc.).[14]

In general, the validity of the registration and, therefore, of the evidence obtained in relation to the use of computer equipment and Internet access, is based on the existence and content of business guidelines on the subject. These are rules that the employer is empowered to dictate, insofar as they refer to the use of computer equipment and media of which it is the owner (telephone, email and internet), and must be known, understood and respected by the employees. In this sense, the previously mentioned STS of 26 September 2007 distinguished two assumptions:

a)　The absence of express norms or limitations regarding the use of computer media entails a greater business tolerance of the extra-labour uses of these tools, contributing to the generation of intimacy expectations in the use of computer equipment. Of course, this does not mean that the company relinquishes its powers of control over the use of such material,[15] but, in accordance with the requirements of good faith, the company must previously inform the workers that there will be control and of the means it is to be applied in order to verify the correctness of its uses,[16] without prejudice to the possible application of other preventive measures, such as the exclusion of certain connections.

b)　On the other hand, if there are express limitations on the extra-labour uses of the equipment or access to the internet, the breach of said guidelines constitutes a disobedient punishable conduct, with the exception "that the

---

13　According to the STS, Criminal Chamber, num. 2844/2014, of 16 June 2014, the control of the so-called "traffic data" or even the possible use of computer equipment to access other network services such as web pages, etc., is protected by the right to privacy (Article 18.1 EC) but not for the secrecy of communications (Article 18.3 EC), which excludes the need for judicial authorization prior to its control. However, Article 90.4 of the LRJS expressly requires such authorization to access "documents or files, in any type of support, that may affect personal privacy or another fundamental right".

14　Vid. the ECHR Decision of 3 April 2007, *Copland case against the United Kingdom*, concludes that the collection and storage of personal information related to electronic mail and the Internet browsing of a worker, without her knowledge, violates her right to respect for her private life and their correspondence, in accordance with Article 8 of the European Convention for the Protection of Human Rights and Fundamental Freedoms, as they may contain sensitive data that affect privacy and respect for privacy.

15　In this sense, vid. the STSJ of Cataluña, num. 841/2011, of 3 February.

16　STS of 8 March 2011 (rcud. 1826/2010).

company has been tolerating this type of breach, or that it has not sanctioned other workers for similar behaviour".[17]

When an absolute and clear prohibition of its use for personal purposes is established,[18] expressly warned in the current disciplinary regime or in the internal guidelines of the company on the lawful use of computer equipment provided by the company, there is no tolerant situation, so that judicial doctrine understands that a reasonable expectation of confidentiality is not generated here. Consequently, if the company decides to carry out a control test of the correct and diligent use of the computerised means made available to its employees, there is no infringement of their right to privacy,[19] and the eventual proof of non-compliance will be considered lawfully obtained, allowing to justify a disciplinary dismissal.[20]

Unlike what happens in cases of tolerance of moderate use for private purposes or relative prohibition, with the existence of an absolute prohibition, the STS of 6 October 2011 denied the requirement of prior communication to the worker that it is going to carry out a control test of the computer[21] (interpretation corroborated by the STC 170/2013, of 7 October) in the terms that will be analysed next.[22] It has even confirmed the validity of the evidence obtained and, therefore, the origin of the dismissal of the worker who, despite the radical prohibition of using the internet for personal purposes in working time, used the company's Wi-Fi password to navigate through certain web pages and watched movies during the work day, through a personal device.[23]

The control of electronic mail by the company can violate the generic right to privacy of the worker (STC 173/2011, of 7 November), as well as its right to secrecy of communications (Article 18.3 CE), although the last right protects

---

17 Antonio V. Sempere Navarro y Carolina Sanmartín Mazzucconi, "¿Puede la empresa controlar el ordenador usado por su trabajador?" *Aranzadi Social 7* (2007): 369.

18 Although the absolute prohibition has been admitted by jurisprudence [v.gr. STS of 6 October 2011 (RCUD 4053/2010)], the use of internet and other computerised means of the company must be allowed for union purposes, since according to the judicial doctrine (STSJ of Madrid, No. 31/2001, of 26 March) has to be considered as a professional use of the network, even if it is not directly linked to the specific labour benefit, because it is consubstantial with the employment relationship [Antonio V. Sempere Navarro and C. Sanmartín Mazzucconi, *Nuevas Tecnologías y Relaciones Laborales* (Cizur Menor: Aranzadi, 2002), 245].

19 STS of 6 October 2011, cit. In the doctrine of supplication, see the SSTSJ of Andalucía/Granada núm. 222/2012, of January 26, and of Murcia núm. 988/2013, of 14 October.

20 STSJ of Andalucía/Granada, núm. 2083/2013, of 14 November.

21 Rcud. 4053/2010.

22 For analogous reasons, the expectations of privacy will be considerably reduced if there are agreements or clauses agreed in a collective agreement, which provide for the possibility of periodic audits of the worker's computer and communication systems, either through remote or face-to-face controls. Such is the case of telework agreements in Telefónica España or BBVA. For a particular study of the matter, see Belén García Romero, *El Teletrabajo* (Madrid: Civitas, Thomson Reuters, 2012), 116–122.

23 STSJ of Asturias, n. 2144/2013, of 15 November.

only certain communications: those that are made through certain means or closed channels. Therefore, the secrecy of communications is not affected when the worker installs a messaging application, without password, in a collective computer of the company, with which access to the content of the messages is open to any user of said computer (STC 241/2012, of 17 December), so that the worker cannot claim an expectation of secrecy of his communication.[24]

Moreover, according to STC 170/2013, dated October 7, it does not entail a violation of the right to secrecy of communications or of the right to privacy, the supervision of employee emails, without the company informing the employees beforehand, when the collective agreement prohibits or sanctions the use of computer tools and electronic mail for private use. This criterion has been rightly criticised by a doctrinal sector, in that it attributes to the company the exorbitant power to convert the mail into an open means of communication,[25] by establishing guidelines that prohibit its use for particular purposes. In addition, this prohibition of the use of mail for private purposes has the potential to exempt the constitutional requirement of judicial authorisation regarding interference in the mail (Article 18.3 SC).[26]

Although referring exclusively to the criminal sphere, the 2nd Chamber of the Supreme Court, in its Decision of 16 June 2014, insisted on the requirement of prior judicial authorisation, "whatever the circumstances or persons, police officers, businessmen, etc., that such interference takes place", rejecting that the business ownership of the communicative tool, the corporate nature of the means of communication used or its use during the workday imply a tacit waiver of confidentiality or the right to secrecy of the communication. However, this resolution has specified that the messages, "once received and opened by the addressee", are now considered data files, so that they are no longer part of the communication itself, nor are the traffic data (circumstances of time, lines used, length of communication, etc.), so that they do not enjoy the protection of the right to secrecy of communications (Article 18.3 CE), nor its reading requires prior judicial authorisation.[27]

However, as it has warned in this same judgment, the fact that they are not covered by secrecy of communications does not prevent the correspondents' own

---

24 However, as regards the right to privacy, it is not decisive that the computer did not have an access code (STS of 26 September 2007).

25 Susana Rodríguez Escanciano, *Poder de control empresarial, sistemas tecnológicos y derechos fundamentales de los trabajadores* (Valencia: Tirant, 2015), 98–99, in relation to the STSJ of Madrid of 29 October 2012 (rec. N. 4309/2012).

26 Unai Aberasturi Gorriño, "Control empresarial del correo electrónico del empleado y relevancia de la información previa a los trabajadores como garantía mínima para ejercer ese control, a la luz de la STC de 7 de octubre de 2013". *Nueva Revista Española de Derecho del Trabajo* 180 (2015): 217. With regard to the need for judicial authorisation vid. art. 90.4 LRJS.

27 However, this doctrine can be subject to abuse, since the worker could mark his mails as unread. In this case, the company must use a computer expert to destroy the presumption that is generated in favour of the secrecy of communication.

guarantees from being applied to both the right to data protection,[28] which requires prior information to the worker on the review and treatment of the data obtained (duration, purposes, etc.), as well as the right to privacy of the persons.[29] The Decision of 16 June 2014 raises a clear discrepancy between the criminal and labour Chambers of Supreme Court (in view of the doctrine expressed in the workplace by the STC 170/2013),[30] as regards the limits to business control of the communications by computer, and reminds the thesis stated by the STS of 26 September 2007, according to which, the fact that the computer has no password and is located in a keyless office, does not imply an acceptance by the worker to have open access to the information contained in their computer, so it is not an obstacle to the protection of their privacy.

Above all, it reflects a different and very significant position regarding the relationship between property rights (of computer equipment and systems used) and freedom of enterprise, on the one hand, and the fundamental rights of workers, as citizens and what they are. Thus, the criminal order of the jurisdiction assumes today the position of guarantee against the exercise of the entrepreneurial powers of self-protection,[31] which in the past was the *leitmotiv* of the social order of the jurisdiction.[32]

On the other hand, some authors have criticised the constitutional doctrine to the extent that it extends the criterion of control of corporate emails to instant messaging systems, installed for private purposes, as they have no professional vocation, hence the non-compliance of guidelines that absolutely prohibit the use of computer equipment for specific purposes may justify the exercise of disciplinary power, but do not enable the employer to monitor its content, or allow him to establish possible penalties based on the statements contained in these messages, unless through the necessary judicial authorisation.[33]

On the contrary, at first the ECHR considered that if a messenger account was installed for work purposes, it would be possible to punish the worker who used it for private purposes. In this regard, the ECHR Decision of 12 January 2016[34] considers that there is no violation of the right to the inviolability of

28 Article 18.4 SC.
29 Article 18.1 SC.
30 Hilda I. Arbonés Lapena, "Grabación de imagen o sonido y control de correo electrónico por el empresario". *Nueva Revista Española de Derecho del Trabajo* 178 (2015): 216.
31 Cristóbal Molina Navarrete, "Autotutela empresarial, secreto de comunicaciones y control judicial: La Sala Social pierde el paso con la Sala Penal. Comentario a la Sentencia del Tribunal Supremo, Sala 2.ª, de 16 de junio de 2014, rec. núm. 2229/2013". *Revista de Trabajo y Seguridad Social. CEF* 381 (2014): 158, 162.
32 Francisca M. Ferrando García, "Vigilancia y control de los trabajadores y derecho a la intimidad en el contexto de las nuevas tecnologías". *Revista de Trabajo y Seguridad Social. CEF* 399 (2016): 58.
33 José L. Goñi Sein, "Los límites de las potestades empresariales vs. Derecho a la intimidad de las personas trabajadoras en el entorno de las TIC. El control empresarial en el espacio virtual. Problemática laboral de las redes sociales". *Actum Social* 95 (2015).
34 Case *Bărbulescuv Romania*, No. 61496/08.

correspondence, nor of the right to privacy[35] by the fact that the company supervises the communications maintained by the worker through a Messenger account, in a case in which the email account was created by the worker at the request of the company for exclusive purposes of communication with customers, and its use for private purposes was strictly prohibited. The ECHR concludes that the company did not intend at any time to check or control aspects of the worker's private life, but to control compliance with their work duties, as it believed that the mail account only contained communications with the company's customers.

The faculty thus conferred to the employer raises, finally, serious doubts of compatibility with the rights to the privacy and the secrecy of communications of the non-linked third parties through an employment relationship with the employer, who receives and sends emails or messages to the worker through the corporate communication medium. For this reason, it has been affirmed the need to comply with the requirements of transparency in the aforementioned control, using elements of mail configuration which allow external communicators to be notified that they are interacting with a corporate mail that can be opened by a different person from the one to which it is addressed,[36] in a manner analogous to the notices that are used in case of recording telephone conversations maintained with customer services.

Subsequently, the ECHR Decision, Grand Chamber, of 5 September 2017, annulled the aforementioned ruling, reinforcing the protection of the worker against the control and surveillance of electronic communications in the workplace by the employer. The Grand Chamber of the ECHR established the concept of "correspondence" that includes sending and receiving messages, applying the right to the inviolability of communications according to article 8 of the European Convention on Human Rights and Fundamental Freedoms. The ECHR thus disavows the doctrine established in the Spanish Constitutional Court Decision number 170/2013, pointing out the need to inform employees, prior to the start of the surveillance, of the scope of the control, although it is forbidden to use it for private purposes. The ECHR considered that the specific reasons justifying the surveillance of communications should be provided.[37]

Finally, it should be noted that the Supreme Court has stated in Decision 119/2018 of 8 February 2018 that the *Bărbulescu Doctrine* (ECHR Decision 5 September 2017) coincides substantially with the doctrine of the Spanish Constitutional Court and with the doctrine of the Supreme Court. In the

35 Article 8 European Convention of Human Rights and Fundamental Freedoms.
36 Aurelio Desdentado Bonete and Ana B. Muñoz Ruiz, "Trabajo, videovigilancia y controles informáticos. Un recorrido por la jurisprudencia". *Revista General de Derecho del Trabajo y de la Seguridad Social* 39 (2014): 24.
37 On this matter, see Cristóbal Molina Navarrete, "De Barbulescu II a López Ribalda: ¿qué hay de nuevo en la protección de datos de los trabajadores. Comentario a la Sentencia del Tribunal Europeo de Derechos Humanos de 9 de enero de 2018, caso López Ribalda *et alli* vs. España (Demandas acumuladas 1874/13 y 8567/13)". *Revista de Trabajo y Seguridad Social. CEF* 419 (2018): 125–135.

aforementioned judgment, the Supreme Court confirmed the admissibility of the disciplinary dismissal of a worker for having transgressed the contractual good faith and abuse of confidence by accepting money from a supplier. The company learned through the casual finding of photocopies of bank transfers made by a supplier of the company in favour of the worker, a fact expressly prohibited in the Code of Conduct of the defendant and charged in the dismissal letter. The company examined the content of certain emails from the worker's corporate email account, not in a generic and indiscriminate way, but trying to find elements that would allow them to select which emails to examine, using keywords that could infer in what emails there was information relevant to the investigation, focusing the search on the dates close to the date of the bank transfers. The Supreme Court concluded that there has been no breach of privacy or secrecy of communications.[38]

Incidence of evaluation of the test in the qualification of the sanction

Probative value of the information obtained through email and messaging

The exercise of the businesses power to control the work activity in the terms outlined above can be translated into the imposition of sanctions, the eventual challenge of which will require providing the evidence obtained to the labour process by reviewing the computer, consisting, where appropriate, in email messages and mobile messaging (SMS, WhatsApp, Messenger, Line, Tuenti,

---

38 The Supreme Court concludes that there has been no breach of privacy or secrecy of communications for three reasons (FJ 6): a) That the casual finding of the aforementioned documentary evidence excludes the application of the Anglo-Saxon doctrine of the "fruit of the poisoned tree", in virtue of which the judge is prohibited to assess not only the evidence obtained in violation of a fundamental right, but also those derived from those (…) b) That the clear and previous prohibition to use the company's computer for strictly personal matters leads us to affirm – as we did in one of our precedents that "if there is no right to use the computer for personal use, there will be no right to do so under conditions that impose a respect for privacy or the secrecy of communications, because, in the absence of a situation of tolerance of personal use, there is no longer a reasonable expectation of privacy and because, if personal use is illegal, no or the employer may be required to support it and also refrain from controlling it" (STS SG 06/10/11 rec. 4053/10); c) That the careful consideration of the electronic mail described in the preceding paragraph, using the company's server and computer search parameters designed to limit invasion in privacy, evidences that the requirements demanded by the company have been scrupulously respected. constitutional jurisprudence and the judgments of suitability, necessity and proportionality have been overcome. It is worth mentioning the ruling of the ECHR Chamber of February 22, 2018, in the case of Liber c. France, in which the ECHR regarding the privacy of the worker and its limits in the workplace has indicated, in application of French law, the difference between the files that indicate the term "personal" and that of "private", indicating that Art. 8 of the European Convention on Human Rights when the company accesses the content of files classified as "personal".

Twitter, etc.). Despite its technical consideration as electronic evidence based on Article 384 of the LEC, the doctrine of supplication is attributing to this means of proof the value of documentary evidence as soon as a printed copy of the capture of the content is brought to the trial. It displays on the screen ("screenshot") or transcription of the messages, in such a way that they support the factual revision in supplication.[39]

However, when the mere written transcription or the graphic representation of the conversation or copy of the information that appears on the screen as a photographic print is provided as a means of proof, the evaluation of the information provided through the instant messaging must be carried out with the utmost caution, for the risk that exists of content manipulation (by creating or editing a document that mimics the logical structure and presentation of messages) or identity theft of its author. In order to give proof of charge or disclaimer to these conversations, article 382.2 of the LEC allows the contribution of instrumental elements of conviction, so it is possible to resort to other probative sources such as testimony or part interrogation, being relevant the ratification of the content by the interlocutors or the silent attitude of the party they are harming.

Regarding the probative effectiveness of instant messaging conversations, it should be noted that different forms of contribution to the trial can be accommodated. It is possible to contribute the original (through the visualisation of mobile devices which have been registered or through judicial recognition) or the recording of the graphic representation (screenshot) in a DVD or pen drive and visualisation in the trial. At the same time, it is possible to print the screenshot or the written transcription of the conversation (in accordance with art. 282.2 LEC, it is necessary to transcribe the words in writing and also to provide all the electronic means that allow their visualization (Article 384 of the LEC)). If it is not the original, it is necessary to warn of the risk of content manipulation or identity theft, so it would be necessary for judicial caution in its assessment, being in any case assessed according to sound criticism (348 LEC).[40] It is possible to provide instrumental elements of conviction such as: the interrogation of a part, the testimony and expert witness in your case (Article 382.2 LEC, notarial acts of presence according to Article 199 of the Notarial Regulation, the testimony of exhibition as provided by the Article 251 the Notarial Regulation etc.) In case of formal challenge of the proof of transcription or copy of the messages, it is expedient to provide expert evidence.[41] In any case, it is necessary to provide evidence to the judicial body that allow reaching the conviction

---

39 In respect with the electronic mail that has been printed, see the STSJ of Aragón 822/2010, of 17 November. With relation to SMS or WhatsApp messages, see STSJ of Aragón, núm. 145/2015, of 16 March.

40 On this matter, vid. Guillermo Barrios Baudor, "La integridad y/o autenticidad de los medios de prueba digital en el proceso laboral: una aproximación al tema a propósito de los correos electrónicos". *RTSS. CEF* 145 (2017): 23–52.

41 In this sense, see the STS of 19 May 2015, with regard to the printing on paper of the screenshots of instant messaging conversations maintained through the Tuenti mobile application.

about the authenticity of the electronic evidence (passwords, mobile phone number, ownership, server and/or computer equipment, photographs, screenshots, trades to companies etc.).

Effects of the illegality of the test in the classification of the sanction

It is necessary to analyse the effects of obtaining evidence with violation of the fundamental rights of the worker and, in particular, the right to personal privacy guaranteed by Article 18.1 of the EC, on the qualification of the employer decision based on the information obtained in this way.

In advance, it must be pointed out that the illegality of the evidence entails the impossibility of being taken into account by the judicial body for the assessment of the facts. In fact, in accordance with articles 11.1 of the LOPJ and 90.2 of the LRJS, evidence obtained through procedures that imply a violation of fundamental rights must not be admitted; its result, as illegitimately obtained, must be considered as not contributed to the records. The use of a test obtained with the infringement of a fundamental right (privacy, secrecy of communications, protection of personal data, etc.) also entails the violation of the right to the presumption of innocence, according to STC 169/2003, of 29 September, which requires the nullity of the evidence and the proceedings, v. gr. the disciplinary hearing and process, based on it.

A first consequence of this would be, unless they can be credited with other means of proof without causal connection with the invalidated test, that the accusations made against the worker cannot be deemed as proven. This circumstance raises what qualification deserves the disciplinary measure imposed, must result in the qualification of the disciplinary measure imposed, the unfairness of the dismissal given that the non-compliance is not proven (articles 55.4 WS and 108.1 LRJS) or the nullity of the dismissal, if it is understood that it implies the violation of a fundamental right (articles 55.5 WS and 108.2 LRJS).

In relation to the question it is possible to identify up to three positions in the judicial doctrine:[42]

a) The so-called "non-communication position" defends that the dismissal is unfair, since the violation of the fundamental right does not come from the disciplinary action itself, but from the means of proof used.[43] According to this thesis, the nullity only operates when the sanction has by consequence the infringement of a fundamental right or implies in itself or directly the

---

42 Systematized very clearly by Carlos H. Preciado Domenech and Miguel A. Purcalla Bonilla, *La prueba en el proceso social* (Lex Nova, 2015), 165–169.
43 STSJ of Castilla-La Mancha, núm. 715/2014, of 17 June. A study on this matter can be found in Jaime Carbonel Murio, "Efectos de la prueba ilícita en la calificación del despido" accessed March 19, 2018, http://forelab.com/wp-content/uploads/Jaime-Carbonell-Murio-efectos-de-la-prueba-ilicita-en-la-calificacion-del-despido.pdf.

violation of that right.[44] In short, the effects of illicit evidence could not be radiated to dismissal.[45]

b) Against the previous thesis, the constitutional doctrine considers that the nullity of the evidence extends or radiates also to the decisions that are based on it, so the dismissal (or minor penalty) will be qualified as null and void for violation of fundamental rights. The so-called "irradiation thesis" rests on the theory of the fruit of the forbidden tree, collected in the STC 196/2004, of 15 November, according to which it is necessary to cancel the dismissal decided by virtue of an proof obtained with violation of the right to intimacy.[46] This doctrine has been reiterated in subsequent pronouncements of both the Constitutional Court[47] and the Supreme Court.[48] Certainly, an interpretation of this issue in light of Article 55.1 c) of the LOTC operates in favour of this thesis, insofar as the infringement of a fundamental right not only involves the nullity of the act constituting the violation, but also the restoration of the situation at the moment before it occurs and the reparation of all the consequences derived from said act.[49] And this is because, as the doctrine has warned, the reinstatement of the worker in the integrity of his or her right will not occur at the substantive level if the dismissal is qualified merely as unfair.[50]

c) Finally, it would be possible to maintain an "intermediate position", according to which the dismissal or minor disciplinary action should be considered null and void, even though it would be possible to maintain the validity of the sanction, when it is based on other independent or totally unrelated evidence to that obtained illegally through the infringement of the fundamental right.[51]

---

44 STSJ of Cataluña, of 5 September 2000 (rec. núm. 2890/2000); STSJ of Aragón, núm. 1097/2007, of 4 December 2007; STSJ of Madrid, núm. 553/2005, of 28 June 2005.

45 Vid. STSJ Madrid, 453/2011, of 30 May 2011; STSJ of Castilla La Mancha, of 12 January 2018; and STSJ of the Basque Country 107/2012, of 17 April.

46 In this sense, see SSTSJ of Galicia, núm. 1607/2008, of 3 March 2008, of the Basque Country, of 12 September 2006 (rec. núm. 1270/2006) and of 10 May 2011 (rec. núm. 644/2011).

47 Vid. STC 29/2013 (FJ 4).

48 Cfr. STS of 13 May 2014 (rcud. 1685/2013). For an analysis of said sentence, see Belén García Romero, "Workplace Privacy and Employee monitoring. Dismissal based on the capture of the employee images on a video camera made without the knowledge of affected worker and with a different purpose from the one declared by the company". *International Labor Law Reports* 34 (2015).

49 Ferrando, "Vigilancia y control de los trabajadores y derecho a la intimidad en el contexto de las nuevas tecnologías", 68.

50 Preciado and Purcalla, *La prueba en el proceso social*, 167, 168.

51 For all those tests connected causally with the one obtained illicitly would indirectly result from the violation of the right to privacy and by virtue of the "doctrine of the fruits of the forbidden tree" (collected in article 90.2 LRJS) would also be invalidated. On the question, see *in extenso*, Preciado and Purcalla, *La prueba en el proceso social*, 99–104.

Conclusions

The use of new technologies for the control and monitoring of work activity has its limit in the criterion of proportionality and necessity. The possibility of manipulation of the information obtained through the electronic mail and the messaging makes necessary a proof of the authenticity and authorship that will normally require support in complementary tests (expert, testimonial, interrogation of part etc.).

Regarding the effects of the unlawful evidence, obtained with the infringement of fundamental rights, in the classification of the disciplinary action, it is concluded that, in order to guarantee a real and effective protection of the violated fundamental rights, it is necessary to defend the irradiation thesis that entails the nullity of the disciplinary decision, considering that the transgression of a fundamental right not only involves the nullity of the act constituting the infringement, but also the restitution of the situation prior to the moment in which the infringement occurred and the repair of all the consequences derived from said act.

At the substantive level, the qualification of the dismissal as unfair does not allow the reinstatement of the worker in the integrity of their rights. Therefore, when in the claim the worker alleges the illegality of the evidence obtained in violation of fundamental rights, it would be advisable to request the nullity of the dismissal decided on the basis of said evidence or, alternatively, its unfairness together with compensation for violation of fundamental rights in obtaining the test.

Index